THE DIARIES
OF
Tchaikovsky

THE DIARIES
OF
Tchaikovsky

Translated from the Russian,
with notes, by

WLADIMIR LAKOND

GREENWOOD PRESS, PUBLISHERS
WESTPORT, CONNECTICUT

Library of Congress Cataloging in Publication Data

Chaĭkovskiĭ, Petr Il'ich, 1840-1893.
   The diaries of Tchaikovsky.

   Reprinted from the ed. of 1945.
   1. Chaĭkovskiĭ, Petr Il'ich, 1840-1893. I. Lake,
Walter, tr. II. Title.
ML410.C4A22   780'.92'4 [B]   79-138104
ISBN 0-8371-5680-7

Originally published in 1945 by W. W. Norton & Company,
Inc., New York

Reprinted with the permission of Wladimir Lakond

Reprinted in 1973 by Greenwood Press
A division of Congressional Information Service, Inc.
88 Post Road West, Westport, Connecticut 06881

Library of Congress catalog card number 79-138104
ISBN 0-8371-5680-7

Printed in the United States of America

10 9 8 7 6 5 4 3

Contents

Illustrations

Preface

PETER ILYICH TCHAIKOVSKY was born on April 25, 1840, Russian Old Style calendar (May 7, 1840, Western New Style calendar) at Votkinsk, Russia. He was the second child of five sons and a daughter. Neither of his parents was a professional musician; his mother played the piano and sang a little. Of the children, he was the only musician, none of the others being inclined artistically except his youngest brother Modest. Tchaikovsky loved his mother passionately and her death, when he was fourteen years old, affected him deeply. The tragedy beclouded his whole life, contributing to the extreme hardship of his youth. At twenty-eight, he fell in love with Mlle. Désirée Artôt, a French opera singer who was five years his senior. Very soon thereafter, she jilted him, marrying a Spanish baritone. When he was thirty-six, his long and voluminous correspondence started with Mme. von Meck, who was nine years older than he. And the following year, his ill-fated marriage to Antonina Ivanovna Miliukova, a conservatory pupil of twenty-eight, took place.

Tchaikovsky was a man of striking appearance. Of more than average height and well proportioned, he was always elegantly dressed. His blue eyes, ever brooding, were his most attractive feature. His manners, retiring and graceful yet masculine, charmed all who met him. He turned prematurely gray, and toward the end of his life he looked much older than his years. The turbulence, the violent struggle within was reflected in his face. He rarely smiled. A man of delicate sensibility, he exhibited the Slavic temperament carried to its extreme limits. He was shy and retiring, yet could plunge into work with ruthless energy. These traits are well reflected in his music which can be suave and elegant but can suddenly grow energetic and even violent. It is nothing less than tragic that such a precariously balanced nature as Tchaikovsky's should have been aggravated by sexual maladjustment.

Tchaikovsky's rise as a composer was slow and painful. While his friends were numerous, he had many enemies. He lived in constant dread of a scandal arising out of his homosexual life and the burden of living under such conditions colored his life intensely. For he, in contrast to others, was unhappy about his erotic nature. Then too, the gossip in connection with his being financed by Mme. von Meck did not add to his happiness.

As a conductor of his own works, Tchaikovsky toured many countries and enjoyed acclaim everywhere. But through it all, an inharmonious note of melancholy and loneliness was ever sounding. His soul was restless: the mad waves of inner dissatisfaction were constantly lashing at his spirit. A peaceful home was never his. He himself is the Pathetic Symphony and the "None but the Lonely Heart."

His death at fifty-three came after nearly five days of horrible torture. It was due to cholera, in spite of unfounded rumors that it was the result of suicide. A quotation from one of his letters best describes his life: "To regret the past, and hope for the future, never satisfied with the present: that is how my whole life passes."

Tchaikovsky's diaries, now revealed for the first time in their entirety in any language other than the original, commence with his thirty-third year and conclude when he was fifty-one, only two years before his death. The years represented are his most important, both biographically and musically. In the translation the diaries have not been expurgated or abridged. Tchaikovsky's personality, as man and musician, is disclosed by his own words and actions, and it is not unreasonable to believe that mankind will love him all the more for his frank revelations regarding his personal life. For these revelations prove only too well that he was very much of the human race; they are the parts that went to make up the whole that was Tchaikovsky.

These diaries have been made available through the co-operation of the composer's brother Ippolit who, following his retirement as admiral in the imperial Russian navy, became assistant custodian of the Tchaikovsky Museum at Klin and of N. T. Zhegin, the late director of the museum. Tchaikovsky kept his diaries irregularly and those missing in the present volume are regarded as lost, for their whereabouts remain undetermined.

To Tchaikovsky, the diaries were extremely personal—his own guarded secret. He wrote for himself. He kept diaries primarily for the purpose of being able to recall the past once again in his memory. As a result, he was not concerned with making his entries clear to outsiders. Certainly, he was least of all concerned with the correct spelling of proper names. This cryptographic character of the diaries presented immense problems—of deciphering the meaning of many passages; of tracking down events and identifying personalities; of correcting countless errors. Nevertheless, certain passages still remain ambiguous, and any information from readers tending to clarify them will be appreciated. The composer liked to intersperse his entries with French, German, Italian, and occasionally English words, at times spelling them phonetically in Russian. Naturally enough the English words will be lost in an English translation, but since they are not significant, the translator has not singled them out of context. The rhapsodic—even capricious —nature of the entries accounts for the jerkiness of the style. No amount of literary doctoring could eliminate this quality; on the contrary, its elimination would deprive the diaries of their most personal tone, which it has been desired to retain at all costs.

In most instances, original Russian names of persons, places, etc. have been retained without translating them into their English equivalents. The dates in the diaries are according to the Russian Old Style calendar, with the exception of those in the final diary, written in the United States, where they have been brought into conformity with American records.

The names in the Register of Personalities identify persons referred to in the diaries; they have been selected with a view toward their general historical significance and the part they played in Tchaikovsky's life. Reference to the Register is strongly urged as it will serve to give the proper perspective or interpretation to entries.

It is a great pleasure for me to acknowledge my indebtedness for valuable information received from Isidor Philipp and Dr. Jan Lowenbach. I am also very grateful to many other persons and institutions for assistance of various kinds whose names are too numerous to list individually, and who must therefore remain anonymous.

To Rhoda, my dear wife, I extend my profound gratitude for help that is incalculable.

WLADIMIR LAKOND

NEW YORK

Introduction

THE DIARIES here published cover, somewhat irregularly, a long period of Tchaikovsky's life, beginning in 1873 and continuing to 1891, most of them relating to the eighties. After his concert tour of the United States in 1891, two years before his death, Tchaikovsky discontinued the diaries. Disconnected though they are, the various notebook entries that have been preserved give an adequately complete picture of daily events and association with an inner circle of friends and acquaintances. Needless to say, all these odd notes, even though many of them reflect only the external circumstances of his life, are of importance as valuable documents, furnishing biographical material.

Readers of Tchaikovsky's diaries should bear in mind that they have here an intimate personal document, a private record written under the direct influence of moods and emotions. It is quite evident that Tchaikovsky intended such a document for himself only and by no means for the inquisitive eyes of outsiders.

Tchaikovsky left a huge epistolary heritage. Publication in the Soviet Union of his correspondence with Madame von Meck (in three volumes), with Taneiev, Jürgenson, and many other friends who had been intimately associated with the composer for many years, perhaps gives more substantial and comprehensive material for thoughts and ideas of the composer. On the other hand, letters do not give such a keen insight into the contradictions of Tchaikovsky's inner world and the tendency to exaggeration so characteristic of his diaries. This is of course understandable when we remember what the diary meant to so impressionable a person as Tchaikovsky. In short notes jotted down on the spur of the moment he gave vent to feelings.

In addition to the many pages of a casual nature, pages touching on chance meetings or describing how he killed time at card tables or other such details, there are many entries that mirror the throbbing, sensitive, and thoughtful nature of the composer, deeply stirred by questions of art and social life. From this viewpoint alone the diaries now being published are of absorbing interest.

Sincerity was an innate and endearing trait of Tchaikovsky the artist as it was of Tchaikovsky the man, and in his diaries too he was wholly sincere and truthful toward himself. Telling of his everyday life or of one or another topic of concern to him, Tchaikovsky is disdainful of attitudinizing or playing up to posterity. He gives voice to everything he thinks and feels. In his dislikes, particularly if they refer to art, so beloved to his heart, he is trenchantly outspoken and straightforward, at times even unfastidious as to choice of expression or epithet. Of the "gods" on his aesthetic olympus—Glinka, Tolstoy, and Mozart—he speaks ardently and passionately, with words of infinite rapture, to the point of tears. These entries show us a full-length portrait of Tchaikovsky— an artist with a heightened emotional perception and a generous, sensitive mind. When speaking of his own creative works he is a stern and responsible judge.

In striking words, Tchaikovsky speaks of his love for his native country and for his fellow Russians. Often traveling and living far from Russia, with poignant nostalgia he recalled the beauties of the Russian countryside which he always saw through a prism of strong, patriotic feelings. "Surrounded by these majestically beautiful views," he wrote while in Switzerland, "and feeling all the impressions of a traveler, I still long for Russia with all my soul and my heart sinks as I imagine its plains, meadows, and woods. Oh, my beloved country, you are a hundred times more striking and charming than these beautiful, colossal mountains that are really nothing more than nature's petrified convulsions. In my country, you are calmly magnificent! But then—distance lends enchantment!"

The memorable reception given him in Prague in 1888 in connection with his brilliant appearance as a conductor induced the following lines (entry dated February 7): "I have become very fond of these good Czechs. And, indeed, with reason!!! God! How much enthusiasm there was and of course all that is not for me, but for dear Russia." This was the manner in which Tchaikovsky accepted the truly triumphal welcome and the world recognition of his works, not in Czechoslovakia alone but also in other countries which paid homage through the person of Tchaikovsky to all Russian music and to Tchaikovsky himself as its most striking and authentic exponent. It should be mentioned that the diaries relating to the concert tour abroad in 1887-1888, in which the composer made entries referring to his meetings with practically all eminent representatives of the western European musical world, are of exceptional interest.

Finally, Diary Eight containing thoughts of broad aesthetic content is of particular significance and value. This diary, giving the characteristics of Tolstoy, Beethoven, Mozart, Glinka and Dargomyzhsky, was designed by Tchaikovsky for his future biographer. He frankly says: "Probably after my death it will not be uninteresting to know what were my musical predilections and prejudices, especially since I seldom gave opinions in verbal conversation." These utterances are often quoted in various writings and give abundant material for fathoming the composer's aesthetic world.

MOSCOW   GRIGORY BERNAND

Diary One

June, 1873 – July, 1873

This diary, a mere fragment, is the only one remaining from the period of the 1870's. It describes a short trip through Switzerland and to Milan and Lake Como taken by the composer with his friend and music publisher, P. I. Jürgenson.

LEAVING RUSSIA

11 June, 1873 Yesterday on the trip from Vorozhba to Kiev, suddenly for some reason or other, everything began to play and sing inside me after a long indifference to music. One theme, an embryo in B major, enthroned itself in my head and unexpectedly fascinated me to such an extent as to make me attempt an entire symphony. I at once decided to abandon Stasov's unsuccessful *Tempest* [1] and devote the summer to a symphony that would eclipse all my previous works. This is the embryo theme: [2]

---

[1] *Despite this decision, he composed his Fantasy Overture Op. 18 for orchestra in 1873. Inspired by Shakespeare's* Tempest, *it was written to a program suggested by Vladimir V. Stasov, the famous critic, to whom it was dedicated.*

[2] *The symphony was never composed but Tchaikovsky used this theme in his piano piece,* Capriccioso, *Op. 19, No. 5.*

I was imagining how I would be delighted with it this summer and how . . . [manuscript torn away]

18 June It is now one week since I wrote the preceding lines. I am still ill and do not yet see the end of my sickness. Was preparing to leave . . . tomorrow, but . . . [torn away]

27 June, Company 13[3] Excellent breakfast. Doughnuts. A neat peasant woman! "The Kremlin in Moscow" and "Evening in Venice" on the wall. Good-by, Kiev province! How beautiful nature usually is.

27 June, 4 A.M., Birzula Parted with Sasha, Lev, and Modya in Elizavetgrad. It was very sad. My stomach feels rather bad. The train is crowded. Could hardly find a seat. Must write Sasha[4] that she positively travel first class. Do not know why we are standing still. Will arrive sometime. Homesick!

On the way from Trsebinia What is more boring than a train trip and intrusive passengers? I am so pestered by an incredibly stupid Italian that I do not know how to get rid of him. He seems incapable of understanding where he is traveling or how to exchange his money. (Karbovance.) I exchanged my money at a Jewish place in Cracow. Am bored. My heart sinks as I think often of Sasha and Modya! There was a terrible excitement at Volochisk and my nerves became upset. Except for the Italian, the rest of the passengers are tolerable. Practically did not sleep all night. An old, retired military officer with eccentric whiskers. At this very moment the Italian is beginning to pester a lady. Oh, God, how stupid he is! I will have to get rid of him in some clever way.

GERMANY

29 June After waiting four long hours at Myslovitz, I am finally on my way to Breslau. The Italian is fully convinced that I am going to travel with him to Liggia. Sickening how he pesters me, and what a blockhead! At Myslovitz I ate dinner without any enjoyment and then took a walk through the interesting town. I can just imagine the Italian's face and his exclamations when I disappear

---

[3] *A village named for a former military camp.*

[4] *Tchaikovsky's sister had intended to go to Switzerland about her daughters' education there.*

at Breslau. Perhaps he may get off too. My money goes just like water.

Jean Procho, Constantinople

Breslau Did not have the heart to fool the Italian. I admitted that I would remain in Breslau. He almost cried and left me his name, written above. I am sitting now in the tower of the Hotel Zur Goldenen Gans.

30 June, Morning Slept well. Early this morning there was a severe thunderstorm. I decide to spend the day here. I am lazy about going to the train again. Besides, something attracts me here. Drink coffee. Except for the roof tops, cannot see anything from my window. How I love to be alone at times! I must confess that I also remained in Breslau so as not to turn up at once in the company of the Jürgensons [5] in Dresden. When alone, you are silent: you can meditate!

Twelve o'clock, noon Roamed about Breslau. Beautiful city! Became awfully tired.

Afternoon There was a terrible thunderstorm with a lot of hail. It is cool now. Typically German dinner; I like it.

1 July Was at Liebigs Etablissement in the evening. A pretty bad orchestra played a fairly good program. Was very bored. Bought an excellent pair of opera glasses. Will leave in an hour.

Near Dresden

(The theme for the first Allegro. The Introduction will also be from it but in ¾.) [6]

2 July, Dresden Arrived yesterday at six o'clock. After getting a room in the hotel, hurried to the opera house. They gave *La Juive* exceptionally well. My nerves are horrible. Without waiting for the end, went to look for Jürgenson in the hotel. Had supper. Went with Jürgenson. Drank tea with him on the terrace. Took a bath today. Roamed about the city with Jürgenson. We had dinner at

---

[5] *Peter Ivanovich Jürgenson, Tchaikovsky's music publisher and friend.*

[6] *This theme was never utilized by the composer.*

the table d'hôte. We leave at once for Saxon Switzerland. I am in a fairly good mood.

3 July, Die Bastei We had a delightful trip to Saxon Switzerland. For three-quarters of an hour we were ascending an enchanting road. Particularly interesting is the bridge near the hotel. The evening went by very pleasantly; the weather was splendid and it was only the Bohemian orchestra that marred the enjoyment. We went to bed early. Awfully disturbing were a drunkard and his two women cousins. Toward morning, we saw a rare sunrise. I slept well. Jürgenson and Sophia Ivanovna badly. The weather is horrible now; clouds are hovering above our heads and we decide to return to Dresden.

An Incident: A carelessly dropped bill of purchase!

Dresden The weather turned bad and we decided to return, making the descent by way of another road lying amidst colossal cliffs. We rested at an inn surrounded by wild territory (Felsenthor). We lunched (*Omelette au confiture*) on the shore of the Elbe and afterward arrived in Dr. [Dresden] by boat. Our former rooms were already occupied and we were given others—I got an abominable one. . . .

6 July, Cologne We saw *The Magic Flute* in Dresden. I felt bad and because of that I enjoyed it little. On the following day, we went to the Holbein Gallery, and at six o'clock we left for Cologne (via Windenburg, Halle, where we had to change, etc.). After traveling almost a day, we arrived at Cologne, where we stayed on the top floor of the Hôtel du Nord. We went to look for Val. . . .[7]

(*Grand Hôtel Baur au Lac*), *Zurich, twelve o'clock, midnight* The Rhine falls are magnificent. Crossing the river is awe-inspiring. But due to tiredness, waiting for the train at Dachsen was dull as was also the road to Zurich. Hoping that it would be cheaper, we stayed in Zurich at the Schwert, where we got accommodations with difficulty and then it was three times as expensive. I was angry. Feel nauseated and bad.

7 July, Near Mainz Am sailing on the Rhine. A charming voyage. The boat is perfect. My health good. Yesterday . . . we traveled very peacefully. It's decided to send the heavy baggage on to

---

[7] *Mme. B. O. Valzek, a singer friend of many years, and a prominent vocal instructor in Moscow.*

Paris. We will continue the journey more easily. We strolled about in Basel. Bought a *sac de voyage*. We are going now to Schaffhausen.

SWITZERLAND

9 July, Lucerne Slept excellently. Zurich is fascinating (Bauergarten, Hohe Promenade). We are leaving now for the Rigi-Kulm by boat.

10 July, Bern The excursion to the Rigi-Kulm was a happy one. The train trip was amazing. With great difficulty, we luckily found a room in the overcrowded hotel. It was hard to get up. The cold was penetrating and I felt bad after sundown. We waited two hours for the boat at Vitznau on the way back and had a very bad dinner. We wandered around Lucerne (The Lion of Lucerne Memorial). We rode here in a scorching heat. On the advice of some Russian, we stayed at the Hôtel de France which was repulsive. Everything was vile, but the supper surpassed all expectations. It was putrid and disgusting.

12 July, Vevey After visiting Bern yesterday and dining there at the Casino, the Jürgensons parted for Interlaken and I for here. (A talkative Swiss politician.) Just as soon as I arrived and stopped at the Hôtel Monnet, I went to look for a *pension* for Sasha. Found an extremely suitable one in the Paradis. Ran off to send a telegram and made a mess of it. Had supper. Strolled along the quay in futile hopes! Read the newspapers. Slept poorly. There was thunder and it was stifling.

13 July, Vevey Visited Miss Peile at the *pension*. I liked her. I wrote a letter immediately to Sasha and sent it off. Lunched. Took a dull walk, long and aimless, through the Terrasse du Panorama; wanted to visit the Hauteville château but did not succeed. Rode to Montreux and the Castle of Chillon; inspected the latter. Dined at the table d'hôte among a multitude of Americans and Englishmen. Was at the circus. My desires are excessive—but I have nothing!

Vevey, Evening Rode to see the Pissevache and the Gorges du Trient. Ascended a certain unfamiliar mountain on the top of which were living two cretins. Had dinner at the Grand Hôtel des Gorges du Trient. It broke me; my money simply goes. Am waiting for a telegraphed reply from Sasha. Surrounded by these majestically beautiful views, and feeling all the impressions of a traveler, I still long for Russia with all my soul and my heart sinks as I imagine its plains, meadows, and woods. Oh, my beloved country, you are a hundred times more striking and charming than these beautiful, colossal mountains that are really nothing more than nature's petrified convulsions. In my country, you are calmly magnificent! But then—distance lends enchantment!

14 July And still there is no telegram! Just returned from Montreux by train where I walked while it was awfully hot. Enjoyed it little. Lunched at the Hôtel du Cygne. To tell the truth, I do not know what to do, I am so bored.

15 July, Morning Was bored all evening and finally the telegram came. Am leaving today at twelve o'clock for Geneva. Am not reserving a room.

16 July, On the way from Geneva Geneva. Jürgenson without his cap. Walked. Discussion, in the evening, about the rest of the trip. Sleep interrupted by women neighbors. Bathing today in the Rhône. Sauntered. Lunch. Departure. Inspection of baggage and passports at Bellegarde. Davidov Koko and his wife. Lac du Bourget. Am going unwillingly to Italy. A pity, because of the money.

18 July, Milan The tunnel. Pain in my abdomen. Early morning in Turin with a severe pain in my abdomen. I remain in Turin; I am taken to a disgusting *albergo* and receive a room with a bed three yards long. With difficulty get some castor oil. Sleep. Departure on the express train. Milan. Galleria Vittorio Emanuele. A visit today to the Brera (The Madonna of Sassoferrato). A walk in the Giardino Pubblico. I am still not fully recovered. Got some medicine at the apothecary's. We are all going now to Lake Como.

Cadenabbia, Lake Como The journey was long and, starting with the boat, was exceptionally pleasant. We stayed at the excellent Hotel Bellevue. We went walking.

Diary Three

April, 1884 — June, 1884

Unfortunately Diary Two for the year 1882 was lost Diary Three takes place in 1884 on the estate of the composer's brother-in-law and sister, Lev and Alexandra (Sasha) Davidov, at Kamenka in the province of Kiev. The composer, surrounded by many relatives and friends, lived in a smaller house on the estate with his valet Alexei but dined at the "big house." He was engaged in the composition of his Third Suite for Orchestra, Op. 55.

12 April [1884] Was still asleep straight up to Fundukleyevka. A cold, biting wind. Was met by no one, but on arriving at the house, I found Levushka up. Conversation and tea (I am in the period of a mad passion for tea). Letters. A visit to the old ladies.[1] A most hearty welcome at the big house. They are lovable!!! Remained long there. Letters from Tasya. Lev came and with him I was at Nikolai Vasilyevich's. There I saw Aksel and charming Varya who has lost weight. Dinner threesome: Lev, cousin, and I. Cousin's incredible stories and complaints about Pelagea Osipovna during and after dinner. A walk to the oak tree grove. Violets. Cold weather. Tea home; letters to Modya, Tolya, Nadezhda Filaretovna,[2] Jürgenson, and Kondratyev. Supper with Lev. Flegont came and we played four rubbers of buy-whist. A cold north wind is howling outside.

13 April Rose late. The cold continues. After drinking tea, went to Lev, who soon left while I remained to strum and think up something new. Hit upon an idea for a *piano concerto*, but it turned

---

[1] *The widow Davidova and her two spinster daughters, Tchaikovsky's distant relations. He adored all three, calling them "our three angels."*

[2] *Nadezhda Filaretovna von Meck, Tchaikovsky's benefactress.*

out too weak and not new.[3] Strolled a little about the garden. Had dinner with cousin—she is ill. Played Massenet's *Hérodiade*. Strolled a little on the road to the Pokrov farm. Drank tea at home. Stayed very long in the big house, at first in the dining room during dinner and later at Alexandra Ivanovna's [Davidova], to whom I brought my portrait. Returned home with Lev. Read Otto Jahn [Mozart's biographer]. A real game of whist with Roman Efimovich Derichenko and Bisterfeld after supper.

14 April Rose late again. Made visits to Father Alexander and his dear little sick son, where I also found Liuba who has grown as tall as a pole and to the Plesskys where I did not find Vladimir Andreyevich at home but saw Boris, Misha, Dolya, Julia Ivanovna, the Englishman with Grigi, Grisha, and Lev.[4] The first three were playing. Cousin and Sabaneiev were at dinner. Cousin received a letter from her debtor-colonel and spoke very amusingly about his honesty but later I was obliged to write a reply to him for her. A terrible, incredible north-east wind continues to blow but I knocked off my walking duties bravely in the Nikolaiev field. Wrote letters at home (to brother Kolya, Levitzky, Tanya, and Taneiev), read the memoirs of Lopukhin. Whist threesome with Lev and Flegont after supper. Terrible luck. Continue to be inactive and not to have the least inspiration.

Sunday, 15 April The weather improved a little; nevertheless, I took my walk in the morning, though with difficulty, to the oak tree grove. Lunch at home with the veterinary and a guest from Smela. Stayed home, read English, and warmed myself at the fireplace. Nikolai Vasilyevich came with Lev. Dinner in the big house. Somehow or other it was dull and sad. The reason for that was probably Vera Vasilyevna.[5] All were tired and dejected. The Englishman frightened me by his proposal of lessons. Whist game at home with Flegont and Sabaneiev. I won. Did not get to Mass today, but met Danya after my walk and gave him the books and the Bible which I brought.

---

[3] *The idea materialized into the Fantasy for Piano and Orchestra, Op. 56, composed in 1884.*

[4] *All were either friends or relations of the composer.*

[5] *Vera Vasilyevna Davidova, sister of Tchaikovsky's brother-in-law. Before her marriage, she was attracted by Tchaikovsky and, to all appearances, her feelings never changed.*

16 April Rose at nine o'clock. The weather is clear and although it is still windy—yet it is spring. Vladimir Andreyevich visited me: the first time I have seen him since his illness. Spent all the time until dinner in the Trostyanka forest picking violets and enjoying it deeply. Danya noticed this and brought me some flowers. At dinner cousin amused me by her astounding peculiarities. Tried to lay the foundation of a new symphony both in the Trostyanka forest and at home, in the afternoon, but still am dissatisfied. Lizaveta, Alexandra, and Vera Vasilyevna came to me. Strolled in the garden and sowed the seeds not of a future symphony but of a suite.[6] At supper the veterinary and Nikolai. Whist threesome with Flegont. My bad luck was colossal.

17 April Despite the bitterly cold wind, went to the Trostyanka forest in the morning where I found comparative peace. Jotted down some ideas. We dined together. Played the piano. English language. Whist foursome with Roman Efimovich and Flegont. My luck was very bad.

18 April In the Trostyanka forest again and the jotting down of shabby ideas. Vladimir Andreyevich was with us during dinner. A visit to the big house and to Mme. Kruaza (during Flegont's lesson). English language after tea. A walk to the mills. The weather is much better today; it's even good. Flegont came to see me. Nikolai Vasilyevich, Roman Efimovich, and Flegont were at supper. Whist. Lev's departure for Elizavetgrad.

19 April Awoke not entirely well—with a head cold and in a feverish condition. Took a walk across the cliffs to the railroad station and back home. Lunched alone in my room. Took another walk (the weather is at last excellent), drank tea, played the piano long (senselessly), dined in the big house, returned home half-sick, went to the garden to look into the distance at a wonderful sunset, read, drank tea, and played whist with Flegont in Lev's study. Was angry because of bad luck. Very dissatisfied with myself on account of all the common ideas that come to me. Is it that I am played out? With difficulty wrote to Nadezhda Filaretovna.

20 April Beautiful weather. All morning in the Trostyanka forest. Was angry on returning home that lunch was not ready. Read English after lunch, became tired, and dozed. Played at home and

---

[6] *The Third Suite for Orchestra, Op. 55, composed in 1884.*

jotted down certain things in my notebook. Dinner in the big house.
Discussions about Schopenhauer, Tolstoy, etc. after dinner. I am
getting more and more stupid! As soon as there is a serious discussion, my head is completely empty. At home wrote to Tolya. The
telegram was received about Sasha's departure from Moscow. Notified Lev. Whist with Flegont. Had good luck—but how boring!

21 April A splendid, slightly grayish day. Walked to Kosar along
the railroad tracks. Lev, having returned from Elizavetgrad at
7 A.M., slept until twelve. On coming back, went to congratulate
Alexandra Ivanovna on her birthday. Dined with Lev, Sabaneiev
and Mr. Obruchev. Was studying English and, before I knew it,
had to go to eat a second time in the big house. Besides us, there
were the Stals. Whist foursome with Flegont and Sabaneiev in the
evening. Nikolai Vasilyevich came and got on my nerves terribly
with his chattering.

Sunday, 22 April Went to meet our people at the railroad station
past the market on the Smelyansk road and the field beyond the
Trostyanka forest. Sat in the garden in the company of others,
waiting for the train. Happy reunion. Bob.⁷ Walked home with
Nata. Bob visited me. Dinner. Read a splendid work for a very long
while (*Shefferd Pasha*). Was a bit lonesome later and did not know
how to kill the time. Walked in the Nikolaiev field; sat on the slope
of the ditch; caught, i.e. killed borage beetles which now make a
kind of migration along the embankment. Collected autographs at
home to present Modya on his birthday. Grigi and Bob compelled
us to watch their sharpshooting. Broun. Sasha was telling, at supper,
about Father Ivan who is now performing miracles at St. Petersburg. Five-handed whist: my luck was bad and I was awfully angry.
Just read the first Book of Kings in the Bible.

23 April Found out, in the morning, that Lev had such a headache at night that they had to call the doctor. A long walk in the
field past the Trostyanka forest. Dust, dryness. Dinner with guests

⁷ *Bob was the nickname of Vladimir Lvovich Davidov, Tchaikovsky's
thirteen-year-old favorite nephew and son of the composer's sister, Sasha
(Alexandra Ilyinishna Davidova). Tchaikovsky was very attached to
him from his childhood and there is reason to believe that in his later
years the attachment was more than platonic. The Sixth Symphony
(Pathétique) was dedicated to Bob. At the age of thirty-five, in 1906,
Bob committed suicide.*

—a bald gentleman and the doctor. Cousin Nastasya Vasilyevna. Went to the big house to congratulate Alexandra Vasilyevna [Davidova]. We sat in the reception room. Sasha was recounting the news of the palace and as for Vera Vasilyevna, she was chattering in her usual manner. Tea home. A walk without any pleasure and sitting about the brick yard. A letter to Emma in answer to her confession. Supper. Vera Vasilyevna and the Stals. The Butakov oppression during whist. Whist twice. There was much Z.[8] Oh, what a monster of a person I am!

24 April Eleven o'clock. Soon I will be forty-four years old. How long I have lived and—truthfully, without false modesty—how little accomplished! Even in my own present *occupation,* why there is nothing—I swear—that is *perfect* and *exemplary.* I am still searching, doubting, wavering. And in other things? I read nothing; know nothing. Only on whist do I spend endless, precious time. And I am sure also that my health will not benefit from it. Today I was so angry, so exasperated, that in another moment, I imagine I would have created an ugly scene and done harm. I was angry a good deal today, in fact, and the time of calm, quiet living, unperturbed by anything, is over. There is much excitement; much that goes against me; much that a madman of my age cannot endure indifferently. Yes, it is time to live in *my own home* and in *my own way.*

The entire morning was passed in pleasant walking. I found, in a ditch in the Rebedailovsky field, a whole cluster of such exceptionally fragrant violets that my room is filled all day with scent from a little bouquet of them. Sat in the reception room after dinner and laughed over cousin's pranks. Her surprise that Katerina Andreyevna Alexeyeva has a *grown-up* son—wonderful! Barely managed to make my evening walk (to the mill) when they called for supper—it is a new arrangement. I suffered from hunger and *lack of attention.* It's petty, but why conceal that even such a trifle can anger me? Then whist and endless anger. Butakova came over. The Elizavetgrad piano turned out to be a bluff; I am without a piano. Sent Alesha[9] to look for one with Vasily; it seems as though there is hope. All day, Bob was a delight to my glances; how per-

---

[8] *This was the secret symbol that, it appears, Tchaikovsky employed to refer to his homosexuality.*

[9] *Affectionate diminutive of Alexei I. Sofronov, the composer's faithful valet.*

fectly charming he is in his white suit. Ury fell off his horse this morning and was bruised. Received an accounting from the Musicians' Fund in St. Petersburg and wrote immediately requesting a loan of 300 rubles.

25 April Alesha congratulated me with great affection. After tea took a long walk in the Nikolaiev field. I thought, judging by yesterday, that everyone had forgotten my birthday—but I was mistaken. They congratulated me and drank champagne. They came in turns from the big house; Roman Efimovich also came. The lady P . . . arrived. Tea in the house. A letter to Modya, and English. Was in the big house and remained there during dinnertime (Alexandra Ivanovna was not there; she is in Prussy). Being frightened by the suggestion of Vera Vasilyevna that it would be good to go walking, I fled. Sat opposite the mill. Destroyed beetles on the embankment. A piano from Mr. Druzhin. Some misunderstanding is threatening to deprive me of it, i.e. the piano. Supper, during which a conversation with P. . . . Whist. Was irritable, but less so than yesterday. Vera Vasilyevna, Varya, and Nikolai Vasilyevich came. Telegrams from St. Petersburg and Moscow.

26 April I am in some kind of seething fury. Because Sasha set me, and with satisfaction, two tricks in hearts, I got angry as a madman chiefly, however, because in the preceding game (it was a threesome) I let her have the bid in clubs out of magnanimity in view of her hard luck at cards today. Why is that? Is this the feeling of an artist benefiting from fame? Oh, Peter Ilyich! Shame, Holy Father! But then, I have not felt well since morning. The obnoxious condition of my stomach is beginning to seriously ruin my life. Worked with great intensity on the Scherzo [10] this morning. I was again a little angry at dinner. Went to the Nikolaiev field. It was humid, windy, and gloomy—but it did not rain. Drank tea in my room. Afterward I wrote a little more. Bob walked around the garden with me and then stepped into my room. Ah, how fascinating is Bob! Whist threesome after supper (was angry). Oh, what a life!

27 April Cold weather again. Worked all morning after a short walk—it went better this time. Was angry during dinner because of the extreme carelessness which reigns in the order of the house. *More than half an hour* passed between the first and second course

---

[10] *From the Third Suite for Orchestra, Op. 55.*

of the dinner. Everyone came in turns. . . . Walked long and very well and thanks to moderation I felt fine. Drank tea with Vera Vasilyevna at home; sat in my room at the window and conversed with Nata and Bob. (Aside: oh, how perfect is Bob!) Wrote letters. All went to the big house after tea. Bob and I looked at the illustrations. Lizaveta Vasilyevna's stories.

28 April This whist threesome irritates me so that I am beginning to be afraid lest it affect my health. Was again furiously angry and malicious. And I have not the strength to renounce the game. Incidentally, had an exceedingly profitable day; first, because my work went excellently and, second, my stomach is in order. On the other hand, the weather was bad: typically Kamenka, i.e. a violent, mad wind with clouds (literally) of dust. Strolled with Bob about the garden in the morning—(what a darling he is!). Went to the Plyakovsky woods through clouds of dust after dinner. *At teatime Sasha was having her dinner;* Broun, Butalenok, etc. were present. I am very delighted when English is spoken at dinner; am beginning to understand it, but cousin always interrupts at the most interesting place. Worked after tea. Was at church with Sasha for vespers (Easter canon). Was much angered by whist after supper. Lev did not arrive. Wrote to the directorate regarding *The Oprichnik.*[11]

Sunday, 29 April Was so absorbed reading the morning newspapers that I got to Mass when the Gloria was already in progress. Stood at the left. Sasha Butakov took the Communion. Stopped in at Alexandra Ivanovna's. Worked. Finished the Scherzo. Walked to the Rebedailovsky field after dinner (Pelagea Osipovna). Enjoyed drinking tea in my room. Went to the Plesskys' with Sasha, Nata and Pelagea Osipovna. Mme. Laskovskaya came. Bob and Grigi astonished us, at supper, by the accounts of their leaps in the *pas de géant.* There wasn't any whist. Sat the whole time in Sasha's reception room. *Bêtes parlantes,* illustrations, Broun. *It rained.* We were waiting for Lev. When he arrived, it was already about one o'clock. Purchased the estate for the von Mecks.[12]

---

[11] *Tchaikovsky's opera* (The Life Guardsman) *written between 1870 and 1872.*

[12] *Mme. von Meck's son, Nikolai, husband of Tchaikovsky's niece, Anna, purchased an estate through the help of Lev, his father-in-law. In later years, Lev was blamed for the unwise investment.*

30 April   And to what purpose do I play whist? Except for being upset and angered, nothing results. Lost again and could hardly suppress my fury during the whole time. The day, as regards the weather, was disgusting. Spent all day writing the valse [13] for the Suite, but feel far from confident that it is entirely satisfactory. Took a walk with great effort on the Smelyansk road to the Trostyanka forest after dinner (not with Sasha but with Vladimir Andreyevich). The wind was terrible. Took part in the *pas de géant* with Bob, Grigi, and Broun after tea. Studied English diligently without interruption until supper. Vera Vasilyevna came. We talked about Faigina, Nadina, Damaln, etc.

1 May   Cold and windy. After reading the newspapers, walked to the end of the Nikolaiev field. Continued the valse. Frightened by the wind, walked up and down in my room for an hour after being in the study (Lizaveta and Alexandra Vasilyevna) in the afternoon. Took part with Bob in the *pas de géant* after tea. Later, made a fire in the fireplace and studied English. There was whist with Roman Efimovich after supper (before that, played duets with my darling, the incomparable, enchanting, ideal Bob to his immense enjoyment). Was not angry but was in a very nervous condition. In the intermission between rubbers, went over to my angel, Bob. He showed me his miniature theater. We played whist until 1 A.M. Roman Efimovich lost heavily.

2 May   Walked the whole morning, being enticed by comparatively better weather. Went far in the direction of Kosar. The valse gave me enormous difficulties. Yes, I am getting old. As Alexandra Ivanovna and Alexandra Vasilyevna were coming, remained in the reception room in the afternoon. Excelled with Bob in the *pas de géant* while they watched and then escorted them home. Fussed with the valse until almost seven o'clock and it did not progress a bit. Strolled in the garden. Met Lev with Sasha. Together visited the beehive at Vasily's. Whist foursome after supper. A miracle—I won! Wrote Modya a letter in a hurry.

3 May   Wrote N. F. [Mme. von Meck] and sent her my portrait after reading the newspapers and strolling a bit in the garden. Then finished the sketch of the valse. Lev came to invite me to Verbovka and I decided to walk there immediately after dinner, but during dinner the long expected thunderstorm broke out with a downpour.

---

[13] Valse mélancolique, *the second movement of the Suite.*

The general excursion did not take place; Lev and Bob rode. I walked about the kitchen garden and in my room, whither I was driven by a fresh rain. Later on, fulfilled my walking obligations in the Nikolaiev field. It was so stifling that I could hardly move and was even afraid I would suffocate. Was at Alexandra Ivanovna's. Arrived during dinnertime and read the *Graphic* in the reception room. Stayed fairly long at the darling old lady's. Nikolai Vasilyevich talked about Raevsky. Went to my room and studied English diligently after a short walk in front of the house, admiring the marvelous evening. Lev and Bob did not return for a long time and I was really becoming worried. We ate supper very late. Vera Vasilyevna and Sasha are scheming to remove sick Anna Petrovna to Kiev. We sat down late to whist (Grigory Grigoryevich). I had very good luck. And still, I was irritable and found the opportunity to act hostile to my opponents.

4 May Decided in the morning after reading some letters (one of which was from Modya with pleasant news about *Mazepa*) [14] to go to Zrubanetz for some lilies of the valley, but when I arrived there and saw a thundercloud, I hastened home. The cloud burst suddenly and although it did not thunder, I was, on the other hand, drenched to the skin. After changing my clothes and sitting down to play Mozart's *Magic Flute* in an extremely peaceful mood, I was interrupted in the middle of the most exquisite enjoyment by the arrival of Bob who told me, with an expression of horror, the news of Tusya Bazilevskaya's death. Deep grief. Festive dinner because of Lev's birthday. Wrote letters until tea, then worked. Went with Bob, Grigi, and Broun to the *pas de géant*. After supper, at which were Nikolai Vasilyevich (he and Lev quarreled about antiquated ideas regarding the sowing of old borage fields) and his daughters, I first loafed aimlessly for a long time, now gossiping with Vladimir Andreyevich and Flegont, now sitting in Sasha's reception room, where cousin told several amusing stories; finally our whist game took place. I am very weary. Darling Tusya! Oh, how unfortunate, how unfortunate! . . . And why? But God's will be done!

5 May The day was soso. In the morning, took a short walk on the road to the railroad station. Worked. At dinner, there was some talk

---

[14] *Tchaikovsky's opera composed in 1881-1883 which had no popular success. However, Tsar Alexander III liked it and much to Tchaikovsky's surprise, he met people sometime after the performance who admired it.*

about a ride to the forest. I declined. Roamed about with Bob and watched him building with blocks in the afternoon. Strolled beyond my strength and without enjoyment, although it was beautiful in the Trostyanka forest. Drank tea in my room. Fussed with one place in the andante [15] until seven o'clock. Became tired. At vespers. Sad thoughts and tears on account of Tusya. Was late to supper. Flegont is ill, and because of that played whist with Lev (very dull). The cornfield. Nikolai Vasilyevich.

Sunday, 6 May Excellent weather. Received a letter with money from St. Petersburg. Attended Mass. Was very affected by religious feeling; stood almost the entire time with tears in my eyes. I am always touched to the depths of my soul by the simple and healthy religious devotion manifested by the common people. (A sick, old man, a four-year-old boy walking alone up to the chalice.) The manifesto about Konstantin Konstantinovich [16] was read. Was in the big house; drank coffee in the dining room. All were stimulated and even jolly. Walked about the market with Bob. Worked very successfully. Walked to the Pokrov farm in the afternoon. Drank tea at first alone, then Sasha and Pelagea Osipovna came over from the big house. Conversation about Julia Plesskaya. Wrote letters at home. A stroll to the mill at sunset. Played some dances for the children after supper. Julia Ivanovna came with Dolly. Conversation about the houses in the neighborhood. Sabaneiev. Dances. There was no whist at all. I confess: whist is almost a necessity for me—even shamefully so.

7 May Magnificent summer day. Tempted by it, walked all morning; was in the Plyakovsky field and in the Trostyanka forest where it was enchanting. Managed to work just a little. We rode up to the big house in the afternoon (Alexandra Vasilyevna left for Moscow today) and from there to Zrubanetz and Solobaichino for some lilies of the valley. Sasha, Nata, cousin, Bob (on horseback), Uka, Tasya and I rode. Picked lilies of the valley with Bob, drank tea, and enjoyed the lovely evening (I rode with Tasya). Whist foursome. When I was lucky, I was embarrassed and tried to lose; when my luck changed—I was angry. Nikolai Vasilyevich, Lizaveta Vasilyevna and Vera Vasilyevna came.

---

[15] *Fourth movement (Theme and Twelve Variations) of the Suite.*

[16] *Grand Duke of Russia who was very friendly to Tchaikovsky.*

Tchaikovsky at the age of thirty-three

8 May A real summer day. Dressed up in white clothes. Worked all morning. My andante is progressing though not without strain, and I think it is coming out very nicely. Despite the heat, walked to the Timashevsky road, in the afternoon, near the cave-in. Drank tea with Sasha and Nata. The tragic details of Tusya's death were received. It's so painful, you weep hearing them. Worked until seven o'clock. Strolled in the garden. English language. Finished reading about Columbus. A rather quiet whist game after supper (Bob returned tired from Verbovka and went directly to bed). Was less angry than usual.

9 May Dressed in new clothes. Was at church but stood a very short time in the door because it was crowded. Vonifaty Sangursky. Dropped in at the big house. Vera Vasilyevna proposed a drive together to the forest. Worked and finished the andante, with which am very satisfied. Bob is ill. Went to the big forest (from the side of Nesvadkov) via Jurchikha directly after dinner. Before reaching Jurchikha, began to suffocate, or at least to get a pain in my heart which frightened me very much. Nevertheless, walked right to the forest. All our people arrived later. A pleasant outing. Vera Vasilyevna. Tea. Uka. Lilies of the valley and night violets. Rode back on the coach box. Bob is well. Supper. Flegont was late. Whist. At this moment, as I write, there is a thunderstorm.

10 May Yesterday's thunderstorm drove me, without reading at all, to my bedroom. Nearly dozed off by candlelight but was awakened by a loud peal of thunder. . . . However, there was almost no rain. Slept excellently. Today there is a coolness in the air. Walked all morning—far in the direction of Kosar. Votya Sangursky came with his drawings and sketches before dinner. Was in the reception room in the afternoon; later, worked a bit, and then, invited by Grigi, was swinging. Worked again. Was playing around the pole with Bob and Alesha for a long time afterward while Ury watched. It was jolly mainly because Bob enjoyed it immensely. Played whist in which Flegont and I were the winners after supper. They are discussing Tasya's and the other girls' performance in the big house. Everyone appeared at teatime.

11 May It was cold and windy again and at five o'clock there was a dust storm without rain. The first movement of the suite called *contrasts,* and its themes,[17]

---

[17] *These two themes were utilized in the composer's Fantasy for Piano and Orchestra, Op. 56.*

has become so repugnant to me that, after spending the whole day on it, I decided to drop it and write something else entirely different. Was in the Nikolaiev cornfield near the high cemetery in the morning. Squeezed from myself the laborious movement of the suite in the afternoon. What is the reason for that? How hard it has become for me to work! Is it possible that it's old age, at last? (Forgot to mention about last night's strange dreams: rambling with Bob, the Tarnovsky governess, Maksheyev, etc.) English language. Nina and Lizaveta Vasilyevna at tea. Whist after supper (by kerosene lamp). Was angry but today, most of all, at Flegont because of his admonishing me. Received news from Pakhulsky,[18] in the morning, about the unsuccessful performance of the *Capriccio* [19] in Paris.

12 May Went for a walk to Tarapun at nine o'clock and returned, walking back as well only toward dinnertime—a grand walk! Sat on the porch, chatted with Nata, tried to ride on the bicycle, etc. Played Mozart. Almost began to fuss again with the repugnant *contrasts,* after tea, when suddenly a new idea struck me and the thing went well. Ran around the pole with Alesha and Bob (he will finally drive me simply crazy with his indescribable fascination). Nikolai Vasilyevich came and talked about the article in *La Revue* on red sunsets. We dropped in at the church (beautiful evening; some Jewish people were strolling; Mme. Kruaza). Nina and Manya at supper. Was consumed with wrath because of the supper menu. Was terribly angry during whist but not on account of cards, but just generally so at something indefinite which may be called Z. Yes, Z is less tormenting and perhaps more steady than X, nonetheless, it is also disagreeable.

Sunday, 13 May A hellish wind, ruining all the seeds sown for beets. Mass was over early and did not know what to do with myself for a long time. Finally I went to Alexandra Ivanovna and sat in her reception room together with cousin. Worked. Was in the studio after dinner and Bob was with me. Walked beyond my

---

[18] *Vladislav Albertovich Pakhulsky, violinist, husband of Mme. von Meck's daughter, Julia.*

[19] Capriccio italien, *Op. 45 for orchestra, composed in 1880.*

strength; yesterday's tiredness still makes itself felt. Wrote a little after tea. Was swinging with Bob and some little girls. After supper, owing to Sabaneiev and Roman Efimovich arriving together, a disagreement took place about who was to be in the game and I left for my room and started to study English but Lev soon came for me. Played with fairly good luck but made many blunders in the last rubber with Roman Efimovich and, even now, cannot forgive myself, that instead of spades I led with hearts!!! Z tortures me unusually today. God spare me such a bad feeling. Modest sent me the portraits of Kolya [20] and the tsarevitch.

14 May Since morning a light, soft rain has been falling unexpectedly, and it has continued until evening. I walked long about the garden in the morning. Worked successfully until dinner. Read Krylov with Bob after dinner. Strolled in the Nikolaiev field. The guard and acquaintance with him. Drank tea alone (Sasha lay down to sleep with Nata). Ran around the pole a little for Bob's sake. Was at cousin's (at her invitation). She was offended because she is being sent to Verbovka; she wished to enter a convent. Sasha came to speak to me about that in the morning. At first (this morning) I did not react sympathetically to cousin, but after visiting her, understood her feelings perfectly. Nikolai Vasilyevich and Verlop at supper. Whist. I was extremely irritable and angry, not on account of the game, but Z was torturing me and what was even more annoying was that it had subsided in the morning.

15 May It rained again a little in the morning. Strolled in the garden. Wrote the last variation (the finale-polacca) [of the Third Suite]. Went to the oak tree grove in the afternoon (the shepherd card gamblers) and returned via the Smelyansk road. Worked again after tea. Noticing Varya going to Sasha, went into the house; later, paid a visit to Alexandra Ivanovna. With her at Vera Vasilyevna's and talked with her about the outrageous commotion of the children. Whist with Roman Efimovich after supper. As usual, I was furious, uncertain at what—however, chiefly at Nikolai Vasilyevich who spoke loudly about various things, for example, how he got his feet wet. Went to sleep without reading and writing the diary: am writing this a day later.

---

[20] *Affectionate diminutive of Nikolai H. Konradi. He was Modest's deaf and dumb pupil.*

16 May Walked in the garden in the morning but later on wandered to Rudnya and returned by way of the brick yard. Was writing until the dinner hour. Dined *en petit comité;* cousin went away to the convent, Lev to his farm. Sat about the reception room in the afternoon, then worked and roamed around the garden. Worked again after tea. Learning that Bob was at the pole, went there and found him with Flegont. We played boisterously. Lizaveta and Vera Vasilyevna came for lilacs. Sat long with Bob and Flegont on the bench by the greenhouse. Beautiful evening. Studied English. My progress in understanding what I read is considerable —but I still don't understand anything when Miss Eastwood [21] is speaking. Had supper without Sasha (she is in the big house). Sabaneiev. Whist. Flegont was *erratic;* I won.

Ascension Day, 17 May Gray, calm but fresh weather. Alesha went to church directly after tea while I, without taking a walk, sat down to work and wrote until twelve o'clock. Walked with great enjoyment in the Nikolaiev field. Had dinner in the big house. Conversation about the catastrophe on the Nikolaiev railroad line. In the afternoon chattered in the reception room with Mme. Kruaza, Alexandra Ivanovna, etc. Mme. Yaroshevskaya came. When I was leaving at four o'clock, Lizaveta Vasilyevna talked about Alexandra Mikhailovna with tears in her eyes. Tea with Nata. Worked with great exertion. Was swinging twice, in the garden. Mme. Vlasovskaya introduced me to Mme. Algzen. The second time, swinging hard with Bob, Alesha, and Apalat. Played Mozart and was in ecstasy. An idea about a suite from Mozart.[22] Mme. Plesskaya appeared during supper and Kruzhilin later. I excused myself from whist and, after sitting at the table, went to my room at eleven o'clock.

18 May I strain myself too much in my work; as though someone were driving me. This strain is unhealthy, and probably will be reflected in the Suite. Went to the Plyakovsky beet field in the morning (beautiful weather); the beets are coming up. Worked very successfully (the variation before the finale). Sat on the roof with Bob afterward (where I would not climb but for the sake of that angel!). Ran around the pole, in the heat, with him as well.

---

[21] *An Englishwoman, governess of the children of Tchaikovsky's sister.*

[22] *The idea developed into the Fourth Suite for Orchestra, Mozartiana, Op. 61, written in 1887.*

Then drank some tea (Vera Vasilyevna and conversation about poor Anna Petrovna), worked furiously later on, so as to be able to start something new tomorrow. Cousin returned from the convent. Stopped in to see her before supper. At Bob's request, played an unusual game—*secret*—after supper; a very stupid game. Whist. I was very tired and played without great pleasure. I lost.

19 May Tasya's sixteenth birthday was celebrated. Tolerable weather. Wrote a variation in the morning. The dinner was festive, with champagne. Went to the Trostyanka forest. Drank tea in my room. Wrote letters. Walked on the cliffs with Bob (the darling), there we joined a boating party, and returned home with him. Dropped in at the greenhouse with Bob and sat there with Em. Fyod. Played some children's songs for Bob. At vespers. A party in the evening with dancing; I played the music. Bob was delighted beyond words when I played quadrilles on themes given by him. At the end, when all had left, Nata, who was very pensive, suddenly said to me: "Oh, Peter dear, life is not worth living!" These words depressed me very much, hearing them from the lips of one with such a wholesome, pure nature as Nata's. In the course of the evening, Vera Vasilyevna recalled the past and apparently with regret. But all that she recalls is to me, personally, repulsive and I did not want it all brought back.

Sunday, 20 May Was late to church. Was about to go walking (confess I was avoiding Danka and *tutti quanti* who were coming out of church) when suddenly I had an unpleasant accident . . . and fled home straight from the Nikolaiev farm. . . . Went to the big house afterward. Was in the reception room with Alexandra Ivanovna and Lizaveta Vasilyevna. The latter was telling about the Pashkovs. Visited Vera Vasilyevna after that. Spoke with her about Tanya. Succeeded in writing a variation at home. Rode in a landau to Verbovka with Lev, Sasha, and Bob in the afternoon. Walked as far as Maidan. Bob and I were walking from Lebedovka where we dropped in at Anna Ivanovna's. At Verbovka we drank tea, rambled about the garden and everywhere with Bob. Everyone greeted us with joy, at home, as they were worried. Whist, after supper, in which I lost seven and one half rubles. Had bad luck.

21 May Typical Kamenka weather: ruinous for farming, atrocious for walking. On the other hand, I worked well today, as I wrote four whole variations. Only made a round of the garden in the

morning and then worked, and finished at twelve-thirty in expectation of Bob who promised to come to study singing but disappointed me. Roamed through the labyrinths and debris of the
big, unfinished house in the afternoon with Bob, because of the
stilts. Strolled in the Nikolaiev field. Tea without Nata, but with
cousin and Tasya who criticized everything and everybody, even
called Miss Eastwood a *fool*. Worked. Went searching in vain for
Bob on the grounds, then went to the Trostyanka field. Was in the
big house with Sasha and cousin; after that we had supper (exceptionally delicious) at the Plesskys'. On returning home, we played
whist and I won a little.

22 *May* Awoke at night with a pain in my throat and nausea,
and was ill all day even though I worked well. Bob came before
dinner and I played some of my songs for him. Walked with great
effort as far as the Trostyanka forest and back after dinner. Was
about to sit down to work after tea, but Bob lured me away with
his stilts. Following a despairing day, clouds suddenly began to
gather; however, nothing or almost nothing happened. Went out
several times searching for Bob. As soon as I do not work or walk
(and that is also work for me) I begin to crave Bob and get lonesome without him. Frightful, how I love him. At supper, the veterinary (arriving shortly before that and received by me), Sabaneiev,
etc. who were taking part in the performance. The rehearsal. I accompanied Tasya's satirical songs. Unattractive performance. Whist
with interruptions. Nikolai Vasilyevich. I won a good deal.

23 *May* Somehow or other, it was particularly delightful this
morning. Met Vera Vasilyevna with Vladimir Andreyevich in the
garden and took a walk with them. Worked successfully. Bob rode
to meet Lev and Grisha and had no dinner. In the afternoon, I
walked to the Trostyanka forest. Cousin (with whom I am often
not affectionate enough) annoyed me considerably today by her
correspondence with Mr. Lody, in which I play the role of a secretary. *Finished the Suite.* Sauntered about the garden and the square
before supper. Wonderful evening. Stilts. At supper, cousin again
with Lody. The rehearsal. *Les Femmes savantes?!* I was very
nervous: everything irritated me, and not without reason. The pain
or, better, the strange feeling in my throat, long in disappearing,
is beginning to worry me; yes, and in addition, a slight suffering
as though from hemorrhoids. When the curious rehearsal was over,
there was whist. I had luck. Despite that, was in a very bad mood.

24 May A letter from Pakhulsky in which he sends me the announcement about the sale of Dvoryaninova. Experienced mixed feelings about that. Wrote a long letter to N. F. regarding the plans about the purchase of an estate,[23] which I decided to put off. Went to the big house and talked long with Vera Vasilyevna. Unless I am very mistaken, she has not, as yet, entirely changed in her old feelings. After dinner, at which were Yakov Isaich and his assistant, we were all disturbed on account of a threatening cloud coming toward us. It gladdened, frightened and disappointed us in turn . . . but finally the long expected rain began to fall. I remained in my room being afraid of the lightning and at the same time admiring it. Lev and Grisha at tea. The examination. A walk to the brick yard. Stilts. Gavriusha Apalat. Read Gogol with Bob after supper and dreamed of a production of *The Inspector General.*[24] Tasya's performance was canceled. Whist. Nikolai Vasilyevich.

25 May All day, still the same *strange* feeling in my throat troubled and irritated me terribly. Worked, in the morning, on the arrangement of the Variations for four hands. In the afternoon, walked to the Plyakovsky beet field past the railroad station. The songs of the workers. Beetles. Sasha was reporting at tea how cousin looks upon my relations with Nata. Later, the veterinary appeared, whom I had to entertain. Wrote, studied English and, all the while, was worried about my throat. Together with the boys, amused myself, before supper, with the stilts, *pas de géant*, etc. We waited a long time for Flegont after supper and, in the meantime, I got a headache so that I played whist with difficulty. Had terrible luck and I was awfully sorry for Sasha. Was very tortured not by the sensation Z itself, but by the fact that it is in me. Retired without writing. Slept restlessly.

26 May Awoke in a very bad mood and frightened about my *throat* after a good but feverishly interrupted sleep. Refrained from eating, thinking that would help but, as a matter of fact, there was no change for a long time, and now (am writing this at 12:30 A.M. after a stroll), it troubles me more than ever. What is it? Most

---

[23] *For a long time Tchaikovsky had ardently wished to own a piece of property where he could live in quiet. At this time Dvoryaninova, an estate, was being put up for sale at a price far beyond Tchaikovsky's means.*

[24] *Comedy by Gogol.*

likely nothing, but it does not make it easier on the nerves. Received a letter from Hubert, informing me about Bessel's proposition regarding the changes in *The Oprichnik*. Was considerably agitated by it. As a result of my slight indisposition and the marvelous weather, did not work but went to the Trostyanka forest through the oak tree grove, and the walk would have been very delightful but for my throat. Dinner took place late. There were Nikolai Vasilyevich and Sabaneiev. Sat on the ladder on the porch with Bob and Tasya, who was combing my hair. Adele Andreyevna (who also dined) was prating about my fame. Later did some writing at home. Only at five-thirty did Nata call me for tea. Cousin's removal. Wrote two variations. Strolled in the garden: the acacias are sweetly fragrant. Met Vera Vasilyevna. It was very pleasant at vespers (it's the eve of Trinity Sunday). Father Alexander wore a skull cap. Bob broke his knee (Apalat and the stilts). My anxiety. The doctor. Whist. Had rotten luck.

Trinity Sunday, 27 May At Mass. Intense, almost unbearable, stifling heat. Was hardly able to last through the ceremony of kneeling. At Alexandra Ivanovna's; drank tea in the dining room. She was, somehow or other, unusually affectionate to me. Mitya's arrival. Met them (Danya) near the railroad tracks. After dinner, the feeling started again. Clouds were hovering and it rained on and off. I succeeded in working. Anna Petrovna's departure. A stroll along the railroad tracks. Dancing after supper. Five-handed whist.

Whitmonday, 28 May The weather was not bad and, even though it rained, it was still too little. Took a marvelous walk through the Nikolaiev field nearly as far as Zrubanetz, thanks to the grayish morning. Bob's fall from the horse was due to the clowning of that good-for-nothing Mitya. It's good that everything is all right. In the afternoon, Mitya was beating the dogs for his enjoyment. At once I detested that mean urchin and was so aroused and upset that I took part with reluctance in the games of *bouts-rimés* and *secrétaire* which Vera Vasilyevna arranged in the big house. Took a walk on the main street on the Pokrov side. Worked a little. Whist with Sabaneiev and Flegont after supper. I had no luck. I was terribly tired and lay down to sleep immediately after returning home. Awoke at night from heartburn.

29 May Took a long walk in the morning to the Plyakovsky beet field. Lev rode away with the *good-for-nothing* (God, forgive me!)

to Chigirin. The teacher arrived. At first, I was busy with the arrangement of the Variations, then, with the selection of my piano pieces for an edition of the *Ausgewählte Werke* which Peter Ivanovich is undertaking. The teacher arrived for the boys. Dinner of boiled meat dumplings with Sabaneiev and the teacher whom I had to entertain. A trip by landau to Prussy: Sasha, Nata, Tasya, cousin and I. It would have been very enjoyable were it not for the *feeling* which appeared to pass at first but then returned with added strength. During the supper at home, the strange behavior of the hostess of the house, openly arousing her children against their close ones or, in any case, against their revered relatives. Oh, why, why all this? . . . Was in the big house. Was present during the game of *the miller* there and conversed with Lizaveta and Vera Vasilyevna.

30 May Since morning, the *feeling*. Took a long walk in the Nikolaiev field. Worked on (1) the Variations, (2) the proofs of the Mozart.[25] During dinner, carried on a conversation with the German (he is very talkative) about classicism, teaching, etc. Considerable rain fell just before dinner. Suddenly and quite unexpectedly the *feeling* vanished in the afternoon—but it came back again in the evening. The proofs in the afternoon. Outfitted Bob for his trip on horseback. Walked to the mill. The insane Jewish man. Sat on the roof at sunset and watched a rain cloud moving away, as well as Nata devouring cucumbers just brought from Verbovka. Whist with Flegont after supper. Lev's return from Chigirin. Tea. Nikolai Vasilyevich; butterflies; Nikolai Vasilyevich dropped in to say good-by. The *feeling*.

31 May All day clouds were hovering and rain was falling, and in the evening, there was a downpour. Managed to do my two hours of walking in the morning; walked from the Smelyansk road near the cemetery to the Plyakovsky fields and while descending to the railroad station had a view of a thundercloud rather near by. Worked on *Figaro* and finished it. Was inseparable for about two hours in the afternoon from my marvelous, incomparable Bob; at first, he lounged about on the porch, on the bench and was fascinatingly *relaxed* and chattered about my works (Kamenka-

---

[25] *Tchaikovsky was arranging for piano four hands his Third Suite and correcting the proofs of the recitatives he had composed for Mozart's* The Marriage of Figaro.

Moscow). Then he sat in my room and made me play. I worked after tea. Intermittent rain. The president of the conference arrived. Our boys left at seven o'clock with the German and the Englishman and returned only toward ten; we were all terribly worried; it turned out that the rain kept them in Prussy. Whist with the president. Heavy rain. A telegram from Modest that he is ill and remained at St. Petersburg. All day the *feeling*. Slept half the night in the studio.

1 June Grand weather. A long walk to the Plyakovsky beet field. Was writing the arrangement of the finale. The *feeling* began to disappear in the afternoon. The trip to Verbovka was extremely pleasant. A little dog was stubbornly following us. Walked with Bob, Grisha, and Uka from Lebedovka. Tea. Horses. Jumping in the brick yard and out of doors. On the way, Nata talked about her fears. Learn during supper that Blumenfeld summoned Vladimir Andreyevich about something. Mad excitement, especially when Lev instructed that he be called. Could hardly finish playing two rubbers.

2 June A walk, still to the Plyakovsky beet field across the Smelyansk road. Was writing the arrangement of the finale. Dropped in at the big house at Alexandra Ivanovna's with the boys in the afternoon; then played *gorodki* [26] with the whole company of boys and teachers and later there was lively leaping in the *pas de géant*. Tea at home (together with cousin; Sasha and Vera Vasilyevna were busy with books). Cousin's stories about her youth, her parents, her courtship, etc. Wrote letters and studied English. Unsuccessful attempt to get in at vespers at the Pokrov church; but at any rate had a pleasant walk beyond the church. A telegram from Modest which disturbed me. Sat with Bob in the studio after supper and conversed about school matters. Whist. No luck; was not angry, but kept breaking out in a cold perspiration. There was a little *feeling* but now I am not afraid of the enemy as I know him; it is still the same thing—my stomach.

Sunday, 3 June Am writing while very tired. A drive to the big forest for the whole day. I *walked* to Podlesnaya. There we rested, had dinner, took a walk with Lev and Kern to the farmstead beet fields, drank tea, etc. I was almost left behind in the forest over-

---

[26] A *game played by striking blocks of wood with a stick. Pas de géant, swinging, and walking on stilts were other pastimes of the group.*

night through a misunderstanding. Supper and whist with Kern at home. Frightfully intense sensation Z. Oh, my God! Forgive and appease me! The *feeling* has passed completely. A telegram from Modest. A strange thing: am *terribly* reluctant to go away from here. I think it's all on account of Bob.

4 June Dreamt about M. and as a result of it was in love a little, even more than a little, all day. . . . it's nothing, nothing. . . . Silence . . . !!! Was in the Trostyanka forest in the morning, and was in a state of horror and sadness as I learned from Nikolai Dmitriyevich Kondratyev's letter about the death of poor, good-natured Mosalitinov. Naturally, it's a pity for him, for he could have enjoyed living longer, but how excruciatingly must Gol. [Golitzin] suffer!!! Kern had dinner and after that I drank some liqueur entirely in vain. Was irritated at tea and throughout the entire day by poor cousin with whom I am not nearly so affectionate as I ought to be. Forgot to mention that at dinner several things happened which react agonizingly on me (about Kruaza, etc.). Dozed during the day, which has not happened to me for a long time. The divine old ladies were also at tea and later, on meeting them in the garden (they were going to Nikolai Vasilyevich with Lev and Sasha), accompanied them to the house. Roamed about aimlessly, on the whole; was also sitting on the roof a while. Nata chatted long with me at the window. After supper, many came to bid Sasha good-by. Whist. I had very bad luck. On account of that, but principally because of a thousand other reasons which constitute what I call Z, I was as angry as a venomous snake. Came home under a melancholy, heavy pressure of this Z.

5 June Awoke with a severe pain in the throat and in a feverish condition. Forced myself to take a walk. Worked at home. Vadim showed up. After dinner the pain began to get worse and I became quite sick so that I did not have supper, while the pain in the throat was so awful that each time I swallowed it was hellish torture. The night was terribly tormenting.

6 June Felt a little better toward morning thanks to profuse perspiration. How much friendship and sympathy Alesha displays on such occasions! Sent for Kulikov.[27] Calmed me, saying there is no abscess. Even though I am better, I still feel bad and do not know how I will travel tomorrow. Slept almost the entire day. Was visited.

---

[27] *A doctor from the hospital at Kamenka.*

Ate very little. Certain visitors (Yak. Mikh.) burdened me. Played whist, just the same, but could hardly last two rubbers. Slept the night brokenly. Heard Sasha's departure.

7 June Remained indoors all day. Visitors again and, incidentally, Lizaveta and Vera Vasilyevna and Baldy. Am much better. Was reading the *Memoirs* of Panaeva all the time. Cold day. Dined in my room. Visit by Mme. Sil. Had supper in the house. Whist with Flegont, Lev, and Dima (who, after all, succeeded in wheedling a subsidy).

8 June Took a walk to the Trostyanka forest. Was in the big house in the afternoon and visited Alexandra Ivanovna with Lizaveta Vasilyevna and Vera Vasilyevna. Rose jam. Tea at home. A ride through the fields in a carriage with Nikolai Vasilyevich and the three teachers. Whist after supper. At eleven o'clock, left for the railroad station with drunken Alesha and the intolerable scoundrel Mitya. One o'clock in Znamenka [Grankino]. The kind general. Peculiarly constructed Pullman car. The sunrise.

9 June [Kharkov] Slept much. At four o'clock Kharkov. Due to the exhibition, stayed, not at the Grand Hotel, but at the Metropole. Wandered about. The Cathedral. The chorus singing. Dinner at the Grand Hotel. Tea at home. With Alesha in the Tivoli garden.

Diary Four

February, 1886 – October, 1886

In the year 1886, at the age of forty-six, Tchaikovsky rented a furnished house at Maidanovo, a village on the Sestra River near Moscow. The natural beauty of the surroundings pleased him, as well as the fact that Maidanovo was easily accessible by train to Moscow and St. Petersburg, where he made frequent trips on musical affairs. Living with him were Alexei and other servants, and he entertained guests often. Throughout this period Tchaikovsky was at work on the composition of his opera, "The Enchantress"; he also finished the Dumka, Op. 59 and the Twelve Songs, Op. 60. In the early spring he went to visit his brother Anatoly and his family at Tiflis. Then he went by steamer from Batum to Marseilles and thence to Paris on the errand reticently described by his brother Modest as "a very important family affair," and now clarified. The diary continues through the summer and autumn at Maidanovo.

MAIDANOVO

1 February, 1886, Maidanovo Almighty God! Give me Thy blessing! Will I ever complete this diary? Only God Himself knows! And how very much I would like to complete this one also and start still many more. How much there is yet to be done! How much to be read! How much to learn! I am terribly reluctant to die as yet, even though at times I imagine that I have lived, oh, so long.

The weather was good (25 degrees [F.]) but cloudy. Was busy finishing the second act [of *The Enchantress*] in the morning, after a walk. Alesha brought nothing from the post office while I await impatiently the letter with the money—I have none at all. Took a very long walk, about three miles from Ya . . ., on the paved road to the right in the afternoon. Alesha drove up for me as agreed upon. Worked and finished the second act after having tea and reading (Shakespeare's *Richard II*). Played Anton Rubinstein's *Nero* after supper.

Sunday, 2 February Rode to Mass in the village with Alesha. Was irritated, as usual, by the choristers and their ugliness. Alesha finally got the *registered letter* from N. F. [Mme. von Meck] at the post office; I was glad and calmed down but at home it turned out to be only a notice of remittance made the day before, which, however, did not arrive. Also received the *statement* (!!!) from Jürgenson. All this so excited and upset me that work was out of the question. Strolled about the garden before dinner. Walked through the rooms, the gallery (was teaching Top tricks) and the garden in the afternoon. Was in low spirits at tea. Nevertheless, worked rather long later (on the Introduction to the opera). Wrote to Jürgenson about the "annuity" after supper, requesting at the same time that the letter be returned afterward. My excitement was aggravated still more by my indecision: to go or not to go to Moscow tomorrow? Luckily, it seems that Alesha (who is celebrating his birthday Tuesday) would want me to leave for he advised that I go.

MOSCOW

3 February Severe frost. Trip to Moscow. Received the desired letter with the remittance at the post office. Railroad station. Tailor. On the way, read, lunched, and spent the time pleasantly; a very quiet trip. Moscow. At home. At the Conservatory concert at 3 P.M. with Anton Rubinstein. Dinner at Zverev's. Madame Pabst and "the bottle." Whist. Arensky's foolishness and his excited condition. A birthday party at the Maslovs' (Anna Ivanovna). Julia Afanasyevna, the Turgenevs, Arensky, and Jürgenson's nephew. Composed a musical jest for Sasha Jürgenson.

4 February Bank. Money. Courteous clerks. Selected some works by Mozart for the suite at Jürgenson's store. Rode to Zverev to fetch the coat. Met Anna Sergeyevna Zvereva and Alexandra Vasilyevna Mo, daughter of Buliginsky. Had dinner at Patrikeyev's restaurant, upstairs at Ivan's at two o'clock. Took a walk. Home. Chattered and played with Sasha Jürgenson. A letter as though from the *Russkaya Mysl*. Brius. Disgusted and ashamed. Anton

Rubinstein's recital.[1] Clementi, Moscheles, Thalberg, etc. Supper tendered to Anton by the professors. Boring. Speeches. Stayed long and drank after most left. Humorous speeches by Laroche. Walked home with Laroche and Kashkin.

5 February Called at the Huberts'. Conversation. Purchased various things. Solo lunch at Patrikeyev's restaurant. Home. Dinner at the Tretyakovs'. Very many guests. Aristocracy. Whist with Perfileva, Laroche and Olga Sergeyevna's brother. Some more whist with Aladina, Elena Andreyevna, and Olga Sergeyevna. At Patrikeyev's restaurant with Laroche.

MAIDANOVO

6 February Boris awakened me. Tea with the Jürgenson couple. Departed. Alone in the railroad car. Home. Dinner. A walk to the apothecary for some soda. A boy hiding in a sleigh. Top.[2] Was eluding beggars. Tea. Letters. Supper. Was selecting from Mozart and am hesitant.

7 February Feel very tired. It's now many years since this happened to me. Wasted much time on several bars with a great deal of effort all day. It was in the Introduction and progress was slow. Nothing unusual. The Jewish bookbinder came in the morning. Strolled on the paved road in the afternoon. Slipped and fell while going down the hill to the river. Just assembled the books for binding. There are rather many.

8 February Clear and freezing but spring is not far off—it's melting in the sun and the gallery is just as warm as the room during day. Wanted to visit the school[3] after tea but there was Mass (funeral services for someone) and so there were no classes. Composed with good results. Walked to the river, after dinner, through

[1] *Tchaikovsky attended the fifth of a series of seven historical piano recitals by Rubinstein whose virtuosity he greatly admired. The program contained works by Clementi, Moscheles, celebrated pianist-composer who taught almost everyone in the generations from Beethoven to Tchaikovsky, and Thalberg, Liszt's rival in his Parisian days.*

[2] *Tchaikovsky's dog.*

[3] *Tchaikovsky was interested in the school for children which he was instrumental in founding. He supported it financially all his life.*

Praslovo (on the side, being afraid of the boys⁴). Read Shakespeare's *King Henry IV* at tea. Like it very much—and I am far from a Shakespearian. Worked excellently in the evening. Was still bothered selecting from Mozart for the Suite after supper; played them through until eleven-thirty. Alexei put my correspondence in order today. Photos.

Sunday, 9 February Yesterday Alesha informed me that there is water in his scrotum again. This makes me terribly sad. When will the poor soul ever recover? Was at church (after an unusually good night's sleep) and stood to the left of the choir. Worked a bit. Two acts are entirely completed. Took a walk on the paved road in the direction of Moscow through Klin immediately after dinner. The dogs followed me as far as Klin, making a great commotion as Rover is away to the hunt. Alesha came for me and drove me back. The weather was beyond all description: clear, even thawing in the sun, while at the same time it was freezing and no wind at all. Went once more to the river after tea. Sasha, the instructor. Home, played through the whole second act. Solitaire. Am brooding and homesick, thinking about the forthcoming long trip. Am getting old and have the desire to stay in one place—at home.

MOSCOW

10 February Left on the baggage train (walked to the railroad station; conversed with the stationmaster, a vender, etc. there). Had a gossipy lady as neighbor in the train but shunned conversation. Enjoyed lunch. Arriving, went straight to the theater, leaving my things at Jürgenson's. Anton Rubinstein Festival. Dinner at the Hermitage restaurant. Sat with Taneiev, Kashkin, Jürgenson, Makovsky and others. Was out of sorts all the time. Wine cheered me up. Opera singers; gossip and squabbles of the Germans. Evening reception at Sergey Mikhailovich Tretyakov's. Whist with Cherinov, Chikagov and Makovsky. Rubinstein was with the ladies. Rode home with Makovsky.

11 February Lunch at Laroche's. Simon's compositions. Visited Max von Erdmannsdörfer with Laroche. "Manfred."⁵ We visited

---

⁴ *At times, boys made walking impossible: they pestered him for money.*

⁵ *Tchaikovsky's symphony, Op. 58 composed in 1885 and inspired by Byron's poem of the same name.*

Albrecht. He was having dinner. Discussed the concert to be given on the evening of March 1. Was at the private opera. *Don Juan* [*Don Giovanni*] in a horrible performance. Anton's recital.[6] I was in a very bad mood. Some lady sat in my seat. Supper at Max von Erdmannsdörfer's.

12 February Visited Taneiev at the Conservatory. Lunched at V. E. Makovsky's. His paintings. His son Sasha, stunningly handsome. At the Shpazhinskys'. The new fourth act.[7] Dinner at the Pabsts' with Anton. Unfinished whist. Noise and yelling. Pauline's advances. Strolled with Taneiev and Laroche on Tverskoy Boulevard. Supper at Patrikeyev's restaurant with Manya. A coachman knowing Ivan.

MAIDANOVO

13 February Tea with the Jürgenson family. Departure. A big, stout, disheveled man and his repulsive wife who took up all the room. The heat was unbearable and the intolerable V. I. Taneiev[8] topped off all the discomfort. Conversed about literature with him after we passed Podsolnechnaya. According to him, Tolstoy is not talented but, on the other hand, Sleptzov has some kind of genius. Hid my complete fury. Home. Dinner. Walk. Was pestered by men and women beggars of all ages. An old woman carrying a thirty-six pound bag of flour. Osip and Sasha. Home. Tea. Dozed. Letters. Bath. Vile night.

14 February Napped intermittently, rather than slept. Why—do not understand. Visited the school. Gentle, shy Father deacon. The children's answers. Gavrila, Ignasha and the little girl, Matrena, were outstanding. Osip was bad. A package from Annette. Embroidery. A tablecloth from Olga. Walked up and down in my room after dinner and later went to the railroad station to telegraph Jürgenson about the ballet.[9] Felt tired as never before and returned by droshky. I am out of sorts, in general. Utmost aversion to work.

---

[6] *Rubinstein's sixth historical piano recital, devoted entirely to Chopin's works.*

[7] *The composer received the libretto of the new fourth act of his opera* The Enchantress *from Shpazhinsky, the librettist.*

[8] *Brother of the famous composer, Sergey I. Taneiev.*

[9] Svetlana (*Amaryllis*), Slavic Princess *by Nikolai S. Klenovsky, a pupil of Tchaikovsky.*

Wrote N. F. and Taneiev. Read the *Vestnik Evropy* after supper.
All afternoon I was morbidly melancholy.

Saturday, 15 February Slept soundly but with a morbid heaviness.
Was downcast, brooding, worked little and with effort (the piece
for Mackar) [10] all day, on the whole. Bitter frost. Walked up and
down in my room after reading the newspapers (*Muzikalny Listok*
and *Novoye Vremya*). Took a stroll by the river under much strain.
Felt better after tea. Was agonizingly lonely and sat in Alesha's
room while he was busy with the bills. Worked a little. Had a headache and no appetite at supper. Feel better now. Played *Nero.*
Strange that I feel an unwholesome aversion now to my latest
works—to "Manfred" and the opera. Decided to leave tomorrow
for the sake of the ballet.

MOSCOW

Sunday, 16 February Slept marvelously. Left on the baggage
train. Superb lunch. A lady constantly laughing and some officers
from Voskresensk. Arrived home. Sasha and Elena Sergeyevna. Tea
with them. Walked to Albrecht. Discussion about the concert at his
place. Photographs from N. [Nikolai] G. Rubinstein's *Nachlass.*
Solo dinner at Patrikeyev's restaurant in Ivan's room. The ballet
Svetlana. First performance. My box was so crowded that I took
an orchestra seat. Sorokhtin. The music of the ballet is not bad but
the ballet itself is poor, although some scenes are effective. Tea with
S. I. [Jürgenson] and the children at home (all including Liuba
Tretyakova had been in the box).

17 February Walked to see Novichikha. Lunched at Savrasenko's
restaurant. Stroll. Conservatory. Session. The new director is very
nice. Took a walk on the boulevard with Taneiev. Called on P. I.
[Jürgenson]. Wrote to J. P. Shpazhinskaya. Dinner at S. I. Taneiev's
with Anton. Concert of some of my sacred works in the evening.
Bishop Peter, etc. Poor program and bad performance. Became
awfully tired. The case of Hubert and talk with Paulina Erdmannsdörfer regarding her husband's anger and excitement, still about
the same matter of the album, which also angered me at the session
as well as the fact that money was taken from me for the trip. Was
at Patrikeyev's restaurant with the Huberts, Zverev, Remezov, etc.

---

[10] Dumka, *Op. 59 for piano, written for Félix Mackar, Tchaikovsky's
Paris publisher.*

18 February Was at the Conservatory. Effects of the matter of the album and the insults to Erdmannsdörfer. N. P. Sitovsky's humor. Called on Shpazhinsky. Tea. Excellent new version for the ending of the fourth act. Lunch at Anton's at the Hotel Dresden. Baratinskaya, the Evreinovs and others. Visited Erdmannsdörfer. Explanation. At the Conservatory. Sergey Mikhailovich. The case of Kommisarzhevsky. Visited Anna von Meck. She was in bed. Katerina Vasilyevna Peresleni. Masha Stahlberg. Dinner at the Hermitage restaurant. Exorbitant prices. Home. Letter about money from Modest. Bad impression. Tea. Boris was offended. Anton's recital. Russian works. Topsy-turvy program.[11] Jürgenson's clerks and I were in the third row. Petersen gave a supper at Lopashov's restaurant. Pompous. Belokha. Cognac with the Huberts.

MAIDANOVO

19 February Slept very little. Boris woke me up. Sent a telegram to S. M. Tretyakov that I cannot come. Votya Sangursky's works. Departed. Priests in the train. A pretty middle-class woman between Podsolnechnaya and Klin. Home. Dinner. Walked about my room. Slept. Tea. In a bad mood. Homesickness and hesitation about the trip. Was driven almost to despair. Wrote letters. Went to the kitchen. Cards. Supper. Ordered dinner for the guests. Wrote the diary for many days.

20 February The wind is howling more than ever; it's hard to imagine that spring is so near. It was bitter cold. After a wonderful night, I felt more cheerful today and decided, come what may, to take the trip, as was understood. Was composing the piece for Mackar after a stroll. Alesha brought a letter from N. D. Kondratyev from Nice as well as from others. Read the newspapers. Instead of a dinner there were just pancakes. And I even had difficulty getting them. Despite the fierce wind, went to the station, immediately after dinner, to telegraph Laroche that he should not come. Was exhausted, but on the other hand, gave my stomach less work. Was drowsy all the while before and after tea. Nevertheless, wrote six

---

[11] *Rubinstein's seventh and last historical piano recital was devoted entirely to works by Russian composers except for eleven études by Chopin. Four of Tchaikovsky's numbers were on the program and, though delighted by their interpretation, he was dissatisfied with the choice.*

letters and worked a little. Played *Nero* after supper. The liberties
taken by the composer merit astonishment but not imitation.

21 February Frightful snowstorm. Was not out at all today.
Finished the rhapsody [*Dumka*] for Mackar in the morning. Received a long letter about family affairs from N. F.[12] Had only soup
and cake for dinner but, in spite of my extreme moderation, almost
became sick and was unbelievably exhausted from the pressure on
my stomach. Yes, I must go to Vichy! Sat down to copy the rhapsody after tea and had several moments of anguish. Dear N. A.
Hubert unexpectedly arrived, probably because of the letter to
Batasha about my melancholy. How good-natured Hubert is! Finished writing the first part of the rhapsody. We had supper; I think
he ate immoderately. . . . We played whist. Gossiped. I recovered
fully. The snowstorm subsided. Believe the weather will be good
tomorrow. Saw Hubert to bed.

Saturday, 22 February Went to Klin with Alesha after rising,
drinking tea, conversing with Hubert, and writing a little. Apothecary. Skating has started. The chef in Circassian clothes. Went home
by droshky (after futile attempts to get a hazel hen). Lunch.
Tonichka overate and went to sleep. I went to Klin again. Stunning,
marvelous, divine weather. After watching the skaters, returned,
drank tea, and played—and Hubert was sleeping all the time. Went
to meet the guests in the big sleigh with him. At the station. Bought
some hazel hens. The train. Batasha, Remezov, Zverev. Home.
Boris Jürgenson. Dinner. Whist. Tea. Batasha's quarrel with her
husband about cards. Showed all to their bedrooms.

23 February Zverev left early. Drank tea with Boris at first; then,
little by little, everyone assembled. The weather is very warm, looks
like snow. I went for a walk with Boris. We conversed. We visited
the cemetery. At the railroad station. Talked with the chef. My
guests arrived. However, the Safonovs did not come, on whose account we all gathered. Dinner, pancakes; all were gluttons except
me. Whist. Why were my nerves very upset and my hands unusually cold? Saw them off. At the railroad station, a telegram from
Modest which disturbed me. Supper at home. Read Olearius.

---

[12] *Tchaikovsky's benefactress wrote explaining her financial position,
which was very secure, and in detail about her eldest son, Volodya, who
took his deceased father's place in aiding his mother retain her fortune.*

Lent, 24 February After rising took a walk (read Gerke's report about matters in the St. Petersburg Musical Society prior to that). Wrote letters. Went to meet Laroche. He arrived. Dinner at home and a walk to Klin for a pair of felt boots. At Skokov's. Acquaintances. Came home by droshky. I was busy copying the piece after tea while Manya was writing an article in his room. Supper. We played Mozart. We were talking until eleven o'clock. I am very glad that he came.

25 February Lovely day but it's still freezing. Wrote a bit after tea (I was shy due to Laroche's presence). Took a walk with him; we were at Klin. Wrote letters after dinner. Rode to Klin with Alesha. Went to the evening prayers in the imperial quarters and in the cathedral. Tea at home. Worked. Supper. Played Mozart and talked with Laroche.

26 February Slept very poorly—my own fault (dreamed about Shchurovsky; very vividly—too much so even). Worked shortly after tea (Laroche had already managed to take a walk). We went for a stroll on the paved road to the right at eleven o'clock. It was bright, clear, and beautiful but cold. We had dinner on returning (was irritated by the pestering of the boys). Laroche was courting Arisha. Read letters and newspapers while lying down in his room. He fell asleep. I had a walk, rested, and then worked in the garden with a shovel. Walked up and down in the gallery—it was warm, like summer. Alesha has returned from the city. My heart breaks as I talk to him lately—I am very unwilling to leave and feel sorry for him. Tea. Work. Letters. Supper. We played a little (Balakirev). He became *drowsy* and went to bed at ten o'clock. Wrote Pobedonostzev about Orlov and his position as chorus master.

27 February Wrote a reply to an inquiry received from Shishkov regarding Orlov all morning. The piano tuner arrived unexpectedly during the most pleasant part of the dinner. Alexei made a scene. His sister. Went to Klin with Laroche; he rode off from there and I went walking. Was at the apothecary, changed some money at Skokov's (talked with a stout acquaintance), heard Andrey Kritsky's entire liturgy at the cathedral and then Ivan, the droshky driver, drove me home. Tea. Laroche was fit for nothing the whole day. In fact, he is seriously shattered intellectually. I was sitting in his room almost up to suppertime. Monteverdi's operas, etc. Letter

to Mme. Kross. I was irritated by the talk about the purchase of an
estate during supper. Was recalling old times, talked about Auber,
etc. with Laroche after supper. He went off at four o'clock and
while bidding good-by confessed rashly that he cannot tolerate my
works. Why is it?

28 February Drank tea with Manya. He left by train. Worked.
Went to telegraph Suvorin after dinner. It occurred to me, at tea,
to read Alexei Tolstoy's *John of Damascus* and *The Sinner* which
unexpectedly made me cry a good deal. While I was in this mellow
mood, which always follows intense artistic ecstasy, suddenly there
came a telegram from Sitovsky saying that the G. D. [Grand Duke]
would be present. It meant that all the plans went to the devil!
Despair, perplexity, fear, and repugnance once more toward my
trip. And in addition to all this, there is the letter from Modest.
Ah! It was a very disturbing day today . . . ! Went to feed Novikova's hungry dog. A cruel feeling of loneliness attacked me during
twilight. Letters. Calmed down. Supper. Played my Second Suite [13]
and was very happy that it is not really so bad as I imagined.

1 March Spring; it's warm and bright. Tempted by the good
weather in the morning, I spent almost all the time walking. There
was a bazaar at Klin. Gave money to various beggars. (Ice cutters.)
Returned about twelve o'clock. Dropped in to Praskovya's to complain that the dogs were hungering. However, managed to work
with good results. Dinner. Walked up and down in the gallery; the
sun was warm and delightful. Played *Nero* and then took a nap on
the couch in the dressing room, yielding to an attack of sleepiness.
Tea. A walk. What sublime weather! Worked with very good results. Played *Nero* after supper. I am still astonished at the impudent liberties taken by its composer. Oh, you ridiculous clown!
By God, I am seized with anger looking at this score. But then I
play this abomination because I am conscious of my superiority—
at least as to sincerity—and that gives support to my energy. You
think that you write vilely, but seeing such trash which nevertheless was performed seriously—your soul feels better. I am ashamed
that I feel so much anger over this work—but why should I make
pretenses in my diary? . . .

MOSCOW

2 March Cold weather like winter. Left Madino [Maidanovo]. In

---

[13] *For Orchestra, Op. 53, composed in 1883.*

the train. The children and their nurse. Lunch. Moscow. Walked to the session [14] which was not at the Conservatory but at S. M. Tretyakov's who has been ill recently. Erdmannsdörfer's foolishness. Dinner at the Huberts'. Zverev, Remezov. Whist. Went home at twelve o'clock.

3 *March* Conversation with Jürgenson. Lunch at Lopashov's restaurant. Overindulgence. Visited Altani. To the Conservatory. At the rehearsal of the students' concert. Called on Erdmannsdörfer. Dinner at the Jürgensons'. A nap; dreamed of Tolstoy. At Karlusha's. Bells for "Manfred." Brius. Andrey. Hotel New Moscow. Drunkenness. Home.

4 *March* Unbearably cold wind. Greeting to the Grand Duke. Razsvetov, Dr. Repman, etc. Visited Altani. Visited Ostrovsky. Visited the Shpazhinskys. Solo carousing at Testov's restaurant. Vespers at Uspensky Cathedral. Felt ill. Home. To the concert with Jürgenson. The Grand Duke. Wonderful students' concert. Konius created a furor. My neighbor was the charming Grand Duke Konstantin Konstantinovich. Supper at the Conservatory. An ovation to Alexeyev. Rode home with Konstantin Sergeyevich Alexeyev. My cheek pained unbearably throughout the night.

5 *March* Was quite sick. Put on my tail coat and walked over to Jürgenson's; but returned home from there and suffered very much from the pain in my cheek all day. S. I. has an attack of heart palpitation. Spent a terrible night; fell asleep really only toward morning.

6 *March* A big swelling formed toward morning. Had less pain but still it pained the whole day and the fever continued. Exchanged notes with Sasha Jürgenson and Elena Sergeyevna in prose and verse. In the morning Popov (Ivan Petrovich) appeared— whom I was obliged to send away, being unable to speak. Batasha visited me. Slept much. Sasha Gudim came toward dinnertime, Laroche much later. Felt bad in the evening.

7 *March* Slept much but not soundly. Popov and a clearing up of the affairs of the Choral Society with him. Lunched alone. As the day progressed I felt worse. Laroche came toward dinner and stayed all evening. We "whisted."

---

[14] *Of the directorate of the Russian Musical Society.*

8 March Feel as though I am better. Wrote letters declining dinner invitations. Sangursky and his painting. Lunched with S. I. Was still exhausted and suffered until four o'clock. Suddenly at about that time my whole sickness vanished as if by magic. Played with the little girls. Had dinner and an immense appetite; played whist with the Huberts and S. I., and had supper.

Sunday, 9 March Rose healthy. Had a discussion about business matters with P. I. after tea. Displayed a most awkwardly organized mind, as usual. Expected Modest who telegraphed that he would arrive on the express train. Modest came. Lunch at the Jürgensons'. I went out for the first time since my illness at three o'clock to attend the rehearsal of "Manfred." Was dissatisfied and embarrassed as everything seemed bad. Dined with Modya and Laroche at the Hermitage restaurant. Returned at twelve o'clock.

Monday, 10 March At the rehearsal at nine o'clock. Was left satisfied. Lunch with Modya and Laroche at Patrikeyev's restaurant. Home. Napped. Awakened by Boris. . . . At five o'clock was at Jürgenson's on account of Kuznetzov's compositions. Korsov. Dinner at the Jürgensons'. Laroche, Modest, Hubert. S. I. is ill. Concert by the Philharmonic Society. Kuznetzov, Arends, Ilinsky and their works. Supper with Sinelnikova at Patrikeyev's restaurant.

11 March Mice. Headache. Rehearsal. Alexeyev with Ushakov. The orchestra applauded. Lunch with Batasha, Hubert and Laroche at the Hotel Slavyansky Bazaar restaurant. A stroll. Home. Dozed. Rode to the Laroches at six o'clock where Modest was at dinner. To the concert together. "Manfred." [15] I stayed in the artist's room. Erdmannsdörfer was pale. My nervousness. A half success but still an ovation. Supper with a large company at Patrikeyev's restaurant.

MAIDANOVO

Wednesday, 12 March At Modya's at Kokorev's hotel. Home. Visited Taneiev. Visited Shpazhinskaya. Her hysterical condition. Visited the von Mecks. [16] Lev. Lunch. Visited Jürgenson. At the railroad station. Christopher is a fool. Shakhovskaya. Travel. Home. Alesha. Dinner. Whist with Novikova. Laroche is also visiting me.

---

[15] *First performance of this symphony, Erdmannsdörfer conducted.*

[16] *Nikolai K. von Meck, son of Mme. von Meck, married Tchaikovsky's niece, Anna L. Davidova.*

13 March   Rose after a bad sleep. Tea together. Philosopher Mikhail Ivanovich Sofronov. A stroll. Horrible weather. Nine letters. Dinner. A stroll. Mailed the letters myself. Tea. Modya had a headache. We played the *Le Gaulois* [17] album together. In my room. Worked. Novikova. Supper. Whist. Decided to take Alesha.

ST. PETERSBURG

14 March   Decided to go to St. Petersburg with Modya. Went to Novikova regarding the horses. Welcomed Katerina Ivanovna Sinelnikova. Dinner. Novikova. Departed for St. Petersburg with Modya.

15 March   St. Petersburg. Conservatory. One thousand rubles. Rimsky-Korsakov, Rubetz, Tur, etc. Visited the von Bülows. His wife. Glazunov. Dinner at home. Concert. Ovation.[18] Tea with Bob and Kolya at home.

16 March   St. Isaac's Cathedral. Lunch at Rimsky-Korsakov's. Setov. Vera's birthday. Mikhailovsky Theater. *La doctoresse.*[19] The dance at Vera's. Supper at Toucet's restaurant. Annette, Apukhtin, Kozlov, Kritzky and Guitry.

17 March   Called on Osip Ivanovich Jürgenson. Lunch at Contant's restaurant with Bazilevskaya and Butakova. At Napravnik's (she and the children). At Kolya's. At Apukhtin's. Played chess. Dinner at Kondratyev's. To Amalya's with Bob and Kolya by carriage. Evening reception at Amalya's.

18 March   Took walks. Lunch at Palkin's restaurant. Mme. Guitry bade good-by. Called on Annette with Modya. Gold. Timosha. Dinner at Bertenson's. Called on Sasha. Big evening reception at Abaza's. My social successes.

19 March   Strolled. Kazan Cathedral. Preconsecration Mass. *Hors d'œuvre.* Lunch at home. Fedya Litke. Carriage. Visits. Visited the Rimsky-Korsakovs and Sasha. Visited Kondratyev. Visited Buta-

---

[17] *The Paris newspaper* Le Gaulois *published a music album which contained the works of famous contemporary composers, including some piano pieces by Tchaikovsky.*

[18] *Hans von Bülow conducted and was the soloist in Tchaikovsky's First Piano Concerto at the concert of the Russian Musical Society.*

[19] *Play by Ferrier and Bocage.*

kova. Dinner at Kolya's. Lily. Annette. To the railroad station with her by carriage. Klimentova, Yakovlev and Shaikevich saw me off.

MAIDANOVO

20 March Rose before Tver. Newspapers. Drowsiness. Home. Horses (*my* horses but no longer *mine*). Tea. Alexander Kiselev. Beautiful weather. Took walks. At Novikova's. Gossiping. Worked. Left instructions.

MOSCOW

21 March Departed for Moscow. Farewell. Arisha wept. Lunch at Patrikeyev's restaurant. At the Huberts'. Home. Dinner at Savrasenko's. Concert. Supper at Patrikeyev's restaurant (*Egmont* and Liszt's *Faust* at the concert).

22 March Arrangements about the passport. Lunch at Lopashov's restaurant. Went to see the Albrechts, the Shpazhinskys, Taneiev, and Katerina Vasilyevna Peresleni (Ermolova). Dinner at the Jürgensons'. Called on the von Mecks. Evening with the Huberts. Played "Manfred" four hands and whist. At the editorial office of the *Moskovskiye Vedomosti* with Laroche.

Sunday, 23 March Visited Erdmannsdörfer. At the railroad station. Lunch, drunkenness, merry send-off. In the train compartment. Read, slept, ate.

JOURNEY TO TIFLIS

24 March Kharkov. Strolled. Lunch at the Grand Hotel. Roamed about. Struggled with sleepiness. Vespers at the cathedral. The choristers. At the railroad station. Dinner. Trofim. His wife and son. Alesha. Crowded train. Pullman car. A fat, repulsive lady; an attractive officer landowner; an old Greek, etc. Slept.

25 March Napped and read all day. Taganrog. Ippolit and Sonya.[20] Conversation and tea. Sight-seeing with Ippolit. Lively on the main street. An old lady lives with them; whist, supper, whist again, and *durachki*.[21]

26 March Delightful weather. Went to the harbor with Sonya (after a telephone discussion). The agency. A sail on Ippolit's ship. Captain Ivan Grigoryevich who had a fever. His ship. Caviar. *Turtle*

---

[20] *Tchaikovsky's brother and his wife.*

[21] *A Russian card game.*

Island. Return. Dinner. Ippolit drove to the garden, to the grove
(Tikhon, a stroll). Tea at home. To the cathedral with Sonya.
Heard the night services. Whist with the old lady. Ippolit is ready
for action at any moment. Supper. Ippolit's stories about his adventures.

27 March Rose early. Tea with Ippolit. Parted with him. To the
railroad station with Sonya. Lingered long before starting out. Departed with the feeling of liking Sonya immensely. Along the sea
coast. Along the shore of the Sinyavka River. The brave, retired
military officer who discussed horses with a cossack. Rostov. Beautiful. Dinner at the railroad station with Alesha. Pullman car. The
civil engineer with either his wife or mistress. Supper in the dining
car. Read. Went to bed early.

28 March, Vladikavkaz, Mineralniye Vody Station Was to transfer
to a car with a direct connection but it turned out that I had to
stay in the same place. A Tartar woman. A dislikable, nonpaying
passenger. A Pole. Uncomfortable and hot. Mountains. We tugged
along everlastingly. Typical Tartars and natives, for the most part.
Delightful weather. Mt. Elbrus. A bundle from heaven inside a
cloak in the third-class car. Vladikavkaz. Bad hotel. Sent an agent,
an Armenian, to the post office. Went to have dinner. The agent
returned, informing me that a post chaise will be available only on
Sunday. Great disappointment. A jolly general. A gendarme and his
girl. A Jewish man is the hotel owner. A stroll along the boulevard
with Alesha. Then alone. Home. Irritable. Tea. And still, it is better
to be alone. It's quite apparent that Alexei made this trip with me
for the sake of adventure and not at all out of those sentimental
motives in which I rather foolishly believed.

29 March Excellent weather. The mountains are clearly visible.
I went for a walk, feeling splendid, after tea and arranging about
the post chaise for tomorrow. Was in church at Mass with the
communicants. The deacon's debut. He was confused, lost his wits
and absolutely did not know what to do. It was pitiable and strange
but also comical. An old priest with a nasal voice. An Armenian
churchman. Left powerfully impressed by the novel character of
that liturgy. Wrote letters at home. Lunched with Alesha in the reception room(!!!). Walked by myself on the paved road toward
the mountains. Russian children. On the way back, the sight of a
poor horse, mercilessly beaten. Met Alesha on the boulevard who

forgot to give me the key and, on returning to the hotel, I was unable to get into my room. Had to go out again. Hired a phaeton and rode along the paved road to a small fortress near where the river (do not recall the name) flows into the Terek. A likable driver on the excursion. He was from Saratov and told me many interesting things about the local ethnography or as he expressed it "about the various religions." It was a very enjoyable two hour excursion. Found Alexei in an unusually gay mood at home. Had dinner with him. His gaiety soon became unbearable for he either argued stupidly or laughed foolishly for some unknown reason. Upset me completely. We walked a little on the boulevard and rested a while. Became worse. Sent him away. But when I returned, he was already in bed and told me that his . . . hurts him again. Am totally upset. Oh, God! . . .

30 March, Mlety It was horrible at the Hotel La France last night. The bed was impossible, fleas were biting mercilessly, while homesickness and disgust were killing me. We rose at six o'clock. A nice guard came at seven. Preparations. Tips. Started out about eight o'clock. First stop at Balta—rode twelve miles. It turned out that the guard was incredibly quiet; just the kind I need. The driver hardly answered my two questions. It was the same later on, i.e. both the guard and the driver seemed dumb. That is what I like on a trip. And not the insufferable chattering of some Neapolitan *guide* knowing nothing. The weather was wonderful. The farther we rode, the more beautiful, interesting, and cold it became. After Lars (the second stop) we began to see the famous Daryal Gorge, the Castle of Tamara, the violently raging waters of the Terek, etc. Dined lightly at Kazbek. There we had to put on our fur coats as we were in the snow country. The entire road reminds me, on the whole, of the one to Davos. After leaving Kobi, we rose unbelievably high, crossed safely the place where there was an avalanche recently and where some Oriental natives were working with spectacles or black rags on their faces, and then descended precipitously to Mlety after Gudaur. The road is marvelous. Here we were given two imperial rooms, appearing extraordinarily attractive and clean, after the filth at Vladikavkaz, which pleased me very much. Ordered dinner. Walked about the balcony (rope) while waiting for it. (Noticed how our *traveling companions:* the officer, his wife dressed in his coat, and the woman cook bravely continued the journey by post chaise.) I was served dinner, very simple and de-

licious. Drank tea with Alexei. A jolly Imeretin [22] servant who had
a characteristic Oriental accent. An Englishman. A lady. Went to
bed at nine.

TIFLIS

31 March Slept well. Rose at six; left at seven-thirty. I enjoyed
the trip greatly all the way. Passanaur (down below; the church;
Kolya Tikhmenev's tomb). The descent to Dushet was breath-
taking. The weather, the trip, everything was good. Only the food
was bad at Dushet. We arrived at one-thirty at Mtskhet. I was to
wait for Panya and Tolya,[23] as agreed upon, but became very disturbed by the endless waiting and decided to travel by post chaise.
Arriving at Tiflis, learned that they had started out! Changed
clothes. Tea. Talked with the nurse. Liked Tatusya[24] very much.
Went to see the city. Shortly after I returned, they arrived. Conversation. Supper. The servants were drunk. I liked Tiflis very much,
on the whole, and it was highly pleasant to see my own again.

1 April The weather was nice starting with the morning, later it
spoiled a little. Drank tea with Tolya. Went out with him, and we
got to the district court in a roundabout way, partly on foot and
partly by horse car. From there I went up from the castle and wandered about long in various lanes and alleys. Was also in Maidan
(native quarter). Lunched with Panya and Taniusha. Talked with
Panya regarding her relations with Tolya. A stroll in the garden.
Ivanov[25] and Korganov. Letters. Kolya Peresleni. Before dinner,
while waiting for Tolya, we sat on the balcony, watching the
passers-by. Dinner. Visit to the Mirzoev Baths.[26] Singular spectacle
of affectation. Sulphur water. It was somehow strange to me and
rather unpleasant. Tea at home.

---

[22] *One of the peoples in South Georgia.*

[23] *Anatoly Ilyich Tchaikovsky, the composer's younger brother and
his wife Praskovya.*

[24] *Tatyana, Anatoly's daughter.*

[25] *Original name of Mikhail Mikhailovich Ippolitov-Ivanov, famous
Russian composer and, at the time of Tchaikovsky's visit to Tiflis, director
of the Tiflis Conservatory of Music. He changed his name so as not to
be confused with Ivanov, a contemporary music critic.*

[26] *Tiflis is known for its many warm sulphur springs and fine bath
houses.*

2 April A gray, rainy day. Read Sarcey's article about Tolstoy after tea and could hardly keep from sobbing . . . out of happiness, that our Tolstoy is understood so well by the French. Walked through the city. Returned with mushrooms for lunch. Changed clothes and went to Ivanov. His wife and others; singers and actors. Gorski. At the French steamship agency. Home. Dinner with Gakel. Symphony concert. Beethoven's (Third) Symphony. My serenade. Smirnova. Borodin's On the Steppes of Central Asia. I was called out—didn't go.[27] Tea with Kolya and Korganov at home. Conversation about music and musicians.

3 April Beautiful weather but it is muddy on the street. After tea and reading newspapers, went to the city and returned for lunch at which Tolya was also present. Wrote letters and many of them. Read the history of the Caucasus. Went for a walk in the Mushteid Garden which I did not like. In the meantime, the piano, rented in the morning, was delivered to me. Kolya Peresleni appeared soon. We waited long for Tolya. Dinner. In the afternoon, we drove to the circus (Gertner, Gavriusha Poltavtzev, Margarita Bratz, etc.). During the intermission, the thing happened for which Kolya and I were watching. Tea at home after the circus. All were sleepy.

4 April Strolled in the Mushteid Garden after tea (during which Tatusya chattered and played with me). Worked. Lunched. Discussed with Panya her mania to arouse passion in everyone. Was at Ivanov's; found his wife and many guests there. Made a visit to Korganov; could hardly find his place, and then he was out; rang his door bell in vain. Home. Worked. Read Ivanov's *Ruth*.[28] Kolya Peresleni just received his funds. Dinner. Champagne in celebration of the wedding anniversary. Joint recital by Korganov and Bichurina. At the Circle. Introductions. We three had tea together at home.

5 April From morning on, the weather was delightful. I went to the monastery of David. That is one of those visits which are never forgotten. There was not a real lunch due to the expected party.

---

[27] *Concert of the Tiflis branch of the Russian Musical Society, conducted by Ippolitov-Ivanov with Gorski as violin soloist playing the composer's* Sérénade mélancolique. *Tchaikovsky desired to remain incognito while in Tiflis; recognized, he preferred not to respond when called out.*

[28] *Biblical opera by Ippolitov-Ivanov, which Tchaikovsky played through.*

Returning home, was busy reading and working. Party at the Vaz (with Panya, Kolya Peresleni, Tolya, Korganov and Gakel). The Georgian cuisine is atrocious—but it was very gay owing to the river being near by and to the miraculous play of colors during the sunset. Nevertheless, it rained later. At home we played whist (Orlovsky) and had supper.

Sunday, 6 April Rain. Went into the city. Was at first at the Armenian church and then at the Zion Cathedral. At the former, was surprised by the novelty of the spectacle and the hideous singing, while at the latter, saw the exarch and heard his sermon. Lunched at home with Vasily Vasilyevich. Guests. Went to my room. Kolya Peresleni and Karnovich. Visit by the whole company to the Goncharovs'. Returning home, walked up and down the gallery with Panya and Kolya. Svinkin. Read. Dinner. Korganov and Verinovsky, an officer.[29] Whist. Experienced a feeling . . . of an unusual sort.

7 April After rising, drinking tea, and reading the newspapers, set out for a walk. Was at the Zion Cathedral (the clock; Panya and Akulya whom I did not recognize immediately). Then went farther on in Maidan and, going across the river, descended to an unusually filthy, although lively, part of the city. (Metekh Prison, etc.) On the way back, dropped in at the Armenian church once more. Lunch (meager! brr . . . !) at home with Panya. Wrote letters. Sat with Panya in the study (just before that she escorted Ivanov and Zarudnaya). Worked. Strolled in the Mushteid Garden. Home. We were awaiting Panya who rode to the exarch. The wager. Visit by Goncharov. Panya. Dinner. Kolya was blue. The little Armenian boy (son of Nikolai, the nobleman). I rode off with Kolya. Evening party at Ivanov's. His songs. His wife sang. Guests. His *sinfonietta.* Supper. They escorted me home. My good Stepan opened the door. The window.

8 April Slept at night with difficulty and awoke with a terrible headache and a feeling of nausea in the morning. . . . Had to undress and lie down. I suffered indescribably until one o'clock. Then fell asleep and rose about three still nauseated. Went to gossip with Panya and shortly thereafter I felt better. Little by little became altogether well. Kolya appeared about five o'clock; he was writing letters to Alexandra Ivanovna Davidova and to his mother. I added

---

[29] *Ivan A. Verinovsky, a young officer, captivated the composer.*

some words. Charming Verinovsky came after dinner; we played whist. Mme. Andreyeva.

9 April Was nervous on account of posing for a portrait. Ivanov drove up at ten-thirty. Photograph studio. As usual, my head was trembling. Lunch at Hotel London. A stroll toward Kodshor. Home. Panya took communion today, also Alexei. Wrote a laborious letter to Shpazhinskaya. Excitement about the first rehearsal of the comedy performance at the Goncharovs'.[30] Gakel, Tebenkov and Karnovich were at dinner. Korganov later. Whist. Macao. Either had hard luck or was winning a lot. Bad tidings regarding Bykov. Joy due to the news about *suffrage universel*.

10 April The weather was excellent, although grayish. Started out for the Zion Cathedral directly after tea. Service conducted by a bishop, the exarch, *washing of feet* (became very tired, but I liked the ceremonies). Splendid lunch at the Hotel London. Walked on the upper path along the ruins of the fortress. *Veiled* women. Home. My people (Panya, Kolya, Karnovich, Verinovsky) went off to the rehearsal of the performance at the Goncharovs'. I worked. Besides ourselves, Karnovich had dinner at our place. With Kolya and Tolya to the cathedral of the exarch for the twelve Gospels. We came in time for the last four Gospels. Home. Panya went to the Goncharovs'. Kolya and I drank tea together. *Korganov's songs* (very weak). Conversation with Kolya.

11 April Gray weather. Went to the railroad station and strolled about in that neighborhood. Lunched at home with Tolya. Before and after that, was busy examining Korganov's compositions in expectation of him. He came first and then Ivanov as well. The poor *Armenian* (a very charming person and good musician) was very chagrined by my criticism. Afterward Ivanov played his works—much that is good. Tolya and Panya came. Went for a walk as far as the bridge when they left (the weather had turned bad). Dinner. Panya is in a too vivacious mood which I do not like very much. Orlovsky. Whist. I was sleepy. Had very good luck.

Passion Saturday, 12 April Went in the city after rising and drinking tea. An Easter egg for Tanya. Lunch at the Hotel London. Mass at the cathedral of the exarch. It took so long to read the vaticination that I decided to go to the Smittens'. Was walking back quite

---

[30] *An amateur performance, in which Tchaikovsky took part.*

Désirée Artôt

full. To the cathedral again. Little girls in blue. The singing was fairly good here. Tolya. Went home. Worked. *Volapük*. Slept. Dinner. Kolya was ingratiating himself. The subsidy. Was lying down in my room in the afternoon, reading the *Istorichesky Vestnik*. Washed and dressed. Matin at the Zion Cathedral. Soon over. Traveling back with Kolya, we either crushed or knocked someone down. Fright, horror, shocking feeling. The doctor was sent for from here. All is well. Thank God! Midnight supper following the fast. Drunkenness.

Easter, 13 April Awful weather, constant rain, turned back on Mikhailovsky Street at the river. Rose at eleven o'clock. Drank tea and lunched alone. Went out for a walk. Rain. Either a lamb or a dog was on the slope under the bridge. Was sitting in the Café Europa. Returned home in a downpour. Home. Worked and read in my room. Dinner. Karnovich, Ivanov, Zarudnaya, Genichka, Kolya, Verinovsky, etc. Whist. Rehearsal. Zarudnaya sang. We had supper somehow.

14 April Excellent weather. Rose late. Worked after tea. Went visiting after lunch (old Sokolov, Gakel, and a doctor with a lump). At the Smittens'. Their daughters are pianists. Heard their playing and gave my opinion. At Alikhanov's, etc. Met Korganov, was in his place; conversed about music. Walked home. Kolya Peresleni told about his quarrel with Svinkin. Dinner. Over display of love again on the part of I. [Ivan Verinovsky?]. We were sitting in the study: I read Feuillet's *La Morte*. Tolya. *Istorichesky Vestnik*. Kolya was sleeping on the sofa. They went away to the rehearsal with the Andreyevs and the Devdorians. I stayed to read and drank tea with Tolya. After he had slept awhile he too went off to the Goncharovs'. I played a little. Am in my room and hear the sounds of a *zurna* [clarinetlike instrument] and drum from the neighboring garden. Disgusting.

15 April Went off in the morning. Was in poor spirits ever since waking. Lunch at home without Panya who rode off to make some visits. Vasily Vasilyevich. Worked. Napped. Tea in my room. Went for a walk with Kolya Peresleni in the Mushteid Garden and in the meadow toward the German colony. Gaiety of the people. Dinner. I invited Verinovsky to whist and Panya was cranky. Whist. The doctor. Macao. After tea and the doctor's departure whist was resumed. *Zurna* and street organ. Verinovsky is attractive.

16 April Worked and left at eleven o'clock for the rendezvous with Verinovsky. Asiatic restaurant. Kolya Peresleni. Perfect lunch. Strolled along Golovinsky Prospekt as far as the descent to the bridge at the paved road. On the way, stopped in at the Russian seesaw place, desiring to amuse myself by swinging, with all my forty-six years and a head of gray hair. Returning, met Tolya riding to the hunt in the company of others. Visited the *Ivanovs-Zarudnayas*. Found them at dinner with guests. Went home. Dinner with Gakel, Fisher, Karnovich. Joint recital by Cesi and Barbi. A box from him. Kolya Peresleni, Verinovsky and Svinkin were with me. A ball at the Circle. Panya, the hostess. Boring. Whist with Karnovich, Orlovsky and a likable Georgian?? Supper. Drunkenness with Svinkin and Kolya. Panya in a cotillion with Verinovsky. *Lezginka*.[31] We returned home about six o'clock.

17 April Rose with a headache and a bit nauseated. Strolled briefly in the Mushteid Garden. Letters. Lunch. With Panya to the Mushteid Garden. Was expecting the formal visit of Ivanov and Alikhanov at home. The invitation to the celebration.[32] Verinovsky. Went to pay Cesi a visit. Found him and others at dinner. Dropped in at the *menagerie* on the way back. Dinner. Kolya Peresleni (whom I saw riding in a carriage) and Verinovsky were at our place. Kolya was telling about meeting the cruel prosecutor. We played whist after dinner. Everyone was drowsy.

18 April Worked. Although slept from twelve to nine, I felt tired. Walked at first and then rode to the castle with Panya after lunch. Visits to Knina (extremely disagreeable) and to Orlovsky. Ascent to the Church of David and higher. Went home tired. With Kolya and Panya on the balcony. Letters. Dinner. Drank too much. With Panya to the recital—canceled on account of Barbi's illness. Went home. The Andreyevs. All left for the rehearsal. I was reading a book on ornithology by. . . . [illegible] Was very tired.

19 April Rising, worked a little but before long went to Svinkin, as agreed, where, in addition to Kolya there was later Verinovsky. Lunch with him at the Hotel London. We had a pleasant time. The giant. The circus and the stables. The seesaws. At Panya's. Her

---

[31] *A Caucasian dance.*

[32] *A special concert of Tchaikovsky's works to be given April 19 by the Tiflis branch of the Russian Musical Society under the direction of Ippolitov-Ivanov.*

unbecoming behavior regarding Verinovsky. Home. Slept. Together to the theater. Tolya. Verinovsky. The theater. Box. Ovation. Deeply touched. Celebration supper at the Hotel London. Formal toasts. Was drunk like. . . . A thousand affectionate greetings with everybody. Was unable to walk as far as home. Was drunk.

20 April Expected a sickening feeling, but rose hale and hearty and without a headache. Took a walk. Traveled after lunch to old Epstein's examinations open to the public. Strolled in an unbearable heat. Home. Panya had guests. Expected Ivanov with the portrait. Autograph. Dinner at the Chirli-Puchurli restaurant. Soso. *La Gioconda.* (The Ryadnovs, Zarudnaya, etc.)

21 April Worked with extremely poor results until lunch. Svinkin came to bid good-by and had lunch with us. He is leaving for two months. News about the card game last night and Verinovsky's losses. Called on Pitoev (he was out), on the Andronikovs (also out), on Rogge. His wife took me to him in his office. Went home. Tea. Worked. It went better. We three dined together. Tolya and Dundukova. Cesi's and Barbi's recital. Tea at home. Discussed the luncheon which I am giving on 25 April.

22 April After rising and drinking tea, went to Savanelli. He is employed at the state bank. Both he and his wife are kind and charming. Home. Lunched with Panya and Tata. Panya began to weep when starting to speak about my departure. I do not recall ever being so touched before in my life. Went to the Mushteid Garden with her and had a long conversation about Tanya (???). Tea at home. Worked. Kolya Peresleni. Dinner on the balcony. Verinovsky. They were dressing him in my clothes. Rehearsal at the Goncharovs'. Talk with Mme. Andreyeva. Supper. Homesick.

23 April Worked—but not without effort. Went to visit Ivanov (found him in and stayed awhile) and Tebenkov following lunch. Felt unusually weak throughout the day with an inclination for sleep and relaxation. Walked in Maidan seeking in vain the Messageries [33] agency. Home. Dinner. Verinovsky. Changing of clothes. Rehearsal. After our performance rode to the theater. *A Life for the Tsar,* the fourth act. Was in V. P. Rogge's box. In the director's office. Pitoev. A supper party at Epstein's. Mme. Ferzing. *Vor-*

---

[33] *French steamship agency.*

schmack.[34] Supper. Zarudnaya beside me. Consul Hermann. The accent recalls the country of either von Bülow or Klindworth. Endless toasts. Ivanov, Korganov, and sweet V. M. Zarudnaya escorted me home. Panya is ill. Was in their bedroom. More drunkenness in my room.

24 April Was badly sick. Awoke in a miserable condition. Mushteid Garden. . . . Home. Sleep. Felt better. Slept again. Awoke at three o'clock practically well. Tea in Panya's room (Tolya rode for the doctor at night). Am improving. At Gakel's with Kolya (whom I met). The garden near the palace. Strikingly beautiful. At the Paquet agency.[35] Almost settled. Walked home. Dinner with sick Panya. Sleepiness. Lounged about. Dressed up. The performance at the Goncharovs'. I accompanied Tolya on the piano. Was concerned about sick Panya. Lavatory. Introductions in the reception room. Prince Dundukov's pleasing manner. Supper. We went to the last table. Goncharov summoned me to the main table. Princess Melikova. Princess Manya. I am completely in love with her. Everlasting cotillions. Drunkenness with the German consul, Tebenkov and Gakel. The nice consul's chattering. The Turkish consul showed me the actual route. Am sailing on a Paquet steamer.

25 April Am forty-six years old today! Rose without a headache but had an empty feeling in my head. Took a walk and bought a cigar. Met the Paquet agent. The guests began to gather about one-thirty at our place. Rogge. The luncheon was cheerful but not particularly successful as to food. Gakel was the life of the party. Prince Andronikov also made speeches. Tea in the garden. Whist was disturbed by old Sokolov. *Mazepa.* Very good performance, especially by Lody and Zarudnaya. (Ryabinin, an amateur, was Mazepa.) Many curtain calls and ovations. Supper at the Hotel London. Weariness.

26 April It is hard to imagine weather more enchanting. Slept wonderfully. Met Ryabinin who not only went walking with me, but even took me to the barber, stayed there and then walked with me still more. However, a very fine man. Partly rode, partly walked back, admiring the stunning beauty of the colors, the blue sky, the mountains and the green. On such days, one does not want

---

[34] *Russian hors d'œuvres.*

[35] *Another steamship agency. Tchaikovsky was planning a trip from Batum to Marseilles and thence to Paris.*

to die. A quarrel with Panya on account of Verinovsky during lunch. Nevertheless, she went to Bykovs' with us. A pathetic impression. Bykova, Andreyevna, Goncharova. At Alikhanov's (he was out). At Genichka's. Was in Dundukov's garden. Dinner at home. The circus. Rain. Tea at home.

Sunday, 27 April After rising, went to the Zion Cathedral. Hot weather. Heard the end of a low Mass. Visited Zarudnaya. Ryabinin, Krasnova. At the rehearsal of *The Mermaid.*[36] Went to the Andreyevs'. Met Verinovsky. Together to the Andreyevs'. We found them in. No phaetons. Home. Avoided seeing Alikhanov and the Andronikovs. Tebenkov. Dinner at Sakharshveli's restaurant. The gaiety and the boundless enjoyment were interrupted by the unbecoming pranks of Praskovya [Panya] Vladimirovna. Mme. Karnovich. To the Café Europa with her and Kolya. Carousal. Card game. Supper. Infinitely sorry for Verinovsky and am angry at that hussy.

Monday, 28 April Rose with painful memories of yesterday. Went to Ivanov. We played his songs and some other things. Photos, coffee, Puzanov, Ryabinin. Group portrait taken at the photographer's. With Karnovich, visited his wife and Bichurina. Dinner at Lody's. Overindulgence. Whist. Home. Melancholy. Tebenkov. Kolya. Went off to my room at ten o'clock to write letters.

TRIP FROM TIFLIS TO MARSEILLES

Tuesday, 29 April Departure. The send-off. An enormous crowd. Unusually tedious and trying. The train was late as though on purpose. We finally left. They were throwing flowers into the train. Karnovich traveled with us. Was urged to remain. The Suram Pass. Tolya's extraordinary appetite. Mikhailovo. I slept after the Pass. Read a marvelous work, although written in a republican spirit, about Carolina, Queen of Naples. Now and then, we went out to admire the wonderful scenery. At last, Panya also lay down. Read. The last stop was Kobuleti. Here Kolya and I had a glimpse of the sea which was at that time beautifully illuminated. We awakened them. Arrival at Batum. It turned out that the Hotel de France was entirely filled. Also the Hotel Impérial. Finally, out of courtesy, they accommodated us. Supper. Gradually, everybody was settled perfectly. I slept with Kolya in the same room. Alesha was next

---

[36] *Opera by Dargomyzhsky, a pioneer of the Russian Nationalist School of Music.*

door. Was beginning to feel the horror of separation. The head clerk was especially likable as also the chambermaids, who were Poles judging by their language.

30 April, Batum Rose and drank tea with Alesha and Kolya. We went to the Paquet agency. Out of weakness, I bought tickets direct to Marseilles and was very annoyed by it later. Went home. Tolya was up; so was Panya. We strolled about the streets, went to the seaside garden after that and then to lunch at the Hotel de France (at Panya's request; I wanted to stay at the Hotel Impérial in appreciation of their accommodating us). Carousal. Went home. Stores. Beautiful site. Tea at home. Tolya (the good-natured Tolya!!!) upbraided Alexei hideously for pure nonsense. To tell the truth, despite all Alesha's tactless and clumsy treatment of people, Tolya was entirely at fault. We left the hotel. Confusion. On board the steamer, at last. Cargo loading. Delay in sailing and an unusually heavy feeling. Champagne. What a precious person is Kolya Peresleni!! Panya wept. Finally they left. Binoculars. Constant waving of handkerchiefs. Depressed feeling. Alesha. He was crying as he explained matters. An inexpressibly melancholy feeling connected with fear of the sea which, however, was more calm than ever before!!! Solo supper. Wrote the diary. Turkish women. Went to sleep. Do not know why the captain walks about here.

1 May, At sea Slept excellently. Went on deck after rising; we were approaching Trebizond. Very beautiful. The Turkish consul, people fishing, the *blagueur* Frenchman from Tiflis whom the consul reproached severely. After a hearty lunch (it is dull at our table for the Italian abbess and her companion do not open their mouths and notwithstanding the captain's efforts, conversation is poor) Alesha and I went to the city by boat. The attractive boatman who was also our guide. Sight-seeing in the city. The charm of the city and streets, but chiefly of its *inhabitants.* For some reason or other, all these things remind me of certain oriental fairy tales. Hotel Europe. Some Russians, recognizing me, came up to my room after their table d'hôte. Trip on horseback to the Greek monastery. Return. *Coffee and a narghile.* An attractive native, speaking Russian. On board the steamer. Napped. Dinner. Commotion. A great number of new passengers especially in the third class. Unusually beautiful sunset. Conversation with the French *blagueur* (however, he is very nice). Am in my cabin. Additional passengers.

2 May Awoke at six o'clock. Stopped at Kerasund; not particularly interesting. The usual hustle-bustle and noise of loading. Sailed after lunch. The weather, still good as ever. Read, tried to write; strolled on deck; saw two ships going in the opposite direction; conversed with the captain. On the whole, continued to be homesick, very much so even, especially when recalling Tiflis and the ugly scene created by Tolya. . . . Was a bit tipsy at lunch and dinner. Additional passengers: a French lady and her daughter; a doctor (who said a few words about music); and a young Turk. We came to Samsun in the afternoon. The mountains are no longer so high here, but still the place is picturesque. Boats, natives, the Greek in a fez with eccentric mannerisms. Wrote letters (after tea). Oh, I am unhappy!

3 May Rose at six. The day was beautiful again. The captain took a seat next to me and talked about literature. He is very naïve and shallow. Walked on deck after lunch, read, and attempted unsuccessfully to compose. Was enraptured long by the beauty of the sea and the distant shore from my nook. After dinner, wanted to be alone in my nook, but a young Turk (from the first class) came up and started to chat. Wrote letters. Tea. Had fewer attacks of homesickness today than usual.

4 May, Constantinople Rose somewhat under strain. It was a little cloudy. The time went by calmly until lunch. Became better acquainted with a number of Frenchmen, several of whom turned out to be Greeks, Italians, or something of the sort, as for instance, the piano tuner. Folk songs. After lunch, almost without interruption kept looking through my binoculars, in expectation of the Bosporus. However, it didn't begin to appear until about two o'clock. The Bosporus, at last. Anchored. The palaces. The Turkish friend, the Georgian from Abkhasia, was my interpreter (afterward) but a living Baedeker in the beginning, pointing out everything on all sides. The sultan's palace, the embassy (Böjük Dere), etc. Finally, we docked at Stambul at about three o'clock. Some boats came to meet ours and among them was one with friends or relatives of the amiable Italian family. Tears. Excitement and noise as the natives left the ship. About four o'clock we too disembarked. *We,* i.e. I, Alesha, the Frenchman from Tiflis and fat Sasha, the Armenian, going to Venice to study. Galata. A Turkish officer helped us much. Carriage. Hotel Luxemburg. No rooms. The obliging *gérant* (smiling *à la* Nikolai Lvovich). Coffee. The Turkish officer forgot the letters entrusted to the Frenchman for Sasha. The *gérant* was accommodating. The officer appeared (who is traveling to Marseilles with us). Letters. They left. Alesha and I strolled while waiting for the agent who went to search for a place for us. We separated. He came. Our room is at a *maison meublée*—the furnishings are vile and wretched. Alexei created a scene. Dinner at a place in the arcade. The Frenchman and Sasha, the Armenian. Strange food. We saw the Frenchman off. The train ride through the tunnel. The boat. We returned by way of a ladder. The meeting with M. Schenet. Home. I was alone in the café. In the garden. Military music, classical concert at the theater. A youth was the conductor, of the Leipzig type. Russians. After the first part of the program (Overture to *Don Juan*, First Movement of the Pastoral Symphony. Song for trombone and dances by Dvořák) I left . . . where to? Went home. Hardly found it. Knocked at other doors in vain. Fright and horror. Found it, at last. Alesha was sleeping alongside. The window. The wind. The dogs. I was a little drunk. Alexei made a scene on account of cigarette purchases. A telegram to Tiflis.

5 *May* We rose. Coffee at the café. Some Greek was the agent. The tower at Galata. The porcelain kiosk of the sultan. The museum. Fatigue. The vista. The plane tree. St. Sophia. Lunch near the bridge. A mosque in the distance with frescoes. At a café near the bridge. Departure for the steamer. Excitement. Customs inspector. On board the steamer. Chickens!!! It is cool. The Turkish woman. The doctor. Dinner. New passengers. Conversation with the Turkish woman and the doctor downstairs. A wonderful, moonlight night. To bed.

6 *May* The rolling began to be rather rough about nine o'clock; all the Frenchwomen from Tiflis are seasick. As for me, at times, I enjoy the view of the sea, at others, I lose my courage a little. The new women passengers (Greeks: a blonde, a brunette and an old lady) are talkative and as a result it became more lively at lunch and dinner. Had a long conversation before dinner with the captain and the Turkish woman about Marseilles. The sea is still rough. The Englishman who has just visited Athens.

7 *May* Rose as usual. Read Bourget's novel (*Un crime d'amour*) which I like very much. Walked with the Turkish woman on the deck. We gazed upon the *hermit* living on Cape St. Angelo after lunch. Strolled on deck. Became acquainted with a charming

Frenchman (a lover of literature and politics). Tea in the second class. George. Read in my cabin. The doctor gave me his treatise to read about the piano he invented.[37] Wild and queer. Conversed at dinner about various countries and customs. My neighbor is an Englishman (traveled about much in his time). In the afternoon, during sunset, the captain was extravagant in describing his enthusiasm for Jules Verne. There was no wind at all today.

8 *May* Read the doctor's treatise about his instrument once more in the morning and expressed my opinion about it afterward. Slept, walked about, and read after lunch. Was moved to tears by the end of Bourget's novel. The captain talked about literature again and gave me Musset to read. Drank tea in the second class. George is ill with a fever. Walked up and down in my cabin. Read Musset. We looked at Mt. Etna, in the afternoon, visible in the distance. Mysterious smoke and flames to the left of Mt. Etna. The captain is perplexed. Lay down to sleep at twelve o'clock, first running up for a look at Mt. Etna and the fire seen near it.

9 *May* Alesha awakened me at 2 A.M. so I could see the eruption. Evidently, the captain was mistaken, assuring us that it was a fire. Am puzzled. The sea was raging, and the smoke and fire were clearly visible. Went back to bed after admiring the sight sufficiently, but was awakened by Maier at five o'clock on orders from the captain that I see Messina. I stood on his bridge and watched the sunrise, Mt. Etna, and the fishermen. The captain says that a new crater has opened. Got dressed after that and waited impatiently for breakfast. Slept. Drank tea in Alesha's cabin. Conversation with Mme. Schirner and her tears while recalling the dead child. Read. Dinner. Rum. *Le rayon vert.* The Englishman related interesting things about his travels. He is very entertaining and makes me laugh, especially when he becomes irritated by the Turk whose boots really squeak mercilessly. I noticed during lunch and dinner that the captain and the doctor were bent on arguing with each other, as though experiencing mutual antipathy. The sea is absolutely calm.

10 *May* Rising, drank coffee and talked with *M. le commandant.* After lunch, walked up and down in my cabin, dozed, drank tea

---

[37] *The doctor invented for each accidental (sharps and flats) its own, individual key. He talked incessantly about his "terrible invention" and gave Tchaikovsky whole tracts to read about it.*

brought by Alesha, counted my gold coins, sat upstairs reading a
book (Suvorov), played with little George and watched over the
heroine of Daudet's novel on and off. We were nearing Sardinia.
Paysage lunaire. Innumerable craggy islands, mountains, etc.
The steamer "Messagerie" passes us. Corsica. Uncommonly peaceful sea. Dinner. We went out on deck during dinnertime. The sig-
nals. *Les bouches de St. Boniface*. The sign on the cliff where
"La Sémillante" perished in 1856. The city of St. Boniface is on a
steep precipice. We sat and walked at the bow of the ship. The
captain gave me the suppressed book *Les mystères du Confessional*.
The chickens are beginning to poison the air terribly. The cognac
bought by me at Mod's. Alexei wore a fez. Experienced something
like falling in love with Daudet's heroine (???).

MARSEILLES

11 May Most likely caught a cold yesterday while in the bow of
the ship. Slept with difficulty and feverishly, and felt ill up to lunch.
Was a bit tipsy at lunch and then felt better. Because it.was our
last *repas*, I ordered that two bottles of champagne be served. Slept.
Tea. We were approaching Marseilles. Commotion and some excitement. Endless procedure in docking. Finally they let us off. In the
tender. Customs. Cigars and cigarettes. Bungling but courteous in-
spectors. Hôtel de la Paix et du Louvre. Table d'hôte dinner. We
sat at the end of the table. It was pleasant. Luxuriously furnished.
Chatted with the English traveling companion after dinner.
Tramped through the streets with Alesha. The Cannebière is beautiful. Café. Newspapers. Sent Alesha home. Roamed about by myself and visited the *palais de cristal*. Lively but not very interesting.
Grog. Went home at eleven o'clock. Could hardly find it.

12 May Slept poorly, awoke with a headache. Tea. Letters. We
went out and first of all I exchanged my money and then bought
Alesha a hat. Walked incredibly far—through Le Prado to Corniche.
We scarcely had the strength to drag ourselves to a restaurant.
Bouillabaisse and a fine lunch, in general. Coffee on the terrace.
Marvelous view of the sea. The horse car. Alesha went home, I
loafed about. Home. Struggle with drowsiness. Tea. Read (Suvorov). Alesha went walking. I stayed home. Dinner. After dinner
(a very tedious one—the gluttonous lady with the mourning head-
dress and coiffure . . . [illegible]). The English traveling companion pressed me to go with him to the *palais de cristal* and to

N[otre] D[ame] de la Garde tomorrow. *Palais de cristal.* Very boring, but there were also some interesting things (Frices Harwez). Comical men and women singers; particularly funny was Coltsolari with his effeminate mannerisms and patriotic acts. Was very homesick all day.

13 May Rose at eight. Tea. *Le Petit Marseillais.* We strolled a little on the streets. *Marché aux fleurs.* Called for the Englishman. With him to N. D. de la Garde. The ascent was not difficult. I was burdened by my companion. Fortunately, he did not prevent us from having lunch together at the hotel. Walked. Joliette.[38] Home. Read. Wrote N. F. The baths. Dinner at the Maison Dorée. Expensive and inferior. We took a walk along the street. I went to the theater. *A Bon Chat, Bon Rat. Gillette de Narbonne.*[39] Merin is charming. The comedian resembles Apukhtin. The tenor is short, young, and awkward but likable. Grog. Home at eleven-thirty.

14 May Slept badly. My own fault(!!!). Alesha left after tea. I rested, read a little and then started out for the Palais Longchamps, and saw the collection of paintings (many of which I liked extremely) and the zoological garden. Lunch with Alesha at home. Coffee in the open. The Englishman. Conversed with him (his name is Arthur Knight). Saw him off at the steamer. The incident at the customs. The steamer was the "San Sebastiano." Spanish language. Rather coarse service. Went back with him also. Again the siege of Belfort. This time the *explication* was in lofty language. Home all the time until dinner. Was reading the most moving part in the life of Suvorov by Petrushevsky. Dinner in the little hall at this time. A gray-haired gentleman from Algiers with his wife and an old man. Was out-of-doors after dinner and felt very calm. The laundress. The incident about the two missing shirts. Sauntered through the city. *Absinth am See.* Read the newspapers. Searched in vain. *Palais de cristal.* The same thing with few changes. The meeting with the lieutenant. The Hatwey brothers.

PARIS

15 May Packing, preparations for the departure, tips, and the usual excitement. The agent arranged the matter about the coupé well. We got a *fauteuils-lits.* We traveled very well. We lunched

---

[38] *The harbor of Marseilles.*

[39] *Operettas by Michel and Audran.*

in the dining car and had dinner (splendid) at Lyon. Read Suvorov (the third volume), as well as the collection of essays by
Bourget on Turgenev, Dumas fils, etc. Retired at nine o'clock. Not
once awakened by the noise of the train. We arrived at Paris at
five o'clock.

16 May, Paris When we drove up to the hotel, old Belard [40] was
already waiting for us. He is not very well. Drank tea (I had my
usual nice 21 *bis*), changed clothes, stopped in to chat with Mme.
Belard and set out for Bicêtre, partly on foot and partly by omnibus.
Georges was sitting at the window when I came and he appeared
to me to resemble his mother so strikingly, that it frightened me.[41]
M. Auclair entertained me until the old lady came. We sat in the
garden. Georges sang, chattered, played, and touched me very
much when he displayed his love for the Auclair couple by refusing to travel with me unless *maman* and *papa* also go along. *"Papa,
va t'habiller tout de suite."* It goes without saying, he speaks
gutturally like the most typical Frenchman. From there, I hurried to the city, returning the same way in order to still the
hunger that was torturing me. The meeting with Achmed-Beem
Totokeridze on the rue de Rivoli. Lunch at the Café d'Orléans.

---

[40] *Proprietor of the Hotel Richepanse where Tchaikovsky always
stayed in Paris.*

[41] *Georges was the son of Tchaikovsky's niece, Tatyana, the oldest
daughter of his sister, Alexandra (Sasha) I. Davidova. Tatyana was a
source of deep sorrow to her parents and relatives. She was a very
beautiful girl, addicted to morphine. At twenty-one, she gave birth to a
son on April 26, 1883, as a result of her intimacy with the music teacher
in her parents' household, Stanislav Mikhailovich Blumenfeld. Her son
was born in Paris where she was taken by Tchaikovsky's brother, Modest,
on the pretense that she was going for treatment for her morphine habit.
Modest I. and Peter I. Tchaikovsky shared this secret, the latter being
in Paris at the time of the birth. Tatyana's child was left to be brought
up by the French couple, Auclair, at Bicêtre, just outside of Paris. Some
years later the boy was adopted by Tchaikovsky's brother, Nikolai (and
even then the rest of the family did not know his parentage). The
opinion was widespread, afterward, in circles close to the Davidov
family, that the boy was Tchaikovsky's son. This was probably due to
the fact that the composer always took a very great interest in the boy.
Tchaikovsky's knowledge of the boy's true parentage was probably the
cause of his excitement regarding Blumenfeld in his entry for June 1,
Diary Three.*

Roamed about. Read the newspapers at the Café Riche. Home. At the Belards'. Mlle. Marie is sweet. In my room. Letters. Alesha. Ate again at the Café d'Orléans. *Variétés*. *Le Fiacre No. 117*.[42] The affected Mme. Chaumont. Baron. Rather jolly. An *américain* [43] in two places. Overdrank a little. Slept well.

17 May Rose with a heavy head and in low spirits. Went to order shirts with Alesha. The balloon. We gave the order and bought a cap. I lunched very well at the Café Riche. Had an awfully long walk, especially along the quay. Sat in a café in the Champs Elysées. Home. Read *L'Œuvre*. Had dinner in the Palais-Royal with Alesha. Châtelet. *Les aventures de M. de Crac*.[44] *Américain*. Went home in a *fiacre*.

Sunday, 18 May Alesha went off to church, while I settled down to read the newspaper, but the Turk came and I hid my displeasure with difficulty. Got rid of him. I went to lunch at the Café Riche. From there went to a matinée at the Gymnase. They gave a very insignificant play: *Le bonheur conjugal*.[45] Home. Was homesick and dejected to tears. Dinner at the Café d'Orléans. Toothache. Went to the Champs Elysées passing by the Tuileries (where they were observing a popular holiday). An unexpected acquaintance, near the *café chantant*, with two very bold Frenchmen. Talked with one of them. Drunkenness. Home. A drunken Englishman knocked at my door by mistake.

19 May Nostalgia, dejection, almost desperation. Went out with Alesha; bought him a pair of shoes. Bought a toy horse for G. Left for Bicêtre in a *fiacre*. Spent five hours there. G. was very cranky today. Strange thing: I do not feel a great affection for this child, although I cannot deny that he is very lovable. Mme. Auclair's superlative cooking. Is she a good woman or merely a *bourgeoise*— a cunning one??? I am unable to decide this question. The eighty-four-year-old woman! Her curious words: *"On est chez ses enfants, quand on est vieux et ils ne pensent pas à nous!"* or something to that effect when I rested in her room. How hard it is to know the whole truth at the first impression; and I had believed that they

[42] *A comedy-vaudeville by de Najac and Millaud.*

[43] *An alcoholic drink.*

[44] *Play by Blum and Toché.*

[45] *Comedy by Valabrègue.*

live in complete harmony. On the way back, gave G. a ride on the carrousel (he and M. Auclair escorted me to the *barrière*). Home. A letter from Glazunov brought by someone named Ovsyannikov. Nostalgia, dejection, desperation. And in addition to that, G. also worries me. What could we do so that his resemblance should not astonish L. and S.??? [46] Had dinner at the Peters restaurant without any enjoyment. Near the *café chantant*. The same queer and bold types. The gentleman resembling Hilf. *Américain*. Home. Terrible dreams.

20 May Rose with a sickly and anxious feeling. Dressing, went to the Champs Elysées. Lunched (with aversion) at the Ledoyen restaurant. Tropical heat. With difficulty located the rue de Bruxelles. Ovsyannikov is a charming boy. When I was walking home from his place, he caught up with me and accompanied me as far as the Madeleine. With Alesha to the Gare St. Lazare. St. Germain. A tour (in a carriage) of the forest. Took a walk. Dinner (complete distaste for food) on the terrace. Many diners. Started for home at nine. A cinder got into my eye. Home. Mlle. Marie examined my eye and said she could see nothing. Nevertheless, it is still there now (eleven o'clock).

21 May Decided to go to Mackar.[47] What suffering I went through and how excited I was—it is impossible to describe. Ten times I approached the place and each time went away—even a large glass of absinth did not help. Finally I walked in. He was expecting me. I imagined him to be otherwise; less tall. His gaze is amazingly similar to Bessel's. We had a talk (while there, someone came to buy my works) and I left. It goes without saying that it was as though a load were taken off my shoulders and I felt easier. Lunched at the Café Riche. Called on Brandukov, he was out. Went to the rue Gay-Lussac on the Left Bank to look up the Turk, so as to notify him in advance that I will not lunch with him tomorrow. The heat was something unbelievable. A terrible thundershower broke out on the Boulevard St.-Michel. I hid beforehand in a café. Located the Turk after the storm. Was frightfully tired, but there

---

[46] *Lev V. Davidov and Sasha (Alexandra) I. Davidova, brother-in-law and sister of Tchaikovsky, parents of Tatyana.*

[47] *Mackar was genuinely interested in Tchaikovsky's works, acquiring from Jürgenson the right to publish Tchaikovsky's compositions for a considerable sum.*

were no carriages. Home. Undressed. Rested. Went to have dinner about eight o'clock in the rue Royale (dull and bad). Loafed near the *chantants.* The same spectacles on a smaller scale. Had an enormous quantity of grog. . . . Was drunk. The *Novoye Vremya.*[48]

22 May The day of Alesha's departure. Ascension Day. Rose in a bad humor, as I was to have lunch at Mackar's. Roamed along the rue St. Honoré, the Palais-Royal and in the Passages. At Mackar's. M. Henri Condemine. M. Mackar. Lunch. I was cheerful. Went home at two-thirty. Met Brandukov. Home. Took Alesha to the Musée Grévin. Thank God, that I got the acquaintance with Mackar off my mind or it would have been hard to part with Alesha. It must be admitted, that with his eternal mania and his arguing about everything, he becomes unbearable *à la longue* in the sense of being pleasant company. This, too, makes parting easier. In general, I value and like Alesha fully only when living in the country, where all is normal and there is nothing to argue about. Just when he was being called to dinner, there was the fuss of transferring the things. I was furious. We started out. The chambermaid of Fredericks, next to whom he sat down in the train compartment. Was very happy about that. Saw him off. Had dinner at the Barbotte restaurant opposite the railroad station. Champs Elysées. The same types near the *café chantant.* Drunkenness. Saw Golitzin near the Café de la Paix. Went home late.

23 May Was expecting Brandukov. Lunched with him at the Sylvain restaurant. Traveled to Bicêtre. Stayed briefly. Mme. Auclair is too flattering. Composed a little. Had dinner at the Royale restaurant on . . . Bouffes-Parisiens. *Joséphine vendue par ses sœurs.*[49] Mily-Meyer. Very gay operetta. Meeting with Marsick and his wife at the Café Glacier Napolitain. Grog. With Brandukov at the Café Américain, where it was crowded. Conversation. Went home about two o'clock.

24 May Was expecting Mme. Auclair with Georges. Went for a walk. Had to wait long for them. Waited at the door with Mme. Belard. Lunch in my room. Georges is an awful *nuisance.* It's terrifying to think about the journey. At his request, went with him and Mme. Belard to get a toy at the bazaar. Rain. Slavyansky's concert

[48] *Russian newspaper.*
[49] *Operetta by Roger.*

at the Trocadéro. *Tribune.* A wonderful seat where it was dark and isolated. Heard an entire part. I liked certain things, although there was faking without limit. "The Little Tiger"!!! [50] Went home, also walking. Worked. Had dinner at the Taverne de Londres. Put on another coat while leaving and had to return from a café. Wandered about afterward. Got a haircut somewhere near the Folies-Bergère. Bought some Russian newspapers and read them inside in the Café de la Paix. Somewhat drunk. Bought books: *Le roman russe* by Vogüé and *L'Emigration* by Daudet.

Sunday, 25 May Rising, waited for Brandukov. Dropped in at Mackar's (why, he is a Parisian Bessel!!!). Lunch at the Café Riche with Anatoly Brandukov. Dropped in at Mackar's again. Decided with Brandukov to go to the *courses.* Traveled in a *fiacre. Tribune.* Continuous rain. Little interesting, at first. Was excited later when they were racing for the *Grand Prix.* The winner was Minting, an Englishman. Went home after waiting long for a carriage. Worked. Dined at an Italian restaurant. Roamed about. Read the newspapers in the Passage de l'Opéra. Drunkenness in the Café Américain and others. Went home. Telegram from N. F. Rain without end.

26 May My head cold is getting worse. Rose in a bad mood. Expected Brandukov and Ovsyannikov. They lunched downstairs with me in the dining room. Ovsyannikov is a liar, but a charming youth. It poured all day without a stop. Took a walk under the Tuileries arcades. Home. To Brandukov at five o'clock. With him to Marsick. We rode on to the Maire restaurant (after an exchange of pleasant words and inscribing some music in an album). Absinth. Marsick was with his wife. A superb dinner in a private room. It was not boring. [Théâtre] Porte St. Martin. Sardou's *La Patrie.* Magnificent production. Effective, but terrible and gloomy. Grog with Brandukov at the Café Glacier Napolitain.

27 May Rain, but there's hope. Letters. Lunch at the Sylvain restaurant. Tramped about. At Mackar's. Made some visits with him. We found Lamoureux (very friendly) and Marmontel at home. We visited also ??? the critic; the pianiste Silberberg and

---

[50] *Valse song by Shilovsky, friend of Tchaikovsky, which was very popular in Russia during the 1870's. Tchaikovsky fled from the concert when he heard it sung by the Slavyansky chorus with its title changed to* Sérénade Russe.

Colonne. All were out. Conversation with Mackar at a café. Went home. Composed a little. Dinner at the Taverne de Londres. Wished to go to the theater, but the weather cleared up and I chose to walk. Stopped in at home to leave my coat. Conversed with the sweet Belard couple in the Champs Elysées. Sat in the Café des Ambassadeurs. A curious incident near the Alcazar d'Eté. A Jewess. The insolence and daring of some . . .

28 May Expected Brandukov and Ovsyannikov. The former came, but the Turk came still before him. The three of us set out for the salon. Merely tired and nothing more. Lunch at the Ledoyen restaurant (but then for lunch, Ovsyannikov did show up). Strolled on the Left Bank. Rain. Home. Waited for Brandukov and Ovsyannikov for dinner. Again, only Tolichka [51] came by himself. Dinner at my place in the dining room. I was in a poor frame of mind. At the opera. The seat was too high up; was uncomfortable and hot. The opera (*Henri VIII*) [52] is worse than mediocre. Drunkenness in the Café de la Paix. My awful headache spoiled the whole evening.

29 May Slept with feverish dreams. The head cold was somewhat better toward morning. Dressed and went to Mackar. His various courtesies and advice. Lunched at the Italian restaurant (with old memories still of 1861!!!). Walked to the Left Bank. Hired a carriage in the Avenue Gobelins. Bicêtre. Georges was unusually nice and attractive today (after his sleep). On the other hand, Mme. Auclair becomes more repulsive to me each time. Home. A letter (from Jürgenson with money) and a telegram from N. F. Worked. Brandukov came at six o'clock. Absinth. (Newspapers, containing a notice that I am in Paris.) Dinner at the Dîner de Paris restaurant. Pierre. The incident with the Spaniard (who knew Russian perfectly). [53] Poor dinner. We were both still drunk from the absinth. Eden-Théâtre. *M. Buatier de Kolta*. The ballet *Brahma*. [54] We left, not staying for the end.

---

[51] *Anatoly Brandukov.*

[52] *By Saint-Saëns.*

[53] *While Tchaikovsky was dining with Brandukov at the Dîner de Paris restaurant, they were sitting near two gentlemen who spoke Spanish. At dinner, they began to make remarks in Russian about their neighbor, believing that they would not be understood. To their great astonishment their Spanish neighbor began to speak Russian to them.*

[54] *Ballet by Dall'Argine.*

30 May After rising, reading, and dressing went out to saunter. Lunched at eleven o'clock at the Café Riche. Took a long walk. Went in to Nicoll and ordered some clothes. Went home to work; but is my mind really on work? Dupont's visiting card disturbed me; I hurried off to him and not finding him in, set out to the Bazilevskys. They were out. At Mackar's. He failed, i.e. he did not get free tickets to the opera. I was very happy. Stayed there awhile. Customers came to ask for my works. A boy had his hat on and Mackar rebuked him for it. Dined at the Botta restaurant. No appetite. Am anxious about tomorrow (lunch at Viardot's). Roamed about. Drank grog. *Expulsion des Princes.*[55] To my surprise, it was quiet on the streets. Returning home, met Mackar on his way to me. With him and his wife at the Grand Café. Soyers. Went home at twelve o'clock. Visiting cards of Réty [-Darcours] and Ambroise Thomas.

31 May Rose in a horrible state of mind. Simply lifeless. Brandukov came at eleven o'clock. His recital. We went to Viardot. Thunderstorm. We were soaked to the bone. What a first acquaintance! However, we were not allowed to go home. This occurrence made acquaintance easier. Lunch. The old Mme. Viardot enchanted me. Her sycophant. In the drawing room. Her pupil, a Russian lady, sang an aria from *Lakmé*. SAW THE ORCHESTRA SCORE OF MOZART'S "DON JUAN," WRITTEN IN HIS OWN HAND!! [56] Went home. Reception at my place. Colonne came first. There were Marsick, Levita, Mackar, Berger; and still earlier, Mme. Boulanger. Levita pestered me and stayed a long time. Dined excellently with Brandukov at the Dîner de Paris restaurant. The Spaniard. Cirque d'Eté. *Promenade.* We stood all the time. Some Russians in a box. Except for the Japanese, everything was uninteresting. Walked. Grog at a café on the corner of the rue Richepanse. In the morning, Brandukov informed me of the death of poor Vladimir Alexandrovich Davidov.

Sunday, 1 June Rose late. Letter from brother Kolya. Lüdzher (a mysterious and enigmatic personality). Brandukov. Played *Mazepa.*

---

[55] *The expelling of the Bonaparte princes from French territory.*

[56] *Pauline Viardot-Garcia. Her husband had purchased this original manuscript orchestra score for very little money many years before. Tchaikovsky spent two hours looking through it; he felt exactly as though he had clasped Mozart's hand and conversed with him. In 1896, Mme. Viardot presented the score to the library of the Paris Conservatoire.*

Lunch at the Sylvain restaurant. Walked to Saint-Saëns. He was out. Saint-Sulpice. Panthéon. *Les caveaux.* A *sergent* was the guide. Firing, screams, etc.—it was nothing. Cold weather. Went home. Worked and wrote letters. Dined at Pierre's at the Dîner de Paris restaurant. The Spaniard came again. Strolled. Near the Alcazar d'Eté. Nothing happened. Fireworks. Went to the rendez-vous with Brandukov at the Grand Café. Grog. We conversed. It was very cold outside.

2 *June* After rising and going through the usual ceremonies (conversed with the Belards), started out to Golitzin. Found him getting ready to go to church. He did not even suspect that I was here. His young gentleman friend is with him. Lunched at the Café d'Orléans. Bought a pin. Roamed about. For some unknown reason, ordered a lot of underwear in the rue du Faubourg-Montmartre. At Mackar's. Condemine. Lefebvre. And some pianist wearing an order. "Manfred" played by Condemine and Lefebvre. Went home. Worked a little. Brandukov. With him to Golitzin. There was still another good-looking (flat-chested) young man; an elegant gentleman and a doctor. Morphine injection. All went to dinner to the Maire restaurant. It was delicious and merry. I paid after a little struggle. With Brandukov to the Alcazar d'Eté.[57] Certain things were enjoyable (Paulus, an English juggler, casting shadows of various things with his hands, etc.). Two Russians were sitting in front of us.

We drank grog in the Café de la Paix. Went home about ten o'clock.

---

[57] *Brandukov, examining Tchaikovsky's diaries later in life and coming across the music above said: "I would not have imagined that he (Tchaikovsky) would write it (the music) down in his diary. I was with him at the Alcazar when this chansonette was sung and he proposed a wager that I would not remember it in a year. And so we agreed that each must sing it in a year's time when we should meet. Meeting after a year and remembering our wager, we both sang it at the same time, so that neither of us won or lost. I remembered it and did not write it down, and only now do I see, that apparently not relying on his memory, Peter Ilyich wrote it down."*

3 June Rose earlier than usual. Letter from N. F. containing money. Dressed and walked to the Russian church to attend the funeral services of V. A. Davidov. Went in for an absinth on the way and felt so uncomfortable after that, that I had to find refuge at a café. The liturgy. The funeral services. I was in a condition not conducive to feeling impressions; but toward the end I was actually crying. Rode home in a carriage with Golitzin. Told a lie. Lunched hastily (at a 2.50 francs restaurant on the boulevard). Bought G. a toy and some chocolate and went over there. G. was very sweet. Mme. Auclair, as always. (Why is she angry at the old lady because she pitches hay behind her back, which I found her doing and told about it?) In the garden. Mme. Bessière (Mme. Belard's sister and her lovely children). Went home to receive visitors.[58] Nobody came. Tried to work. Brandukov. A misunderstanding with Viardot. He went to explain. Dinner at the Dîner de Paris restaurant. The Spaniard. Coffee downstairs in the café and conversation about Anton Rubinstein. Rode off as though to Bicêtre. Instead went to the Odéon. *La vie de Bohème.*[59] Boring, antiquated, and stuffy; besides that, even the actors are third rate. Walked home through the boulevards. Elegant shoes. Grog at two cafés.

4 June A crazy day. Rising, went to lunch (at the Café Riche); bought various gifts and necessities (received the money at the bank); then obtained the tail coat; then was at Mackar's (how he tires me!); then at Boulanger's (there was singing, etc.); then at Brandukov's, and with him to Bogomoletz and Nicoll to try on some clothes. Dinner in the open at the Sylvain restaurant. We sauntered. Appointment with Mackar at the Grand Café. His pestering and questioning. A telegram from Guitry. Acquaintance with M. Maréchal. Terrible drunkenness. Meeting with Golitzin. We walked with him as far as my place. A surprise: Olga,[60] whom I expected tomorrow, has already arrived. The poor thing was waiting for me. Conversation with her. We went to sleep very late. I am like a madman from all this excitement.

---

[58] *Tchaikovsky was so tired out by visits that he reserved only specific hours for visitors at his hotel.*

[59] *Play by Barrière and Murger.*

[60] *Olga was the wife of Tchaikovsky's brother, Nikolai. She arrived at Paris to take Georges, for she and her husband were adopting him.*

5 June God, what a horrible day! I think it took two years of my life! Slept restlessly and little. However, it turned out that Olya slept even less. After drinking tea with her, entrusted her to the care of the Belards, while I went off to a café across the boulevard to write some letters (to Colonne and N. F.) and drink absinth. Got drunk. Next to me turned up the kindhearted German (the handsome friend of the late Mosalitinov). Indifferently, without enjoyment had lunch at the Sylvain restaurant. Went to ramble a while. Sat in the Eden-Concert café. Memories of Gonsalès. Guitry was at Mackar's. Went for a drink with him at a café. Chatted with that amiable person and then he brought me home. Slept. Put on my tail coat. Olya. At Mackar's. At Marmontel's. We arrived before any of the others. Little by little, a lot of guests gathered. Cornély from *Le Matin* . . . ; Detroyat, the librettist, a stout jolly fellow offering me a libretto; the composer, Guiraud (very charming ladies, writers, Barrias, the famous sculptor, etc.). I suffered inexpressibly, very, very much. Cornély was lying about Russia, very sympathetically, however. Detroyat was orating about music. Marmontel's pleasant son tried in every way, after dinner, to show his friendship toward me. Discussions about Wagner. Disputes. Shouting. Detroyat's story of how he never became a singer. In the music room. Intimate talk with Guiraud. Smart and likable chap. We left. Old Marmontel was touchingly affectionate to me. With Mackar as far as the Chaussée d'Antin. Drunkenness, all the same. Acquaintance with a strange Russian at the Café de la Paix.

6 June It is hard to imagine a more unfortunate person than I was all day today, and until evening. . . . After rising and drinking with Olya, brought her, in the morning (rain), to Mme. Auclair. We talked in the carriage. We found G. asleep. When he awoke, at first, he was shy and cranky, but later, although rather nice to Olya and me, he was mischievous and troublesome beyond reason. Olya displayed exemplary patience and strength of character. We lunched. Walked to Mackar (Maréchal) with whom I chatted and went home. Nevertheless, I worked a bit. At six o'clock, rode to Golitzin while it rained. Two nice young men, unusually dark. Café de Paris on the Avenue de l'Opéra. Brandukov. We waited long for Guitry, but it turned out that he was in a private room upstairs. Angèle. At first, the dinner was not lively; afterward it was better. Guitry (what a smart and wonderful man) advised me not to go tomorrow to Marmontel's class and even drafted a letter for me. After separating, went with Brandukov to the Café de la Paix and copied the letter there with some changes. We sent it off. Poor Tolya Brandukov; he is out of sorts today. Grog and newspaper reading at the Grand Café. Some more grog. What a drunkard I have become here! Went home. How glad I am that I got rid of M. Detroyat, but at the same time it looks exactly as though I'd done an ugly thing. Oh, what a hideously split personality I am! More and more I am becoming convinced that I must live a country life.

7 June After rising very late went to have lunch at the Maire restaurant. Strolled. Executed Jürgenson's request. Casual acquaintance with M. Brandus (lost my visiting cards) and a talk about Jürgenson. Home. Stepan's letter to Alexei, accidentally opened by me, in which I read the news about poor Verinovsky. Deeply grieved and upset. However, went to Mackar to go visiting with him. Rain! Called on Bourgault-Ducoudray—he was out; on Lemoine—he was in (eccentric personality; showed various curios, served tea, etc.) and on Marie Fayan—she was out. Had to concentrate terribly for, during the noise, was obliged to talk to Mackar and listen to his tender words. Oh, how hard it was for me! Barely managed to ride home to change clothes and set out for the dinner given me by Mme. Bogomoletz. Rather many guests (among them Lefebvre, Fauré, Benoît, Lalo, the Marsick quartet, Boulanger with his wife, and a crowd of unfamiliar ones). Magnificent dinner. Had a smoke and talked with Camille Depré. M. Bogomoletz's charming daughter and son. My quartet; Fauré's quartet; singing by Mme. Boulanger, Mme. Lalo as well as Lefebvre. . . . Acquaintance with the charming Fauré, Benoît, etc. Walked with Brandukov along the boulevard. Grog at 2 A.M. at the Café Américain. Found flowers from Mlle. Fayan at home.

Sunday, 8 June When I had dressed and was about to leave, an attractive gentleman, who turned out to be M. Bourgault-Ducoudray, entered. He spoke about Glinka, Tolstoy and Russian art in general with exaltation. Jean-Marie whom I sent to Olya. Lüdzher. He accompanied me as far as Colonne's (Passage Jouffroy, M. Guiraud, Editeur). Colonne was extremely pleasing and kind. Lunch at the Rougemont restaurant. Pouring rain. A bouquet of flowers for Fayan. At Mackar's. (A violoncellist???) At Condemine's. M. Emile Bernard. The younger Condemine is very taking. I played a good deal. So did Bernard; he is not talented. Dined at the Maire restaurant: all of their company and Brandukov. It was

gay. At eleven o'clock with Brandukov at the Café de la Paix. Golitzin. Found the visiting card of Léo Delibes [61] with an inscription
at home.

9 June Almost losing my mind with excitement and did not know
what to do first. Left at nine-thirty o'clock and went to have some
photographs taken at Reutlinger's. The proprietress (a German)
has a torn lip. Friendly gentleman photographer. Six poses. Lunch
at the Café Riche. Home. Olya and Mme. Auclair. The documents.
Letter to Nikolai Ilyich and the request to telegraph Ostrovsky.
Visited Delibes. Returned home for the *Extrait de naissance* [birth
certificate]. Mme. Viardot's letter canceling today's dinner invitation and inviting me for tomorrow. Replied. At the Consulate General. Talked with the secretary. Went home. Sent Jean-Marie to
make arrangements. Rode to fit some clothes; to Mackar; to Brandukov; to Marie Fayan. Visited her for an hour and a half. Charming
character. Went home. Dinner with Brandukov at the Dîner de
Paris restaurant. We sat in a café; tramped about the streets. Grog.
Went home early. Conversation with Marie and Jean-Marie. Lay
down to sleep earlier than usual.

10 June Excitement. At Mackar's. Messrs. Philipp *et* Alliod. At the
Conservatoire. Ambroise Thomas is very friendly. Piano playing
examinations in Marmontel's class. At Mackar's. Lunch at the Café
Riche. Brandukov came in unexpectedly toward the end. Walked
home with him; bought certain things. Encountered Jean-Marie and
Auclair. Difficulties about the passport. Olya. We sent for Georges.
I went for a walk so as not to go crazy. Returned about four o'clock.
At the *commissaire's*. We had to wait. Curious procedure. They took
my height, etc. Thank God, we got the *certificat!* Called on Kleeberg. She plays nicely. At the Sleeping Car agency. Postpone my
departure. At Golitzin's. Dinner at Dr. Michelon's. The Count??
An amateur pianist played one of my songs. Boredom. The three of
us including Golitzin walked to a café after dinner. Grog. Saw an
old gentleman acquaintance.

11 June Awoke early. Went out at nine-thirty with Jean-Marie
to walk there. Olya was waiting for us with G. and Mme. Auclair.
At the passport bureau. The courteous clerk. He is delighted with
G. He promises and deliberates how to arrange it. The *Sous-chef*

---

[61] *Tchaikovsky considered Delibes, after Bizet, the most gifted French
musician.*

orders us to come once more as he does not make the decision himself. G. is entrancing and, incidentally, sings the *Marseillaise* at the top of his voice. Traveled home by boat. Lunch. Auclair cries and is a bit drunk. We ride to the *Préfecture* again. Everything settled. Return. Take a stroll and purchase some water colors. Home. Sleep. They delivered G.'s passport. Olya rests near by. Leave at five o'clock. At the Sleeping Car agency. Absinth. At Brandukov's. Meet him. Dinner at the Café Riche. *Café chantant.* Grog. Went home. Packed. (I still managed, during the day, to run in to Mackar and travel up to Gounod, whom I did not find in.)

TRIP TO RUSSIA

12 June Day of departure from Paris. Tea with Olya. We left together. I to Mackar. Discussions and sweet attentiveness. Solo lunch at the Maire restaurant. Made certain visits. Found Bernard in. Finished packing at home. Visit to Mme. Conneau. Absinth at the Café de la Paix with Brandukov (we address each other familiarly). G. arrived at home with the Auclair couple. Creates a scene. I suffer. Dinner. Departure. Mme. Belard saw us off. Brandukov and Mackar came. Golitzin. Young Russians and a Brazilian. I am unnaturally talkative. Fell asleep. Georges did not sleep almost the whole night, nor Olya either.

13 June It was more fortunate and calm than I expected. Cologne. Tea. G. slept twice in the course of the trip and the second time a good deal. Very sweet but too high-spirited. Dinner in the dining car. Golitzin. Hannover. Was obliged to spend some time alone with him; create fairy tales; talk nonsense. Berlin at eight o'clock. We strolled and took a ride. Supper at the railroad station. He ate well. The train left at 11:05 (I went to walk a bit before that). He lay down to sleep at once. I, too, near by. Anniversary of mother's death.

14 June Awoke and dressed hurriedly before Dirschau. Coffee. G. slept well. . . . Am writing a telegram while it is quiet alongside: must be G. fell asleep again. We had dinner in Königsberg. The time passed rather quickly. Eydtkuhnen (money exchange). Verzhbolovo. Dinner. G. suddenly fell asleep at dinner. Carried him while he was sleeping to a small ladies' compartment. Well, at last in Russia! This evening both Olga and I were unusually tired and I actually had a feeling almost of despair. However, we had supper in Vilna.

ST. PETERSBURG

Sunday, 15 June A long drawn-out day. Was obliged to entertain much and fuss with Georgie. By the way, I gratified him particularly by inventing a slapping game. Coffee in Ostrov and Pskov. Dinner in Luga. (Fellow passengers: a Russian gentleman traveling from Berlin and speaking all languages well; a dirty . . . who almost took a seat beside me and a St. Petersburg Englishman.) St. Petersburg, finally. Kolya met us. I went to the Hotel Europe. God, how little you feel that you are in Russia at this hotel! Dressing, went to Nikolai Ilyich. Georges looked very happy and played as though Bicêtre and *geo-tilliez* never existed. After conversing and putting G. to bed, went to have supper at Palkin's restaurant. A white night! Strange, but beautiful. . . .

16 June Rising, read the newspapers and wrote letters. Dressed at eleven o'clock and went out. They are whitewashing and painting the corridor. Lunch at Ernest's. A stroll through the Summer Garden past the school of law, etc. Haircut. Was composing at home the agreed upon letter about G. Drank tea. Went out. Thunderstorm. Waited at Dominick Street. Dinner at Nikolai Ilyich's. Georges is sweet beyond recognition; has a haircut and is spick-and-span! . . . He became angry at Olya after dinner and cried convulsively in my arms. When I was leaving, he cried bitterly and wanted me to stay. Read the draft of the letter to Olya and Kolya. At eight o'clock we traveled to Pavlovsk. Damp weather. Strolled. They played uninteresting music. Left at ten o'clock. It was light as day. At Timosha's. Somehow it was not cheerful. Not like before. Had supper at Palkin's restaurant. Went to bed shortly at home.

17 June Liza knocked when I was getting up. Brought a letter that I was expected at twelve-thirty at Kolya's. After dressing, went in to Leiner's restaurant to have lunch. Was angry. At Nikolai Ilyich's. Georges was pale. The christening was fixed for two o'clock. Walked. Found three rubles near the Bolshoi Theater. Bought some little pictures for G. Returned to Kolya. The priest and the sacristan. The documents. The birth certificate. The ceremony. G. was fascinating in his wide peasant coat. He was understanding and patient. Cried a little during the font rite. After conversing with the priest, rode home to pack. Paid my bill. Traveled to the Cathedral of St. Isaac. Vespers. The lady from Tiflis. Toys for G. Dinner at Kolya's. G. was very pleased with his toys, especially with the little soldiers entering the fortress. Left him secretly to avoid tears. Railroad station. The nonprofessional doctor from Moscow. Train compartment. Lay down to sleep after Luban. Slept until Tver.

MAIDANOVO

18 June Drank tea in Tver. Took a nap before Klin. Alesha. Home. Gifts for the servants. N. D.[62] was in my room. Dressed and went to Kondratyev. Mary and Emma seemed to me to have aged very much. At Novikova's. Miss Albedil. Empty gossip. Solo dinner at home. Strolled; was in the forest. Tea at the Kondratyevs' with Novichikha [Novikova]. Just after coming home in a calm and happy mood and conversing with Arisha, Vasily and good Sasha Legoshin—there arrives a guest, Vadim Peresleni. There was no end, no limit to my anger. Was completely upset and said so. Took a short walk with N. D. and Dima. Novichikha. Supper in my room. Whist game at N. D.'s. After my return, Dima departed at twelve o'clock. . . .

19 June Ever since morning it has been cool, but toward evening it turned so cold that I don't remember anything like it at this time of the year. Now at twelve o'clock midnight it is 37 degrees [F.]. After rising late in the morning and drinking tea on the balcony, went to have a talk with N. D. Worked fairly well until dinner. Strolled in the forest opposite Klin after dinner. Mushrooms. Drank tea in the gallery at my place and felt excellently. . . . Wrote Modest. Read. Talked with Sasha Legoshin and Alexei while they had tea. Was at the Kondratyevs' during their dinner. Strolled with N. D. about the garden. Home. Watched the people having supper through my binoculars. Took a stroll about my domain. The game of *goat* out of doors. The Kondratyevs drank tea in my room. Albums. Escorted them to their home and stayed awhile with N. D. He was cursing the Russian climate.

20 June Still cold though not so cold. Walked around the property in the morning. Worked successfully. Went to the railroad station after dinner to send the telegram to Shpazhinsky. Stopped in to see the Kondratyev ladies; then N. D. escorted me and remained while I made some tea in the gallery. Was writing a letter to Nikolai Ilyich almost until supper, as though from Mr. Krüger(???).

---

[62] *Tchaikovsky's friend, N. D. Kondratyev, lived with his family in a house near by the composer's for the summer.*

Strolled; dropped in at N. D.'s. Supper. Legoshin. Was in the Kondratyev reception room and in his room. Solitaire.

MOSCOW

21 June Departed for Moscow. Rode to the railroad station with Alexei and Sasha Legoshin. Moscow. Rode up to Jürgenson. Twelve o'clock at the Shpazhinskys'. Poor woman! She does not have long to live now! Lunch. Sasha read the fourth act.[63] I was very satisfied. Bade good-by. Went to my hotel. At Jürgenson's. The statement. A surprise (4000).[64] Visited Brius. Andrey. Took a walk. Dined at the Hotel Moscow. Another Dmitri. At the Uspensky Cathedral for vespers after dinner. Orlov saw me. We went for a smoke in the pavilion. Dobrovolsky. Hermitage Garden. Boring. It stank. Went home. Drank tea in the public room downstairs.

Sunday, 22 June Mass at Uspensky Cathedral. The singing was good, but the selections were horrible. Orlov and Dobrovolsky were in the pavilion with me. Conversation. The incident with the exchanged umbrella. At Vladimir Dmitrievich Konshin's. Found only Irina Fyodorovna, but on leaving met Nikolai at first alone, and later with Grigory Grigoryevich. Lunch at the tavern, in Dmitri's public room. Bought wine and food at Lapin's and Depré's. Home. Letters. Prepared for the trip. The provisions in a lot of vats, boxes, and barrels. Local train. I was in a bad mood. Egor Egorovich was in the same car with me. Afterward I was alone. Slept until Podsolnechnaya. Alesha met me. Lots of mail; home. Among them, one from Antonina Ivanovna[65] which agitated me, though not very

---

[63] *Of the libretto of* The Enchantress.

[64] *Royalties from Jürgenson; in this instance, four thousand rubles.*

[65] *Antonina Ivanovna Miliukova, wife of the composer. Before their marriage, she was a student at the Moscow Conservatory and wrote him a letter of adoration. Although he informed her that he did not love her and told her the facts about his sexual nature, she nevertheless persisted, even to the point of threatening to commit suicide. Out of weakness he proposed marriage; she accepted immediately. However, six months before he received her letter, he expressed a wish to marry in order to still gossip regarding his homosexuality. And there is proof that she was not sincerely in love with him, of which he was aware. For a very short while he was her husband in name only; the marriage was interrupted by his complete nervous breakdown. After their separation she continued to plague him with letters. She suffered from nymphomania, imagining her-*

greatly. At Mary's. At N. D.'s. I was melancholy. Went home at eleven-thirty.

MAIDANOVO

23 June Changeable day, but very pleasant. Was writing letters all morning, among them one to Antonina Ivanovna. After dinner, walked to the railroad station to mail them. Tea in my room. Legoshin. Preserves. What pleasure there is in Legoshin's frequent presence; he is such a wonderful personality! Good God! And there are people who turn up their noses at a valet because he is a valet. Why, I don't know anyone whose soul is purer and nobler than Legoshin's. And he is a valet! That people are equal regardless of their position in society was never so absolutely apparent as in the present instance. Was at the Kondratyevs' during their dinner. General excitement on account of Egorka slipping his chain. They gave him bread after Vasily tied him again; however, he got loose once more. Walked in the park together with all the Kondratyevs. Had a hasty supper and hurried to the card game. I saw Novichikha appear before supper for the card game (ridding herself of two women guests from Rzhev). We played. N. D.'s idiosyncrasies. I bear them more patiently than before. Lost a little. We escorted Novichikha as far as the turn to her house.

24 June It rained during the day, but it was warm. Worked. Lunched at twelve o'clock. Strolled in my hunting boots. Was depressed but do not know why. Tea. Read an article about Tolstoy's philosophy. Letters. Went to the Kondratyevs' to have dinner. Novichikha came and chattered about all kinds of nonsense and incidentally related some interesting things about Shakhovskaya. Whist. Tea. The illumination at the Schillings'. We escorted Novichikha and then I returned to the Kondratyevs' with the ladies again. Conversation about Tolstoy. For some reason or other, I was in a bad mood.

25 June Slept excellently. Went bathing for the first time. The water was wonderful. Worked straight through to dinner. Had dinner without enjoying it. Walked along the bank to the right. A

---

self to be the center of attraction for all men. Although refusing to divorce Tchaikovsky, subsequently she entered into a common-law marriage herself and gave birth to three children. Eventually, showing signs of insanity, she was confined to an institution in 1896.

thunderstorm was approaching and I did not walk, but fled back. Escaped the rain in time. Learned from N. D. of the arrival of Sanya von Vizin. A vaudevillelike episode. Went to my room. Novichikha soon arrived with Sanya who has lost much weight and was fascinatingly pretty. She remained with me. We drank tea. We sauntered around the garden. At N. D.'s. At Novichikha's. Was present during her dinner (i.e. Sanya's). Thunderstorm. Home. Splendid evening. At the Kondratyevs' after supper. In his room. Visited Mary. Telegram from Olya. Leaving tomorrow to meet her.

26 June Had such a horrible dream last night that it was frightening to recall during the day (indefinite whose mass suicide; the desire to escape by train; the impossibility of finding my things; hurt constantly by everyone and everything, etc.). This dream turned out to be the sign of a feverish cold, which asserted itself markedly toward evening. At six o'clock, Alesha awakened me. Rode to the meeting with Olya and G. Saw them. Georges was more likable than ever. Could not find a nurse. Liza serves as one. Went home. Tea. Was in an ailing condition. Had no desire for work. Went for a long walk to the river opposite Klin. A shepherd. Mushrooms. Dampness. Went home. Flower bouquet. Stopped in at Novikova's. Quarrel with little Albedil about an incident. Shouted at her. Went away upset. Bathing. Dinner. Letter from Novichikha containing the insulting letter of Kondratyev. At N. D. K.'s. He was furious at Novichikha. The piano. Visited Novichikha. Discussion and my shrewd advice to repay N. D. by sending money. Explanation with Albedil. Subtle words. She is a nihilist. Tea at home at the window. Dozed. Talked with Legoshin (I forgot to mention about his jest with the shirt while I was bathing). Worked (end of the third act). N. D. appeared and was fulminating. Took a stroll with him. He soon calmed down. Emma escorted me. Supper. The Schillings in a boat. At N. D.'s. Conversed with him and Emma in his room. I was feverishly animated and talkative. My teeth ache.

27 June A hot, good day. Slept well but was still feeling ill. Worked with some effort. The gardeners were tidying the garden. An Italian boy. Went for a walk, nevertheless, after dinner, and even walked far (on an obscure path in the forest near the railroad) but was dead tired. Could not fight off drowsiness after tea and lay down on the divan. Terrible nightmares. Worked. Strolled a short while; dropped in at Novikova's. After supper (all waited for

Legoshin) went to the Kondratyevs' who just returned. N. D. began talking again about Novichikha. After that, sat on the balcony rather long. Vasya escorted me to my door.

28 June After rising and a walk (briefly with N. D.), worked as well as wrote N. F. a letter. Letters before dinner. One from Antonina Ivanovna unnerved me completely. Could not eat anything and was in a bad humor all day. Only in the evening began to feel better. What can one do with this madwoman??? [66] Walked to the railroad station at Klin. Met the stationmaster going to bathe. Talked with him. Tea at home. Mikhail Ivanovich. Ransacked letters for the address of Maria Markovna.[67] N. D. came over. Was present during their dinner. Rambled with N. D. Conversed with the drunken Mikhail. Supper. Visited the Kondratyevs. Tea on the terrace. Dina made us laugh. Emma sulked with me a little because I did not approve absolutely and entirely of Modest. Nervous fear while returning home.

29 June My Saint's day. At Mass at our place. *Te Deum* at my home. Solo lunch. Mikhaila. Walked. A cloud. Ran home. Detained by Novikova. Was perturbed at home and throughout the whole day on account of Antonina Ivanovna. At four o'clock N. D. and Novikova came together. Shortly, the von Vizins and all the rest appeared. Whist. Dinner. We walked a little. Whist again. I was in a bad mood all the time. Antonina Ivanovna's letter was the cause. Hemorrhoid pains. At times, during the day, imagined that I was dying. Wrote my will.[68]

30 June Rose late. The entire morning and all the time between tea and evening spent writing drafts of letters to Antonina Ivanovna. Could not write anything decisive. Intense moral suffering. Hatred and pity at the same time. Took a good walk in the forest beyond the village after dinner. Osip and Gavrila. Strolled alone before supper and with Novikova. She introduced me to Vizler and some other summer residents. The chef's gossiping at N. D.'s. He traveled to the New Jerusalem. Supper. Walked. Was upstairs at the Kondratyevs' to look at the former rooms. Visited Mary. The chef's gossiping again. Oh, how much I suffer from Antonina Ivanovna! That is what will finally kill me!

---

[66] *She was being very difficult about a proposed divorce.*

[67] *Maria Markovna Palchikova, Tchaikovsky's first music teacher.*

[68] *This will was superseded by another, made on August 30, 1887.*

1 July Was bathing. A gray, windless pleasant day. Went bathing. Finally wrote a letter to Antonina Ivanovna (Oh, how difficult it is neither to insult nor to indulge) and several others besides that. Went to the railroad station after dinner to mail the letters. Tea. Read and played *Parsifal*. Watched my people playing the game of *stukolka*.[69] Walked in the near-by forest. At Mary's. Talked about Dina and Emma (whether she should work for Tolya). Supper. Arisha wept??? At N. D.'s who was in the city today. On the whole, I was more cheerful today than all these past days. Still have hemorrhoid pains.

2 July Rain in the morning when I awoke. The whole time until noon was somehow very sad. I was busy finishing something in the third act. Still, all my thoughts were on Antonina Ivanovna and about the letters. Went to Klin; stopped in at Skokov's. N. D. came over with the little dogs after tea. We sat near the flower garden (there was no longer any rain but the sun was behind the clouds). Legoshin. A lady with some children. Escorted N. D. home and remained during their dinner. Home. Supper. Played bezique. Received the fourth act [libretto] today. Will start tomorrow.

3 July Started to write the fourth act today and very *successfully*. Excellent weather. The incident with Antonina Ivanovna is beginning to disappear into the realm of the past. My conscience is clear —but still, in spite of all, even the fact that she is the most worthless creature in the world, I pity her. No luck, poor thing. After dinner and a stroll to the grove opposite Klin (dropped in at Novikova's . . . who returned yesterday), played whist, during the day, at the Kondratyevs' with Novikova. Worked, whist again. Was angry at N. D. K. Moonlight night. We escorted Novikova.

4 July Met N. D. while walking and learned that he had a severe attack of asthma at night. He was very pale. Worked with not particularly good results. Forgot to mention that I was so angered by Emma (secretly entrusted letter and the question: *why am I angry at her?*) that I could not fall asleep for a long time and purposely told everybody (half-jokingly but in effect angrily) about it today. Went to the railroad station after dinner. Just after my return the thunderstorm began. One thunderclap was awfully loud; they say that a tree was struck by lightning near the Sytins'. Was at the Kondratyevs' during their dinner and inscribed photos in the study.

---

[69] *A Russian card game.*

Home. Worked, nothing very exceptional. Supper. At the Kondratyevs'. The doctor telegraphed that he would not come. But then, N. D. was well. Anna Yakovlevna. Tea in the reception room. At N. D.'s. Solitaire. Am angry at Emma and feel how very unjust and cruel it is.

MOSCOW

5 July Left on the express train. The Choral Society. Popov. Ivanov. Karlusha. The chorus sang in the hall (colorful program). I was very satisfied. Again at Popov's. Dinner at the hotel in a private dining room. Something was not good as I did not feel well the entire remainder of the day. Park. Walked. A pond near Zikov. Kiselev appeared unexpectedly. Went home. Synod bureau. Hermitage garden. At the Antæ theater. The fairy play, *The Pullet*. Rather amusing. Supper at the Hermitage restaurant. Brius. Very pleasant.

6 July Uspensky Cathedral. *My Cherubim* chorus song.[70] Dobrovolsky. At the Synod bureau. He, Orlov, Ivanov. Coffee. Conversation. Inspection. Took a walk. Rain. In the Kremlin under the arch. Dinner at the hotel; strolled a bit around the city. Home. Settled my bill. (Misha was in a tail coat.) Railroad station. Alone in the car. The poor third class passengers! Arrived safely. Supper at home. With the Kondratyevs. Nechaeva. Whist. My stomach was out of order; as a result, I was more angry than usual at Emma and *tutti quanti*.

MAIDANOVO

7 July While out walking, looked at the oak which was struck by lightning four days ago. Serezha Sytin. Novichikha. Wrote letters. Went over to the Kondratyevs' at twelve. They were having lunch. Levenson. Her weeping and ill health. Dinner. Kiselev arrived at the railroad station and sent for Sasha Legoshin. I went walking. To Klin. To the apothecary. Voronov with some company; the architect friend of S. I. Taneiev. Chloric lime. Home. Tea. Whist at the Kondratyevs'. Home. Played *The May Night*.[71] N. D. Kondratyev and the little dogs. Supper. Strolled. At the Kondratyevs'.

---

[70] *During divine service, he heard one of his sacred works for the first time. He was very pleased.*

[71] *Opera by Rimsky-Korsakov.*

A. A. Lvova. She chattered all evening and very interestingly, I must admit.

8 July Worked with not particularly good results. (Mme. Erdmannsdörfer's letter, happy for Brandukov, and a letter to him.) Walked after dinner (Olga, Mikhail's wife arrived) but not far as a thunderstorm threatened. Tea. Went to the Kondratyevs'. Lvova was having dinner and, after giving her blessing to everyone, departed. A walk to N. D. through the garden and with the ladies (Mary, Dina, Annette) to the village and farther. Beautiful although cool evening. Supper. Bade Olga good-by. Whist—a *monstre* (six rubbers at Kondratyev's). I won. Escorted Nadezhda Vasilyevna [Novikova].

9 July After rising, took a walk. N. D. and Dina. Letters excited me (one from Modest, U. was concerned) and perhaps because of that I worked so poorly. Worked very unsuccessfully. Dinner (prior to which I managed to write several letters). Went to the railroad station. Rain. Mary, Emma, Levenson, and Dina drank tea in my room. N. D. sat in the reception room. The thunderstorm was approaching. All left except Levenson. She stayed a while and then went away with Vasya. Worked again with awful results. And they say that I am all but a genius??? Nonsense! Was at K.'s. Suffered because I am cruel to Emma and Annette—but what can I do? Emma is simply becoming unbearable. And the more sympathy she deserves, the less she arouses in me. Had supper. Played my Second Suite with Annette. Was at N. D.'s recalling old times.

10 July Worked somewhat better thanks to no disturbing letters. But I felt bad all day; had pressure on my stomach and something else vaguely painful. Walked almost exclusively around my home and in the garden after dinner. Tried to go to the forest but the downpour was imminent and I returned home in time. Letter to Dima Peresleni. Tea. Went to Kondratyev's. Levenson was departing. Because of her departure, stayed during the Kondratyev dinner so as to see the effect of my cake. More pouring rain. At home, with good Legoshin, overheard and watched the people having their supper. (Legoshin told the story, during tea, how they arrested him in '81, thinking that he was a "student.") Supper. Whist with Novikova at Kondratyev's. I was very irritable because of illness. Boring to go home with Novikova.

11 July Slept restlessly. Awakening, heard the sound of rain. (Left a note on the door for Alexei that he should not awake me until nine o'clock.) Rose late. The weather was killing. I was sick. Pressure on my stomach and aversion to work and reading. The rain was violent and lingering; it was impossible to go out. Wrote letters. Walked up and down the gallery and a bit in my alley after dinner. Sasha Legoshin. Looked in at N. D.'s with him. Returned home to tea. The trunk from Tiflis and memories regarding it. Conversation with the friendly Legoshin. Read. Slept directly after tea. Banners. Emma and Dina came. Showed them the souvenirs of Tiflis. Supper. Complete lack of appetite. At the Kondratyevs'. Whist with Novikova. Though I was lucky, nevertheless, was terribly angry at N. D. What a riddle that man is! Good and evil alike give him pleasure. I am ill.

12 July Spent a horrible night. Vomited all the time and had a feeling of anguish and disgust toward everything whatever. Took some castor oil. Fell asleep with difficulty. Reaction of the medicine. Slept again. Rose with effort at ten o'clock. Slept once more and without interruption until dinner. At that time, had something like an appetite. Finishing Tolstoy's magnificent work, *The Cloth Measurer.* Was melancholy. Went to the Kondratyevs'. Stayed there during dinner. I did not feel bad during the day. But toward evening, the feeling of pressure on my stomach started again. (Could it be a tapeworm?) There was not even a trace of appetite at supper. Sasha Legoshin brought me a thermometer (it turned out that I had fever; the temperature was 100.4) and the twelfth volume of Tolstoy's works. Started *The Death of Ivan Ilyich* at once and finished it. I do not feel quite well; the pressure still continues on my stomach. *The Death of Ivan Ilyich* is a work of genius about suffering.

13 July Slept wonderfully, but I still had the feeling of being sick. Awoke late. Beautiful day. Went walking. Stopped in at Novikova's and talked with her and Albedil. Strolled through the fields across Praslovo. Began to feel bad. On the way back, went in to Novikova again. She was having dinner. Home. Dinner. Read, played *Judith* [72] and conversed with Sasha Legoshin, to whom I told the story of Verinovsky. The fatal news was confirmed by Stepan's letter to

---

[72] *Opera by Serov.*

Alexei.[73] Tea in a hurry at four o'clock. To the Kondratyevs'. Soon the von Vizins and Novikova arrived. Whist. Dinner. I ate and felt better; even thought that it disappeared, but it became worse again toward evening. Novikova confused and angered me terribly today (the Suvorins!). We finished playing at twelve o'clock. They want the von Vizins to stay for the night and someone in my place. I am angry inwardly, but being afraid of the darkness and danger, I invite them sincerely. Declined. Escort them to Novikova. We sit about. My stomach hurts more than ever. They ride off. Go to my place and after drinking some cognac with water, feel no more pain. What a strange thing that is!

14 July Slept wonderfully. Awoke and came to tea feeling my nerves rather pleasantly stimulated. But still was not able to work. Lunched without any appetite. That was due both to ill health and to the fact that I finally received the details of Verinovsky's death; wept, sobbing violently, almost hysterically—food was not at all on my mind. It occurred to me, after lunch, to read Tolstoy's *Forest Felling* and I wept again. All the time it was raining terribly. Put on my raincoat about five o'clock and went over to the Kondratyevs' and then to the railroad station. Met Kashkin but Jürgenson did not turn up. We sat down to dinner together at home and Kashkin's cheerful conversation had a good effect on me. We dropped in at N. D.'s. After that we drank and conversed for a long time.

15 July A good day. I still felt unwell. Walked under strain with Kashkin to Ivanovo. Ivan the coachman and his father were in front of their new hut. Church. We were seated. I could hardly walk back. We hired a coach with little bells and rode home in a gig. Drunken driver. Lunch. Albrecht arrived unexpectedly. Whist with both the N. D. K.'s [74] and Novikova. Telegram from Kashkin's wife. We started out for the railroad station. Jürgenson arrived. Mary and Emma were nearly late. Kashkin departed. I rode home alone in a phaeton. Jürgenson and Karlusha walked. Supper. Conversation.

---

[73] *Ivan A. Verinovsky was a young artillery officer who became acquainted with Tchaikovsky during the latter's visit to Tiflis. They became very attached to one another, Verinovsky to the point of adoration. Failing his examinations for a higher military position, he shot himself.*

[74] *Kondratyev and Kashkin had the same initials.*

A stroll in the park. Drunkenness. Metronome. *Ruslan and Liud-mila* and *A Life for the Tsar.*

16 July Rose almost well. Tea and coffee with the two guests. A walk through the village, the forest near the river and mill and back home along the embankment. Dinner. Drunkenness and talks. Metronome to *Ruslan and Liudmila* and some songs. Walked to the railroad station. Met Altani while seeing them off. Vasily drove me back. Ill again. It's nothing. Home. Read the newspapers. Legoshin. Conversed with him. He visited me. Supper. At Kondrat-yev's. Nastya, the lovable, adopted child of O. S. Pashkova. Home. Read the *Memoirs* of Grech (bought from the spinster at the rail-road station). Haircut. Am well.

17 July Awoke at night with an indescribably excruciating pain in the chest. Could not lie, sit or stand. Alexei became frightened seeing me in the studio in the morning. Mustard plaster. Wee bit better. But still suffered intensely throughout the day. Golitzin. He visited me with N. D. I received them though it overtaxed my strength. Read Grech. Dinner without appetite. Rested at their place. Golitzin visited me again. Was present during their dinner. Golitzin was slightly drunk. Saw him off. Emma visited me. Un-dressed. A night of torture. Hardly slept, sitting up now in one, now in the other chair. On Golitzin's advice, put on a blister beetle during the day and that helped very much, for when the abscess opened due to the blister beetle, I could then lounge in the chair in which I slept until morning. From that time on, I got better and better. Alesha was very solicitous.

18 July Rising, had the blissful feeling of a person ceasing to suffer after being terribly tortured. Walked a little after tea. Saw Emma and Dina. Wrote letters. Despite weakness and the effects of fever, walked to Klin, after dinner, to drop certain letters in the letter box (on the main street) about which Alesha must not know (to Tim., to Kart., to Ant[onina] Ivan[ovna]). At Kondratyev's. Teplov, whose cavalry guardsman's cap I saw from a distance. Tea at home. N. D. came over. Conversation with good Legoshin. Alexei with some cherries. At Kondratyev's. Emma with her tenderness and unnatural playfulness. She and Dina escorted me home and were looking all the time into the lavatory. Mary and Nastya. Supper. Whist with Novikova at Kondratyev's. Awfully dark. Candle in a glass. Escorted her; walked home frightened, as a bat was pursuing me.

19 July A gray, cool morning. After a difficult sleep and a head-ache, rose at ten o'clock (left a note for Alexei). Walked to the forest after tea and returned by way of Praslovo. Was at Novikova's. Met Emma and Nastya. Dinner. Letter to Jürgenson for La Mara.[75] The Sytin girls sent some mushrooms with Serezha. Went to thank them. Stayed and conversed with Mme. Sytin. At the Kondratyevs'. Tea. Worked a little. Beautiful sunset and evening. At the Kondrat-yevs' after their dinner. *Les gentillesses d'Emma!* Watched people walking on the embankment by way of the mill. Strolled long on the path in the arbor, enjoying the view. Home. Met the boys (Serezha Sytin, Schilling, etc.; their new way of pestering). Read at home, sitting near the flower bed. Supper. Whist. I was angry at N. D. even though I won. No real feeling of sleepiness.

(*Tchaikovsky's footnote*) And now it's more than two months that he [Verinovsky] is no longer alive!!!

Sunday, 20 July Father would have been ninety-one years old today. Was late to Mass. Strolled a bit; saw some people at a dis-tance going to a baptism at Klin, but also worked. Went to the forest after dinner and walked to the distant forest on the left of Belavin. Wrote letters and visited the Kondratyevs after tea. (Emma went away to the Stolpakovs' this morning.) Whist. I walked home with great fear. It was dark and in addition I was afraid of Kiselev, who turned up again and asked N. D. and me for money. I sent nothing.

21 July Beautiful day. Worked rather well. Took a short walk after dinner along the embankment (Top was unfaithful to me; slipped away from me to Legoshin and Trantin who were walking ahead). Sat about and conversed with the Kondratyevs. Tea. Home. Letter

---

[75] *La Mara (pen name for Marie Lipsius) was a writer on music, notably an editor of anthologies and letters. She requested Jürgenson to procure from Tchaikovsky a specially written letter that would portray him as composer and musician, which she wished to include in her book entitled,* Musikerbriefe aus fünf Jahrhunderten, 1886. *Tchaikovsky an-swered Jürgenson and asked that his (Tchaikovsky's) letter be given to La Mara. The letter did not characterize him as she wished but she used it, nevertheless, in her book.*

to Mackar. Walked far along the railroad tracks to the right; saw three trains fly past; Emma was returning in one. Wonderful weather and a wonderful tramp. Emma was telling some interesting things about the Stolpakovs. I was chilled to the bone and afraid of catching a cold. Drank two large glasses of wine at supper and warmed up. Whist. N. D., and indeed even Mary, played with unusual greed. Escorted Novikova again and was still afraid. Really, returning home after whist in this way is unpleasant.

22 July For some reason, I vomited and felt bad at night. Rose at ten o'clock. Went to congratulate Mary. *Te Deum.* Took a little walk in the garden. Lunched at twelve-thirty o'clock. My servant girl went to the birthday lunch for Kondratyeva in the arbor. Went for a walk through Klin and Praslovo and back home. Worked. Whist at Kondratyev's. Arrival of O. S. Pashkova and Maria Iva-novna. Dinner. Was angry at Emma who has become awfully in-trusive. Strolled around the garden. Whist. Maria Ivanovna and a gentleman guest whom I introduced to her. Novichikha was more confusing than usual. It was very dark on the way home.

23 July I felt somewhat bad after rising. Strolled with N. D. a short time and was in his room for a little while and also in the dining room with the rest of the company (Pashkova and Maria Ivanovna). Worked. All the ladies came from the other house. After dinner, search for the pin that was lost yesterday in the meadow near Alexei. (They were carousing in my place yesterday; Legoshin, the priests, etc.; it was a farewell evening party arranged by Sasha.) Took a short walk in the forest. Home. Tea. Vasya. At Kondratyev's. Fuss due to N. D.'s departure. I saw him off. Sasha Legoshin. Awaiting the train. Bade good-by. Sat a little while also with O. S. Pashkova and Maria Ivanovna. Home. At the Kondratyevs'. Was at the Kondratyevs' after supper. Emma irritates me more than ever. Poor Emma! Went home as early as I could. Feel empty and rather sad on account of N. D.'s absence. Among the letters in the morning was a huge and vicious one from Pavlovskaya from Montreux, but a still infinitely more strange and vicious one came from Antonina Ivanovna, in which she asked that I dedicate something to her as well as that I undertake to bring up her children.

24 July Quite an autumn day. Worked successfully. Went to the town gate, after dinner, by way of Klin (looked at the big, gray house [76]); then returned home through Praslovo. Met the chamber-maids of Kondratyev and Khodunov. Dropped in at Novikova's for a moment. She is becoming absolutely unbearable with her stupidity. Tea. Letter to Pavlovskaya. With the Kondratyevs during their dinner. Absence of N. D. is felt very much. Walked with them as far as the paved road. Arisha served supper. Alexei rode off for . . . Waited for him. Emma, of course, turned up near the house. Was at their place. I was chattering rather volubly. It was terribly dark.

25 July After a walk, sat down to write letters. Received several letters. Expected the guests, i.e. first, the Kondratyev company who dined at my place (I looked on) and second, Mary, Emma, Dina and Nastya. Walked with effort after dinner. Following tea, worked briefly. Went to the Buzon silk factory with the Kondratyevs. Supper. Escorted them. The moon and the sunset. Glorious evening. Postponed my trip to Moscow until Sunday.

26 July Slept excellently. After taking a walk, worked and with success, but how far it is still to the end!!! Mary, Emma and Dina came to dinner for the last time. Nastya has already left. We went to Novikova after dinner. She had an ugly quarrel with Mary. What a fool she is—impossible to describe! Strolled in the forest; marvelous weather. Tea with the Kondratyevs in my place again. Departure. Saw them off. Bought them presents from?—what's his name. Walked back along the railroad tracks. It was sad. Sat in the arbor at home watching the sunset. Home. Supper. Read the Moscow newspapers. Feel a kind of depression and a strong sense of missing the Kondratyevs.

MOSCOW

27 July Took the express to Moscow. Alesha saw me off. Starokopitov and the saleswomen. Traveled in a compartment. Was about to go to Jürgenson. But his place is so deserted and desolate that I went to the Hotel Moscow. Kotek's letters from Mme. Stal. Tears. My room number ten. Just as I was about to have lunch, Ivanov arrived. All the secrets about Rukavishnikov. Could hardly get rid of him. Lunch and drunkenness. Lingering rain. Brius, even though

---

[76] *The composer's future home which he occupied on May 5, 1892. After his death, it became the Tchaikovsky Museum and contains most of his manuscripts, pictures, furniture, and other Tchaikovskyana.*

it was Sunday. Gratification and stings of conscience. Home. Ennui.
Ivan drove me in a carriage to vespers in Dolgorukovsky Street.
Was standing near the choir. They sang rather well. Smoked in the
darkness. Left after the holy water ceremony. Patrikeshka [Patri-
keyev's restaurant]. Arrival of Zverev and Co. Drunkenness.

28 *July* Rose early. Visit by I. I. Popov. Mass. Our chorus sang
very well. Ivanov is an able person. My Cherubim chorus song.
Boy soloists. At Jürgenson's. Lunch. Played piquet with him and
Pechkovskaya. Money. Home. Continuous heavy rain. Indecision.
Remained. Visited Ivanov. Gratuities to the soloists. Visited Zverev.
Dinner. Three rubbers of whist. Still the same guests. At Testov's
restaurant in the large dining room. Little drunkenness. Came home
at twelve o'clock.

29 *July, Moscow* Slept fairly well. After reading the newspapers,
wrote letters. Was unusually nervous, almost to the point of being
dizzy. Was angry at everything and everyone. Finally went out at
about twelve o'clock. At the piano tuner's. Made certain purchases.
Heartlessness and even enmity toward the beggars near the Kuz-
netzky bridge. Lunch in the hotel on the balcony. Drove with Ivan
for the purchases. Cigars at Andreyev's. Rain again. Home. Disgusting condition: either sick or frantically nervous. Absolutely insur-
mountable repulsion toward Moscow and everything that's here.
That is strange. Departed. Ivan hardly drove as far as Lanin when
he said that he was ill and could not drive any farther. My poor
Vanya! Railroad station. Litvinov. Mazurin with his wife. Conversation with Litvinov as far as Khimok. Acquaintance with Mazurin.
Did not feel well during the trip. Klin at last. Tavern. Rain again
and was completely drenched. Home. Changed clothes. Supper.
Letters from Tolya, Modya, and J. I. Shpazhinskaya. Tolya's and
especially the one from Shpazhinskaya excited me very much. Poor,
unfortunate J. I.!!! Walked a long time up and down in the gallery.
Wouldn't get a chance to work tomorrow again. Imperative to
answer J. I. She is probably dying—perhaps already dead. During
the last few days, my thoughts have been gloomy. I imagine that I
will not complete *The Enchantress*.

MAIDANOVO

30 *July* Learned in the morning, after a wonderful sleep, that
Dima arrived. Little by little, during the course of the day, I yielded

to his affectionate behavior. After tea and conversation with him, wrote poor J. I. Shpazhinskaya and to Emma about Tolya's letter. Went to Klin in the afternoon with Dima. It was sultry. We drank some water at Skokov's. Returned via Praslovo. Tea. Conversation. Dima rode off. I was seized with a kind of incomprehensible sorrow and a craving for people's company. Went for a walk. Beautiful evening. Wished to encounter the village children and gladly gave them some money. Met Baron Schilling with his family. Was on the paved road. Marvelous sunset which I enjoyed looking at from the church wall. Sasha, the deacon's son and his strategic methods of obtaining honey. Along the way, stopped at the terrace of the big house where Albedil, Lena Sytin and Vizler were sitting and conversed long with them—that is what the craving for people's company has come to! The core of the matter is that I miss the Kondratyevs very much. Supper. Played Massenet's *Manon* after supper. A talk with Alesha and Vasily concerning Rover, who was unchained (talked in the dining room at the window). Put the books away. The feeling of loneliness has disappeared—but boredom has replaced it! How to drag it out until sleep! . . .

31 July Slept marvelously. But it's a strange thing! I have noticed now for a long time that I always feel bad in the morning. What could it be? Why is it that instead of the morning vigor, there is the feeling of weariness, sadness, and the reluctance for activity? . . . Wept while reading the essay of Vogüé (*Le roman russe*) about Turgenev. Walked a bit. Good day, although it rained intermittently. Worked, without any inspiration, but successfully. Went to Klin through Praslovo, after dinner, and had no pleasure. Walked along the other side to look at the house but did not reach it. Was only near the grove. Tea. Visited by Albedil and Elena. Worked again. Played *Harold*.[77] Enjoyed looking at the sunset again from the wall. After supper, read Bourget (on Turgenev, Amiel, the de Goncourts, etc.). Walked with Alesha about the garden. The moon in all its glitter. Indefinite feeling of loneliness and depression. . . . Seems that Alesha also feels it vaguely.

1 August Gray and cool. I felt so bad in the morning that I imagined myself to be quite sick. Later on, it passed. Read Vogüé on Dostoyevsky and wept again. Was late to consecration of water;

---

[77] *Opera by Napravnik.*

saw the procession from a distance. Worked well. Went to the city
with Alesha after dinner to look at the house about which there
was some talk recently. The location is good, but the house is bad.
We returned through Praslovo. On the way, Alesha was telling
about Vasily's quarrel with Arisha. We found the latter gaudily
dressed up for some unknown reason. Tea. Worked doggedly until
seven o'clock. Letter to Antonina Ivanovna. Watched the sunset at
the church. Cool weather. Took a stroll in the garden after supper.
Moonlight. Jolly voices from everywhere. Played *Manon Lescaut* at
home. Like it better than I expected. Today, too, had momentary
pangs of solitude.

2 August Today it was not merely imagination, as yesterday, but
a fact that I slept restlessly at night and felt a vague discomfort
all day. However, after a short walk (in the forest), worked well
uninterruptedly until dinner. No appetite whatever. The piano
tuner arrived. I went (without enjoyment) to the grove opposite
Klin. The shouts of the shepherds. On returning, found a big party
outside. Vasily's birthday and he had guests. After tea, heard and
watched the merry guests. Wrote letters to N. D. Kondratyev,
Emma, and Panya on the terrace. Went to look at the sunset again.
It was singularly beautiful today. Observed the Schillings having
supper, through my binoculars. A strange inquisitiveness! Talked
with Alesha, after supper, about Arisha's quarrel with Vasily.
Played *Manon*. Today, again, Massenet seems to me nauseously
luscious.

Sunday, 3 August Excellent weather but cool. Felt quite well in
the morning, which hasn't happened for a long time. Walked to
Mass at Klin. Was in Uspensky church (the odd priest with effeminate manners) and for a short time in the cathedral. Worked before
dinner. Commenced the other half of the fourth act (the Princess
and Kudma). Read the newspapers after dinner. Went to the near-
by forest and cut out a shady path. Arranged about the climbing
plant in my gallery. Tea. Work until seven-thirty. The sunset. Some
unfamiliar people were in our garden. Read Vogüe for a long time
after supper. Moonlight. The singing of the girls. Rode to the railroad station to meet Nikolai Ilyich who was passing through.
Arrived early. Read the newspapers. Saw my brother. We succeeded in talking a little. Izvolsky. Aksakov at the news dealer's.
Cold and clear weather.

4 August Slept poorly and had a little pain in the abdomen but, thank God, it passed completely during the day. Rose at nine. Read the newspapers and some letters (L. [Laroche?] asked for money again). Took a walk. Worked well. After dinner, went to the nearby forest and was very delighted, especially with the shady path I had cut. Thank God, I have again become fully receptive to nature seeing and comprehending in each leaf and flower something unattainably beautiful, reposeful, peaceful, giving me again an intense love of life. . . . At home, too, I have begun to occupy myself with flowers more than formerly even though it's only with the climbing plant in the gallery whose amazing growth I watch with great interest. . . . Mystical and magnificent! Tea. Letters (to N. F. and Lvova). Worked. Went to Malanino. Herd of cattle. Spied on the Schillings??? And why is it that I like to see and know so much how others live? Supper. The quarrel during the *pas de géant* between Arisha and Novikova's cook. Disgraceful. I heard everything. Swinging. Played *Manon* at home. Oh, how nauseating is Massenet!!! But what is most aggravating is that I feel a certain kinship with the *nausea*.

5 August Grayish day. Felt excellently and, while awakening, joked with Alexei *as formerly!* How long since I have awakened with a joyous consciousness of health and happiness! After a walk (saw a place near the cattle shed where it would be good to build myself a little house), worked intensely but with good results. Took Alesha to show him my place after dinner, but he showed me a still better one. Strolled in my forest and went over to the Dmitrovsky road where I discovered a *new and beautiful* place to build a little house. The little girl carrying mushrooms and singing. Went home. Tea. Worked persistently until seven-thirty. The sunset was gray and somber. Home. Supper. Read Starchevsky's article on Hahn. Went to the *pas de géant*. The cursing of the laundresses was not heard today but that of Colen, the Frenchman, the Sytins, etc. Played *Manon*.

6 August The rain started yesterday evening (at eleven o'clock), and continued all night and nearly all day, destroying the wild climbing vine in the gallery which concerned me so. It cleared toward evening. Walked up and down in the gallery. Worked. Mme. Stal's letter angered me before dinner. Walked in the garden, in the afternoon, and to the village along the embankment. Was drenched. ("Uncle, did you see the horses?") Worked after tea. Sunset at the church. The boys. Ignasha, etc. Going roundabout past Novikova, saw her on the balcony. Conversation. Supper. Read Belov's article on Russian soldiers. Played the end of the nauseating *Manon,* and the rubbish of M. Lefebvre.

7 August Cold weather. Just like autumn. However, resumed the baths. Worked successfully. As a result of yesterday's damage, the gardeners were working today. Rain. Went to my place in mud boots after dinner. What a sight! Met the grandchild of Kabach (or is it Tabach?). Tea. Read Pingaud's good book, *Les Français en Russie et les Russes en France.* Worked very successfully. The sunset. The priest and his nephew. Went to the priest's to look at the sordid rooms. *Le Roi l'a dit.*[78] Supper. Read the *Istorichesky Vestnik. Le Roi l'a dit.*

8 August Worked very successfully again which is the case of late, on the whole. Went to the village via Praslovo after dinner, hoping to see the person of interest to me. While walking on low ground, noticed people running. It was a fire and was extinguished immediately. Crossing the Dmitrovsky bridge, came upon an entirely new place, a forest near the brick yard. Back via Praslovo once more and saw no one this time. Tea. Alexei had a guest from Klin; a former railroad-station waiter; I listened secretly and believe they spoke about courtship. Worked with self-oblivion until seven-thirty. With Alesha to the church wall. The sunset. A talk about his marriage. Supper. Read. *Le Roi l'a dit.* Emma was in Klin en route; left gifts: a book and a letter containing the usual sweet words. It's really shameful to respond so to such kind thoughts. But I cannot help it. Angry.

9 August My teeth pained at night a little, and pain now. Slept excellently. Took no bath. Walked only about my own grounds after tea. Worked well. After dinner (lost my appetite due to a lot of letters) went to look at the house in Klin which Alexei thought of purchasing. Absolute trash. Returned through Praslovo. Saw Egorushka; asked and got twice as much. Tea. Was writing. The work has progressed unusually fast recently. Wrote to Catoire and Emma. Went out; enjoyed the flowers and took a walk with Alesha around the grounds. The priest, his nephew and son were fishing for carp. Conversed a little. The sunset. Was at church, and after-

---

[78] *Opera by Delibes which Tchaikovsky played over.*

ward walked along the edge of the field in the direction of Praslovo, admiring the beauty of the view. At home, played my music. Telegram. Must travel to Moscow tomorrow for the jubilee of Jürgenson.[79]

MOSCOW

10 August Beautiful day. Trip to Moscow. Direct to the Jürgensons'. Celebration of his jubilee. *Te Deum.* Lunch in the garden. Speeches. Alexeiev. Yakovlev. Whist. Yakovlev, a German, his wife, S. I., and I. Unpleasant incident concerning money. Left. Boris borrowed ten rubles. Walked. At Testov's restaurant. Loneliness and disgust. Drunk. Home. Drank again.

11 August After reading the newspapers, went to Emma. She was out. Also Stolpakova. Was at the Conservatory. Dined at the tavern in Dmitry's room. I am disgusted with taverns in general, and with this one in particular. An excellent walk far into the Petrovsky park. If only there was something like this in Maidanovo! Drank tea at some grove. Home. Letter from Emma and angry at her. Rode there and found her out again. Stolpakov is a friendly and engaging person. Visited Karlusha. With him and his wife to Lentovsky's Hermitage. The fairy play *The Devil's Wife.* It was good but I was sleepy. A lady whom I let sit down in the box. Supper in the Hermitage with the Albrechts.

12 August A knock at the door awakened me at ten o'clock. Farsky. Settled a misunderstanding in the orchestra score of *Cherevichki.*[80] Catoire came, but I asked him to return later. Saw the Stoyanovskys, i.e. Emma, off. Lunch at the Kursk railroad station. Home. Charming Catoire. His variations and quartet. Karlusha. Money from the Musical Society.[81] With them at Jürgenson's. Budkevich. Home. Departed. Ivan has been driving me around in a carriage all these past days. Practically alone in the first class the

---

[79] *The twenty-fifth anniversary of Jürgenson's activities as a music publisher.*

[80] *Tchaikovsky's opera composed in 1885, first known as* Vakula, the Smith *as well as* Oksana's Caprices, Oksana *being the heroine in the opera.* Cherevichki *is the name of a kind of shoe with high heels worn by the women in the Ukraine section of Russia.*

[81] *Probably performance fees.*

whole trip. Klin. Vasily, the coachman. Alexei was grumbling about the purchase of a cabinet. Letters. The small bottle broken.

MAIDANOVO

13 August Beautiful weather. Slept well but felt my stomach upset all morning. Took a walk. Letter from Modest. He'll arrive shortly. Wrote letters. Took them to the railroad station after dinner. Worked after tea. A stroll in the open country. Stopped in at Novichikha's. The superintendent was there. We chattered about all kinds of nonsense. She escorted me home. Supper. Played Korsakov's *The Snow Maiden.*

14 August Superb weather. Read the newspaper in the playground. The little Schilling girl going for mushrooms with her nurse. Worked well but intensely and became very tired. After dinner went to the grove opposite the village. Tea. Was amused watching the chicks and the hens. Work again. Took a walk to the open country beyond the farm. Good news in Klin: it is Dedication Day. Worked a little before and after supper; finished the *arioso* of the godmother. Am reading Loti's *Pêcheur d'Islande.* Not especially pleased. The tone of the writing reminds me of that repulsive Zola. (Et . . . after the period.)

15 August It was such a fine day; there has been nothing like it all summer. Was tempted by it and walked as far as Klin through Praslovo (there was a religious festival in the Uspensky Church). Worked at home. Worked after dinner also (a rarity!). Strolled a little. Worked after tea. Went to the village with some coins and distributed no little amount of money today. On the paved road. Played Fauré's quartet before supper. Read an interesting article, *The New Land,* in the *Vestnik Evropy* after supper. Telegram from Modest. He will come tomorrow.

16 August What a change; windy and cold. Worked (last scene!!! . . .). The cabinet was delivered. Went to the forest after dinner and returned across Praslovo. Did not see Egorka but tried to see him. Met Novikova near her place and visited her. Home, transferred the music to the cabinet. Wrote letters to Brandukov and in regard to him. Took a walk. Home, worked a bit. Watched the fire from the tower. Supper. Alexei drove off to the railroad station. I waited at home. It was dark. Arrival of Modya with Kolya. Conversation. Tea. We parted late.

Sunday, 17 August After tea, took a walk with Modya to Klin and returned via Praslovo. I spoke to him about the Caucasus, my travels, Paris, Georges, etc. Dinner. Strolled by myself a little way. Was pestered by the Maidanovo children. Tea. Walked through the bright country during the sunset. Supper. Read the first two acts of Modya's comedy.[82] Liked it very much. The weather was windy, bad.

18 August We strolled around the garden. I worked and, *today, entirely finished* the rough sketches of the opera. Thanked God for this kindness. Walked alone after dinner along the embankment to the right; it was raining all the time. Tea. Talks. Kolya . . . was placing and nearly set fire to . . . Letters. Visit by Baron Schilling. Was at Novikova's. Home. A talk with Kolya. *Russkaya Starina.*[83] Supper. Read the third and fourth acts of Modya's play. The third act is excellent; the fourth, I criticized.

19 August Very cold weather. Was about to go and see the Schillings off but they were already gone. Showed Modya and Kolya the tree which was struck by lightning. We strolled about. Was composing the songs for the empress.[84] Began by not being particularly successful. Took a walk after dinner between the forest and Praslovo. Tea. Novikova visited us. She chattered and made us laugh with all kinds of nonsense. A song. A walk in the open. Supper. Novikova. Whist. Kolya was excited very nicely.

20 August Cold weather. We took a walk together in the morning. Was composing a song. Walked by way of Praslovo to Klin after dinner and there went down to the right of the bridge, going as far as Demyanovo along the embankment. After returning, we drank tea and the four of us rode off in a *troika* to look at the Selensk property. We found the proprietress very surprised. It turned out that Novichikha lied about it all. The property was not for sale. We stayed a while. Unbecoming behavior. At the railroad station. A

---

[82] *Probably the play* Lizaveta Nikolaievna *by Modest (Modya), Tchaikovsky's younger brother.*

[83] *A Russian magazine.*

[84] *Tchaikovsky dedicated his Twelve Songs, Op. 60 to Maria Fyodorovna, the tsarina of Russia, at the suggestion of the Grand Duke Konstantin.*

crowd from three trains. Walked home. Read. Supper. Modya read me *The Afflicted Woman.*[85] I like it.

21 August Warmer weather. Was composing a song after tea and a stroll. At dinnertime, when we were already at the table, Hubert arrived unexpectedly. Was very glad. Walked by myself in the direction of Shchapova. Tea. Conversation with Hubert. He brought some tricks with him. The three of us sauntered together. We watched the trains. There was whist after supper. Kolya was excited very nicely.

22 August After rising and all drinking tea together, we took a stroll. I worked until dinner composing a song, not without some strain. After dinner (I was a little angry at Hubert all day because of his fastidiousness) I dropped in at Novikova's (she invited both Modest and me) and went down to Klin to buy a mouth rinse for Kolya; his gums hurt him. Tea. They all left for the railroad station to meet Nata, who however did not pass through. I was working. Rain. Played Napravnik and Lefebvre four hands with Hubert. Supper. Novichikha. Whist. We went to sleep late.

23 August After having tea (with unusually tasty rolls) we all took a walk together. With Modya to Novichikha. Shakhovskaya. While Modya and Hubert went to the railroad station, I wrote a song. Dinner. Went through Praslovo (something draws me all the time to that village) to Klin, from there along the road to the brick works, but again I returned by way of Praslovo. Saw Egorka Tabach flying a kite. Talked with him and some other boys and girls. These children, although ugly, are so charmingly engaging in their display of the pure Great Russian spirit, that I could not help being moved. (One of the girls asked for twenty kopeks; then one hundred rubles and later a *five kopek piece!!*) Tea. Wrote again or tried to. Rambled along the paved road with Hubert. To a question of how I should act (about a fundamental problem in my artistic life) I received as an answer an account of a concert by a nine-year-old wonder child, etc. etc. However, seldom have I liked anyone as much as good Hubert. Home. Expected the guests. Novichikha and Shakhovskaya. The former is more than ever unbearable, stupid, fussy, etc. Shakhovskaya is on the whole a clever and impressive woman. Supper. Whist. Kolya took part and triumphed. They left.

---

[85] *A drama by the composer's brother, Modest.*

I overdrank. A telegram came from Taneiev. Why is it, I ask my-self, that I was dissatisfied for some reason on receiving the news of his arrival tomorrow morning? For I do not really know any-one who stands higher in my regard and sincere friendship than T??

Sunday, 24 August Was at Mass at the Uspensky church together with Modest after tea. The effeminate priest. Tried to compose another song in expectation of Taneiev. Taneiev. Dinner. A walk with him. His stories about the Maslov sharp wit. New quartet.[86] Much that is good. After tea, the quartet again for Hubert. We went in the company of Novichikha to look at the place for my house. Through the park. Novichikha's stupidities. Taneiev played the quartet again and some small things. Supper. Angry because it was meager. Taneiev was demonstrating various piano tricks. He departed. An errand to Hubert. We parted at eleven o'clock; I was very tired.

25 August Cold but clear weather. Was in a bad mood in the morning for some reason. Walked alone. Wrote a song and a letter. Went to the near-by forest after dinner; returned earlier than usual and watched them flying a kite, which was excellently pasted to-gether by Nazar. (He is very attractive.) Novichikha. We went to meet Mitya and Bob. Both have become very much more hand-some. Bob has grown a great deal. They ate and rode off immedi-ately. A talk with the mayor of Klin. Came back, so as to pay the money. Starokopitov. The woman news dealer. Walked back by myself. Grand evening. Newspapers. Interesting events from Bul-garia. Supper. Meat dumplings. Modya read me the end of *The Afflicted Woman.*

26 August Terribly cold weather. After tea and a walk in the garden, wrote almost two songs. Went to Klin across Praslovo after dinner. Met Tabach's grandson with a school bag. Conversation. We made preparations for Kolya's departure. Saw him off. A fire in Vershutin. Purchases at the railroad station from Starokopitov and the woman news dealer; conversation with them and Egor Egorovich; drank coffee; waited for the train; Perfilev, etc. Arrange-ments about a seat for Kolya. Departed. Home in a carriage. Read Nata's letters and the newspapers. Supper. Afterward I played *Parsifal.* The little dogs.

---

[86] *Taneiev's third, D minor, Op. 7. Sergey I. Taneiev was a pupil and close friend of Tchaikovsky.*

MOSCOW

27 *August*   Trip to Moscow with Modya. Lunched solo at the rail-road station. At Jürgenson's. My uncomfortable financial relations with him. Conservatory. Visited Taneiev. With him to the Huberts'. Met Batasha after a separation of five months. She presented me with some embroidery. There was much laughter. We drove to the Hermitage. Dined there in Andrey's room. A play at the Maly Theater. *The Husband of a Famous Woman.* What rot! What vile acting except for Ermolova and Sadovskaya! Weary. Tea at Testov's restaurant. The actor Davidov.

28 *August*   Modya and I had to sleep in a stuffy room. Practically did not sleep. Rising, went to Altani at his new apartment. Conversation about various matters. Felt bad. Matilda. Conservatory. The examination. Purchases. Dinner at one o'clock at the kind Huberts'. Went home. Modya lay down to rest. Vanya drove me to Jürgenson for the purchases. Went home. Meeting with Lody. Visit by A. N. Shishkova. At the railroad station. S. I. Taneiev was in the train (his acknowledgement and portrait). Doctor Benzenger. Tedious journey. Home. Supper. Alexei told me the result of the trip to Podsolnechnaya. Brought the manuscript of the first act of *The Enchantress* and examined it.

29 *August* [*Maidanovo*]   Rose early. Beautiful weather. Took a walk with Modya around the garden after tea. From the arbor we saw something strange in the river. It turned out to be a corpse. Was contriving a song with reluctance. There is no inspiration, but how can I dedicate less than ten songs, at least, to the empress? Went to my forest with great difficulty after dinner. Tea. Feeding of the chickens, little dogs, etc. Worked. Taneiev. With him to Vizler. Found her in the garden with Koln. A walk. A boy sent for the pince-nez. Portraits of the girl with whom S. I. [Taneiev] is in love and whom I can in no way recall. Tried to all evening but without success. Taneiev played very well before supper (Polonaise Fantaisie and two Schubert-Liszt transcriptions). Was still trying to recall the girl through the diary after supper. Wonderful moonlight night. Taneiev invited me to Demyanovo [87] tomorrow.

30 *August*   The weather was never before so beautiful. However, I wrote a song after tea and a brief stroll. We immediately started

---

[87] *The estate of Taneiev's brother.*

out for Demyanovo after dinner. Lovely park but the house is bad, resembling an old barn. A walk through the park and to the river. Tea. Maryanna Sergeyevna. A long walk in a beautiful section. We returned by way of the paved road. Marvelous evening. Moonlight. Stopped at the church with Modya on the way back. Came in at the end of vespers. Home. I read *The Stage Coach*,[88] after supper, and also played Catoire's attractive quartet.[89] How talented he is!

Sunday, 31 August Divine weather. Modya went to church. I copied over the first song. Dinner. Went to my forest. Ant hills. The boys were following me. I became angry. Tea. Preparations. Saw Modya off. There were no tickets. Later everything was all right. Egor Egorovich. Colen. Modya got in a compartment where there was a youth (seemed like Golitzin) with unbelievably beautiful eyes. Walked home on the railroad tracks. Boys. Supper. Played the two new acts of *The Enchantress*. Good.

MOSCOW

1 September Trip to Moscow on the express train. Lunch at the station. *Te Deum* at the Conservatory. Reading of the report.[90] Kashkin's speech on Liszt was endless. . . . Set out for Petrovskoye-Razumovskoye. Unforgettably beautiful excursion. Dinner in honor of Jürgenson at the Hermitage restaurant. Speeches. Boring. In the Hermitage garden with Zverev, Remezov and the Nekrasov brothers. *Grigory Grigoryevich Nosov*. Lounging around at the Patrie restaurant. The Nekrasovs are good but intolerably narrow-minded. Stayed at Jürgenson's.

2 September Rising after a night's sleep, conversed reluctantly with P. I. For I detest conversing in the morning. Conference at Shishkov's. Razumovsky, the priest, Hubert, I, Orlov and Dobrovolsky. Useless talk. Lunch with Hubert at the Slavyansky Bazaar restaurant. At P. I.'s store. Catoire and his quartet; Taneiev, Hubert. How kind and noble S. I. Taneiev is! What interest he shows in Catoire! Tired. Ivan, unexpectedly. Glad. Park. Long trip in the forest. At the Bolshoi Theater with the Huberts and Sasha Gudim, who arrived today. *Ruslan and Liudmila*. Went on the stage during

---

[88] *By Count Vladimir A. Sollogub, novelist and librettist of Tchaikovsky's early opera Undine.*

[89] *String quartet, Op. 23.*

[90] *At the opening of the new school year at the Conservatory.*

the intermission. Kashperov. In the office. Meeting with old acquaintances. Supper at the Patrie restaurant. In love with V. . . . Hesitation. Virtue triumphs.

MAIDANOVO

3 September Slept very little. All morning, one thing after another awakened me. Departed. At the railroad station. The angry colonel and his daughters. The chatterbox wife. The kind military officer and his valet. Klin. Vasily Belavinsky. Home. Dinner. Letters. In my forest. The superintendent and a talk with him. Tea. Letters. Stroll. Looked at the trains. The weather is turning bad. A dry, sharp but warm wind. Gave tips; was at the inn, etc. Both old and small. Home. Letters. Supper. Shel's *Tamara*.[91] Letters. Tired.

4 September Slept nine hours almost without interruption. It rained at night. Astonishing change in weather. Walked up and down in the gallery in the morning due to the rain. Copied over a song. After dinner walked in the gallery, the garden, and to Klin. Constant pestering by all kinds of beggars. Tea. Another song ("Simple Words"). Walked about the garden. And here too were beggars, who had lost all in a fire. Finished the correspondence. Played Fitingov's rot after supper.

5 September The weather was excellent again, although cool. I slept restlessly and had strange dreams (naked flight with Nazar;[92] the necessity and at the same time the impossibility of doing something due to Sasha; the deacon's son, etc.). After a walk (Polkashka slipped his chain) copied over two songs until dinner. Went to the forest near the railroad beyond Malanino after dinner. Tea. Chickens and cats. Another song. Short stroll. I was gripped with fear, imagining that the mad dog would come back. Returning, worked some more. Read an article on freemasons. Supper. Played the third act of Fitingov's opera and was amazed by the emptiness and worthlessness of its music. Why, anybody could compose like that!

6 September Cold weather. Autumn. After walking, worked with exertion. Walked about the garden and the terrace of the big cottage after dinner, avoiding the endless downpour. Strange at-

---

[91] *Opera by Fitingov-Shel, Russian composer.*
[92] *Modest's valet.*

tempts to break into the empty house.[93] After tea, feeding of chickens and working, walked to the cathedral. I like vespers! Came back in a carriage. It was dark. Supper. Finished copying over one song. Searched futilely for more texts.

Sunday, 7 September Went to Mass at the cathedral after tea. Quite autumnlike weather. Was very moved, after Mass, by the attention shown me while meeting the railway singers. Praslovo. The rich man wearing rubbers and the diplomat. The darling little girl. Copied over the last song, but decided to compose two more new ones. Rain. Strolled on the terrace and a bit around the garden. Was composing. Tea. Feeding of the chickens. Worked. When it was already turning dark, went to the sentry booth and saw a mail and passenger train. Returned, not without being afraid. Supper. Correspondence. Fireplace burning for the first time. The eleventh song, to the text of Khomyakov, is ready.

8 September Do not recall weather more horrible. Wind, rain, and even snow all day. Walked about the gallery after tea. Composed with considerable labor and exertion the twelfth song to the beautiful text of Khomyakov. Walked an hour each through the rooms and in the garden in the afternoon. Climbed into the big, empty cottage, opening the center door with some effort. Went around the empty rooms. On the card table there was a note that had been lying there since 22 July. Tea. Finished the song and copied it over. Worked continuously up to supper. Cold weather. The fireplace is burning. Received many letters today. As usual, they disturbed me. Among them, the letter from N. F. from Pleshcheyevo.[94] She just returned.

9 September The weather is somewhat better but still very cold. Nevertheless, I am never so well in the summer as now, when one rises and lies down shivering. Wrote letters in the morning, including one to Konstantin Konstantinovich about the songs. Took them to the post office after dinner. Looked in vain for Egorka in Praslovo. Tea, chickens, reading. (A story by Vinitzkaya in the *Vestnik Evropy* and an article by Pavlov on Lzhedmitri in the *Russky Arkhiv*.) Strolled with Alesha in the garden as well as on the Praslovo road up to the descent. Discussed household affairs. Home, put

---

[93] *The composer lived in this house during the summer of 1885; his friend N. D. Kondratyev occupied it the summer of 1886.*

[94] *The estate of Nadezhda Filaretovna von Meck.*

the finishing touches to the *ensemble* of the first act of *The Enchantress*. Supper. Played R. K.'s *The Snow Maiden*. Bonbons; reading; etc.

10 September The weather is still bad, cold, and rainy. The big house is being boarded up. Saw Praskovya Ivanovna and confessed to her my stealthy visit to the house the day before yesterday. Fussed all day with the *ensemble* of the first act of *The Enchantress* and became very, very tired. Walked up and down in the room after dinner and toward Klin while it rained but did not reach it. My stomach is bad today. Cold weather. The fireplace is burning now. I just undressed. Furnace. Charcoal fumes.

11 September Somehow did not sleep normally. Perhaps was poisoned by the charcoal fumes or was simply very tired from work. Did not bathe. It all passed after tea. After a walk, worked and finished what was necessary. Went to Klin after dinner. Egorka was in Praslovo. . . . Went walking immediately after tea as the weather cleared up. Walked long through the high meadow, past the cattle shed, admiring the unusually beautiful sunset. The sun was setting behind a cloud under which it appeared on the horizon and then there took place a really extraordinary play of violet and blue colors. Home, sat in the darkness for a long time and was lost in reveries. It was a little melancholy. Telegram from the G. D. K. K. Alexei's sister and her husband arrived. He will work for me as a stovetender. Played the entire first act in one sitting and noticed to my horror that it was frightfully long. And long operas are not good for anything. Watched people having supper through binoculars. Supper. Read with great enthusiasm Aksakov's *Family Chronicle*. Met Alexei's sister and her husband (Alexei, despite pitch darkness, managed to walk and send off my telegram for it was to the G. D.!!!!)

12 September Instead of working (but then, owing to lack of music paper there wasn't any work) I took an extremely long walk straight up to dinnertime. (Klin; beyond the bridge, to the left; in the village; the brook; the forest; the meadow at the brick works; etc.) Returned just before dinner. Walked around the gallery in the afternoon. Wrote letters. Tea. Chickens (a real joy to me, this feeding). Sunset. Played through the second and third acts and was in such a state of horror on account of their length that I lost my temper. Shouted at Alexei because of some nonsense during supper. For comparison, played the first act of *A Life for the Tsar* after supper. Still, it is shorter. But mine is at least fifty minutes and that's straining a point!!! Am very upset. What shall I do? Moreover, I do not see the possibility of shortening it!

MOSCOW

13 September Departure for Moscow. Cold weather. Lunch at the railroad station. Session of the Synod choristers. A thoughtless priest was the chairman, etc. At the Conservatory. At Jürgenson's. At Hubert's. With him to the Uspensky Cathedral. Vespers. Shishkov's chattering. The choristers. Ceremony of erecting the cross. At the Conservatory. Supper at Testov's restaurant. Sasha Gudim.

14 September Family tea. (Oh!!) Mass at the Uspensky Cathedral. I was in a corner near a column. The Irkutsk bishop. Lunch with Gudim at Lopashov's restaurant. We sent for Laroche. Society and drunkenness. Laroche and I were in the park. My Vanya. All possible occasions of entering taverns. It was shameful. At Klimentova's. Unexpectedly, a . . . happening. I run to the tavern. Tidy myself carelessly. Return. Lonesomeness. With Laroche at the Hotel Moscow.

15 September Rose feeling incredibly lonely and disgusted with myself. Visited the von Mecks. My worry and fear on account of Anna.[95] Everything is all right so far. New house. Afraid of the dog. Lizaveta Mikhailovna, Anna. Lunch at Lopashov's restaurant. At S. I. Taneiev's. With him at Catoire's. His mother. Visited the Huberts. Tea. Taneiev and the study of the pedal. A performance of *Don Juan.* Supper at the Huberts'. Misunderstanding with Vanya. Find him near the street door on returning. A very pleasant and happy moment in life. On the other hand, had a sleepless night, and then, what torture and anguish I experienced in the morning— I am unable to describe it.

16th instant Votya Sangursky. Lunch at Pechkovskaya's. Old Malvinskaya. Feeling of loneliness. Searched for Vanya near the hotel. Ezer. Rode past the Triumphal Gates and took a walk. Abatement of erotic feelings. Puzzling phenomenon—as I imagined it would be the opposite. Home. Lounged about a bit. Dinner at the von Mecks'. Tonya, etc. At Popov's at eight o'clock. Session. Drunkenness at Patrikeyev's restaurant. Drunkenness in a tavern

---

[95] *Anna L. von Meck, Tchaikovsky's niece, who was pregnant.*

on a street leading to the Solyanka. Onlookers. Returned absolutely drunk. . . . Disgusting night.

17th instant Sickening feeling on waking. Catoire. S. I.'s congratulations. Books. Walked. At Jürgenson's store. *Don Juan.* Taneiev was right. Lunch at Patrikeyev's restaurant. Meeting with Taneiev. Conservatory. Letter to the student . . . [name illegible]. Sitovsky. Home. Sleep was hindered. Lay down afterward and slept until six o'clock. Rode on Tverskaya Street. Coffee. Visited Peresleni. She is a darling. Dima escorted me as far as Petrovka Street. Lapin. Vanya. Went home. A big crowd. Whist in the studio. Supper. I was at a separate table in the company of others. It was gay. Headache. Simon.

MAIDANOVO

18 September Slept poorly; rose with a headache. Tea with everybody. Vanya. Departure. Lunch at the railroad station. Perfilev. Slept from Kriukov on. Vasily, the coachman and conversation with him. Home. Dinner. Strolled in the forest. Tea. Warm bath. Supper. Read and played the first act. Shortened it. Slept badly. Alexei was fussing with the gun and revolver all day.

19 September Felt a weakness all day, probably from the bath. Did not go farther than the gallery, being afraid of catching a cold. Started, after praying, the orchestration of *The Enchantress.* Sat upstairs. Could hardly walk one hour in the room after dinner. Slept an hour and had terrible dreams. Roamed about the room after tea. Letters; incidentally, one to Misha Klimenko who moved me very much by his letter. During supper, read everything relating to *Don Juan* by Otto Jahn. Read *Family Chronicle* after supper. Solitaire. Tried to read the old diaries. Disgusting. Why is that?

20 September Worked excellently. I like working in Modest's room very much. Was in the village after dinner; there and back via Praslovo. Egorka wore an overcoat. Tea. Worked upstairs. Went to meet Laroche, but he did not arrive. Cathedral. Vespers. From there, a most charming coachman drove me back, whose voice and manner of speaking completely enchanted me. Something like that of Karataev (Tolstoy's). Returned for supper. Arisha. Macaroni. Quarrel about the quality of the macaroni with Alexei who was for the Milan kind. I was possessed today by a rather unusually strong feeling of contentment and even happiness. But still I must travel the day after tomorrow for the sake of that intolerable Anton Rubinstein and his mania for organizing celebrations for himself. Admit that he is an ace and is deserving of ovations, but why it does not sicken him—I do not understand.

Sunday, 21 September Today I no longer felt yesterday's complete contentment—and why, even I myself do not know, although that is not Laroche's fault. After working upstairs and reading letters (one from P. I. J. concerning the passport of Antonina Ivanovna disturbed me very much), went to meet Laroche. Boys and tips to them. Meeting. We arrived. Dinner. Walk to Belavin and through Praslovo. Egorka and his friend turned up near us. He delivered Laroche's coat. Met them again on the way back and they walked as far as the house. Tea. Laroche slept. I worked a little and went to enjoy the beautiful sunset. Home, on Manya's [96] awakening, we played Mozart four hands and conversed. Supper. Torpid. We gossiped. Must go to Moscow tomorrow. Laroche remains here.

MOSCOW

22 September Trip to Moscow on the slow train. Lunch in the train. Home, i.e. at P. I. J.'s. Walked to the office of the governor general for the passport (Prince Vasily Trubetzkoy). Conservatory. Visited the Albrechts. Visited P. I. J. Pabst. Document for Antonina Ivanovna. Dined solo in the Hermitage restaurant. At Albrecht's for the ticket. Went home to change clothes. Performance of *The Demon* under Anton's [Rubinstein] direction. I sat in the first row. Tarnovsky and his chattering. Ovations. On the stage. Had a smoke with Anton. Chaev. Minsky, the poet. Endless talking with Aibozhenko, Klenovsky, etc. Supper tendered to Anton Grigoryevich by the artists. I was between Svyatlovskaya and Belokha. Drunk. Made toasts and speeches. Object to Maikov, etc. Walked home.

MAIDANOVO

23 September Peter Ivanovich awakened me at eight o'clock. Awful *katzenjammer* [hangover]. I was quite sick in the train. Felt better near Klin. Laroche was in the park. Dinner. Slept excellently after a half-hour walk about the rooms. Tea. Stroll with Laroche. He departed. Letters. Supper. Reading, playing of my fourth act of *The Enchantress*, etc.

---

[96] *Nickname of Laroche, derived from Herman, his first name.*

24 September Worked all morning upstairs after a walk. Fussed with the cabbage today and because of that dinner was a trifle late. Stroll to Klin. Back across Praslovo. Egorka and his brother met me just over the bridge. A kite, which I held and let go. Pestering of the children (for some reason, I am not angry at them in Praslovo). Egorka's mother invited me tomorrow—they have a holiday—Dedication Day. After tea and reading (*Family Chronicle*) worked upstairs again almost until supper. The quarreling, crying and cursing of Arisha whose disposition, it turns out, is getting worse and worse. And that spoiled my enjoyment during supper. Forgot everything while reading *Family Chronicle* (the death of grandfather Bagrov). Am still worried about the length of the opera, in addition to St. Petersburg opera affairs.

25 September Slept very long and well. Chopped cabbage after a walk. It was lively and pleasant. Worked without interruption until dinner. Letters before dinner. Walked along the embankment in the direction of the other mill in the afternoon. Cold and bad weather. As before, was delighted by Aksakov's *Family Chronicle* at tea. What a beautiful, original work and how I like books of that kind! To penetrate down to the most intimate depths of strange lives and in addition into the remote past—that is an immense satisfaction to me. Worked upstairs on the orchestration almost to the supper hour. Supper. Played *The Power of Evil*.[97] Wrote letters!!! (that has not happened at this hour for a long while). Solitaire.

26 September A stroll. Work. In expectation of mail, was awfully excited for reasons which I am ashamed to write, but which I will not forget. Pride!!! . . . Walked far in the forest, after dinner, through the swamps along the road to see Old Shchapova. After tea and reading Aksakov, walked about the rooms (witnessed an amazing play of colors during the sunset from upstairs) and worked once more. Went downstairs half an hour before supper. Mikhailo Ivanich was in Alesha's room. The Host; the sermon; laughter. Supper. Played *The Power of Evil*. One telegram after another. One from N. D. Kondratyev that he will come tomorrow; the other from N. [Nikolai von] Meck. Thank God! A daughter was born to them.

27 September Rose at seven-thirty. Appointment with N. D. Kondratyev and Sasha at the railroad station. Suvorin's letter and

---

[97] *Opera by Serov.*

my reply. Calmed down in *other* respects. Walked. Worked upstairs. Alexei brought the *check* from N. F. toward dinner. A stroll about the rooms and the garden in the afternoon. Tea. Worked some. Went to meet the guests. Kashkin alone. With him to the cathedral. No vespers. Went home. Gossiped. Supper. Roamed in the garden. Gossiping and drunkenness. Frightened on account of the Musical Society.[98] Melancholy impressions from the conversation.

28 September Set out for Klin with Kashkin after tea. Cathedral. Vasily, the coachman. We rode to Ryzhov. A pleasant trip; walked it partly. Magnificent house. Big park. Little owner. Inspection. We saw all and managed to return for dinner almost at the usual hour. Dinner; drunkenness; a first walk; drunkenness again; a second walk and constant chattering. Kashkin is a nice person; I am awfully fond of him but, nevertheless, I got tired and cannot express the blessed feeling of solitude that I am now experiencing at home. Saw him off. Voronov, the Taneievs, talked with the mother of the woman news dealer, the Taneievs, etc. Vasily drove me home. Newspapers. Supper. The blessing of solitude.

MOSCOW

29 September Traveled to Moscow on the express. Lunch *on credit* at the railroad station. Money from the bank. At Laroche's. He was eating cutlets. We planned about the evening. Conservatory. We decided to give a dinner for Karlusha. I was with S. I. T. at A. Leontevna's. Brius. Visited Jürgenson. Simon. Dinner at the Hermitage restaurant. Usatov and his request. A play at the Korsh Theater. Splendid theater. I was in a box with Manya, Karlusha and Kashkin. Endless intermissions. Supper at the Hermitage restaurant. We decided Laroche's problem. He will take a year's leave of absence.[99] Home late.

30 September Awoke late. Tea and discourse with P. I. Dressed and left. Letters in the store. Dima. With him to Lopashov's restaurant. In a private dining room upstairs. Ordered the dinner for the

---

[98] *Tchaikovsky was elected an honorary member by the St. Petersburg Society of Chamber Music.*

[99] *Laroche was practically forced to take the absence, for on account of his laziness and degeneration he was neglecting his teaching duties at the Conservatory.*

fourth of October. Stroll. Dima saw me off. A big crowd. Koko and Vasya Davidov. In a Pullman car. Irritated by my neighbor and his coat. *Revenge*. Klin. A. I. Starokopitov and my debt. Home. Letters to Shpazhinskaya. Emma angers me. Supper. Money. Mikhail. Bible.

MAIDANOVO

1 October Grand weather. Rising after a wonderful sleep, took a walk, and worked. Felt a kind of weakness. Went to Klin via Praslovo after dinner. Met Egorushka in Klin. He and his friend accompanied me up to the house. Chatted pleasantly. Tea. A stroll and the sunset. Worked. After supper was thinking all the time about the cuts in *The Enchantress*. Alexei's bill is unbelievable. I am in a bad mood. Am riding at once to the railroad station to meet N. D. Kondratyev arriving on the express train. Twelve o'clock midnight. Rode there; it was bright moonlight. We saw each other. Returning not without effort, succeeded in falling asleep.

2 October Worked very diligently (still on the arrangement of the first scenes). Newspapers. Excited. Ivanov wrote unsympathetically about *Mazepa*. Walked in the direction of Pervushin. Tea. It's beginning to grow dark early. Worked nearly until supper. Became tired. Joked with Arisha at Alexei's expense. The weather was beautiful today. Saw a hawk over the ducks in the garden in the morning. A telegram from Emma!!!! Wept without stopping, later, on account of Vanya Verinovsky.

3 October A striking day; gray but windless. Somehow, I was unusually delighted today with the autumn and nature. I must say that for some time past I have not felt normally, one way or another. Particularly in the mornings (sleep soundly but it's difficult) I feel bad. So that I scarcely enjoy the country and my freedom. But I felt well today. However, not throughout the day. Dinner and newspapers after work. Strolled around the house and garden, in all, until three o'clock. Worked once more. After tea, walked to the railroad station to meet Emma. Was awfully angry because of the disturbance. But was affectionate to her. Transferred her to the mail train. Vasily drove me home. Work. A telegram from Karlusha declining tomorrow's dinner party. I was angry. Supper. In a bad mood. But should I travel or not? Don't know. The second act of *Nero* lasts more than an hour. Finally, found an act longer than mine. Feel out of sorts.

MOSCOW

4 October Express train. Moscow. Lunch at the railroad station.
Haircut. At Jürgenson's. Stroll. Was at the Huberts'—he was out.
At Jürgenson's again. Flerov was there. Simon and I were hiding.[100]
Dinner at the Hotel Moscow restaurant. Saw Vanya through the
window. Called for Jürgenson with Vanya. Session.[101] Erdmannsdörfer. I was bored and disgusted. Visited Anna Leontevna (Albrecht fled to Ryazan).[102] Laroche. With him to Testov's restaurant. Conversation and drunkenness.

5 October Rose very late. Letters to Evgeny K. Albrecht. Boris.
The drawing teacher. Walked to Jürgenson's store. Lots of piano
four-hand music for Laroche, who promised to travel with me, but
fooled me. Lunch at the Hotel Moscow in a private room upstairs.
Vanya drove me home. Conversation with S. I. and the children in
the dining room. Departed. Vanya got a ruble yesterday and today.
Laroche was at the railroad station. Slept, on the way, sitting in
the corner of the car. Home. Lots of letters. Oh, those letters!

MAIDANOVO

6 October The weather was grayish, nice. Worked. Met Laroche.
Dinner. Walked alone, not far, nevertheless dropped in at Praslovo
but did not see E. [Egorka]. A muzhik asked to work for me. Wrote
while Manya dictated to me after tea.[103] Worked upstairs. Supper.
Brahms' symphony.[104] *The Cloth Measurer.* My nerves. Wished to
cry.

7 October Worked so intensely that when I rose, I was as un-
steady as a drunkard. Dinner without enjoyment. Forced myself to
take a walk. (Enchantingly attractive incident. The send-off. The

---

[100] *From Flerov, music and dramatic critic.*

[101] *Of the directorate of the Russian Musical Society.*

[102] *Konstantin (Karl) K. Albrecht, whose affectionate diminutive was
Karlusha, violoncellist and professor at the Moscow Conservatory. He ran
away from the birthday dinner planned by Tchaikovsky a few days
earlier.*

[103] *Laroche was writing an article on Liszt which he was dictating to
Tchaikovsky. He was so lazy that Tchaikovsky undertook to write at his
dictation.*

[104] *Tchaikovsky and Laroche played the symphony four hands.*

hand clasp.) Home. My head began to ache. Worked beyond my strength. Sat idle near the table on which Manya was writing his article on Liszt. Saint-Saëns' septet. Supper. Tolstoy's *The Cossacks*. Terribly tired. But my head hardly pains at all any more. Slept excellently and very long.

8 October   A rainy day. With Manya to the school. The priest and the head deacon. Very few children in the school. Worked and although I was less tired than yesterday, yet I became very tired. After dinner walked in the rain to Klin along the embankment. Never before was I so pestered for money as today by everybody and from all sides. Gave out a lot (a painter; a clerk; a man whose children were burned; women; old men; etc., etc.). And the main thing is that all accost me from a tavern while I am passing by. Bought a lamp for Manya. Tea. Dictation. It went poorly. I worked until my head ached. If it continues like this, then I really believe that I will be unable to finish the opera. We played Rubinstein's symphony (*dramatique*) four hands until supper. Tolstoy's *The Cossacks*.

9 October   The first snowfall. Walked around the gallery with Manya after tea. Worked without strain. Walked about the gallery and garden after dinner. Almost immediately after tea, went and worked a bit. Wrote Kross's obituary notice (one year after his death!!) from six-thirty to eight while Manya dictated. We played Brahms, the villain. What a talentless s . . . ! It angers me that that presumptuous mediocrity is recognized as a *genius*. Indeed, in comparison with him, Raff is a giant, not to mention Rubinstein, who is still a big and vital personality. But Brahms—that's a kind of chaotic and wholly empty dry matter. A telegram from Napravnik during supper. The opera [105] is postponed. Undecided whether or not to go to Peter [i.e. St. Petersburg].

10 October   A real frost. After tea, strolled about the garden with Manya and we were also down below (the river flows amidst the snow). Worked well. Took a walk in the gallery (despite the frost, the blazing sun warmed it up) in the afternoon and on the paved road beyond Malanino. Awoke Manya. Tea. Conversation. The time for departure arrived. Saw him off in spite of the cold and *verglas*. A big crowd of people at the railroad station. Mail and other trains. The books, ordered through Praskovya Fyodorovna. Saw Manya

---

[105] The Enchantress.

off. Preparations for meeting Grand Duke Sergey Alexandrovich. Went home. Read the newspapers. Alexei's (who has a headache) surprise at the books. Supper. Played my vocal and piano score.

11 October Got to sleep with difficulty but slept soundly. I exerted myself so in my work that my head ached and I was upset in general. Arisha served the dinner as Alexei got stuck in the village. Despite the heavenly, wonderful weather, strolled with extreme effort and in the worst state of mind. I would not have gone but I promised Egorka to buy him a cap. Saw Alexei and Vasily proudly driving by with my new horse. Egorka. The cap. Tops, and bonbons for him and his friend. Drove off with Tabach. But at the turn in the road, was up again and walked home with difficulty. The boys and money. Lounged in the easy chair after tea. Wrote letters upstairs. Oh, those letters! Played Massenet's *Le Cid*. Became angry at Alexei and his arguing over a trivial matter. *Le Cid*. Cui's article. How absurd he is and what a high opinion he has of himself. Somehow, the whole day was unprofitable.

12 October An absolute invalid. At the least exertion, it seems to me as though I have a nail in my brain. My stomach refuses to function. And to die, oh, how I dread it! Overcast day. Worked well up to dinner. Ate practically nothing at dinner, and still felt bad. Strolled in the fields. Tea. Work. Exertion. The nail. Massenet's *Le Cid*. Supper. The fireplace was burning. Solitaire without a stop. Cannot read. In general, everything is an exertion for me and my head aches.

13 October Slept long, yet awoke with the sensation of the *nail*. Was exceedingly careful all day both in eating and working. But still, I felt the nail all the time. Now what can that be? Have I lost the ability to work hard? Why, that is death indeed . . . ! The weather was calm, windless. However, I have lost the gift for enjoying nature. Worked through the whole morning. Learned from the newspapers, that *E. O.* [*Eugene Onegin*] is playing this week. Am very glad. After dinner (strict diet), walked in the room and the garden. Tea. For some reason or other, I was in a bad mood and responded angrily and irritably to all of Alesha's jokes. Worked. Played *Le Cid* before and after supper. Not so very wonderful! Still the same thing! Looked in *A Present for the Young Host* with Alesha, in search of sago.

14 October It was a good day and though my head pained at the slightest effort at concentration, yet my health was better. Before dinner (worked successfully and without any unusual tiredness) *drank no vodka* and was very glad afterward. How easily I walked! The dogs (Top and Rover) hindered me in going to Praslovo. Tried to escape from the dogs and was successful but in the end Top found me. Read and smoked a cigar at tea and enjoyed it all, thanks to temperance. Worked on the arrangement and got a headache, but it was not severe. Played *Le Cid*. How Massenet has written himself out! Read Wolff's *Les Gloves à Paris* [106] after supper. This book is coming to an end. It lasted eight and one half months.

---

[106] *Possibly Wolff's* Les Thugs à Paris.

Diary Five

October, 1886 — June, 1887

This diary is continuous with the preceding one, beginning where that left off in the autumn of 1886 and carrying on through the next winter and spring. Its events take place at Maidanovo with trips to Moscow and St. Petersburg where the opera "Cherevichki" had its first performance, Tchaikovsky conducting. He also finished his opera "The Enchantress." The diary ends with a trip by boat down the Volga to Tiflis for another visit with his brother.

MAIDANOVO

15. October, 1886 Rose, after a wonderful sleep, with the sensation of the *nail* in my head. It passed later; a walk helped it especially. Worked well. After dinner (without vodka), walked to Klin by way of the paved road and returned through Praslovo. The weather is grayish, but delightful, with a slight frost. Did not see Egorka, although the others were there. Tea. Work (*Décimète*).[1] Read. Supper. Played the second act. Lasts forty minutes. That is all right. Thinking all the time about the other cuts.

16 October Awoke at night with a headache. Rose well, though with the feeling of the nail. It was gone later. Worked well. Finished the *Décimète*. Dinner without vodka. New dishes discovered by me in *A Present for the Young Host*. Strolled in the garden, as the wind (during clear weather) blew sharply, and outside of the garden it was bad. A Hussar count inspected the estate. Walked along the path at the arbor in front of the big house. Sasha and Osip watched me like a rabbit. Amusing. Showered them with good things. Tea home; reading. Worked so diligently that the *nail* appeared. During

---

[1] *The Finale (No. 7a) from Act I of* The Enchantress.

the time between finishing work and supper, amused myself watching people eating supper, through the binoculars. Played the fourth act with the cuts indicated after supper.

17 October Worked in the morning and finished everything up to the dances. After dinner, walked again on the road to Praslovo with the result that Egor ran out to me, unfortunately not alone. Talks, promise of skates, etc. Tea. Preparations. Departure with Alesha in a gig. At the railroad station. Mail train. Shishkov and Sabler. Oh, for the night compartment! Neighbors are officers. Read the *Russky Arkhiv*. Slept with difficulty.

ST. PETERSBURG

18 October Arrival. Modya informs me of the news about the death of N. D. Kondratyeva. Very upset. Decide not to go there. Lunch at Nikolai Ilyich's. Georgie. Went home with Modya. Bob, Mitya, and Anna Merkling dined at our place. Mikhailovsky Theater. *Fromont jeune et Risler aîné.*[2] Butakova, the Bazilevskys, the Zhedrinskys, etc. Tea at home.

19 October Funeral of N. D. Kondratyeva. Endlessly long service. Painful. Followed the coffin to the monastery. The grave of Gruzinsky. Home. Boys. At Apukhtin's. Prince Lob.-Rostovsky. Pivato restaurant. Dinner at Nikolai Ilyich's. All of us and Anya. Entrancing Georgie. With Anya on Sergeyevskaya Street. Evening at the Kondratyevs'. Conversation all the time about the deceased woman. Went home early.

20 October Learning that guests were to lunch here, I went walking after tea and read the newspapers. Beautiful weather. Summer Garden. The quay. Nevsky. Carousal solo. Vasilyevsky Island. St. Petersburg side. Again the Vasilyevsky. *Kinshi.* Went home. Tea. Writing up everything for four days. Dinner at the Kondratyevs' and whist. At Meshchersky's.

21 October Morning at brother Kolya's. Georges. Dinner at the Bazilevskys'. *Ruslan.* Supper at brother Nikolai Ilyich's. All this with Bob.

22 October Took a photograph of Bob. Dinner home. The boys—friends of Mitya—are very nice. In the evening: Apukhtin, Guitry, Meshchersky. Our supper.

---

[2] *Play by Alphonse Daudet and Adolphe Belot.*

23 October Lunched at Nikolai Ilyich's. Morning at the Conservatory. The kindness of Karl Julyevich.[3] Beethoven's septet. Liadov, Rubetz, etc. Dinner at the Zhedrinskys' (with Apukhtin and Kondratyev). Whist at N. D. Kondratyev's.

24 October Morning at Napravnik's. Olga Edwardovna. At Pavlovskaya's. Dinner at Annette's. Mme. Klingenberg. Her severity. *Une reine manquée*(!!!). Evening reception at [Rimsky-] Korsakov's. Liadov, Glazunov, Dütsch.

25 October Rehearsal at the Conservatory hall. Ovation by the orchestra. Stasov, the Blumenfelds, Glazunov, etc. Lunch at Ernest's. At Balakirev's. The baths. Dinner with Bob at Butakova's. The evening quartet concert did not take place. Again at Butakova's. Evening reception at Guitry's. Angèle, Sicard, Litvinov, Benckendorf.

Sunday, 26 October Mass at Kazan Cathedral. Lunch at the Miliutin store. Rehearsal of *Harold* at the Marinsky Theater. A lot of people and talking. Hindered listening. Dinner at home. Annette. Bob. *The Daughter of the Pharaoh.* Zucchi.[4]

27 October Rehearsal of the symphony concert at Kononov Hall. The Stasovs, Balakirev, Glazunov, etc. I liked Korsakov's symphony and Glazunov's overture very much. Lunch at Romanov's. At the Grand Duke Konstantin Konstantinovich's. Gave my autograph and, due to drinking, acted foolishly. At brother Kolya's. He is ill. Georges. Elena Georgyevna. At the Olkhovskys'. Slept at home. Bob (my joy!) is ill and stayed home all day. Dinner at Kondratyev's. Whist. Home at ten o'clock. Bob. Wrote the diary for a whole week. Just wrote a letter to Mackar. He angered me a little by reproaches.

28 October In the morning, *worked* (a miracle—contrived to work a little in St. Petersburg!). Good weather. Strolled after the family lunch (Bob stayed home again). Was at Vsevolozhsky's. The doctor, Albrecht. Met Glazunov on the Nevsky and had to walk the whole of Sadovaya Street with him. At the Olkhovskys'. Home.

---

[3] *The composer probably attended a concert, through the courtesy of Karl Julyevich Davidov, 'cellist, composer, and at that time the director of the St. Petersburg Conservatory of Music.*

[4] *The famous ballerina, Virginia Zucchi appeared in this ballet by Cesare Pugni.*

Dinner at Napravnik's. Charming Volodya.[5] At the opera. *Faust.*
Was on the stage. Zinovyev, my neighbor. In my box, Annette,
Lily, Katya, Kolya. At Meshchersky's, tea, three together.

29 October Work. Mikhailov, the singer. Lunch with Kolya. Went
for Bob's photograph. Home. Took a box at the Maly Theater for
Alexei and Co. At Vera Vasilyevna's. The Grand Duke, unexpectedly. I withdrew to Vladimir Fyodorovich's room. They called.
The Grand Duke's attentions and my awkwardness. Home. Dinner
at Pavlovskaya's. Kondratyev. The concert. Rimsky-Korsakov's symphony; Glazunov's overture; works by Shcherbachev, etc. Rain. I
was at Palkin's restaurant. Appearance of Glazunov, Dütsch, etc. I
was with them. *Champagne.* Went home late.

30 October Terrible headache. Slept until lunch. Went to see
Kondratyev. Sat in the study of N. D. (who was out) and at Dina's.
Home. Slept. Wished to go to Bob but could not, as I did not feel
well. Appearance of Tanya and Bob. They had dinner. Dressed and
went at six-forty-five in a carriage to Her Grace, the Grand Duchess,
Elizaveta Mavrikyevna. The amiable Dmitri Konstantinovich and
the fascinating Konstantin Konstantinovich. All is well. *Lohengrin.*
I was in a box with Modya, Kolya, and Annette. Was on the stage.
At Vsevolozhsky's. Good performance. Laura Lvovna Ivanova and
Korsov's sister.

31 October Lunch at Bessel's. Liadov. Home. Borrowed three hundred rubles from Kondratyev. Legoshin. Meeting with Sonya
Drashusova after a lapse of ten years. We dined at the Bazilevskys'.
Evening reception at Balakirev's. The whole Group [6] except Cui
and Borodin. The two Stasovs, etc.

1 November With Modya, lunched hurriedly in the arcade. Dress
rehearsal of *Harold.* I was in O. E.'s box. Napravnik. Volodya and
Kostya. Dinner at Malya's. We stayed long. Supper at Guitry's.
Again the same people. Angry that Bob did not come to Litke's,
and jealous of him.

Sunday, 2 November Overslept. The end of the Mass at the Kazan
Cathedral. Lunch at home with Kolya and Bob. I conceal the fact

---

[5] *Napravnik's son.*

[6] *The Group consisted of Balakirev, Cui, Mussorgsky, Borodin, and
Rimsky-Korsakov, representatives of the New School of Russian Music,
and popularly known as the "Mighty Five."*

that I am jealous of Bob on account of Tanya, and angry with him. At Tanya's. Franz's children. Home. The schoolboy Radin. Tatarinov. Dinner at Ponse's. Grabbe. Evening reception at Pogozhev's. Whist with Pavlovskaya, Kondratyev, and an officer. Supper. Felt a little ill.

3 November Felt ill in the morning. Conquered myself and went to the rehearsal. Glazunov's symphony. Rimsky-Korsakov's *Fairy Tale.* Lunch and rehearsal of the quartets at the Albrechts'. Became quite ill. Quinine. Slept at home. Dined and stayed at the Kondratyevs'. My cheek pained. Slept at home and had nightmares. Felt better toward morning.

4 November Learn from the newspapers that *Harold* is canceled. Home all day. A pleasant feeling to be a bit ill and free. Sent out declinations. Jürgenson came twice. Worked. Lunched with Kolya. Sasha Bazilevskaya and Sonya Drashusova came. Bessel. Toward dinner Anya and N. D. Kondratyev, as well as an unexpected guest, Taneiev. Whist. Petersen. Oh, what a rarely pleasant day!

5 November Lunch at L. A. Lavrovskaya's. Besides myself, Albrecht, Verzhbilovich, Taneiev, Malozemova. Dinner at home. Excitement. The concert by the Group. The first movement of Glazunov's symphony. Balakirev. Platonova. Celebration in my honor at the Chamber Music Society. Lavrovskaya. Arma Senkrah. Supper at Donon's. I drank a lot.

6 November Katzenjammer. Better. At Davidov's in the Conservatory. Class in orchestration. In his place downstairs. At Ivanov's, the critic. Sickening and humiliating, although not based on anything. Laura Lvovna. At Tanya's. At Butichikha's, essentially kind. Dinner at Nikolai Ilyich's. Modya, Kolya, Tanya. Slept in the easy chair after dinner. Felt nauseated and vomited after leaving. At Kondratyev's. He has a *jour fixe* (Chertkov, Stoyanokov). I was with the young ladies. At Timosha's. The sore. Painful. Palkin. Morek and his two questions.

7 November With Modya to Bob. Sanya von Vizin. In the school. Lunch at Romanov's with Petersen. At Osip I. Jürgenson's. At the Napravniks'. The children; Volodya; Olga Edwardovna. Am worn out by the new postponement. Bade good-by. At Angèle's. They did not receive me. Home. Dinner at A. A. Davidova's. Cultured Lyda. Charming Koko. Fuchs. The widow of Aug. Julyevich. At

Balakirev's. He was out. Home. Tea. Modya went walking. I busied myself. Supper. (Today, Kolya became eighteen years old.)

8 *November* Lunch at the Kondratyevs'. Dropped in at Butakova's. She was out. At home, where everything was already packed for departure, found a letter from Vsevolozhsky with an invitation for Sunday to talk over the ballet. Fell into despair, but decided to stay and made arrangements accordingly. Ran to Vsevolozhsky. Here too both Petipa and Frolov turned up and we immediately started discussions.[7] My rejection of *Salammbô. Undine.*[8] Appearance of Dizeni and my quarrel with him. Went away. At Pavlovskaya's. Kondratyev. Lelya. At Thomas'. (In the morning there was already a letter.) The formalities of dedication. Home. Nerves. Apukhtin. Tanya and the boy were late. My anger and a scene. Dinner. When all left, I chatted long with Bob. Accompanied him to Liteiny Street. I have a strange feeling when I am with Bob. I feel that he not only dislikes me, but really feels something like antipathy toward me. Am I mistaken or not? Strolled. Had supper at Palkin's restaurant, without needing it.

9 *November* At the Church of the Transfiguration. The choristers are good, but the repertoire!?!? Fled from some terrible concert. Meeting on the bridge with Sanya von Vizin. At our place. Lunch. Bob was present; on leaving, he bade good-by and said that he would not come to see me off. God bless him! At Aly Ivanovna's. She was out. Home. Worked. Finished what I wanted. Awaited Modest. Went away alone. He caught up with me on the bridge. A carriage. Wonderful dinner at Sanya von Vizin's. Bobyk [Bob], i.e. not mine but Sanya's son (soulless, although affectionate). Anya has neuralgia. To the railroad station with Sanya in a carriage. Seeing me off were Sanya, Anya, Modya, Kolya, O. E. Napravnik and her son Volodya. Compartment. Very small. The offended Frenchmen. Slept with difficulty.

---

[7] *About a suitable subject for a new ballet which Tchaikovsky was invited to write.*

[8] *Tchaikovsky considered Fouqué's Undine as a subject for a ballet but never composed it. However, he used this subject for an opera in 1869 which went unperformed and which he destroyed except for five excerpts.*

MAIDANOVO

10 November Arrival. Alesha. Rain. Went home in a cart. Happiness. Tea. Dressed. Letters. Dinner. Due to the rain, strolled in the gallery. A letter. Tea. Letters. Proofs of the songs [Op. 60]. Supper. Played all kinds of trash in the Bessel edition. Cui, etc. the pretentious rubbish. Am angry. Writing the diary for many days. Silence. Am I happy, though, having attained the desired homecoming? A question that it is as well not to decide.

11 November In the school. A new location downstairs at the priest's. Good. Worked successfully. Dined with extreme moderation and suddenly immediately after dinner I began to feel so bad that I could hardly drag my feet. Am I out of my wits? Made myself stroll in the garden. A little better. Beautiful, gray weather. A fight between two turkeys amused me very much. Worked again after tea. A headache again in the form of the nail. After supper played, read, played solitaire—but my head still ached. Slept with difficulty.

12 November Rose half sick. It was better later. Worked successfully. After dinner (beautiful, gray weather), walked to the railroad station and back along the tracks. I felt well. Tea. Talks with Alesha about various plans. Somehow, I feel sorry for them—because of me they are vegetating in a dull place. The work went excellently, but my head ached all the same. Supper. Played the C-sharp minor quartet [9] and the first act of *The Oprichnik*, which I intend changing in the summer. Several times today, despondency came over me because of dissatisfaction with the present. Feel more and more a coolness toward Moscow. Will think about Peter [St. Petersburg].

13 November Worked fairly well, but ever since morning there has been something not quite normal; I was already up at seven o'clock. Nevertheless, walked to Klin, bought skates, and took them to Egorka. Meeting with Tabach, the father. Egorka accompanied me to the house. Worse and worse. The pain in the intestines is unbearable. Castor oil in a large dose. Fever, delirium. Dozed. Slept through the night at first on the divan in the bathroom, then in the studio. Rose—it was still dark. Lay down on the bed at seven-thirty and slept an hour. Became better.

14 November The castor oil did wonders. Although I was weak all day and felt the effects of fever, yet I felt well in general. The whole

---

[9] *Probably Beethoven's String Quartet, No. 14, Op. 131.*

day was given over to letters. In all, I sent off eighteen of them, and two are still unfinished. Strict diet. Read first Renan (*Les Apôtres*), then Aksakov's recollections of Gogol. Portraits.

15 November   Thank God! Toward evening, I began to feel quite well, even the headache (the nail) disappeared. However, did not sleep well at night; I left Alexei a note that he should not awaken me. Fussed too long before sleeping with experiments in conducting. Rose reluctantly. Strolled a little around the gallery. Worked very well. Letters from Kolya Konradi, Volodya Napravnik (concerning *Harold*) and Modya. After dinner (just before dinner Alexei's mother and sister arrived) strolled about the room and the garden. Tea. Worked very well and easily, exactly as I used to in my youth. And what does all this depend on? Supper. Played the third act of *The Oprichnik*. Bad. If I change it, then I must be thorough.

Sunday, 16 November   Real winter. Eighteen degrees [F.] and several times during the day a snowstorm. Was at our church. Came in at the end. Sasha, the teacher, and Ignasha. Worked. After dinner (newspaper accounts about *Cordelia*,[10] etc.), walked about the rooms, the gallery and a little in the garden. Egorka (the dog) bit a shepherd. Alexei in a rage. Went to Praskovya to return the dogs, but came back reconciled and with some furniture. Tea. Work. By the way, showed Pelagea Ivanovna Sofronova about my rooms. She said "like Heaven." Supper. Played Glazunov's symphony and the fourth act of *The Oprichnik*. Poor.

17 November   Rose, after a hard night, ill again. Headache, disgust toward everything. Overcame it in the morning. Walked an hour in the room and a half hour in the garden after dinner. Slept. Tea. Work. Bath. Supper. Struggled with the *nail*. Did practically no reading. Looked through *Cordelia*. Idled the time away.

18 November   Quite sick. Simply to the point of madness. Worked beyond my strength. Disgust toward everything in the world. A telegram in the evening. Feel better. Informed Alesha that I am going to the rehearsal of *Cherevichki*.[11] Slept well.

---

[10] *Opera, also known as* Revenge, *by Soloviev.*

[11] *The composer's opera, in rehearsal at the Bolshoi Theater in Moscow.*

MOSCOW

19 November A miracle! Completely well. Left on the express. Rehearsal of *Cherevichki* with piano. Soso. But am well. At Laroche's. Dinner at my place (in the Hotel Moscow). *Cordelia.* At Patrikeyev's restaurant. George Kartzev. *Les tribulations d'un mari de cantatrice.* The right hand of Katkov is dead drunk. George and talks concerning Tatusya.[12] Slept soso.

20 November Rose with the *nail.* But it's not bad. Better and better all the time. At Jürgenson's store. At Batasha's. Both are home. Cold chicken. At the Bolshoi Theater. The scenery for *Cherevichki.* Rehearsal. Mostly by the understudies. Became tired. Home. Good feeling. Worked. To Jürgenson. Vanya. Dinner with Sophia Ivanovna Jürgenson. The Huberts after dinner. Whist. Supper. Jürgenson's boorishness in the quarrel with Hubert. Laughter just the same. In the main it was jolly. God! What do I want then? What? Where? How!!!

21 November Lunch at Lopashov's restaurant. Rehearsal. Disorder. Klimentova pestered me, even coming in and gossiping with me nearly half an hour. At Panaeva's. At the von Mecks'. Dinner. Anna's girl friend and Petya Henke. Kira. At Taneiev's. Vladimir Ivanovich. Tea. Arensky's Fantasy [13] and the shrewdness of Varvara Pavlovna. Supper at my place in Dmitri's room. A lot of people from the students' concert.

22 November Rose late. Went out at ten-thirty. Met Baron Schilling. Slavyansky Bazaar. Rehearsal. Disorder. Korsov. Alongside, the rehearsal of *The Barber of Seville* with orchestra. Belokha. At Jürgenson's. At Shpazhinsky's. He was out. Waited. Dinner at Patrikeyev's restaurant. Home. Drowsiness. Evening reception at Klimentova's. Lots of guests. My trio. Singing of Handel and Mozart. Goltzev. Chaev. Supper. Went home late.

Sunday, 23 November Disinclination toward carrying on the diary. Lunch at V. D. Konshin's. Home. Dinner at S. M. Tretyakov's (after an unsuccessful attempt to decline). Tatusya Panaeva and George. Evening reception at the Huberts'. Siloti. Zverev. Whist with

---

[12] *The composer's cousin, Tatyana (Alexandra) V. Panaeva-Kartzeva, wife of George Kartzev.*

[13] *Also known as* Margarete Gautier (La Dame aux Camelias), *dedicated to Tchaikovsky.*

Sophia Ivanovna Jürgenson, Siloti, and Batasha. Supper. Alexei arrived.

24 November At Peter Ivanovich Jürgenson's. Lunch at Natalya Nikolayevna Pechkovskaya's. Rehearsal. Still the same thing, i.e. nothing. Dinner at the Hermitage solo. Walked. Home. Worked.

25 November Lunch at the Slavyansky Bazaar. Rehearsal. Gave everything to P. N. Grigoryev. Went away. Visits to the Synod choristers (they were out); to the Conservatory (Taneiev, Papendieck); to Anna Leontevna Albrecht. Home. Tea. Work. At Kartzeva-Panaeva's. The opera *The Huguenots*. I was in a box (complimentary) with George and Tatusya.

26 November Worked. Lunch at my place in the hotel. Rehearsal. Gloria and *Slavsya* for tomorrow's jubilee. My rehearsal. Almost all. Better. Courage and the desire to conduct. Home. Tea and work. Dinner at V. D. Konshin's. The Alexeievs. A stroll. Got a carriage under compulsion in order to get by *Paradise*. Home. Alesha is not here (he is at Matvey's). Letters. Drunkenness privately. Disinclined toward the diary.

27 November Disinclined toward the diary more than ever before. Ordered a laurel wreath for the evening. After that at the Synod choristers. Explanation with Dobrovolsky concerning the program of their concert. Listened to a part of the chorus rehearsal there. Went home. Sat down to work, when suddenly was called from the Conservatory to attend the session. Became angry but went. The question about Panaeva, Mamontov, etc. Jürgenson was rather blusterous. Home. Dinner at Shpazhinsky's. Changes. The laurel wreath. Jubilee performance of *A Life for the Tsar*. Kashperov's impudence. Shostakovsky, Ilinsky, etc. Nervousness. Presentation.[14] To the private opera after the second act. Empty. Fearful for Tatochka. She is excellent although she has no experience on the stage and does not know what to do with her hands.[15] Lyarov, Lopukhin, etc. Supper at Patrikeyev's restaurant.

28 November Worked. Lunched at my place in the tavern. At the theater. It turns out I was mistaken. There is no rehearsal. At

---

[14] *Tchaikovsky presented a laurel wreath in honor of Glinka.*

[15] *Tchaikovsky also attended a performance of* A Life for the Tsar *at a private opera in which Tatyana V. Panaeva-Kartzeva (Tatochka), an amateur, and his niece, appeared.*

Arends'. At Laroche's. Not at home. Went home. Worked. Dinner at the Taneievs'. Talk with Vanya [16] on the way. Flood. Dinner and Sergey Ivanovich Taneiev's quartet.[17] The Maslovs. Left after two performances. The Maslovs, Taneiev, and Hubert walked as far as the Arbat Gates. Talk with Vanya. Somehow he is unusually talkative today. Home. Watched the people from the tavern from upstairs. Jolly. Forgot to mention that I almost quarreled at dinner with stupid V. T. [Taneiev]. Cannot stand the provoking stupidity of that bully. But he thinks no one is as clever and original as he.

Saturday, 29 November Popov. Examining Magistrate Keiser. Jürgenson. Rehearsal. Discussions with Altani. Korsov and his invitation. Strolled a little. A telegram to the von Mecks. Concert. Supper with Batasha and Tonichka. Zverev and Remezov appeared later. Drunk as a sailor. Could hardly hold the pen in my hand.

Sunday, 30 November Terrible day. Morning at the Soother of My Sorrows Church. Dima. Could hardly find it. At Mass. Lunch. Order and cleanliness. At the Chamber Music Society. Mozart's wind quintet. The session. Nonsense and squabbles. At home with Taneiev. Arends and his symphony. Dinner at my place. Concert of the Synod choristers. Urusov. Shimantsky. I was with Hubert. Evening reception at Pabst's. Arma Senkrah. Luxurious supper. Sad, but I livened up, thanks to the wine. Snow, but it's melting.

Monday, 1 December Slush and warm again. Expectation of Altani. Lesson in *conducting*. The excitement subsided.[18] Lunch at home. At Anna's. She was out. Home. Worked. Dinner at my place. At Laroche's. Vanya. At the Erdmannsdörfers'. German company. Arma. Music. Pabst's sonata. Supper. Not as gay as yesterday. Endless slush and mud. God does not send us winter.

Tuesday, 2 December Worked. Lunched at my place. A stroll. At Levenson's. Ordered some shirts. At Pchelnikov's. Home. Worked. To Yasha at five-thirty. Vaniusha. Hands. Dinner at the Gartungs'. With Yasha to the Duma. Session. Very interesting. The incident with Osipov-Przhevalsky. Tea at the Alexeievs'. At Manya's. Kar-

---

[16] *Tchaikovsky's coachman in Moscow.*

[17] *The Third String Quartet in D minor, Op. 7, was twice performed for Tchaikovsky.*

[18] *Tchaikovsky decided to take some lessons in conducting from Altani, the conductor. The first lesson excited him.*

lusha. Supper at Lopashov's restaurant. Walked, Abominable slush. Knocked at Brius'—he did not respond.

Wednesday, 3 December   Rehearsal with piano. Hardly anybody. Nevertheless, all went through. Shpazhinsky came to the rehearsal, spoke about the incident with Kashperov. Dinner at the Maslovs'. Sick all day, due to nervousness at the thought of the forthcoming rehearsal with orchestra. *Israel in Egypt.*[19] At Popov's. Arma's concert. Solo at Patrie's restaurant.

Thursday, 4 December   Slept restlessly. Preparing myself. Vodka. Rehearsal [of *Cherevichki*]. How I thank God for giving me the strength to conquer myself! Not bad—fairly good. Happy to the point of self-oblivion. Home. Dinner. At Panaeva's. At the Conservatory. My sonata. (Magnitzkaya, Pabst, Liebling.) Home. Tea. Letter to Modest.

Friday, 5 December   Rose half sick. Worked nevertheless. Waited for Liebling and Shpazhinsky; however, only the former appeared. Did not know what to do with him. Heard Pabst's fantasy. His overture. Left. I had lunch and went off. At Batasha's. At Anna von Meck's. Home. Slept two hours. Worked. Dinner here at the tavern. Performance at the private opera.[20] Panaeva. Empty. The Huberts in my box. Anna alongside. Sad impression. She sang excellently. Tea at their place. Lelya Apukhtin (he was sitting in the governor-general's box).

Saturday, 6 December   Worked at home. A new, model shirt. Went on foot after lunch to Shpazhinsky. Went home from his place. Worked until six o'clock. Dinner at Korsov's. Aria. Sickening feeling. Von's [Erdmannsdörfer's] concert. *King Stephen,* Arma Senkrah, Siloti (superb performance of the sonata), Ninth Symphony. Excellent performance. Supper at Patrie's restaurant with the Huberts (he is ill), Zverev, Siloti, Remezov, Safonov, and Zverev's pupils.

Sunday, 7 December   At home worked a little, although very unsuccessfully (a change in the second act of *The Enchantress*). Lunch at V. D. Konshin's. Walked to his place in a wet snowstorm that tortured me terribly. At his place, were Volodya with his wife and some other people. Chamber music matinée. My sonata.

[19] *Handel's oratorio.*

[20] *Verdi's Aïda with Panaeva.*

Taneiev's quartet. Took part in the *professors'* dinner. I was between Kashkin and Blaramberg; Goltzev (toast!!!), Boborykin, Stoletov, Kovalevsky and others. Afterward at the Conservatory. Handel's *Israel*. Boring. Intermissions. Nevedomskaya. At Patrie's restaurant.

8 December Rose very late. Amiable Sasha Siloti and the question about his future. Solo lunch. Dropped in at the theater. At Jürgenson's. A stroll. The schoolboy Schilling. Home. Dinner at the von Mecks'. Evening at Zverev's. At the von Mecks' were the Kartzevs and Kapnistikha.

9 December Rose late. Was busy writing a letter to N. Fil. [Mme. von Meck]. At Lopashov's restaurant. Order for the dinner. A stroll (it is freezing today) on Taganka Street. Haircut. Discussions. Home. Worked. At Erdmannsdörfer's. Arma was late. *My* dinner at Lopashov's restaurant. Panaeva did not arrive. Dining were: P. P. Kartzev, George, Lelya Apukhtin and I. We sat long. Vanya. The hand. At Laroche's. Katerina Ivanovna arrived. Went home. Drinks at my place upstairs. Chorus master Ivanov.

10 December Felt well on rising. Worked after tea. Had lunch at home. Walked a little. Stepped in at the Erdmannsdörfers' in order to avoid the visit to me planned by Arma and Polina. We played through a small piece. Went away. Had a good walk. Came to work at three o'clock and stayed until six o'clock. Dinner here at the hotel. Nausea. Walked as far as the Yar. Vanya. The hands. Evening at Safonov's. His father. Whist. High-spirited old man; very charming. Walked to call for Zverev and Kashkin. They quarreled.

11 December Rose. Worked. Lunch at home. Branduchek. Walked to the Conservatory with him. The violoncello. At Peresleni's. Found Dima alone. At the Huberts'. Sat alone and read. Finally he showed up. We had dinner. Went home. Electricity. Worked. Drunken Vanka. *Der Freischütz.* Supper at my place: Polina Erdmannsdörfer, the two Senkrahs, Brandukov, the Pabsts. Sleepiness.

12 December Rising, waited for Altani. He, as usual, was late. But that kind person gave me an excellent lesson in conducting. We waited for Brandukov and Laroche. Lunch. Drunkenness. Shishkov. Walked. Crimean Ford. Recalled the promise to Shpazhinsky. A dinner at his place (did not eat) and discussions about the opera. Home. On the way, beggars. Worked. At Sophia Ivanovna Jürgenson's. The Huberts, the Safonovs. Yesterday Vanya provoked anger. Today he was melting with kindness. Must mention about an important episode. Strolled after lunch, met (A. N. Shishkov). He has a drawback—a pug nose is not always attractive. At the Jürgensons'. Was drinking alone. Paid the bill. Preparing for tomorrow.

13 December Rehearsal. Conducted. Tired to the point of exhaustion. Dinner at the Alexeievs'. Soon left for the concert of the Philharmonic Society. My serenade. Nevedomskaya. Blaramberg, Malm, etc. Timanova. Glinka's and Ilinsky's choral works. This chorus is very nice. In the artist's room. A. V. Panaeva and George. Shostakovsky and champagne. Lay down to sleep fairly early.

Sunday, 14 December Klimenko. Rehearsal. Dinner at K. V. Peresleni's with Dima. At the ballet. *Giselle.*[21] I was in a box with the Huberts. We sat in Testov's restaurant and in the Hotel Moscow.

Monday, 15 December Rehearsal. Less shy. Decided to decline the dinner at the Ilins'. Declined it. Worked at home. Dined at my place at three o'clock. Strolled. Was excited on account of *Mazepa.* Home. Letters and the diary. Alexei announced that he is to be a bridegroom. Went downstairs, seeing Dobrovolsky and Orlov, and sat with them.

16 December Slept well. Alesha was packing for his trip to Maidanovo. I was busy working in preparation for the rehearsal. Lunched at ten-thirty. Rehearsal. Lost my temper—even with Altani. At Jürgenson's. Simon. Money. At Panasha's. She was out. Went home. Worked. Dined at seven o'clock. Was drinking. Strolled. Got in to the Bolshoi Theater. *The Demon.*[22] The second act and part of the third. Strolled. Had my drink. A lot of people, but yesterday (M . . . a)[23] few. Jealousy.

17 December Rising (without Alesha—he departed), I worked. At eleven-thirty had lunch. Went for a walk. At Jürgenson's. S. M.

---

[21] *Ballet by Adam.*

[22] *Opera by Anton Rubinstein.*

[23] *Probably Tchaikovsky's opera* Mazepa, *which was given the day before with few people in attendance in comparison with Rubinstein's* The Demon.

Tretyakov. The news about Vera Tretyakova and Siloti.[24] Worked at home. Dinner at the von Mecks'. Henke (Lyda and Vera). Their strange effect on me. George and Tatusya. Stayed long after the dinner. We drank tea. I was painstakingly talkative. How charming a person the good-natured Kolya is. Walked. Hermitage. Champagne. Home. The news about the little Bazilevsky.

18 December At the Synod choristers at ten o'clock. My works and those of others. Spiteful Sokolov. Orlov and Dobrovolsky. At the Conservatory. At the theater. Dances from *Cherevichki*. Bogdanov (the question about the benefit performance). Visit to Ilina. A stroll. Home. Dinner at the Hermitage at three o'clock. Worked. Ivan, the coachman and the fifteen rubles. Evening reception at the Huberts'. The Mamontovs and the Ugrimovs. Was angry. Whist cheered me up. Supper.

19 December Fell asleep at four o'clock. Rose at about nine o'clock disgusted with sitting up all night, but mastered myself. Last proofs to correct. Felt courageous and bold beyond my expectations, as I feared the effects of a sleepless night. Good. Strolled. Worked. Dinner at the Gartungs'. The session of the Duma. Boring. Tea at the Alexeievs'. Sumbul. The secretary of the Duma. Gartung. Sat upstairs at home and had my drink.

Saturday, 20 December Lunch at eleven o'clock. Rehearsal. Briullov. Despite the sleep, was in a bad mood and made awful mistakes. Worked. Dined at home. Concert of the Musical Society. Panaeva. Failure. George. Had supper. Overslept very much as I had retired late. We were celebrating Siloti's engagement.

21 December Rehearsal. The principals were not present. Rehearsed a little with the chorus. Home. Brandukov. My songs.[25] Panasha and George were late. Dinner. In Panaeva's box at the Maly Theater. Evening at Nevedomskaya's.

Monday, 22 December Lunch at eleven o'clock. Went out. The scenery for the first act. Rehearsal. After that the explanation with Korsov. Freed myself. Went straight home to have dinner. Lobro.

---

[24] *Alexander I. Siloti, pianist and Tchaikovsky's close friend, became engaged.*

[25] *Op. 60. Numbers one to six had just been published by Jürgenson.*

Forgot. A note to her.[26] Strolled after dinner. Went home. Worked on the piano and vocal score.

Tuesday, 23 December Lunch at ten o'clock. Rehearsal. The entire opera. Was satisfied with myself. Made fewer mistakes. Some things went well. Drunkenness during the intermission. After which, I left. Tavern at Lubyanka Place. Home. Dinner at the Tretyakovs' across the Moscow River. Siloti. Whist. Home.

Wednesday, 24 December Rose at nine. Finishing the piano and vocal score of the second act of *The En'ress*. Visitors: Yasha Gartung—he left. Ippolit and Kolya von Meck. Later Dima, Laroche, Hubert, Kashkin, Brandukov. Lunch. With Vanya to the park. Walked. Twice at Jürgenson's. Home. Letters. At Patrikeyev's restaurant. A Christmas tree at the Jürgensons. At Batasha's. A Christmas tree. Whist. Supper. Laroche. He escorted me and stopped in with me.

MAIDANOVO

25 December Rose late. Letters to influential people regarding the benefit performance for the orchestra. A stroll. Lunch. Drunkenness. Distributed the tips. Departure. Drunkenness at the station. On the way, walked and drank at the stations. Klin. Alesha. Vasily, the coachman. Home. Modya. Talks. Supper. Calendar. Discussions with Modya from the other room. Reading.

26 December Wrote letters all day (it was freezing and bright). Wrote eighteen of them. After tea, Praslovo folk came to praise Christ. Went for a walk after dinner. Egorka escorted me with his two friends. We chattered merrily. About the woodsman: "Alesha, Alesha, your mother is not good." Played Blaramberg's opera,[27] before and after supper. Very poor.

27 December Rising (after a wonderful sleep), for some reason I was in a bad mood; with Modya drank tea and strolled. Cold weather. Worked upstairs. Walked on the paved road after dinner. Strolled more than I should. Was sleepy and felt feverish following afternoon tea. Nevertheless, went to work. Struggle with sleep. Slept restlessly about an hour. Worked. Laroche's arrival. Supper.

---

[26] *J. F. Ter-Manuk Lobro, a French singer to whom Tchaikovsky offered the role of Olga in his opera* Eugene Onegin.

[27] Maria of Burgundy.

The second act of *Maria of Burgundy*. We escorted Laroche upstairs. Gossiped.

28 December We rose fairly late. We all took a walk together. Worked in Modest's room. Dima's arrival. Dinner. A stroll with Modya and Dima. Masks. Boys from Praslovo accompanied us as far as Maidanovo. Tea. Laroche dictated the beginning of an article on *The Stone Guest*.[28] Worked. Supper. Whist. Laroche and Dima went to play bank. Watched. Undressed at twelve-thirty.

29 December We all took a walk except Laroche, who was ill and whom I could hardly get out before dinner. Strolled alone after dinner. Modya is with Dima. Encountered Egorka, after all, who was waiting for me. He accompanied me up to the house. Wrote after tea at dictation. Dictated brilliantly today. Supper, whist. Among the letters in the morning, was an arrogant one from B. in regard to my letter and telegram in defense of Napravnik.[29] Wrote B. that once and for all am severing all relations with him. What vermin both he and his C. [Company] are. A more loathsome *accouplement* is difficult to imagine.

30 December Still sleep with difficulty, but know why—too much eating. Worked painstakingly until dinner. Had no desire for strolling. Walked about the rooms and strolled a little. Tea. Dictation. It was not so good. Worked until supper. Whist. Dima is leaving tomorrow.

31 December Dima left in the morning. Worked. Not quite well; my head ached. Walked only in the room and slept an hour. Dictation after tea. Good. Played duets with Laroche after supper.

1 January, 1887 Beautiful winter day without wind. Worked. Strolled after dinner. Boys pestered me. Came across Modya toward the end of the walk. Tea. Dictation. Laroche's crankiness. Our servants were all dressed up and came over to us. Nazar is drunk. Laroche made love to Arisha. Became tired.

---

[28] *Opera by Dargomyzhsky.*

[29] *An article in the* Musikalnoye Obozrenie, *of which Bessel (B.) was editor, stated that Napravnik, a Czech by birth, disliked Russian music and had tried to dissuade Tchaikovsky from having* Eugene Onegin *performed. The latter resented the article and denied the charge. Bessel still maintained his position and, in addition, attacked Tchaikovsky.*

2 January Did not go walking in the morning. Worked diligently. Toward dinner, Dima arrived. Brought the news of the death of Mitya Bazilevsky. Walked, after dinner, up and down in the room and a little in the garden. Tea. Dictation. Work. Supper. Whist.

3 January Poor Dima is played out. After tea walked up and down in the room, then to Klin. Money to the beggars. Below, near the factory on the height above the river, stumbled upon our boys: Egorka and his suite. Egorka's mother. They escorted me home through Praslovo. Tea. Dima and Modest went to meet the *darling* who was passing through on her way to the Bazilevskys'. Worked. Supper. Lively. Whist. Maskers from the city. Our people dressed up.

4 January Nothing unusual. After dinner strolled with Dima. Pestering. Worked. Whist.

5 January It was drizzling. Strolled a little. We all drove to the railroad station. Kolya Konradi. Went home. Supper. Whist. Anxiety.

6 January The priest conducted the services and drank tea with the deacon and the children. Preparing for *Cherevichki.* Katerina Ivanovna Sinelnikova. Dinner. Slept. Strolled a little with Dima. Tea. Whist before supper. Nervousness. I don't feel well.

MOSCOW

7 January Departed alone in a compartment on the express. Had a bite at the railroad station. Straight to the rehearsal. Welcome. Made a little slip in the conducting. After the rehearsal, a clarification with Korsov about the Musical Society. Dined at the Hotel Moscow. No appetite at all. (Dropped in at the von Mecks'.) *The Huguenots.* I am in the first row. Angry at the usher. Tired and in a bad mood. Arriving home (on Myasnitzkaya Street),[30] found Modya and Alesha already there. In poor spirits. Went to sleep at once.

8 January Kolya von Meck. Walked to lunch at the Saratov restaurant. Rehearsal. Dissatisfied both with myself and others. Talked

---

[30] *Tchaikovsky wrote to Mme. von Meck requesting her permission to stay at her house on Myasnitzkaya Street, pointing out that he would have much more privacy than at a hotel and it would facilitate his work. She was very happy to grant his request.*

it over with Altani. Home. Tea. Dinner at the von Mecks' with Modya. Dropped in at the Hotel Moscow. Home.

9 January Rehearsal of Arends' symphony. Shostakovsky and *tutti quanti.* At the Conservatory. At the examinations. My rehearsal. In very poor spirits. Was angry. Home. George. Dinner at Laroche's. Walked home.

9 January God! How old I am—and I still write the diary! Why!!!! And remember nothing, as I write three days later. Home. Tea. George. Dinner at Larocheva's. Went home tired.

10 January Everything the same. Lunch at the Saratov restaurant. Rehearsal. Was tired. *Modulations* with Usatov. Concert of the Philharmonic Society. Arends' symphony. Went away.

Sunday, 11 January Litvinov with a request. Rehearsal without orch. . . . Shpazhinsky. Dinner in his place. At the Huberts' (Batasha's birthday). Maly Theater. Supper. Returning home, found out about—Alesha's action. However, gave in and was at the engagement party.[31]

12 January Rose at the usual time. Walked to the theater. Jürgenson. Tartar restaurant. Rehearsal. Maikov. Shpazhinsky. The question about the delays. Solo dinner at Patrikeyev's restaurant. A stroll. Piggishness. Meeting of the directors of the Musical Society. I demanded *satisfaction???* for the theater. The meeting took place at S. M. Tretyakov's. Was upset (on account of the Korsov and Butenko matter). Walked with Taneiev. Solo dissipation. With Artem. . . . Forgot to mention that before the meeting, I watched the students' dinner there. Simeon was a waiter. *The other side.* Kakurin.

13 January Rehearsal. An explanation with Altani and Korsov due to a misunderstanding. Dinner at the von Mecks'. George. Sasha Kartzeva. The sick Tatusya. Performance at the Korsh Theater. *Grief from Wisdom.*[32] With Modya and Dima at the Yar restaurant. Lonesome.

14 January Rose with a bit of a headache. Full rehearsal [of *Cherevichki*]. Modest and Laroche. Shpazhinsky, etc. Good, but I am afraid for Krutikova. She is ill. Dinner at Bezekirsky's. They

---

[31] *Of Alesha, Tchaikovsky's valet.*

[32] *Play by Griboyedov.*

drove me up. *The Snow Maiden* [33] at the private opera. Talks with Mamontov.

15 January The day of rest. Bessel (Ivan), arriving to talk it over with me. . . . Prokunin. At the box office of the theater for the tickets. Lunch at Arends'. Painful situation. His lovely wife and very pretty little girl. At V. D. Konshin's in the store. Yasha. At the Conservatory. Sitovsky and the letter to the artists of the theater. Went home. Laroche. Dinner at the Hotel Moscow (luxury and money!!!). Lonesome. Whist at Manya's request. Walked home.

16 January Rising, went out for a walk. Lunch at the Nikolaiev railroad station. Rehearsal. Terrible disappointment: Krutikova is sick and is unable to sing at the first performance. Discussions. Maikov. Was very dejected, as I very much dislike Svyatlovskaya in this role. Maikov. Meeting of the directors of the Musical Society. Went straight to Altani. Home. Vanya. Dinner at the Jürgensons'. In a bad mood. Modest, Batasha, and Tonya, etc. Whist. Supper. Left with Manya and Hubert. I had Vanya drive them home. The lost money. Walked with Manya. A little tavern on Myasnitzkaya Street. I am very drunk.

17 January The day of the dress rehearsal. Rehearsal with piano for Svyatlovskaya. Solo lunch at the Hotel Moscow. A stroll in the park. Vanya. Nausea. Home. Was excited. Rehearsal as though without the public. But a large public collected. Good. Was tired. Supper with Modya, Laroche, and Taneiev at Testov's restaurant.

Sunday, 18 January Dima. We three walked together as far as the Prechistensky Gates. Dima envied the paupers. Lunch at V. D. Konshin's. The pride of Lord Vladimir Konshin. Concert (during the day) of the Musical Society. D'Albert. Incredibly tired. Home. To the Hermitage with Dima, Laroche, and Modya. Stepped in to the Hotel Moscow alone. Tarnovsky.

19 January The day of the first performance. Rose quite sick. Met my brother Kolya and Niks at the railroad station. At Maikov's. At Dmitri's at the Hotel Moscow. Got drunk. Past the Tver Gates. Yar restaurant. Meeting with Klimentova. Home. Slept. *First performance.* [34] Nervousness. Ovation. Supper. Fatigue.

---

[33] *Rimsky-Korsakov's opera.*

[34] *The performance was a huge success; however, it remained only two years in the repertoire of the Bolshoi Theater.*

20 January Slept little. The news about *Tanya's death* [35] communicated to me by Modest. We waited for Kolya von Meck. At my brother Kolya's at the Slavyansky Bazaar. Lunch. At Laroche's. He was sleeping. Katerina Ivanovna Sinelnikova. Home. Kolya von Meck. Depressed feeling. Saw Modya off. Home. Dozed. Dinner at the Hermitage with my brother Kolya and Manya. The former left, but Manya got drunk. Jesters' Boulevard.

21 January A strange feeling. Tanya's death—like something tragic bursting into my life—was haunting me. In the morning, by the way, was at the Conservatory. S. I. Taneiev went out with me. Altani not at home. At Krutikova's. She was out. (At the theater and at the chorus rehearsal of *Tamara* [36] before the Conservatory and lunch.) A telegram at home from Bob and Modest. The details of Tanya's death in the newspapers. Solo dinner at the Hermitage. D'Albert's recital at the German Club. Intermissions. Had supper (or rather, sat) at the Patrie restaurant with Hubert. Zverev and N. N. Mamontov joined us. Was angry, but later it was all right. Drunkenness there and home.

22 January Rose at eight-thirty. Kablukov. Prokunin. Tortured me with his rubbish and his "yessing." Could hardly get rid of him. Saratov. At the Conservatory. At Altani's. Unpleasant discussions concerning disagreements. Karlusha. Meeting with Andrey at Brius'. At Korsov's. *Ciarlone* and his *nonsense*. At Krutikova's. At Anna von Meck's. Pale and shocked. Solo dinner at the Hermitage. Home. Telegrams. Letters. Evening reception at the Tretyakovs'. D'Albert (a young genius). Panaeva. The Moscow *beau monde*. *Kapnistikha*. Vanya. At the Hotel Moscow. Home. Drunkenness.

23 January Worked. Lunch at the Hotel Moscow. Park. Slept at home, and rose, not as on the nineteenth—but in a sickening state of mind. Tea. Was nervous the second time more than the first. Fear and horror at first. Later it passed. Cold audience. It warmed up in the third act. Became warmer and warmer after that. Supper at the Patrie restaurant with the Huberts, Zverev, Remezov, Jürgenson.

---

[35] *His niece, Tatyana L. Davidova, died quite suddenly while attending a ball at St. Petersburg.*

[36] *Opera by Fitingov-Shel.*

24 January Worked. At Jürgenson's. Money. Embarrassed. Lunched at Pechkovskaya's. At the Bolshoi Theater. Fyodotikha's rehearsal. At Anna's. She spoke about her father who passed through yesterday. Sad. Worked at home. Solo dinner at the Hermitage. Sent for Laroche. Spent the evening at the Huberts'.

Sunday, 25 January The son of A. F. Frolovsky. Worked. Lunch at the Slavyansky Bazaar. At the Conservatory. Simon's quartet and the C-sharp minor [Beethoven]. Meeting. Argument about the letter. Was angry. Dinner and evening reception at Lesly's. Whist with Batasha, Laroche, Ugrimova and Mme. Lesly. Went home at twelve o'clock.

25 January Rising, waited for Prokunin and Kochetov. Neither of them arrived. And I had an orchestra rehearsal at eleven o'clock for Borisov. Why??! Don't understand. At the theater. At Pchelnikov's. Nice person. At the Conservatory. Meeting. Useless talk concerning the contract with Mamontov. Went away. Home. Worked and not bad. . . . Dinner at N. K. von Meck's. He told about the incident yesterday(?) with Tanya. God! How much misunderstanding there is here. After Kira's [37] bath and combing (thinking I would frighten her) went . . . had dinner at Br. [Brius'?]. Was sitting and sitting. . . . Supper at the German Theater. What trash . . . !

26 January Rehearsal of Borisov's parts at eleven o'clock. My arm is tired. Lunch at Veydel Tagliaboué's. At Pchelnikov's. Stormy meeting at the Conservatory still about the same matter of the theater. Left incensed. Home. Worked. Dinner at Kolya von Meck's. He reported the details of Tanya's funeral. Stayed long at their place. Went home.

27 January At eleven o'clock at Batasha's. The proofs of *The Enchantress.* Lunched at her place. At Laroche's. A stroll along the Moscow river. Taganka Street. Tavern. Home. Slept. Tea. Visit by Mamontov and perplexed: which one called? Imagined that it was Victor coming to announce the cancellation.[38] Sent Alexei to the theater. Came. Terrible nervousness (more than previously). Soso. Finished all right. The audience is warmer than the one before.

---

[37] *Little daughter of Anna von Meck.*

[38] *Of the third performance of* Cherevichki.

28 January Rising, received Donskoy and rehearsed the character scene with him. K. is talentless. Lunch with Manya at the Hotel Moscow. *Will find out who, how, and what.* (What does this mean? Must have been drunk when I wrote it.) Conservatory. Requiem Mass. Home. Worked. Dinner at the Hermitage. At I. I. Popov's accidentally on the *jour fixe.* We chatted a while. At N. F. Dobrovolsky's. V. S. Orlov. At the Grand Moscow Hotel. Loan of one hundred rubles to Laroche.

MAIDANOVO

29 January Departed at 9 A.M. Slept on the way. (The officer and his discussion with a girl about opera; also, with a student about politics.) Home. Laurel wreaths. Dinner. A stroll. Letters all evening. Reading after supper. Blissfully happy.

30 January Rose at the usual time. Grand day. Walked. Worked. A long walk after dinner. Worked diligently after tea until I got tired. Supper. Read Pypin's article on Dukhinsky. Poor Arisha is living her last days at my place. Alexei is perfectly satisfied and happy.

31 January Beautiful weather. Felt the usual bad condition less this morning; i.e. nausea and coughing. Worked with frightful intensity. After dinner (the new dish, jellied hazel grouse, created a furor) strolled. Egorka and his brother were waiting and found me. His birthday and I bought him presents. After tea, due to illness, walked only a little upstairs, admiring the beautiful view. Worked to the point of stupefaction. Supper. Read Kostomarov's article, etc. in the *Vestnik Evropy.*

Sunday, 1 February Good weather in the morning, later on a snowstorm broke out. Worked. Was immoderate at dinner and regretted it afterward. Went walking despite the snowstorm (not terrible, however). Egorka and his company still caught me all the same and it was necessary to walk with them all the way home. Then tea, work, supper, and reading of Turgenev (*The Song of Triumphant Love*). It made a deep impression on me. Strange dreams at night: *Mme. Viardot* [39] *and Laroche.*

---

[39] *Mme. Viardot and Turgenev collaborated in writing* The Song of Triumphant Love.

2 February   Worked. Tried to go to church, but there were heaps of snow. After dinner (avoiding the snowstorm) walked some more at home. Later on, even took a walk along the river. Was pestered in spite of the snowstorm. Worked downstairs at the piano in the evening. Correcting the beginning of the fourth act [of *The Enchantress*]. Letter from Wurm about *my* concert and a reply. Farewell to Arisha. Tears. Read Vogt on amphibia.

3 February   Divine weather. Fourteen degrees and windless. Was busy today with changes in the fourth act as a result of alterations in the libretto. I found it surprisingly difficult. I am already very tired with all this fussing. After a wonderful walk, to the right on the paved road, came home and learned the sad news of the death of Mikhail Sofronov's two children and about some awful disease (hand) of his own. Grievous doubts! And that on the eve of Alesha's wedding!!! Worked all evening still on the same thing. Very difficult. Read *Klara Milich* [40] after supper. This morning Arisha left definitely! Sad.

MOSCOW

4 February   The day fixed for Alexei's wedding. While I was working in the morning, Vasily brought a telegram from the bride that she is ill and cannot come. Excitement. The village relatives of Alexei. (Egorka, who had a birthday, came.) Agitation; gossip; the details of the death of Mikhail's children and about his disease. Strolled briefly. Worked. Left at seven o'clock for Moscow. On the way, read Turgenev's short stories and was enraptured. On Myasnitzkaya Street. Supper at the Hermitage. Slept poorly. Headache.

5 February   At S. I. Jürgenson's and to the engraver's. At the Synod choristers. Singing. Shishkov. To the Conservatory with the bass soloist. Arranged the matter. At Galvani's in his class. At Anna Leontevna's with Zverev. Lunch. In Jünker's at the bank. Received funds. [41] Got in to the rehearsal (dress) of *Tamara*. Fitingov [-Shel]. Talked with Altani about Panaeva. Discussions with Korsov. Sat through the third act. At the Conservatory. Singing by the Choral Society. Poor selection. Dinner at the Hermitage with Karlusha. Laroche. Apathy. Went home at twelve o'clock. Slept well.

---

[40] *A story by Turgenev.*
[41] *Money sent by Mme. von Meck.*

6 February At Batasha's. Lunch at the Hotel Moscow with Dobrovolsky and Orlov. At Pechkovskaya's. At Panaeva's. Kashperov. Meeting of the directors. (We three.) With Taneiev to my place. Discussion about Taneiev's directorship.⁴² Changed to a tail coat. A hurried dinner at the Hermitage with Taneiev. At Siloti's wedding. In the church. At *their place* (Hotel Diusso). At the opera. First performance of *Tamara*. At Batasha's. Corrections.⁴³ Supper. Dropped in at the Hotel Moscow to pay the debt. Drunken Gradov-Sokolov.

MAIDANOVO

7 February Rose with a headache. At the railroad station. Hot in the railroad car. Alone. Home. Found no one in. No dinner. Rage. Lunch from the dinner leftovers. A stroll on the other side of the paved road. Tea. Worked. Letters. Alexei's bill is tremendous. Fatigue and in a bad mood in general. God, how I have squandered money!

Sunday, 8 February Worked like a horse. Contrived to take my walk after dinner through the forest in the direction of Belavin—it was in order to avoid the pestering of boys and all kinds of women. Heavenly weather. Arisha arrived. Everything is the same. Letter from Wurm. Worked. Supper. Read.

9 February Worked again like a horse. And again beautiful weather. And again strolled toward Belavin in the snow and on a little-traveled road. Wandered through the snow. Home. Tea. Work. Finished the piano part to the very end. Supper. Played. Read Boborykin's novel. There was a letter from Shpazhinsky from St. Petersburg about *The Enchantress*. A strange notion—in September.⁴⁴ . . .

10 February Everything is as usual. Walked again, after dinner (to avoid pestering) to Belavin, but was noticed from somewhere and four of them walked on the road crossing mine and then

---

⁴² *On Tchaikovsky's recommendation, Taneiev became the director of the Moscow Conservatory of Music in 1885 only to retire four years later to devote himself to composition.*

⁴³ *In the proofs of* The Enchantress.

⁴⁴ *He was informed that* The Enchantress *would be performed in the autumn of 1887.*

stopped. Tried to go in to the forest but sank in the snow. There was nothing to do. Went past, swearing at them. Gave them nothing. (Egorka, Sasha, the teacher, etc.) Worked until I was tired. My dinner consisted of eight *pancakes*. Succeeded, before supper, in writing a lot of letters to Paris concerning the *audience* for my works.[45]

11 February   Was hurrying to finish the fourth act, so as to send it to Moscow and worked all day until I got a headache. After dinner walked mostly about the rooms and a little in the garden and along the river. Received a telegram from Altani before supper about the success and packed houses of *Cherevichki*. Am awfully gratified. For I, as usual, was imagining just the opposite: emptiness, etc. Even saw distinctly in my sleep an empty theater. He informs me also of the successful debut of Panaeva. Alexei is going to Moscow early tomorrow morning.

12 February   Nothing unusual. Alexei took the early train to Moscow—on an errand to Sophia Ivanovna Jürgenson (the manuscript of the fourth act). Alas! Jürgenson himself returned and, as expected, mixed it all up. To mix up things—that's his specialty and what's more, because he is ambitious, he intrudes at the wrong time. Alesha returned when I was working upstairs in the evening. Strolled after dinner about the house, the garden, and a little by the river. Wrote several letters in the evening. Started the orchestra score of the second act. It came hard.

13 February   The weather is beautiful but cold. Worked diligently but did not get very far. Walked to Klin after dinner, thinking I would watch the skating—but there wasn't any. Handed out a lot of money—but eluded the most intrusive. Letter from Grand Duke Konstantin. Nice person. Worked. After supper, Alesha left to dissipate in the village—I am horrified.

Saturday, Shrovetide, 14 February   Although in the morning I was just the same as always or even better (not nauseated; ate eggs) after dinner, went from bad to worse. All our people set out for the skating at Klin. And I intended to go, but *slept* instead. How-

---

[45] *He received a letter from Mackar, his Paris publisher, requesting that he come to Paris as soon as possible as Mackar was arranging an audition of Tchaikovsky's works before an invited audience in the Salle Erard.*

ever, worked in the evening as usual. Supper without appetite. Thought that I would be quite ill but, thank God, felt better and better. It is now 1:30 A.M. and I am playing solitaire.

Sunday, 15 February The last day of Shrovetide. I am completely broken up. Again as in November: pain in the head; nausea, etc. Wanted to go to church but changed my mind and regret it, for probably my head would not pain if I led a less sedentary life. After dinner went to the skating in the village though it was an effort. A band of boys, among them Egorka and repulsive Sasha, the teacher. We went to see the military hill past the prison with the whole band (as well as those at the railroad station). Skating. Vespers. Egorka. Went home by carriage and in a bad mood. Arisha alone. Tea. Headache. Worked against my will. Became better at supper. Played *Judith*. Became tired and felt unwell again. A telegram from Laroche that he will come tomorrow. Worried about N. F. on account of the earthquake in Nice.

16 February A clear Monday. The trip by D. Tolstoy [46] to Podsolnechnaya. Did not feel well. We watched. It was soso. Laroche (for whom I was waiting in the train) did not show up. Home. Tabach, the father. Dinner. Felt bad again. Walked about the room. Tea. Slept in the easy chair. Worked. Laroche. Supper. Conversation. I am out of sorts, but then, it's not bad.

17 February Slept as usual. Still felt a little ill in the morning. Worked fairly well. Went with Manya to the village after dinner. At Skokov's. Manya rode off; I walked. Nevertheless, Vasily drove me up. Meat for the dogs. Tea. Vespers at our church. It's absolutely spring out of doors. Work. Bath. Supper. Talks with Manya. Reading of Gogol. Letter from Paris about the *audience*.

18 February Am writing much later (19 March) and certainly do not remember what happened. Worked, of course. Dined with Laroche; strolled alone. In the evening, we read Gogol's *The Marriage* together.

MOSCOW

19 February Departed with Laroche. On the way, Tolstoy's drama.[47] Weinberg, the inspector, came into our compartment.

---

[46] *Count D. A. Tolstoy, secretary of the interior.*

[47] The Power of Darkness.

Lunch at the railroad station. At Sophia Ivanovna Jürgenson's (to whom I wanted to apologize because I would not stay at her place). At Peter Ivanovich Jürgenson's. We quarreled and shouted at one another. At Batasha's.[48] At the Conservatory. At the Albrechts'. Hotel. Dinner at the Hermitage with Laroche, Katerina Ivanovna Sinelnikova, Kashkin. At the von Mecks'. Went home. Drinking. Tarnovsky and Gradov-Sokolov.

20 February Rehearsal of the students' concert. Kashkin, Pabst, Siloti. Excerpts from *The Enchantress*. I was satisfied. At Shpazhinsky's (he was out). At the Huberts'. They are absorbed in my proofs. The fuss with Jürgenson and the proofs. At the Conservatory. Dined alone in the tavern at my place. At the Bazilevskys' (Vargin's house). K. V. and Dima Peresleni. Home. Drunkenness.

21 February Rehearsal again. Shpazhinsky. Lunched with him at the Hotel Diusso. Taneiev and Safonov also there. At Jürgenson's. At Altani's. His wise advice regarding conducting. Home. Tea. At Panaeva's. She was out. Dinner at P. I. Jürgenson's. Grisha is ill. At Panaeva's again (waited until she came and talked it over). She is invited by Wurm to sing at my concert. Again at Jürgenson's. The Huberts. Whist. Supper. Dropped in at the Patrie restaurant. The only one in the whole tavern. Sasha and the Sumy hussars.

Sunday, 22 February Alexei, the engraver. Dima. At Erdmannsdörfer's. *Francesca*. Lunch with Dima. Concert. Excerpts from *The Enchantress*. Home. Alesha. Dinner at Zverev's. Siloti with his wife. Kashkin, the Huberts. Whist. At the railroad station. Avoided S. I. Taneiev and P. M. Tretyakov, being afraid of discussions. Slept straight up to Maly Vishera.

ST. PETERSBURG

23 February Arrival. Kolya has lost weight. He has been ill as a result of an injury. Lunch at home. Brought the music to Christopher. At N. D. Kondratyev's. He has changed terribly. At Rahter's. Tickets. Dinner at home with Annette. With her at the concert of the Musical Society. The symphony and songs of poor Borodin.[49] D'Albert. Went to Rubinstein in the artist's room. Lavrovskaya, etc.

---

[48] *Tchaikovsky went to Moscow to help Batasha work on the proofs of* The Enchantress.

[49] *Borodin had died suddenly of a heart attack one week before.*

Met Kiselev while leaving; he was annoying today. Shouted at him. Tea at home.

24 February Korsov at my place. Rehearsal at the court gallery. Dance from *The Enchantress*. Stakelberg, Napravnik, E. K. Albrecht. Lunch at Butakova's. At my brother Kolya's. Georges. L. M. Molas.[50] Was not received at Pavlovskaya's (she is ill). At O. E. Napravnik's. Home. Dinner at N. D. Kondratyev's. Whist. At first, he was all right, afterward, a weakness. Zasyadko. Dima from the rehearsal. Went home. Was busy preparing the suite.[51]

25 February Korsov. At the bank. Lunch with Korsov. At Vsevolozhsky's. At the theater.[52] Examination of the debut singers. Dinner at Wurm's. Evening at home. *Bob* (my joy!) and Mitya.

26 February At Mass at the Kazan Cathedral. Lunch at home. Lizaveta Mikhailovna Molas. At the theater for the examinations again. Princess Beloselskaya. Count Adlerberg. Blond tenor. Home. The rise of spiritualism. Dinner at our place. The Briullovs. At Vera Vasilyevna's. She was not home. Tea at home. Bob.

27 February Nervousness. Strolled. Exhibition. Lunch at Kondratyev's. He is not better. Home. At Grand Duke Konstantin Nikolaievich's. His wife, son, and bride. Muromtzeva and her four women pupils. Kündinger, Napravnik, etc. Dinner. Home. Worked. Retired early.

28 February Rose at eight. Nervousness. Bob. Went out. At the Nikolaiev railroad station. *First rehearsal* [concert]. Nervousness, horror. Later it went all right. Ovation by the artists. At Palkin's restaurant. At Nadezhda Nikolayevna Rimskaya-Korsakova's. The children were frolicking. Slept at home. At the baths. Mokhovaya Street. Dinner at home. Butakova. Apukhtin. Concert. *Romeo and Juliet*.[53] Ovation. Bob's delightful chatting.

---

[50] *Companion to the composer's niece, Tatyana, the sole person among Tchaikovsky's relatives and friends who shared the composer's and his brother Modest's secret regarding Tatyana's child.*

[51] *Number 2, Op. 53, for orchestra. On March 5, Tchaikovsky was to conduct the first performance at a concert of his works by the Philharmonic Society of St. Petersburg.*

[52] *First rehearsals of* The Enchantress.

[53] *Fantasy overture for orchestra by Tchaikovsky which he heard at a symphony concert conducted by Napravnik.*

1 March At Mass at St. Isaac's Cathedral. Lunch at home. (Before that, at the Traveling Exhibition again. Surikov.) Bob and his coachman. Strolled. At N. D. Kondratyev's. Countess Konovnitzina. Mosolov. Dinner at my brother Kolya's. Went home. Was working in preparation for the rehearsal.

2 March Second rehearsal. *Francesca.* Stasov. The program. Lunch at Romanov's. Oysters. To the Church of the Apparition. Tim. not home. A new acquaintance. Dinner reception at Lavrovskaya's. Malozemova, Iretzkaya, Albrecht, Doctor Vladimirov. Rumors about the attempt.[54] Came home at twelve o'clock. Worked.

3 March Third rehearsal. Balakirev and his whole company. A large audience. My conducting passable. Lunch at home. Davidov, the actor. The portrait of the empress.[55] At Vsevolozhsky's. At the office. At Thomas'. Dinner at the von Vizins'. *Ruy Blas.* Supper at Guitry's. Angèle, Jumar.

ST. PETERSBURG

4 March At Osip Ivanovich Jürgenson's. At the bank. Received the money. Lunch at Ernest's. At N. D. Kondratyev's. Cavalli. N. D. in the bath. Rehearsal of the songs at Panaeva's.[56] The Saburovs. Home. Dinner at Butakova's. Lelya. Mme. Gogel. At Balakirev's. The usual guests. Olenin, the landowner, and his child, extremely odd. Supper. At Palkin's restaurant with Nikolai A. Rimsky-Korsakov, Dütsch, Glazunov, Lavrov, and Shcherbachev.

5 March In the morning at N. D. Kondratyev's. Lunch at Palkin's. Slept at home. Bob. *My concert.*[57] A complete success. Immensely delighted, but why is there a drop of gall in the honey on this occasion??? A formal, boring supper.

6 March Rehearsal of the Pustarnakov quartet at Heine's. Prince

---

[54] *To assassinate Tsar Alexander III. On March 1, some students were arrested carrying bombs.*

[55] *Tchaikovsky dedicated to the empress of Russia his Twelve Songs, Op. 60, and in appreciation she sent him her autographed portrait.*

[56] *She was to sing some of Tchaikovsky's works at the March 5 concert.*

[57] *This concert introduced Tchaikovsky as a conductor to St. Petersburg. It was an all-Tchaikovsky program and very successful.*

Georg. Lunch at home. Lizaveta Mikhailovna (a step-mother). Slept. Palkin's. Evening reception at Rimsky-Korsakov's. Shestakova. A lot of guests. Ippolitov-Ivanov and Zarudnaya. At Pogozhev's from eleven-thirty on. A big crowd. Pavlovskaya. Supper. Dragomirov. The curious Mme. Krivenko. Pavlovskaya sang. (On the way to Rimsky-Korsakov's, dropped in at the railroad station to see Panaeva and George off.)

7 March Catoire. Shapiro. Oysters. At the academy. At N. D. Kondratyev's. Home. Bob. At Ippolitov-Ivanov's. Misunderstanding. Home. The schoolboy Radin. Dinner at Napravnik's. At the Kondratyevs'. The angry Meshchersky. Home. Bob in the bath.

Sunday, 8 March Awaited Stasov in vain. Was glad that he did not come. At the Kazan Cathedral. The bear. Catoire. The academy. At Glazunov's. B, La, F.[58] Home. Bob. Walked with him as far as N. D. Kondratyev's. Sivers. Dinner at our place. Chess. Volodya Napravnik. The Pavlovskys dropped in at eleven o'clock. Evening reception at the Suvorins'. Ivanov, Skalkovsky, Kutuzov, etc.

9 March At Catoire's. His compositions. Lunch at home. Baron and Vasilyev. At my brother Kolya's. Bought perfume. Dinner at the Briullovs'. Evening reception at Dütsch's. Whist with him, Lavrov and Liadov. Supper. Conversation. Drove Liadov home.

10 March Wrote letters. Lunch at home. With Modya at the Olkhovskys', at Wurm's, at Litke's. Home. Dozed. Dinner at the Kondratyevs'. Evening reception at Pavlovskaya's. Called for and brought Ivanov and Zarudnaya. She sang. Pogozhev. O. E. Napravnik. The opera *Ruth*.

11 March Mad excitement. At Vsevolozhsky's to whom I brought the assignment of the roles. In the arcade. At the Marinsky Theater. The choruses from *The Enchantress*. In the monastery at Tanya's grave. At Gerke's. At N. D. Kondratyev's. At Bob's. Home. Dinner at Nikolai Ilyich's.[59] Relatives. Departure. Seeing me off were Anya,

---

[58] *Rimsky-Korsakov, Liadov, Borodin, and Glazunov collaborated to write a quartet on the notes B (B natural), La, F, which when spoken quickly sound Belyaev, the name of the music publisher.*

[59] *Tchaikovsky's older brother.*

Emma, Napravnik, the Pavlovskys and indirectly Vsevolozhsky and Pogozhev. Read *The Season* and a novel by de Maupassant. Slept well.

MAIDANOVO

12 March Drank coffee in the train at Tver. Home. Glad. Letters. Dinner. A stroll. Much snow. Freezing and sunny. On the way back, Egorka with his brother near my house. Arranged my music and papers in good order. Worked. Bath. Copied the diary from the other little notebook (from February 17) for nearly a month!!!

13 March Devoted the whole day to the proofs and strained myself to such an extent that I felt bad. Did not feel like eating, even slept with difficulty, but strolled a little and very unwillingly in spite of the beautiful weather. Waited with some excitement for the news as to whether the Ivanovs would come or not.

14 March Ivanov and Zarudnaya arrived very late, i.e. at ten o'clock. I met them while strolling. At first I was displeased by their arrival and was angry particularly at the thought that they would interfere with my work; but afterward, these lovely people (she especially is rarely charming) forced me to forget everything, except that the company of kind and good people is a priceless blessing. Did not work at all. We walked to Klin. The fair. We dined merrily. Then chatted. Ivanov played and she sang fascinating excerpts from his opera (the duet charms me especially). They departed at six o'clock. I immediately got down to the proofs. Worked until supper and after. Read the newspapers. Was excited, but then, it was pleasant.

Sunday, 15 March Walked to Mass at Klin. Rode back in my carriage from there. Worked on the proofs. Walked up and down in the room after dinner, and then slept, as I felt tired, and the tiredness is due to the fact that I sleep poorly, and the latter is due to the fact that I work too much. Walked a little after tea and worked again. After supper, tired myself as usual with reading, etc. Slept soso. Alexei's bill. I was angry as always.

16 March Started to work very early and succeeded in becoming awfully tired from the proofs by dinnertime. Dumplings. Walked in the room, in the garden, and along the river. Was awfully tired. Read the novel of de Maupassant. After tea, tired myself with the proofs again, awfully. After supper, killed time playing the piano

Nadezhda Filaretovna von Meck with her daughter Liudmila

(*Le Cid*, Bach's Mass), reading, solitaire. I need not hide from myself that, truly, all the beauty of life in the country and in solitude has somehow vanished. *Nowhere do I feel so bad as at home.* My stomach is always out of order; always my head aches; and besides, just as soon as I stop working—then lonesomeness, fear for the future, etc. Is it so crowded that I must live in solitude? When I am in the city, I imagine it is bliss to be here, yet here I feel no happiness. But then, I am generally depressed today. The thought of N. D. Kondratyev alarms me.[60]

17 March Slept better. In the school. The priest. A lesson in the Old Testament. Few children. The deacon. Worked. Dinner. Strolled at home and on the paved road. It is thawing, but not enough. At home, worked so hard after tea, that I was tired out. Killed time in every way after supper. Burned perfume.[61] Slept with a headache.

18 March A spring day. Felt very bad all morning and a stroll did not help. A feeling of being broken up and of weakness. Walked in the room after dinner, then took a walk in the direction of Yamly and became so tired that, literally, I could hardly reach home and came back angry and irritated. Napped in the easy chair. Mikhaila arrived. Worked again (still on the proofs). Supper without appetite. Played the Galitzin Quartet (B flat major).[62] *Cordelia.* Strange work. Thinking all the time about how to arrange my plans and the trip and am unable to come to any conclusion. Must work.

19 March Snow all day. In the morning, after listening to Mikhail Sofronov's sermon, walked in the room and in the gallery. Worked all morning until dinner. Strolled about the room and a little in the garden and on the embankment. Meetings with beggars. Impossible to walk. Petka, the little spy and the vodka for the deacon. Tea. Conversation with Alexei about plans for the future. Played a little. Work. Finished the proofs. However, corrected certain things over again after supper. Endless solitaire. All day hesitation about how and where to travel and on what to decide.

---

[60] *Kondratyev was fatally ill with dropsy.*

[61] *Tchaikovsky was very fond of perfumes and liked to make mixtures of various scents.*

[62] *String Quartet, No. 13, Op. 130, by Beethoven, dedicated to Prince Nikolai B. Galitzin.*

Just read the *diary* for these same days two years ago.[63] My God! At that time my imagination was still beautifying all the misery and bareness of Maidanovo. How I liked everything. How affectionately I treated the children here and how I have dropped them now.

MOSCOW

Friday, 20 March Departed on the express. Pullman. Reading. Lunch at the railroad station. Walked to the Conservatory. At the Huberts'. He is ill. Conference with Erdmannsdörfer about the concerts. Home. In a bad mood. Dined. Erdmannsdörfer's concert. Supper at the Hermitage. Slept well.

Saturday, 21 March Rose at nine. P. I. Jürgenson. Talks. Read the newspapers. Wrote Panya. Dinner at Batasha's. Her sister. Arrangements about tickets for the Shostakovsky students' performance. In the editorial office of the *Russkiye Vedomosti*. Lukin, Blaramberg. At Taneiev's. He left. Kind Varvara Pavlovna. Home. Tea. Strolled on Tverskaya Street. Coolness to Vanya. Desire to get rid of him. Mamontov's Italian opera.[64] Russell was Linda. Manya and Katerina Ivanovna in my box. Karlusha in the stall. Supper in the Hotel Moscow until three o'clock. Kashkin came over.

Sunday, 22 March Angry at disagreeable Ivanov, who came just as I sat down to read the newspapers. Popov. Talks about their concert and about all sorts of their nonsense. They stayed a long time. Lunch at V. D. Konshin's. His speechmaking. At Batasha's. At Orlov's. Fyofanov's shrewdness. Home. Telegram from Laroche about his broken hand. Horror and fright. At Laroche's. A. M. Davidova. Thank God! It's all no longer so terrible. Mamontov with Zina. At the Maly Theater. At Laroche's again. At the theater again. Performance of excerpts from comedy operas. The first act from Blaramberg's *The Buffoon*. With Batasha, Tanya, Zverev and Remezov at the Patrie restaurant.

MAIDANOVO

23 March Took the morning train to Maidanovo. Was twice angry: 1) a gentleman remarking that smoking is not permitted and 2) the stupid conductor with regard to the women's car. Slept.

---

[63] *Tchaikovsky's diary for 1885 has been lost.*

[64] *Donizetti's* Linda di Chamounix.

Klin. Home. Dinner. Felt bad. Slept. Strolled more than I had strength for, feeling nauseated. After tea read and wrote letters. Tiredness. Quarrel of Alexei with Arisha during supper. Played the E-minor quartet,[65] Rimsky-Korsakov's *The Snow Maiden* and Delibes. Reading of Boborykin's stupid novel.

24 March Bad weather. After a stroll, got down to the orchestration. Did not feel well after dinner despite extreme moderation. Amused myself burning perfumes. Walked. The deacon's grandchild. Chatted with Alesha during tea. Alexei Fyodorov arrived and brought the proofs. Busied myself with them. After supper, read the orchestra score of *A Life for the Tsar* and various other works.

25 March Beautiful day. Was at Mass here at Madino. Stifling. Host. Worked four hours on the proofs of *The Enchantress*, for which Alexei Fyodorov came. Walked along the embankment after dinner. The spring waters have already begun flowing. A waterfall at the mill. Met both Alexeis. Worked at home until the departure of Alexei. Provided him with what was necessary. Strolled at sunset. Sat and conversed by the church wall on the hill with the priest, surrounded by various people. Very enjoyable. The water rose rapidly. At home, wrote an answer to Sophia Ivanovna Jürgenson's letter about Peter Ivanovich's grief; he noticed my coolness. It's true, though I try to assure her in every way that he is mistaken. Played the fourth act of *The Enchantress*. A whole hour!! That's terrible!

26 March Am good for nothing. Work with incredible difficulty. My stomach is poor, and in spite of extreme moderation, still don't feel quite like myself, feel lonesome and strange, and at times, really dreadful. The weather is divine. Walked along the embankment in the morning. Migratory birds. Spring. Worked diligently until dinner. After dinner (ate almost nothing) walked to the large village along the embankment (meeting with the grandfathers, etc.) and returned by way of the paved road. On the bridge, surrounded by boys, watched them catching fish with *nets*. Sanka, the teacher, and Ignasha. Gave no money, although my fingers itched to do so. Tea and work at home. Went to watch the sunset. Work. Had supper reluctantly. Read Korsakov's *The Snow Maiden* and marveled at his mastery and was even (ashamed to admit) envious.

---

[65] *Probably by Beethoven, Op. 59, No. 2.*

Read that poor Kramskoy died. What should I do in order to be normal? . . .

27 March Rain. Felt much better today than for days past. Was at preconsecration in the morning. Worked. Letter from Katerina I. Sinelnikova (about Laroche), from Klimenko and from Gerke. After dinner strolled on the Praslovo side and went across the overflowing brook courageously in a narrow but deep spot. The Praslovo children pestered me (but not Egorka). Tea. Chat with Alesha. Letters (to Shpazhinskaya, etc.). The work went well. After supper played through the third act. Solitaire. Perfume and experiments with *eau de violette.*

28 March Snow!!! Strolled in the gallery and a bit in the garden. Worked as usual. Letters and newspapers excited me. After dinner walked again (crossing the brook courageously) in the direction of Praslovo along the lowland. Egorka with his brother. At tea, conversation with Alesha and hair grooming. The weather cleared up. The sun appeared. Worked (changed my mind about riding to the Palm vespers in the village). A note from Taneiev. Played *Harold* (first act) and Mendelssohn's overtures.

(Palm) Sunday, 29 March Cold weather. Was late to church. Worked. After dinner, walked about the rooms (fussing with the perfumes; my mania is becoming stronger and stronger) and then in the field and on the paved road across the ditch. (Alexei was driving to Lukanov.) The boys were waiting in hope of money, but I became hardhearted. Worked after tea. Went to watch the sunset from the church wall. A crowd of boys and girls in expectation of money. Had pity and gave some. Awaiting Taneiev. He arrived on horseback with his nephew. Conversation. Supper. He played excerpts from his opera (trilogy based on Aeschylus).[66] Nuts and all kinds of sweets.

30 March Passion Week. I am fasting. The weather is excellent, although a little cold. Worked. After dinner walked on the paved road to the right and felt light as I did not drink vodka, but toward the end of the walk began to feel ill. At tea, conversation with Alesha, and grooming. Letters to Anton G. Rubinstein (a reply to his proposal to write an opera) [67] and to Wurm. Worked. The sun-

---

[66] Orestes.

[67] *Tchaikovsky refused the offer to write an opera for the next season*

set from the arbor. Worked. Was tired. After supper, read the orchestra score of Glinka's *A Life for the Tsar*. What mastery! And how did he accomplish it all? Incomprehensible, that from such an extremely limited and commonplace dilettante, judging by the autobiography, there should develop such a colossus??!!

31 March Beautiful weather. Strolled. Worked diligently, but progressed little. Letter from Modest with the news that Bob is coming tomorrow. After dinner strolled behind the house; it was impossible to cross the brook in the direction of the forest. Gazed at its mouth, where the snow arch under which it disappears had already collapsed. Alexei (in a chef's costume) was cleaning the house all day. At tea, conversed with Alesha and read Amédée Thierry. Worked. Went out at seven o'clock to watch the sunset from the wall. The priest. Conversation. Worked until I was tired. Supper unusually Lenten. After that (Arisha still pestered Alesha jokingly) straightened out one place in the orchestration which presented difficulties today.

Wrote a letter to Sasha today, who, it seems, is grieved by my silence.

1 April *Bob* arrived!!! We drank tea together. We walked along the embankment to the cathedral at Klin. The deceased (likewise in our church, where we dropped in). At Skokov's. Walked home on the paved road. Worked little. Dinner. Stroll with *Bob* again. Brooklets, dams, large brook, etc. Bob's indescribably lovely chatting. Tea. Worked. Alesha brought letters. One from Arensky, an angry one. Went with Bob to see where the dam burst. Letter in reply to Arensky.[68] I have a headache. Supper. Looking at drawings and talking with Bob until eleven-thirty. Telegram from Albrecht and Kashkin.

---

[68] *Arensky was hurt by Tchaikovsky's opinion of the former's fantasy for orchestra*, Margarete Gautier. *Tchaikovsky replied that he could not comprehend why Arensky, so gifted a composer, should select Dumas fils' unworthy subject when there were Homer, Shakespeare, Gogol, Pushkin, Dante, Tolstoy, Lermontov, etc. Such a selection was understandable with Verdi (his opera* La Traviata) *who sought a subject that would react on the nerves of people in an epoch decadent in art.*

2 April Did not sleep well. A short stroll with Bob. Expecting Kashkin and Albrecht. With Bob to meet them. Karlusha's delightful story about the "censure" at dinner. A long tramp for *building up* Bob, to Praslovo. Tea. Examination and playing through of Albrecht's *études* and *ballet* excerpts. Whist with Bob after supper.

Passion Friday, 3 April Karlusha departed. Worked. In church and a stroll in the forest with Kashkin and Bob after dinner. Worked after tea. Played duets with *Bob!!!* After supper, played Arensky's symphony with Kashkin.

Passion Saturday, 4 April Was coughing all night and slept badly just as the night before. Got up alone at five-thirty o'clock. Awoke Bob at six. Saw him off on the mail train. Mitya. Went home. Worked. Dinner with Kashkin. The weather turned bad. Slept. Tea at seven o'clock. Letters. Talks with N. D. Kashkin. Terrible cough. Matins. Easter morning dinner.

Easter, 5 April Rose at ten o'clock. Tea with N. D. Expecting the priests. The priests. Eating and drinking. Strolled with N. D. in the direction of Yamly. Tea. Arrival of Taneiev. He played his piece. It is very lovely. I like it very much but he likes it still more.

6 April Taneiev stayed overnight. We separated and worked after tea. The three of us walked together to Demyanovo after dinner. Varvara Pavlovna; Elena Sergeyevna; Dzhanshiev. Tea. Went home partly riding, partly walking. Apothecary. Mme. Selenskaya, the wife of a landowner??? Worked at home. After supper S. I. Taneiev played excerpts from his opera.

7 April The cough is beginning to disappear. Worked after tea. After dinner, S. I. Taneiev was busy guessing my melodies in *The Enchantress* from the accompaniments. I walked a little. Tea. Lively chat with lovable Taneiev. He left finally at six o'clock. I escorted him across the ditch as far as the road leading to Klin. Beautiful evening. Boys and girls pestered me. Home. Worked. Supper. Borodin's letters.

8 April My head ached at night. Woke with awful pain and vomiting. Could hardly rise. Dozed right up to dinner. Felt better little by little. Finished with difficulty the *markings* in the second act and sent it off to Taneiev. The weather is terrible. Did not go out all day. In the evening played *Ruslan* and an act from *Nizhe-gorodtzy.*[69] Slept well.

9 April Immediately after the morning walk up and down in the room, got down to the fourth act and worked diligently and success-fully all day. Walked in the direction of Praslovo after lunch. Boys kept pursuing me. I hid near the river. Egorka by the house. Work. Tea. Work. Bath. Supper. Put the books brought from the bindery into the cabinet.

10 April Snow. Cold weather. Worked intensely in the morning. Was angry during tea at Alesha because of the argument about *cooking.* According to him, curd is cooked—well, from that an argu-ment arose. Ate almost nothing at dinner due to Vasily's failure. Walked in the room, on the terrace, and a little in the garden. Hair grooming during tea. Work. Went out a little for a breath of air. The work is advancing. Letter from Batasha. Played *Nizhegorodtzy* and Schubert's quintet.

11 April The weather is still bad. Surprised to have no answer from Bob. Worked. After dinner walked in the room and to the forest on the other side. Tea. Hair grooming. Conversation with Alesha. Worked so hard that I thought everything within me would burst from strain. At supper, it seemed as if I did not understand what to do or how to go about the routine of eating. Suddenly voices from the pantry . . . What happened? It turned out to be S. I. Taneiev and his two nieces. All soon left. Conversation with S. I. Taneiev. He gives me good advice concerning the orchestra-tion of the duet between Kudma and the godmother. No one came for him. He stayed overnight. Had nuts.

Sunday, 12 April Grand weather. After tea S. I. Taneiev went away to Demyanovo. I went with him as far as the incline. Work. To the forest after dinner. Ditches. Home. Reading. Tea. Worked. A stroll around the garden about seven o'clock. Magnificent sunset. Work. Supper. The malice of Arisha. Alexei and the postman *were dissipating.* Went out to the garden after supper. Beautiful evening. Played the scores of the quartets in the Payne edition. Tired.

13 April The weather is simply heavenly. In the morning, went strolling longer than usual, namely, to the right along the embank-

---

[69] *Opera by Napravnik.*

ment. After work and dinner, walked (without a coat) again along the embankment to the mill. Returned across the forest. Top frightened me with his wild barking in the forest. He was hunting apparently. Worked after tea and conversation with Alesha. The girls were cultivating the garden and with them Ignasha. Later, around sunset, I was with him also, in the arbor. Work. Supper. Tiredness. Early to sleep.

14 April Am a little ill. A gum boil, but suffered very little, only in the morning and in the evening while eating. Strolled farther than I felt like though it was not particularly far, in the forest. (At this moment as I write, am frightened by a mysterious knock. . . .) Worked. Strolled again. The superintendent. By the wall during sunset. Osip, saying that he is going to the factory. Sasha and *tutti quanti*. Handed out money. Worked. Supper. My tooth ached. The work advances soso.

15 April The beautiful weather continues. Slept, but a headache—my own fault. Strolled in the garden. Worked. After dinner, forced my way to Klin through Praslovo (the bridge is built). Sat on the boulevard and enjoyed it. Returned the same way. The pestering went on as usual. Egorka appeared toward the end. Lost my pince-nez. Gypsies, and in addition a boy from Madino, and all of them crave my fifteen kopek piece!!! Letters. Intense work. Sunset. Watched the work at the dam and the *priest* who was fussing over something with a fish, together with Vasya and the guard. After supper, felt tormentingly hungry. I have become too obstinate.

16 April It's still finer; it's quite warm. Often now I experience a great and deep joy from the spring, birds, butterflies, the bright sunshine, the warmth, and all the beauty of spring. . . . Still worked just as diligently, but a certain absent-mindedness seized me and I kept making awful mistakes. . . . Walked in various directions after dinner; in the field past Praslovo, etc. Tea. Work. A stroll in the arbor during sunset. The impertinence of boys. The work at the mill. After supper (even though Arisha has a birthday, she still quarreled with Alexei) played *The Power of Evil*. A sort of sickening musical mutilation and at the same time there is *talent, sensibility, imagination*. To tell the truth, there is infinitely more of all these in Serov than in the notorious *mighty Group*. But on the other hand, they have *good form, a striving for grace*—in a word, externally more attractive.

17 April Still the same beautiful weather. After dinner and a stroll went to see Novikova, who arrived yesterday. The pretentious architect (not likable). Tea. Work. A stroll. Played *The Enchantress* from a new copy received today.

18 April The weather is tropical, but windy and with cloud drifts. It was thundering. Dropped in again at Novikova's after a stroll (Egorka and Co. angered me yesterday as they embarrassed me before Novikova and the architect.) Tea. Work. Tired. Read Wolf's history of the theater in the evening.

Sunday, 19 April It's hot but the wind is strong and it's gray. Walked to the Sobolevsky forest after dinner. Petka, the boy annoyed me. Afterward, as usual: *drudgery.* Klimenko's letter to Alexei about the *clerk* who swore at me. Am very upset. Cannot go to sleep without drinking heavily.

20 April As a result of yesterday's episode (Klimenko's letter about the clerk and his "monstrous" stories) was so upset that I slept poorly and was in a bad mood all day. Work is a savior. Novikova's gift. Dropped in at her place after dinner and a stroll (in the direction of Sobolevsky). Lizaveta Grigoryevna (*alter ego* of Princess Shakhovskaya) with her daughter. Chatted with them with great pleasure. Novikova led me to the carriage shed. Tea. Work. Evening stroll. Supper. Arisha is going away tomorrow. Read *Chronicle of the Theater* by Wolf from nine to twelve-thirty and did not notice how the time passed.

21 April Slept rather poorly. Arisha's departure. Tears. She did not say good-by to Vasily. A stroll. Work. After dinner (I stopped drinking vodka entirely and am quite happy) walked in the direction of Belavin and returned via Praslovo. Not possible without being pestered. Letter to N. F. Tea. Work. A stroll. Two gentlemen frightening me turned out to be strollers. Bath. Supper (without vodka).

22 April Rose, walked, worked (very hard: the very end of the fourth act). Read letters after dinner. One from Emma. I was very grieved. Botkin declared Nikolai D. Kondratyev's condition is very serious—he is incurable. I am terribly grieved by this. The stroll in the forest calmed me. Tea. Novikha sent an invitation. Went to see her; with her to Sobolevsky. He was boating on the water on the estate. Baron Cherkasov. Worked with incredible intensity. Evening at Novikova's. Whist could not be arranged. Watched them playing preference.

23 April The weather is hot, even stifling. Worked. Finished the fourth act. Began to make the markings. Dinner with guests. Sobolevsky and Novikova. Strolled about the garden. Met Novikova and had a chat. Home. Went walking at an unusual hour, namely, at seven o'clock; watched the mail train from the guard booth. Home. Work. Supper. Went to Novikova (who invited me because of Shakhovskaya's arrival) but they were just going to bed. Read Du Camp.[70] All day I have been grieving a little and am perplexed.

24 April The day is grayish, but good. After work (markings) and a stroll in the garden and on the lowland to the left (the leeches in the stream; a strange old pauper) went to Novikova's. She had gone out with the princess; I caught up with them. We went to the village together; saw how Andriushkinov's father was situated in the hut rented by Mme. Bushman; dropped in at the school and at the teacher's. Tea at home. Work, a walk. Went to Novikova after supper. Conversed with her and the princess about Mme. Gelbig, Tolstoy, life in the future, etc. A wise and interesting woman, this princess.

25 April Forty-seven! Hm! Hm! Have lived through a lot! The day is bad; wind, rain, snow, sleet. Rose unusually late—at nine o'clock. Novikova and Shakhovskaya were at dinner. Strolled about the gallery and in the garden or near by. Work. Beautiful sunset. Taneiev appeared during supper. Triple counterpoint. Conversation about the subject of his opera. Very tired.

Sunday, 26 April The day of remembrance of what happened four years ago in Paris.[71] Drank tea with S. I. Taneiev and we were talking animatedly about important matters. Worked straight through until dinner; almost finished the fourth act. All my hesitation about how and where to travel has been solved unexpectedly with the realization that what I want is to remain here until I finish the third act. S. I. Taneiev is the cause of my making this apparently sensible decision. After dinner, escorted S. I. as far as the paved road (a walker is a bad companion for a rider). His

---

[70] *Maxime Du Camp (1822-1894), French traveler and man of letters much read in Europe.*

[71] *The birth of Tatyana's son.*

promesse. Letter from Emma with the same sad news about N. D. Kondratyev. Am very grieved. Was at Novikova's to bid good-by to Shakhovskaya. Home. Finished the fourth act and sent it off to Demyanovo. Strolled. It's awfully cold. Read M. Du Camp. Supper. Played Haydn, Mendelssohn, *The Maccabees.*[72]

27 April Terribly cold weather. Started the third (i.e. the last, as regards work) act. Worked successfully. After dinner, walked about the rooms, the garden, and in the vicinity of the homestead. Saw the *observatory,* constructed by the boys of Praslovo, but in such a way that they did not see me. Tea. Work. A stroll. Work. After supper enjoyed the fireplace and fussed quite a while with it. Maxime Du Camp.

28 April Woke much earlier than my usual time and could not sleep any more. Korsov's telegram and letter concerning operatic matters. Did not work as well as yesterday. After dinner walked to the forest along the right bank of the brook. Kept sinking in the swamps. The weather is damp and windless although not very warm. The insurance agent and insurance. Work. A beautiful, striking sunset! Work. Supper. *Parsifal.* An invitation from Karlusha to the silver wedding.

29 April Rose at seven o'clock in the morning and worked until time to wash up. Then later met Novikova in the garden. With her to the mill and along the embankment. The likable miller ("an old man"). Worked. Toward dinner unpleasant letters. N. D. Kondratyev is quite bad. Very upset. Stasov's letter about Borodin.[73] Strolled (rain) about the garden and the gallery of the big house. Worked. Did not go out for a stroll in the evening. Awfully nasty out of doors. Going tomorrow to Moscow for Albrecht's silver wedding. I am very melancholy and crushed because of the news about N. D. Kondratyev.

MOSCOW

30 April Departed on the express to Moscow. Lunch and drunkenness at the railroad station. (Alesha Obolensky and Glazunov, with

---

[72] *Opera by Anton Rubinstein.*

[73] *Tchaikovsky thanked Stasov for his letter and biography of Borodin and expressed his high regard for Borodin and grief over his recent death.*

his father, were in the train, but I was saved by the compartment.)
A long walk. Got into a show booth on the Zvetnoy Boulevard—
very amusing (a satirical singer performing Russian songs "Oh,
Vaniusha, now stop fooling around"), puppet show (a merchant
is banished to hell, an odd orchestra—well, in a word, very entertaining). At Jürgenson's. At Sophia I. Jürgenson's (Grisha was lying
down while Sophia I. read to him). At Laroche's. At Hubert's. The
dinner and speeches at Karlusha's. Silver flowers. The celebration.
Left on the express. In the compartment with me were Mr. Voskre-
sensky, a Greek tobacco merchant, and a handsome Italian. Was
very tired. Home. Alexei drove to fetch me. Could hardly calculate
how to walk up to the entrance—darkness set in. A letter from
Modya; N. D. Kondratyev is better.

MAIDANOVO

1 May Marvelous weather. Worked. Went to the Sobolevsky
forest after dinner and had a wonderful walk, although felt a tiredness as a result of yesterday's dissipation. Work until seven-thirty
after tea. A stroll about the garden. Nightingales. After supper read
the newspapers. There was a letter from Emma, confirming the improvement in N. D. Kondratyev.

2 May Warm weather, rain in the evening. Strolled briefly after
dinner. Visited Novikova. After tea and work, rambled about the
garden with Catoire who had arrived. Clouds came and it rained.
Supper. Two fugues. Catoire's *The Mermaid.*[74] A talented young
man. S. I. Taneiev arrived. We played and examined the works of
Catoire again.

Sunday, 3 May Beautiful weather. Both guests left. Took a walk
with indescribable pleasure. Andrey left today for the village.
Worked hastily and impatiently. In the forest after dinner. Hiding
from Top. Worked intensely. Strolled before supper. Beautiful evening. Read the new *Istorichesky Vestnik.*

4 May The weather is simply too wonderful to describe. After a
stroll and work, received a letter, before dinner, which disturbed
me. N. D. Kondratyev, as Modest writes, is in fact worse although,
thanks to Father Johann (from Kronstadt), he is spiritually better.
Will have to go there. After a stroll in the forest, visited Novikova.
She got on my nerves awfully today. Gave her the money sent by

---

[74] *The two fugues for piano and* The Mermaid, *a cantata.*

Mamontov. Worked intensely after tea until eight o'clock. A walk. Some strangers were strolling. Strolled after supper. Dropped in at Novikova's. Gossip about Mary Kondratyeva (whom she upbraids without regard), about Suvorin's son who shot himself, etc.

5 May A divine day. The work went very hard (the Introduction). Letters of which some are comical (a request to harmonize a song), the others sad. Nikolai D. Kondratyev is worse and worse. Afterward took a vast walk in the forest. I saw Top chasing a rabbit; the exhaustion of the poor dog. Tea. Feeding the chickens. Work. A stroll. After supper (talk about N. D. Kondratyev with Alesha and the drunkenness of Vasily) went for a walk while it was still light. Was at Novikova's and gossiped with her about all kinds of nonsense.

6 May A little windy, but the weather is still good. Worked well, so that toward evening *finished everything!!!* [75] Glory and thanks to God! After dinner walked on the road to the Shchapova forest through swamps and my forest. Tired. Worked steadily until supper. After supper walked along the embankment as far as the place the miller had broken open and then was at Novikova's, gossiping, as usual, about the most unbelievable nonsense. Laughed about Praskovya overhearing my talk with the gypsy's son from whom I had bought a fish. The stars. Novikova's imaginary comet tail.

7 May Hot weather. Wrote letters in the morning. After dinner walked to the railroad station to post them. Returned via Praslovo. The boys. Followed by Egorka and his brother. I am tired of them. Made some markings after tea. How tiresome that is! Took a walk after supper and was at Novikova's. Sobolevsky. Conversation about literature. Strange and wrong feelings were exciting me.

8 May Finishing the work. The markings. After dinner (*stufato*) got sick with a terrible pain in the intestines. Castor oil. I worked at night. Punished for being a glutton.

9 May Feel better. At Novikova's. The aunt of Simon's wife. They both drank tea at my place. Novikova saw me off. Left on the mail train.[76] Korsov and Krutikova in the train.

---

[75] *The orchestration of the entire opera was finished; he also noted that event on the manuscript of the opera.*

[76] *To St. Petersburg where he was called on account of the critical condition of Kondratyev.*

Sunday, 10 May Bob and Kolya met me. Home. At N. D. Kondratyev's after lunch. Horrible impression. He has changed so much
that he is unrecognizable. At Annette's. At the Tavrichesky Palace.
Dinner and evening at the Kondratyevs'. N. D. played whist.

11 May Did not sleep all night. Was crying. A stroll to the island.
Lunch at the Félicien restaurant. At N. D.'s. Was present during
Shershevsky's visit. Dined there also. N. D. was drowsy. Went home
at nine o'clock. Bobushka, my darling.

12 May Lunched at the Pivato restaurant. Strolled on the Vasilyevsky Island. Dinner at home. At N. D. Kondratyev's. Mme.
Markevich. There was no game. With Modya and Zasyadko at
Palkin's restaurant.

13 May I feel poorly. The Summer Garden. Lunch at the Contant
restaurant. Martinov and Musman. Home. N. D. seemed more
cheerful in the evening. Whist.

14 May Kazan Cathedral. Grace. Lunched at Palkin's restaurant
on the balcony. A stroll. The Neva at the Kalashnikov pier. Tsar's
Meadow. The show booth. Dozed. Dinner at Butakova's. At N. D.
K.'s. There was no game. He was complaining about his endless
suffering. Terrible to hear. Zhenya Kondratyeva. Home. Pestering
of boys.

15 May (Coronation.) At St. Isaac's Cathedral. The grace did
not come off. Lunch at the Grand Hotel. At St. Isaac's Cathedral
again, heard the *Te Deum* with twelve bishops. Thunderstorm.
Small tavern. At Litke's. Niks is quite bad, no better than N. D.
Kondratyev. Home. At the Apukhtins'. Dinner at the Donon restaurant with Panaeva and George. Evening at Kondratyev's. N. D. is
awfully weak and inexpressibly pitiable.

16 May At Pogozhev's—he was out. Strolled. Lunch at our place:
there were Olya, Kolya, and Georges. At Olga E. Napravnik's. Conversation at first with the boys, then with her. Church of the Apparition. Timofey. Home. Kolya's examination in history. At N. D.'s
with Bob. He is more lively, but I found out from Zhenya Shershevsky that there is no hope. Degeneration into *wax*. Dinner. The painful farewell went off better than I expected. Was almost late. Bob,
Kolya, and Modest saw me off. I was extremely upset. Drank a
lot as a result of which (*see following*).

MOSCOW

Sunday, 17 May Woke near Tver with a terrible headache and in low spirits. Became somewhat better after Klin. Stayed at the Hotel Moscow. Alesha was there, I was very glad. Lunched. Went to the good Huberts'. Found both home. After the visit, rode home and had a nap. Thunderstorm. Waited. To the park with the Huberts by carriage. Walked in the Petrovsky-Rasumovsky Park. Supper at the Moorish restaurant.

Monday, 18 May At the Conservatory. Langer's and Ladukhin's examinations in harmony. At Jürgenson's. The problem about money. Lunched at Testov's restaurant. Strolled. The illness commenced (pressure on the stomach and lack of appetite as in Rome). Walked to the Jürgensons'. Tea and whist with the Huberts in the arbor. I felt very bad. We went upstairs.

Tuesday, 19 May Rose apparently well, but afterward it became worse and worse. Lunch with Jürgenson at the Diusso restaurant. At the notary's. Money. The Laroches. Slept. Examination in the class of advanced piano. Supper in the company of others at Testov's restaurant. On coming home, took a laxative. Ate almost nothing all day.

Wednesday, 20 May The illness continued. Dropped in at Lopashov's restaurant but could not eat. Meeting of the directors. Examination in violin (the younger Konius). His counterpoint as well as that of his brother. Went home. Preparations and payments. Dinner with the Laroches, Kashkin, and Jürgenson at Lopashov's restaurant. Nizhegorod railroad station. The Huberts, Peter Ivanovich Jürgenson, and Boris P. Jürgenson saw me off. Departure. The weather is bleak. I got a bit better but later felt bad again. Drank tea at Pavlov. The actor, Varlamov, the actress, Vasilyeva (her husband, Taneiev, came up to me), etc. Slept a great deal. The pain in the intestines practically unceasing.

TRIP DOWN THE VOLGA

Thursday, 21 May Nizhnii [Novgorod]. Disappointment regarding the cabins on the "Kavkaz" and the "Mercury." We took a cabin in the second class. On the ship. The usual commotion until we were settled. I felt ill. The weather is bad. Enjoyed it little; stayed mostly in my cabin. Table d'hôte. (Women neighbors: a slender mother with a cranky boy and nurse, a pert girl telephone operator, afterward the boisterous girl of the captain's assistant, etc.) Felt ill and was seized with homesickness at times. The weather is bad. Noise in the cabin. The only attractive ones are a stout and apparently very kind lady with her family and an old retired military man, who turned out to be very smart. The rest are very unattractive, especially three student tourists. The first-class passengers act superior. The steward gave me a pillow—slept excellently, although my abdomen pained.

22 May, Kazan　I did not feel well in the morning. Went on shore. Kazan is very beautiful from a distance. Lunched soon after sailing at eleven o'clock. Then was depressed all day and from time to time, a singular homesickness came over me and a consciousness of being alone and scorned by all. Certain passengers arouse something like hatred within me, particularly, the three students and a fourth student in uniform, accompanying the amiable schoolboy Sasha. A third-class passenger had an attack. The weather is nasty. My dinner at six o'clock without any enjoyment. Simbirsk. Went for a stroll with Alesha. Later, we drank tea and conversed. Slept tolerably well. My health is still not very good. Some sort of weakness (pain in the stomach); feverish condition.

23 May, Volsk　Woke (they had the heat on—it was very hot) in Samara. After dressing and drinking tea, went for a stroll through the city with Alesha. First rate city. Notices all over about *Onegin*, given yesterday. Reformed Church; odd kind of singing (I liked it very much since it is not the usual deacon bass as with us), old women, the little deceased woman, breads, etc. We returned. Lunch. Syzran and before that a bridge. Walked a long time on deck. At Syzran an important person got on. Suddenly, soon after that, caught sight of Emanuel, the conductor. Made believe that I did not recognize him; he was pointing at me. I was running away after that all the time. Reading (account about the institute in the *Russky Vestnik* and Poznyak's abominable novel!!!). Khvalynsk. Tea with Alesha. Volsk. The captain's assistant. To the city at his suggestion. Charming little city. Garden. An important personage. Restaurant. Unusual interior. Reception room. We ate well. I am still not quite all right. Walked to the ship. Magnificent moonlight night.

Trinity Sunday, 24 May, Saratov　After dressing we went to the city. By no means liked it as much as I had expected. The cathedral. Mass. Kamyshin was notable among the next stops. The whole city is laid out on the shore, very different in its own way (boards and balustrades above the precipice). The railroad station. Yesterday I became acquainted with a likable cadet, a very entertaining conversationalist. I conversed so much with him in the evening that I did not even notice that Alesha had transferred all our things to first class. Tea. Slept very well.

Whitmonday, 25 May, Tsaritsin I did not like this city. It is strange somehow! For example, on an immense vacant precarious square, in which one's feet sink in the sand, all of a sudden there is an enormous house in Viennese style! Lunched with Alesha on board ship in first class. Not until two o'clock did we set out from Tsaritsin. Farther on still flat. Sarepta. Ginger cakes. My tooth ached. Dined by myself at six-thirty. After dinner, a talk with a smart Georgian (wearing eyeglasses), who had traveled through Siberia. And all day, in our salon, there is music by two not very attractive young ladies, one of whom sings vilely (although the selections are good) while the other thumps on the piano.

26 May We arrived at Astrakhan in the morning. Drove with Alexei to see the city. Much better than Saratov. Transfer to a small ocean ship. A Russian captain with his mother, who poured tea when we were having lunch. No whist. My friendship with the unusually likable schoolboy is progressing *crescendo.* Conversed also with the smart Georgian-Siberian many times and pleasantly. Nine feet. Transfer to a schooner. A large cabin in which we are alone. Table d'hôte. I finally talked with the young lady singer [77] from the conservatory, who has been sailing with us straight through from Nizhnii. All the talk was about singing, music, and opera. The young lady asked *whether I saw Pavlovskaya in Onegin?* A gray-haired gentleman said that *"Tchaikovsky"* kissed Lody several times last year for his performance of Orlik [78] in *Mazepa.* All together it was very jolly. Later, conversed with the Georgian, and then sitting

---

[77] *On board, the passengers organized an improvised musical evening and Tchaikovsky offered to act as accompanist. No one on board knew his identity. There was an amusing incident when the young lady singer placed before Tchaikovsky one of his own songs and began instructing him how to accompany it. To his difference of opinion, she retorted that she surely must know better as Tchaikovsky himself went through the song with her teacher!*

[78] *The gentleman was slightly in error for Orlik's part was for a bass while Lody was a tenor.*

down in the buffet to drink some coffee, became acquainted with the inspector who told me his whole life story including how he squandered four thousand rubles in oil. Beautiful night; moon, sea. . . . Could hardly tear myself away. The inspector again; in his cabin. In my cabin. Spent a terrible night. It was tossing frightfully; it seemed now . . . now it would turn over. . . . A terrible fear seized me. It was not until four o'clock, when it seemed to me that the tossing was subsiding, that I fell asleep.

27 May, At sea Rose at eight o'clock. Tea. There is less tossing. The Georgian-Siberian. Mountains. Shore. Petrovsk. Bade good-by to the cadet. The bay. People came to meet the other lady singer, our neighbor (at table). Table d'hôte lunch. An attractive seaman with whiskers. To the city. It is hot. The garden. Empty streets. The meeting with my cadet (his name is: Mikhail Alex. Shelemyatev). We barely arrived in time. In a boat with the whole company of our fellow travelers. Until dinner, read, walked, conversed with the Georgian, played solitaire, etc. After an exceedingly scanty and poor dinner at the common table (I am by now conversing amicably with the lady singer), the captain remained with me and tormented me with his talk about politics. And just then, as if for spite, there was a glorious sunset. Derbent. Flames. The noise and shrieks of the natives. Sat long on the second-class deck, conversing with two charming Georgians. The beauty of the moonlight night was beyond all description. I slept excellently; there was no tossing at all.

28 May Rose at eight o'clock. After tea sat on deck. How vexing that it's impossible to sit alone and enjoy the sea and the beautiful day! The weather is excellent today, would like so much to give myself over to contemplation without interference, but here and now I am afraid they will force conversation! It spoils all the pleasure. Wrote letters and the diary until lunch. I do not have the least urge *to create*. That is strange. Lunch. Watching the captain's whist with the captain himself (it resembled a money-changer's). Expectation of arrival. Baku. Grand Hotel. Not bad. Went strolling alone. The bazaar. Mikhailovsky Garden. Everything burned down. Met the Georgians on land. Together to the bazaar. Dinner with Alesha. A quarrel. Reading of the newspapers. The circus. From there to the garden. The circus again. Went home. Slept soso.

29 May Awoke Alesha. A ride to Balakhana. Oil derricks, or better, a forest of oil derricks. The gusher. Boring for oil. Went home. Lunch. Railroad station. Disorder. I am in a compartment with a German. *Smoking not permitted!* A curious predicament. My anger. Fell asleep. Ate at some railroad station. Visited friends in third class. They know who I am. Gave Grelaev ten rubles. Went to sleep at ten-thirty. Slept well.

TIFLIS

30 May Tiflis. Tolya, Panya, Tata, and Kokodes met me. Conversation and tea. I went to the baths with Alesha. A terrible old man. Vile. Lunch at home with Panya. Tatusya and the dolls. Strolled about in the Mushteid Garden and the streets. Went home. Devdoriani. Thunderstorm. I am in a phaeton with Panya and Tolya. A downpour, hail. Dinner at the Hotel London. My people and Tebenkov with Karnovich. Jolly, but Tolya and Tebenkov had arguments. Went home. Thunderstorm. Alesha opened the door himself.

Sunday, 31 May Mass at the Zion Cathedral. Bishop Alexander. Lunch at home. Gakel, Orlovsky. It is hot. With Tatusya and the nurse to the Mushteid. Rain. I am at home. Dinner at six o'clock. Kolya Peresleni. Thunderstorm and rain. At the theater. "The way you make your bed, so will you lie in it." [79] At the Circle. Supper. Rain. All the same company.

1 June It is hot. Slept badly. Tea on the balcony. The Mushteid. Home. Lunch. Korganov and his sister. Bykov. Letters. Dinner on the balcony. At the theater. Benefit performance for Savina. [80] Ovation. Frenzy. Kavkaz restaurant. Supper reception. Annenskaya, the actress, Adamiyantz, the speech by Opochinin, etc. A toothache all evening.

2 June The heat is maddening. Tea on the balcony. The Mushteid. Toothache. Lunch at home. Slept until four o'clock. In the Mushteid and in the city. Thunderstorm. At the beer saloon. Home. At dinner, a public prosecutor from Kutais (a cigar), Opochinin, Gakel, and the doctor. The Turkish consul. At Rogge's. Judgments on *The Enchantress.* Tea. Supper. At home, a telegram from Modest. N. D. Kondratyev is dying. Poor Modya. My curious heartlessness. Thunderstorm.

---

[79] *Another title for Dumas fils' play* La Dame aux Camélias.

[80] *Tchaikovsky saw a performance of Shpazhinsky's play* The Enchantress *and thought that Savina, the actress, was beneath all criticism.*

Diary Six

June, 1887 — September, 1887

This diary carries on from the preceding one. At Tiflis, Tchaikovsky received the news of the critical illness of his friend Kondratyev and set out to join him at Aachen, Germany. His stay at Aachen with his sick friend was broken by a brief visit to Paris, after which he returned to Maidanovo. During the time of this diary he was at work on the string sextet, Memories of Florence, the Mozartiana Suite, Op. 61, and the Pezzo Capriccioso for 'cello and orchestra, Op. 62.

TIFLIS

3 June, 1887   Home. It is hot. The Mushteid [Garden]. Lunch. Reading. Korganov's sister. She sang many things. Took a walk. After dinner at the theater with Kolya Peresleni. We looked at the scenery of *A Life for the Tsar*. Performance. *The Unsocial Woman*.[1] Supper by the entire company at the Circle.

4 June   Storm. In the Mushteid with Tata. Dinner at three o'clock. A stroll with Kolya. Beer in the Rotonde. Evening card party at our place. Lidov. Peshkesh. The poems of Grand Duke Konstantin Konstantinovich. Tebenkov's criticism.

5 June   Home all morning. After lunch went for a stroll through the city; dropped in at Lanko's for Mozart. After dinner went to the Circle with Kolya. Reading. Whist game with Orlovsky, Korganov and Kolya. Supper. Savanelli.

6 June   Rose in a tired condition and out of sorts. Went strolling in the city and returned by way of the Verisky Bridge. We dropped in at the theater for the box. Pitoev. Looked over Verdi's *Otello*

---

[1] *Play by A. N. Ostrovsky and N. Y. Solovyev.*

at home. Dinner in honor of Savina at the Circle. Speeches. Whist game (Opochinin and Rogge). Home. Retired early.

Sunday, 7 June News about the death of Niks Litke. It is sad. Mass at the Zion Cathedral. An ordinary priest conducted the services. The end of the Mass at the Cathedral of the High Priest. The Bishop Alexander. Asiatic restaurant. Matinée performance. *Grief from Wisdom.*[2] Dinner at Slovesnik's. Strange people. A stroll in the Botanical Garden. Home. The Rotonde. Beer. The vagabond boy. The Circle.

8 June Went to the city. Home. Kolya Peresleni. With him to the Rotonde to drink beer. We are alone. Bakradze. He was conducting a potpourri from *Onegin.* After dinner I was with Kolya at the theater. Farewell performance of Savina. *Divorçons.* The Circle. Supper for the entire company.

9 June After tea went with Panya to the Goncharovs'. Talks with her and the Turkish consul. I go visiting the Andreyevs, the Orlovskys, the Smittens. Pribik's quintet at his place. Dinner at home. Gakel and the doctor. All of us at the Rotonde. Dark beer. Tolstoy. The Italian consul. At the Circle. Newspapers. Supper.

10 June The Mushteid (Panya departed this morning and tea was served me by Yakov, the messenger). At eleven-thirty Kolya Peresleni. With him for the purchases; at Tebenkov's at the Café Europa; I visit Rogge; together we are at Gakel's; at Smitten's; at Mme. Karnovich's (she was out) and dinner at the Bykovs'. A stroll in company in the Botanical Garden. Borya and Misha. A *whist game* at the Circle with Tebenkov, Kolya, and Smitten. Supper with Mme. Bykova. With Orlovsky, Kolya and then directly to the Café Europa. Stepan. Girls.

BORZHOM

11 June We rose early. Departure. The usual excitement. Kolya Peresleni. Crack, the puppy, accidentally found. Compartment. Admiring the wonderful views. Tolya was sleeping all the time, and I too gave my contribution to Morpheus. Dinner at Mikhailovka. Marvelous road to Borzhom.[3] Rather painful feeling due to the narrow outlook and limited horizon. A quarrel with Alexei, who is sulking on some account; the devil with him. A stroll in Vorontzov-

---

[2] *Play by Griboyedov.*
[3] *Famous watering place in the Caucasus.*

sky Park. Dinner. Riding with Tolya. Tiredness. After tea we slept.
Had nightmares all night, but enjoyed the cool air. The incident
with the chefs.

12 June Rising, went to Mineral Waters Park and had a glorious
walk up from the last bridge, then through the forest, afterward
on the long road to the village, etc. On the way back, met Tolya.
He showed me the baths. Took a wonderful bath. After dinner we
remained at home. In the garden after tea; we went to hear the
music. Stepped in to see the doctor. He ordered me to see him
in the morning. We met Pryanishnikov. Home; soon after supper
we dispersed. Nightmares again.

13 June Was excited before the visit to the doctor. Was at his
place at ten. He tapped and felt me—it pained in certain places.
He found that my liver has moved somewhere that it shouldn't
have. At once began to take the waters. The meeting with Alexandra A. Davidova and her children. Mikhailovsky and Akimov.
Tolya. Coffee. Strolled. Bath. Elizaveta's Eye. I got lost. Returned
entirely unexpectedly by way of the Vorontzovsky road. Read after
dinner. Alexandra A. Davidova drank tea. Rain. Took the waters
in the park. At vespers. Telegram from N. F. von Meck. Retired
soon after supper.

Sunday, 14 June The waters. Tea at home with unusual enjoyment. Read *Razumovsky*,[4] wrote a letter. Bath. After dinner with
Panya to the park. Struggled with sleep at home and felt generally
weak all day. Alexandra A. Davidova appeared with her whole company to take a trip somewhere together. I declined and gladly
stayed home and drank tea. The waters in the park. Went to the
post office, via the bridge to the left, both ways. Home. Supper.
Talks about this and that. The apothecary's bill by the chef. Excitement. Retired early to my room.

15 June Rose at seven o'clock. Dressed without Alesha's help and
went to take the waters. Tea. Reading. Complete reluctance and
incapacity for work. Letters. Bath. A stroll through the park. The
whole day my entire body ached, especially my feet. Dinner. Rain
threatened, but I succeeded, in order to ward off sleep, in taking a
walk along the road to the Black River. Tea. Rain. During rain, to

---

[4] The Razumovsky Family *by* A. A. *Vasilchikov*.

the park to take the waters. Music under an awning. Received a letter at home from poor N. D. At supper talk about the servants.

16 June Excellent day. Rose at seven-thirty. Felt during the whole time of taking the waters a kind of heaviness and reluctance toward activity. Tea and reading. Composed a little (the beginning of the sextet).[5] Bath. A marvelous walk upward and return home across Vorontzovsky Park. Soon after dinner we saw Tolya off, who left with Alexandra A. Davidova. Hotel Marseilles. Mikhailovsky. Home alone at the piano. Tea. With Panya to the Vorontzovsky and from there to hear the music. Nikolai Bezhanovich and his wife. Panya forced us to walk along the avenue, where there were people. Home. Interesting newspapers. We had supper together, talk about a variety of things.

17 June Rose at seven-thirty. The waters. Beautiful weather, fresh. After tea was finishing the fourth [volume of] *Razumovsky*. Letter to N. D. Kondratyev. After the bath, returned home again via Vorontzovsky Park (with deviations). After dinner commenced the orchestration of the Mozart Variation.[6] With Panya and Tolya to the farm. From there I climbed to the palace park. Unsuccessful ascent. While descending a narrow path, encountered a snake. A long struggle with myself; a mad desire to kill. Returned finally. Came upon some ruins. Beautiful view. To the park in a carriage. Panya. Went with her and took the waters. At home, newspapers and letters from P. I. Jürgenson. Supper. Talks with• Panya about the Solovtzovs, etc.

18 June For some reason, every morning it is awfully hard for me to walk; somehow today it was especially hard. After tea, read and orchestrated one variation. Bathing. Walked in the park. While going home met the Turkish consul. He paid a visit to Panya as a result of which dinner was late. Wrote a letter to the tsar.[7] Tea.

---

[5] *Tchaikovsky commenced composing the sextet, scored for two violins, two violas and two 'cellos, in June, 1887, and finished the first version in August, 1890. The second version was made between December, 1891, and January, 1892. This work is titled Memories of Florence, Op. 70.*

[6] *Theme and Variations, the fourth movement of Mozartiana, a Suite for Orchestra, Op. 61, completed on July 28, 1887. It is interesting to note that Tchaikovsky started to work first on the fourth movement.*

[7] *Tchaikovsky petitioned Tsar Alexander III to assign funds for completing the construction of the opera house in Tiflis.*

Strolling with Panya to the ruins and along a beautiful, restricted road. The waters. It was already dark when I returned. Secretary Vannovsky is here today. We saw Devdoriani among the persons in the suite on the balcony of the Cavalier House. The servants (Stepan and Annushka) are quarreling about something and have now also involved my poor Alexei. Was slyly watching the neighbors having supper.

19 June Overslept a little. After taking the waters, a stroll and tea, orchestrated the Mozart Suite. Bathing. The Turkish and the German consuls dined at our place. They left with Panya for Vorontzovsky Park. I busied myself a little at the piano. A beautiful walk through Vorontzovsky Park, along the road and on the distant slope. The music. Crowd of people. A lot of letters at home. Moonlight night. Walked a bit with Alesha. Panya's fears on account of the chef.

20 June After taking the waters and tea, wrote letters. Returned home by way of Vorontzovsky Park after bathing. During dinner, visitors dressed in tail coats, teachers from the high school. Did some orchestrating after dinner. Went with Panya to the Black River after tea. Gypsies, their dogs, and pestering. I am in the park with Milor. Loss of a button. The supper too light. About the garden with Alesha. The schoolboy neighbor at times scratched on the violin, at other times, he sang. Talk with Panya about Moscow and the Moscow people.

Sunday, 21 June After taking the waters and tea, rode with Panya to church. Bath. A stroll in the park. Dinner. Letters. A chat with Panya. Tea. Alone in the palace park. Walked throughout it. Beautiful. At home found Tebenkov. After supper, we drove to the evening ball. We watched.

Monday, 22 June The waters. Fatigue. A visit to the doctor and a renewal of the tickets for the baths. After tea wrote a letter to N. F. Bath. Tebenkov. On the road to Torsk. Grosman's visit. Dinner. Arrangement of rooms for Modest and Kolya [Konradi]. The Mozart variation. Tea. A ring salesman and a decorator. With Panya and Tebenkov to Grand Duke Park. *"Please bring no dogs!"* Glorious view. By the time I took the waters, it was already dark. When we finished supper, Modest appeared unexpectedly. Kolya. About Litke and Kondratyev. Escorted them. Decided to move upstairs.

23 *June* The waters. Tea with Modest, not in my room this time but in the dining room. Walked with Modya in Vorontzovsky Park, on the main road and on the bridges. Bath. Dinner. A variation. Tea. Tebenkov. A stroll on the road upstream along the right bank of the Kura River. The waters. Supper. Rain. Conversation about carpets, collections, painters.

24 *June* Overslept. Tea in the new place for the first time, on my little balcony. Letters. On the way to the bath, met Panya. A stroll beyond my strength (I felt unusually weak today, having been awakened at night by terrible nightmares) via Elizaveta's Eye and straight home along the road. Dinner. Tebenkov. About literature. In my room upstairs. Thunderstorm. Fright. Modya visited. After tea we wanted to go for a drive, but it rained. Took the waters. Took a walk to the Armenian church in the mud. Read, at home, Emma's letter about N. D. K. (he is on the eve of departure abroad) and the newspapers. Before and after supper, also later on, talk about spiritualism and Englington. Candy. Rain. Tricks. Alexei constructed a screen.

25 *June* Weakness, but better in regard to constipation. Letters. Tebenkov at dinner. They arrived while I was working. Tolya and Kokodes. Tea. A stroll by the entire company to the mineral waters and on the Torsk road. It was very damp. Rainy day. Worked a little. After supper whist with Tebenkov.

26 *June* Slept on a spring bed and probably due to that feel somewhat better. After tea wrote letters (God! How this correspondence sickens me!). With Kolya Konradi at the baths. A stroll. A visit to the sick Pryanishnikov. A beautiful view from their place. After dinner worked and struggled with sleep. Tea in Vorontzovsky [Park]. From there to the waters. Elizaveta's Eye. Take the waters. Kokodes. Went home. I worked a little. Supper. Poor Tebenkov has a migraine headache. Whist in which Kolya Konradi took part.

27 *June* Slept better. Still the same thing: the waters, a stroll, tea, reading, letters. (Oh, those letters!) Bath. A stroll. Dinner. All day my stomach has been as before—bad. Was working. Tea. On foot with Tolya, Modya, Kolya Konradi and Kolya Peresleni (whom we met and dragged along with the promise of a phaeton) to the Likansky monastery. Very interesting. Tired. The waters with Kolya between nine and ten o'clock. After supper, whist in which Teben-

kov also took part. *Palm reading* (?!?! Is it possible?). I've lost confidence.

Sunday, 28 June A long excursion on the Torsk road. Dinner on the height. Became very tired. My health is not as good as at first. In general, the waters affect me rather poorly. Dined in the evening between six and seven o'clock and whist. Kolya had very bad luck.

29 June Not an especially happy Saint's day. After Mass and the bath, lunch at Bakradze's hotel. Solo stroll to the ruins. The guests whom we were expecting (Orlovsky and Karnovich) did not arrive. We dined alone (and, of course, Tebenkov and Kokodes). A stroll to the Black River. Whist. Departure. Throughout there sounded an unhappy tone. I sent a telegram to N. D. Kondratyev which inevitably would have to be delivered before his departure, but concealed that.

30 June Alexei is drunk and has a *katzenjammer*. Rose unusually early. It is cold! Worked. Bath. A stroll very far through the park. Read after dinner. After tea with Tolya, Modya, and Kolya in Grand Duke Park. The waters. Panya is with the ever present Tebenkov (perhaps he is an excellent person, but that everlasting tête à tête with Panya is beginning to annoy me). After supper a telegram from N. D. Kondratyev. Decide to go.[8] Whist with exertion. Tebenkov's departure. Errands given him.

1 July Feel bad; slept, it goes without saying, and rose with the roosters. The waters. Letters. After dinner nearly fell asleep on the divan downstairs. (Tata was entertaining us.) Slept in my room until tea. A stroll by the three of us (Tolya and Modya) on my restricted road. The waters. With Modya and Kolya at the children's ball. *Lezginka.* Acquaintance with a lady resembling Tanya. Supper and whist for a short time. Retired early and slept excellently.

2 July The waters. After tea was busy with the Mozart [Suite]. Suddenly a visit by three incredibly stupid gentlemen with a request for a chorus. What could be more stupid!!! All due to that unbearable Mr. Volshevsky. Hid my anger with difficulty. Bathing. A ride with Panya and Kolya to the very end of Mineral Waters Park. After dinner walked to the Black River and farther on the paved road. After tea rode with Panya and Modya to the same place

---

[8] *Kondratyev begged Tchaikovsky to visit him at Aachen, where the former had gone for medical treatment.*

to go boating. The mineral waters. Anxiety about *Kolya* who went horseback riding and had not yet returned. We went over there. Little by little the anxiety reached utter despair. It was nine o'clock when he finally appeared. We were sitting way beyond the eye hospital, in the darkness, when it happened. God! What happiness it was! Supper (the chef was dismissed and Stepan cooked!). Retired early. A professor came with some poems, before the ride. A fine fellow!

3 July Rose early. The waters. The usual shunning of General Yankovsky, etc. After tea had hardly commenced work when that unbearable and disgusting Mr. Volshevsky appeared. I controlled myself in every way in order not to insult him. Where can one run away from people like that??? Could hardly get rid of him. After the bath went home across the Vorontzovsky. The dinner Stepan prepared was very successful. Struggled with sleep after dinner and could hardly conquer it. After tea alone to the Vorontzovsky. Listened to the music from the Panin Eye. Running away from the public into the park. At home found a letter from Tebenkov and a passport for abroad. After supper short game of whist.

4 July The waters. Tea. Newspapers. In the *Novoye Vremya* I was called for the first time a "venerable" composer. Was angry. Letters. Bath. Tolya with Panya at the springs. To the Torsk road. Descended to the left toward the camp. After dinner worked on the *Ave verum.*[9] Kolya Peresleni arrived. Tea. To the Panin Eye. We were watching Tolya who was on the Torsk road. Down below. A juggler. Not a bad performance. *Pridanov and money.*[10] We had supper after the performance.

Sunday, 5 July Took the waters. Stepped in to see Dr. Heidemann. Bade good-by and paid. Home. Various business matters. The order to Alexei.[11] A stroll in Vorontzovsky Park. Visit to Professor Markovnikov. About eclipses. Home. Dinner. Heidemann and Pryanishnikov. Ice cream and cocoa. With Pryanishnikov looked through

---

[9] *Tchaikovsky utilized this work by Mozart in his suite.*

[10] *The composer borrowed money for his trip to Aachen, returning it when he received his funds from Mme. von Meck.*

[11] *Tchaikovsky explained to him about going to Pleshcheyevo, the residence of Mme. von Meck, for the funds. Mme. von Meck, fearing the inefficiency of the Russian postal service, suggested that the money be called for.*

the whole of *The Enchantress* and came to an agreement. Tea. A ride to the Green monastery. Guides. A Greek. Home. Guests at our place: Pryanishnikov with his wife and niece, Juzefovich, the singer (she turned out to be Stepova, a friend of Anna's) with her teacher. She sang. Very good voice. Supper.

TRIP FROM BORZHOM TO AACHEN

6 July The waters. We started out at ten o'clock. Tata (who was shy with me this morning) escorted us a little way. We rode in a carriage (Panya, Tolya, Kolya Peresleni, and I). Modest is ill and did not come. Talk about the Kondratyev family. Dinner at Mi-khailovka. The train. No seats, but I got into the car of an important person and rode in it as far as Batum. Bade good-by. With Tolya and Kolya as far as the Suram. Journey farther on. Read. It was good, but toward evening was seized with intense lonesomeness. Later it passed. I napped until we reached the sea. Admired the sea. Batum. Hôtel Impérial. Supper. Alongside Prince Chavchavadze, an important general, and his corps were having supper. Remember distinctly it all happened exactly ten years ago!!?? [12]

7 July (Batum.) After rising and drinking tea went off to ramble, while I charged the porter to get the tickets for the steamship. The garden by the sea in comparison with last year is overgrown and has a neglected appearance. Was in the harbor; drank Turkish coffee at a café. Walked on the shore along the railroad tracks and went as far as the battery. Excessive heat. At home wrote Panya a letter. Bath with Alesha. A coachman from the Orlov muzhiks. Lunch. Walked through the city again and drank Turkish coffee. Bought various things. Home. Tea. To the steamer. We sailed between five and six o'clock. On deck. Dinner soon after. (Fellow passengers: a gendarme with a stout, filthy wife and child (the same ones who got into my car yesterday); an Armenian family with long-nosed young ladies; a young man with black whiskers, mawkish and courting the young ladies; three indefinite gentlemen dressed in *tussah silk;* an elderly, foppish gentleman, recalling Count Shartrsky, acting aristocratic and youthful—that is all, I believe.) The captain dined with us. He resembles the late tsar, but is very short; extremely talkative, rather affable, although of limited intelligence it appears. The usual feeling of animosity toward passengers. After dinner, all the time on deck and talked only with

---

[12] *On July 6, 1877, Tchaikovsky's unfortunate marriage took place.*

Alesha. Beautiful sunset. Tea. Went to bed very early, at ten
o'clock. Slept so soundly that I did not even hear that we stopped
at Sukhum and unloaded. Ivan, the cabin steward, is extremely
attractive.

8 *July* Rose between seven and eight o'clock. Drank tea alone.
Read on deck the talentless *Moscow Conflagration* of Danilevsky.
Went downstairs to my cabin—was about to start reading *Pugachev*
[*and his Associates*] by Dubrovin but fell asleep immediately and
slept about an hour. That is strange. Wrote the diary and letters
in the salon. I managed to sit at the end during lunch; talked to no
one, and achieved complete seclusion, which, however, depresses
me at times. So I seem to sail between the devil and the deep blue
sea, having—at the same time—an indescribable repugnance and
horror toward *making acquaintances* and yet a feeling of depression
in solitude. Walked, read, killed time any way. Drank tea at two
o'clock. At four-thirty, dinner. In expectation of the sunset walked
on deck in the bow. Kept an eye on the passengers. After tea
waited impatiently to go down to my cabin. We were approaching
Kerch; I did not wait and left. But my sleep was poor. Something
like an itching nettle rash over my whole body was torturing me.
Ivan came to shut the porthole as we were loading coal. Poorly,
but slept the night through somehow.

9 *July* Rose at six-thirty o'clock. We were lying in sight of Kerch.
From a distance it produces on me an impression of an ancient
Greek city. It is hot. Sat on deck all the time after tea. Eyed what
was going on about us. (The pretty blonde and stout wife of the
captain's assistant.) A small ship arrived with new passengers. Went
to walk in my cabin, like a tiger in a cage. Quite a number of curious types are sailing with us. The youthful acting bewhiskered
gentleman (a Pole?)—why is he alone? And that swarthy Russian
(a type like Shakhovsky) chattering continuously with the Armenian young ladies and evoking constant laughter from the older of
them, the plump and gossipy one! But these Armenian young ladies
themselves (attractive, however)?!! And the gentleman like the
Klimenko type? And the retired colonel from Baku? And the Sukhum gentleman, either a Jew or a Russian, telling much about
Ashinov? etc., etc. And all of them behave as though they were
antagonistic toward me. The weather was hot and stifling while we
were lying in the shipyard. We set sail during lunchtime (very
late). Lots of new passengers. I was sitting, at first, by the column,

facing the captain, then transferred to the very end of the last table. A father with his daughter; a thin, sickly looking clerk; a sprightly, handsome old Greek (a bit of a braggart), etc. After lunch and coffee hid in my kennel doing physical exercises. Exchange of pleasant words with the captain, unexpectedly. Tea. Dinner. Theodosia. A long walk with Alesha. A talk with an old porter in an upper cottage. The Aivazovsky Gallery. Ridiculous, this Aivazovsky and his laughable gallery. We sat in a restaurant by the seashore; we drank tea. On board ship. After sailing at ten o'clock, I turned in and soon lay down to sleep.

10 July Woke at five o'clock from the noise of the chains. We were lying in Yalta. Dressed, rode across to the city, and walked through it considerably. Flowers. Returned at seven o'clock and drank tea. Stayed long on deck before and after the ship's departure. A huge number of new passengers. Three Frenchmen (very elegant), a gendarme with his wife and child, explaining very courteously all that we were passing. Livadia, Orianda, Alupka, etc. Went down to the dining room and wrote the diary. At lunch there was an immense crowd of people. I sat at the very end of the table and opposite me were the youthful acting Pole and a lame colonel, with both of whom I talked for the first time. Sevastopol. It is hot. Hardly found Shpazhinskaya. She saw me off. We sailed at three o'clock. Newspapers. Dinner. Opposite me the Frenchmen. I talked with them. We were sailing along nicely. In the evening a conversation with the handsome old Greek. Smart. Went to bed early.

11 July Alesha awoke me at five o'clock. At night I kept waking up from the tossing and the squeaking. At six o'clock we began to near Odessa. Very beautiful city. We stopped at the Hôtel du Nord. I did not feel well. Later, when I strolled through the wonderful city, it was all right. Lunched excellently with Alesha. Walked long through the main streets. Hesitation as to when and how to travel farther. Home. Tormented to hot tears by lonesomeness. It is sad to think of Borzhom and sad to part with Alesha. Tea. A stroll with Alesha. Down below, in the harbor. Dinner. We got a little drunk. In the municipal garden. Mr. Lenk's orchestra. They played pretty well and it was a fair program. Kozlov's chorus; their songs and dances. Went home via the quay. Retired at eleven o'clock.

12 July We rose at eight o'clock. Telegram from N. D. K. After the newspapers and tea, as well as futile searching through railroad

timetables (we are all mixed up), went to church. The cathedral
is grand but not pleasing. The singing is insignificant; the selections
are simply shocking. As always, I was angry because of the singing.
Only in a village can one listen to deacons without being angry.
The weather turned bad. Strolled during the rain and sat in a café
on the boulevard. Home. Wept from lonesomeness. Departure. It
was horrible to part with Alesha. I am in a compartment with a
Jew and with a very young, dark, Odessa Englishman. The J. was
led away somewhere. I remained for the night with the youth, very
attractive. Slept well. Volochisk. Confiscation of one hundred cigarettes.

13 July Departure. In my part of the car are a youth, a pair just
married, and a gentleman, who turns out to be Vrangel.[13] Am despairing beyond compare. But got used to it. All the same, I read
more than talked. Dinner in the diner in Lemberg. Boredom and
lonesomeness. Cracow. Supper. The seats were opened up; slept
with difficulty.

14 July, Vienna Got rid of Vrangel who invited me to go with him
to the Grand Hôtel. Goldenes Lamm.[14] Read the newspapers and
drank coffee. Walked through the city. Bought various things. It
is hot. Lunch. The waiter recognized me and was so courteous that
I considered it my duty to buy a tremendous amount of cigarettes
from him. Departure at four o'clock. Bade good-by to the Odessa
Englishman. Rode in a sleeping car. In the compartment with me is
a Hungarian. At first I avoided conversation; later it was necessary;
very much so, in fact. Passau. The customs. Wine. A stupid but
kind conductor.

15 July Rose early. Inconvenience. The incident with the ticket.
The Hungarian. A fussy old man for a neighbor. The road is along
the Rhine. Cologne. Washed, left my things in the lavatory and
went for a stroll. Dinner at a small restaurant. Loafed about the city
and killed time. Departed at six o'clock. Arrived in Aachen at eight.
Neubad.[15] The meeting with Sasha[16] and N. D. Joy. A good im-

---

[13] *He and Tchaikovsky were together at law school and had last seen
each other in 1859 when the latter graduated.*

[14] *The Viennese hotel where the composer stayed.*

[15] *The establishment in Aachen where Kondratyev and Tchaikovsky
stayed.*

[16] *Kondratyev's valet, Sasha Legoshin.*

pression. Conversation and recounting of all endured by poor N. D. He is awfully thin, but is a whole lot more cheerful. When he went to sleep, I had supper and chatted with Sasha. We returned between one and two o'clock. Nice room.

AACHEN

16 July After drinking tea, reading the newspapers, and dressing, went to N. D. The doctor. I was waiting for him in order to find out the truth. *"Il est sauvé!"* My happiness. Letter to Modya. Dinner at the Grand Monarque at a separate table. A stroll. A ride in a landau with N. D., Sasha, and Pick. Beer. On returning, I went for a stroll alone. Supper in N. D.'s room. The doctor and his lengthy discussion. After ten o'clock I left for my place and then went to drink beer with Sasha. Conversation about the ailing one, Mary, and so forth.

17 July Rose at seven o'clock. Drank tea and read the newspapers a long time. Letter to Emma. At N. D.'s. He looks worse today and his spirits were low all day. He quarreled with Sasha in my presence. Went with Sasha to buy him and N. D. hats. A short stroll. Dinner at the Grand Monarque. Three lads are awfully attractive to me. Girls. Took a walk in the heat. At four o'clock we started out in a landau. A long ride in the suburbs. N. D. was very irritable and gloomy practically all the time. The wooden tower that I ascended with Sasha. Beautiful view. On returning, took a stroll. Tea was later, as the doctor was changing the dressing. At tea, N. D. was terribly depressed as a result of the removal of the abscess and the operation. Afterward, I succeeded *décider* him. See, more and more, that I was very necessary to him and that I did a good deed by coming.

18 July After tea started the orchestration of the Gigue [of the Suite]. At N. D.'s. He is more cheerful today, although very uneven. At ten o'clock went strolling. Suddenly the lower part of my abdomen began to pain severely. Walked about the city with difficulty. At home, napped on the little divan right up to dinnertime. Took a bath. Dined, after all, as well as a healthy person. A ride to Lousberg. Unsuccessful attempts. . . . As a result of that N. D. was very cranky and in a bad mood. On returning, went to the bank to get my money. Visited N. D. Supper (a commotion.) Talks with the doctor about Laroche. A frightful thunderstorm. N. D. was very irritable with Pick.

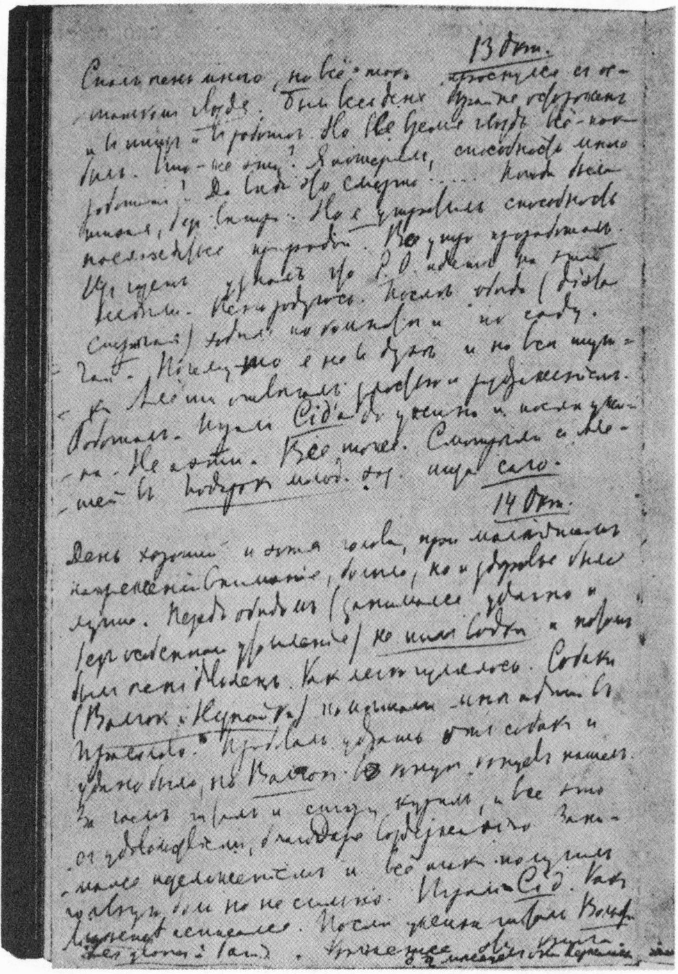

Last manuscript page of Diary Four

Sunday, 19 July Rose at the usual time. Nine-thirty at N. D.'s. He slept poorly and, on the whole, he has become worse than he was three days ago. Strolled. A procession. Watched from our street. Wrote letters downstairs at N. D.'s. He dozed and was weak and melancholy. Went to look for a mattress for him: his whole bed is disarranged. After dinner (*Moselle-mousseux*) went to the garden. Due to the races no one was there and I had a good walk. Returning, visited N. D., read *Une vie*.[17] N. D. was dozing all the time, but said that he feels more calm and better than yesterday. Took a stroll. Supper. Schuster came and stayed awfully long. Talk about various treatments and the new discoveries in medicine. After N. D. went off to sleep, I was with Sasha at the exhibition (beer) and in the Viennese café (beer).

20 July Rose at the usual time. Sasha, at N. D.'s. He slept poorly. A stroll to the Zoological Garden. Sat at N. D.'s and wrote letters. N. D. napped and was delirious. Bath. Dinner (too hearty). Had a beautiful stroll, past the gates and near the forest, where it had a village smell. At four-fifteen was at N. D.'s. Found Mr. Moravsky there. Then N. D. napped again. Ordered shoes and bought others. The doctor. Before that, a whole scene of N. D.'s terrible rage at Sasha on account of the beer and especially at poor Pick. In general, N. D. has become worse, more irritable. I think that the situation is bad again. The doctor is very solicitous and painstaking. Went to drink *Maiwein* with Sasha. Illumination at Clirenbrunnen.

21 July Finished the Gigue in the morning. At N. D.'s. He slept poorly again. When he went for the bath, I started out for a stroll and landed in the Zoological Garden again. The lions with a dog, parrots, and monkeys. Bought a knife for N. D. and neckties for myself. At N. D.'s. Bathing. Dinner. A walk. Coffee twice. In Hochstrasse, some repulsive man pestered me trying to get acquainted. A ride. N. D. is in a good mood, but between him and Pick there is a stupid hostility. N. D. constantly quarrels with him and that affects me painfully. It will end with some serious quarrel; indeed, it nearly happened this evening, but didn't. Visit by Radziwill. I strolled. The doctor before supper. *Stukolka* with Sasha. I had good luck. N. D. became tired and quarreled with Pick. I left early to go to sleep.

---

[17] *By de Maupassant.*

22 *July* A cool night and a cool day. Sasha came, conversed and drank tea. Letters. Went to N. D. Informed him about the death of Katkov. The doctor arrived while I was there. Went walking. Went to Lousberg. Watched the sights. Home. At N. D.'s. Bathing. Dinner, etc. Returning, was getting ready to work, but Moravsky appeared. Had to converse. Shortly after that took a walk and did a little work. N. D. is still the same: naps, weak, but not angry today at Pick. He is worried about *fluctuation*. A letter today from Alesha and many others. The doctor. I am upstairs. Supper. *Stukolka*. I am now home and am remorseful about something. The idea of this remorse is: life passes, is coming to an end while I have reached no conclusions; I banish vital problems, or run away from them when they arise. Is that how I live? Am I acting right? For instance, now: I am here and everybody is admiring my *sacrifice*. But there is no sacrifice at all. I am complacent, am a glutton at the table d'hôte, do nothing and spend money on nonsense, when others are in need of necessities. Am I not a real egoist? Even as regards close ones, I am not what I ought to be.

23 *July* Today N. D. was operated on. He was very excited all morning. Schuster appeared while I was present and said that he would come with the surgeon in an hour. I encouraged the poor sick man and left for my room upstairs. All was over quickly and well. Went to him. Waited afterward for some clothes. After the bath put on the new clothes. Dinner (an attractive family) at the center table. A walk beyond the city. Home, sat at N. D.'s and was finishing the *Menuet* [of the Suite]. He was dozing. My bill. Herr Klassen. N. D. requested that they reduce my bill. A walk. Found Schuster at N. D.'s. We had supper after him. *Stukolka*. N. D. is more cheerful and more fresh.

24 *July* An unpleasant, sad day. In the morning N. D. was in a good mood. After a stroll I sat in his room and worked; he was writing letters. After dinner and a walk, I found him talking with Sasha saying that there was really no improvement. He cried bitterly. Oh, how painful it was! What I said to him I no longer remember; only little by little did he become more calm. Moravsky came and chattered long, tiring us. Took a short walk. We waited for the doctor. Supper. The doctor was late. A prolonged discussion from which N. D. received some reassurance, but a terrible sadness

fell upon me. *Ramsch.*[18] God, how sad I am! Want to rail at my
fate—but am ashamed!

25 July Yesterday I overindulged in alcohol. Did not sleep well
and felt bad in the morning. Poor N. D. did not sleep at all. Strolled.
Worked at N. D.'s. He was to lie down to sleep in his bed after
the bouillon but did not sleep. After dinner, went to the Rosenbad,
at N. D.'s request, to find out about the apartment and the terms.
Looked over everything. A ride in a landau to Lousberg. Read at
home. Took a short walk and bought a pineapple. Schuster. Rather
calming talk. Supper. *Ramsch.* I was unusually bored and my
nerves were capricious. Though N. D. did not complain of his fate
today, still I feel sorrier for him than ever.

Sunday, 26 July Slept well. Sasha at teatime. N. D., it turned out,
slept not badly. I went to Mass at the cathedral. I do not like the
Catholic service. It is quite different from ours. A walk. N. D. took
a bath (*Schwitzbad*) today; I saw him perspiring in bed. After
dinner (I was in new clothes) I walked with difficulty to the Pontthor. At four o'clock a drive to the forest. The heat abated as the
sun hid behind the clouds. It was pleasant. We were watching the
archery. Arriving home, N. D. felt a terrible tiredness. I went to
take a stroll on the promenade. Beautiful views. Returning, found
N. D. terribly disturbed. He cried awfully and expressed his gratitude to me unusually fervently. After tears relief came. We sat
down to play after supper. Kobchik came late. We played in his
presence. *Moselle-mousseux.*

Monday, 27 July An accident happened with my bowels. . . .
No sooner did I sit down to drink tea when Sasha came in. I like
Sasha, but like still more . . . to be alone in the morning. Hid my
displeasure. N. D. slept poorly. At his place. A foot bath. A walk
straight across the Pontthor and up the hill to Lousberg. They were
enjoyable moments. At N. D.'s. He took a foot bath while I was
there. Then he lay down and perspired. I worked a little. Bathing.
Dinner. Lack of appetite and a kind of endless boredom gripped
me. After walking a little, went home. N. D. slept soon after I came.
Shirts. Home. N. D., having slept, became very cheerful. Supper.
A game. The doctor. A game again. N. D. was sulking at me as I
had good luck. Parted very coldly and he answered ironically to a

---

[18] *German card game (skat).*

sympathetic question of mine. I left for a walk. Punch. Home. Fuss with a new shirt.

28 July N. D. slept excellently, Sasha informed me when he came between nine and ten o'clock. At his place. A walk to Lousberg on the usual road. Home. N. D. had a foot bath; he perspired freely. Became emotional. I finished making the markings in the Suite. Bath. Dinner. The son of the lame lady. Coffee. A stroll. Home. N. D. is exhausted from perspiring and is complaining. Napped. Moravsky came. An odd chap. Walked a bit. Watched some Russians going to the juggling exhibition. Home. N. D. is still exhausted. The doctor. He is satisfied. *Ramsch.* I had two glasses of punch in a café. Home. Had attacks of lonesomeness.

29 July Sasha, making his morning call, informed me that N. D. slept excellently. I found him rather happy in expectation of the doctor. Walked to Lousberg again on the same road, making some deviations. N. D.'s foot bath. He perspired little, and became very angry at Hubert when the latter said that there was little perspiration. The perspiration came; he was happy again. My bath. Dinner. Strolled. At four o'clock found N. D. in a very tolerable state of mind. He napped. I talked with Sasha in his room. We have come to the conclusion that things look bad. I went for a walk. Payment to Cook's Tours. Coming home, found N. D. very low in spirits. Long weeping. Singular tenderness toward Sasha. The doctor found him crying. The doctor, as usual, pacified him, but kept making mistakes and contradicting himself. However, it turned out all right. At supper the appetite appeared. All the rest of the evening N. D. was very cheerful. A game.

30 July Sasha came during teatime. N. D. slept well. The calomel reacted strongly. Sat a little while in his room. He is very yellow and weak. A walk. It is cold. Home. N. D. suffered from colic—the result of the calomel. He could hardly last until the bouillon. Slept. My bath. Dinner. A walk. Found Moravsky at N. D.'s. A singular chatterer. Even though N. D. speaks about him with scorn, yet he is glad when he visits him. N. D. said, during the day, that he is better, that he breathes more freely, but later on he began to suffer. Prince Radziwill. I took a stroll. On returning, found N. D. in terrible agony. Before supper, weeping again. I understand him: he abhors the death that approaches him—and I too abhor it deeply. The doctor during the weeping. A gradual calming. While the doctor was there, we had supper. The kind doctor calmed the sick one. A game. *Monsieur le chef* and talks with him. A game again. I strolled. Swedish punch.

31 July Rose early. Sasha. At N. D.'s. He felt well despite the imminent operation. I took a long walk outside the city on a beautiful road in the direction of the mountains. When I returned the operation was over. N. D. was in a most pleasant state of mind. Unfortunate man! If he knew how futile are his hopes! All day he was in a good mood. I sat in his place and almost forgot about the bath. Dinner. A walk. At N. D.'s. He was enraptured with his dinner and evidently drank too much. Agony. Toward evening it was again a little trying for him, but less than before. I decided to drop a word regarding Paris. It was all right.[19] The doctor came early. Unde spoke with me privately. I understood little of the details, but did understand that although there is hope, it is still very bad. *Ramsch* with an effort. Coffee. Punch.

1 August Sasha at my place. Sad talks. Letters. At N. D.'s. He was still in his bedroom. The doctor. I left for a stroll. Returning, found him under the effects of a strong dose of mercury. His heart was palpitating; his head as if in the clouds. A new plan for his meals upon my advice. At twelve o'clock, lunch. At one o'clock I left to bathe. Returning, found him in bed feeling very cheerful. Moravsky. The urine flowed well today. His dinner. His gauntness and yellow color surprised me. He had a good appetite. I lay down. Found that he had enjoyed his food thoroughly. We conversed. There were no hysterics at all. The doctor. One cannot make out: is he glad or not? My supper. *Ramsch.* N. D. became tired and dozed. I am with Sasha in a café. Swedish punch. Sasha is somewhat strange.

PARIS

Sunday, 2 August Departure for Paris at 10 A.M. At N. D.'s. Excitement at the railroad station. In the compartment with me, a Rumanian (fussy) and an attractive German. Verviers. Lunch. Reading of Tolstoy. Paris at seven o'clock. The Belards. Surprise and joy. Vermouth. Conversation. Dinner in the Café Riche. Near

---

[19] *The composer felt he had to seek relief, if only for a few days, in Paris.*

the Alcazar. Everything the same. Café de la Paix. Grog. Home. Brandukov.

3 August According to their calendar, it was the fifteenth, the Assumption of the Virgin Mary, and everything was closed. Did not find Mackar. Home. Brandukov. With him to Mackar again. He is definitely not in. Lunch at the Sylvain. I was in Bicêtre. The Auclairs were very happy. Tears. Went home practically all the way on foot. Dinner with Brandukov and Botkin in the Dîner de Paris. *Café chantant.* Café de la Paix. Very tired.

4 August At Mackar's. Found him in. His joy and kisses. Conversation. Lunch in the Riche. Roamed about and made purchases. At two-thirty at Mackar's again. Mme. Mackar. A walk. Home. Packing. Mackar, Brandukov and Botkin dined at my place. Seeing off. Excitement. Drunkenness. Uninteresting fellow passengers. Slept with difficulty.

AACHEN

5 August Fruit and cake at the customs. Home. Sasha. Tea. Slept but tossed about. At N. D.'s. He is very weak and goes from bad to worse. Dizziness. Walked. Bath. Dinner. Walked. Home at four o'clock. N. D. awfully weak and his gums hurt. However, had an appetite at dinner. The doctor. The gums were cauterized. *Ramsch* with indifference. *Gewerbe Ausstellung.* Wrote the diary for four days at home.

6 August Rose late. Sasha did not come. All that is the result of the steaming and the changes he has made in his manner of living. At ten o'clock found N. D. having coffee. We waited for the bath. The doctor. I walked a little. Home. As a result of d [drinking] or I do not know what, I departed from my *habitus* and slept until one o'clock. Bath. At N. D.'s. He is soso. Dinner. A short walk. At N. D.'s. He was writing letters and was, on the whole, stronger and better than yesterday. For dinner he did not have the appetite he had yesterday—however, for a sick person it was not bad. During dinner, he spoke in a very disturbing way about himself, even something about suicide. But at the same time spoke about both life in St. Petersburg and treatment by Vrevsky. I walked. The doctor came in at the same time I did. A strange relationship between us. The news about the bed which must replace the *baths* gladdened N. D. very much, to such an extent that he grew angry with me when I said there would be baths later on. I had supper at his place. Afterward *Ramsch* and all the while N. D. was in a good mood. Still he was sleepy. At nine-fifty left for a walk. Viennese café. *Schlummerpunsch*. *Figaro* and *Le Gaulois*. A talk with the *Ober-kellner* about punches. Purchase of Swedish punch.

7 *August* A very hard day. After waking with a headache, drinking tea, and talking a little with Sasha, went downstairs. Found N. D. at coffee. His expression is not good. Stayed a while. A short walk. Found N. D. very weak and extremely short of breath. At lunch he had no appetite. It is generally bad and goes from bad to worse. At times it seemed that any moment would be the end. After my dinner and walk, found him still weaker and decidedly in a bad condition. Stayed with him. Unexpected rage at me. Even though one must not be angry, yet I was awfully *froid,* and all the more because his unjust and impossible attitude toward Pick this morning was terribly painful to me. It was over later but not easily. Pity got the upper hand. He was suffering horribly. After dinner the pain in the gums became worse. Frightful hysterics. He felt better when the doctor came. The bed from Düsseldorf. Calmed down. I had supper downstairs in an empty room. Schuster. *Ramsch*. A walk. Swedish punch at home with Sasha. Embarrassing.

8 *August* N. D. is a whole lot better. A very good day for him on the whole. Due to the steaming and his reaction to it, he at once became better. I received Modest's interesting letter about Tzkhra-Tzkaro.[20] Walked to Lousberg by my route. Wrote Slavina, who requests some changes in the part of the Princess.[21] Walked after dinner. At four o'clock N. D. *perspiring* in the new perspiration bed. My long conversation with Mlle. Tasbender. N. D. perspired. He is completely cheered up. Walked before supper. Came at the end of the doctor's visit. Supper. *Leberwurst. Ramsch.* How grudging and cruel I am! Ashamed to confess why I write this. Read *Le Matin* and an excerpt in it from an article in the *Moskovskiye Vedomosti,* where it is proven that Katkov liked the Germans. After all that's happened, it is unpleasant to me.

Sunday, 9 August N. D. slept well. Went to Mass at the cathedral, they sang something in the style of Palestrina and very well. Coffee at the railroad station. Home. N. D. in the perspiration bed. During

---

[20] *Tiny hamlet in Transcaucasia.*

[21] *In his opera,* The Enchantress.

my visit there was no perspiration. Went away upstairs and was waiting nervously. The perspiration came after an hour had passed. Thank God! Was at N. D.'s during his lunch. An enormous appetite. N. D. in the best of spirits. Dinner and a walk. (Watched a mouse in a store window.) Bought N. D. a melon and some other food, and busied myself about his oysters. His dinner. After dinner he is in an unusually good state of mind and talks about his sickness as something entirely gone. His absolute belief is a bit unpleasant to me. How many disappointments there have been already! I took a short stroll. Supper. A game. The doctor. He played with us. Punch with Sasha in a café. Cold weather.

10 August N. D. slept poorly. In the morning I found him looking worse than yesterday. Strolled along my favorite route and saw the arrival of the express train. Lousberg. I was in the *steam* room at N. D.'s. It went badly. I left for my room and after staying a while went down to N. D. He was still in the steam room. I was very worried about the perspiration; even my own nerves were upset. Finally learned from Sasha that there was perspiration. With N. D. during lunch. He is in a bad mood today as the urine is bad and Schuster had told him, for some reason, how surprised the surgeon was that he had not died yet. Bath. Dinner. Drank coffee in the Elisenbrunnen, the Viennese coffee has become repulsive. At N. D.'s. He is worse than yesterday. His dinner. Has an appetite. Read the splendid *Thousand Souls* by Pisemsky. Took a short walk. It is cold. The doctor. My supper. During the game I felt tired, nervous, and irritable with everybody.

11 August Well, what an evening! Sasha's abdomen hurt and terribly severely. Disturbed by this, N. D. was so disgustingly furious and unjust with Pick that neither pity for his condition nor the knowledge that Pick is in fact clumsy and not very bright could suppress the indignation I felt. I had to go away. N. D. aroused painful thoughts in me in general. His egoism and lack of real kindness assert themselves so harshly and in such a disagreeable form that I no longer have any feeling for him now, except pity. Will I tear myself away soon from this hell? The moment when I was with Sasha during the vomiting, while beside us N. D. was shouting and carping at Pick, was horrible. Well, why write it down? It cannot be forgotten! The day was soso. Even though N. D. both perspired and ate a good deal, yet it seems to me, for all that, everything is going bad!!! In the morning, I went to Burt-scheid, then became enthusiastic and went to Siegel. In the forest and in the fields experienced beautiful moments. It hurts and vexes me that I can't help being surprised and indignant at N. D. But it is beyond me.

12 August It passed. Sasha is better today. Although N. D. says he did not sleep at night yet he did not feel badly. I took a walk to Siegel again and drank coffee in the *grove* once more. Returning, found N. D. after perspiring. There was perspiration. He was wait-ing for Schuster. I went to my room and worked a little on the violoncello piece.[22] Downstairs. Bathing. Dinner. Exchanged smiles with the lovely Spanish children. There was no *Campo Sangrado* today. Coffee in the Elisenbrunnen. About four Russian young per-sons today. A walk. Home. N. D. dozed in the easy chair and coughed terribly. I wrote Emma (about Sasha's fifteen thousand). The doctor. Supper. *Ramsch.* A quarrel with Pick again. *Ramsch.* At nine-thirty, N. D. retired. I was at the *Wintergarten* on the Hochstrasse and drank grog. Boring.

13 August An abominable day. N. D. was all right in the morning. I took a walk and, on returning, found him at lunch, not like yester-day but in a very bad mood, as there was very little perspiration. His frame of mind is vile and everybody is to blame because he is worse. My talk with Mlle. Tasbender and her friend. She disclosed to me who Schuster is. It turns out he's obnoxious . . . nothing less, even though good as a doctor. N. D. had wished to take a ride and I came at four o'clock, but he was sleeping. I told Sasha the opinions of other doctors regarding perspiring. Walked some more. N. D. was in a sleepy mood all the time, both before and after dinner (he said he had no appetite but ate a good deal). During the doc-tor's visit, he behaved as though we all, and especially the doctor, had conspired to let him die in Aachen. It was awfully painful and unpleasant, all the more so because the doctor was really making mistakes, contradicting himself and finally provoking us with his pronouncement that the disease might last *three months.* I tried in every way to help the situation, but managed poorly. *Ramsch,* all the same. I was lucky. N. D. was angry. Punch in the Viennese

---

[22] Pezzo Capriccioso for *'cello and orchestra, Op. 62, dedicated to Tchaikovsky's friend, Brandukov.*

café. Terrible time. Had a telegram from Zasyadko; [23] he asks when to come. My nerves were very upset. Drank too much. Vomited.

14 August N. D. is better today, but still not the way he was some days ago. I remained a while with him. He sulked a bit on account of yesterday. Took a walk on the Jacob Strasse. Home. Was present at N. D.'s lunch. Unsuccessful (Tartar beefsteak). Bath. Dinner. Coffee in the Elisenbrunnen. Home at four o'clock. N. D. in the garden. His gauntness amazed me. Modest's story. N. D.'s dinner. Sat with him the whole time. Finished the sketch of the violoncello piece. Supper in room number six. The doctor. Today the roles changed: the doctor is not entirely satisfied, N. D. is completely so. *Ramsch.* A kind of unusual boredom oppressed me. The telegram to Zasyadko was sent.

15 August A very hot day. Downstairs at N. D.'s. He complains of terrible weakness. Nevertheless, he walked three times around the room with me. A walk on Lüschmirovsky Highway. It is hard to breathe (it happens frequently to me now). Dropped in at a modest tavern; drank beer. Was very worried about the question: would there be any perspiration or not? The perspiration turned out to be splendid. Was present at N. D.'s lunch. Bath. Near to me was a man with a woman—they were English. Dinner. Coffee in the Elisenbrunnen. A walk. Home. Still the same endless procrastination. Copied the violoncello piece. Supper. The doctor. He's a *liar. Ramsch.* A hellish, frightful homesickness and impatience amounting to a desperate desire to leave. Café Küppers. *Dissipated.* Home in the darkness. God! There are still ten days to live in this hell!!!

Sunday, 16 August N. D. much worse since morning. Strange! Yesterday the perspiring and the urine were good! He is in utter despair. Cannot describe the scenes that took place, surely, I will never forget them. Doctor Schuster. N. D.'s demand to say *yes* or *no.* Schuster displayed much strength and bluntness in this instance. The consultation. Doctor Meier. I ran to the apothecary. Inconceivable nervousness. After the consultation somehow everything got better. However, dined without enjoyment and could hardly drag my feet for a walk. And in addition to all that, the *feeling* in my left side becomes constant as soon as I am upset. Found N. D.

---

[23] *Kondratyev's nephew. The composer had written his brother Modest asking: "What do you think about Zasyadko? Should not I write him to relieve me?"*

making himself walk with Sasha. Torturing hours. A strange thing!
I was completely depressed by *horror* and *lonesomeness,* but not
by *pity!!!* It may be due to the fact that N. D. displays fear and
faintheartedness toward death, and even though I myself may be
just as cowardly in regard to death, when he starts to *whine* in
despair like a child or a woman, I am more frightened than pitying.
But in the meantime, God, how he suffers!!! And why I am so bitter
—I do not understand. Yes! I know that I am not wicked nor hardhearted. But it is my nerves and *egoism* that whisper louder and
louder in my ear, "Leave, do not torture yourself, take care of yourself!" . . . About departure, I still dare not even think. Drank after
the doctor's visit (*compresse échauffante* and calomel) and a short
game of *Ramsch.* Punch in the Elisenbrunnen and in the Viennese
café.

17 August Sasha informed me that N. D. is better. And he really
was better today than yesterday—but, my God, how bad off he is!
Waited long in Sasha's room during the dressing. Sat a while.
Walked! Wrote out the piece for the violoncello at N. D.'s. He is
quiet, calm and humble today. I pity him more when he is in that
condition. My dinner. A stroll. At four o'clock at N. D.'s. He is still
so meek and pitiful today. There was no appetite. I worked in his
place. A talk with Dremel. At N. D.'s. My supper. Sasha came.
Sasha worries me. He is fatally melancholy; it is clear that he is
suffering terribly. Why if he becomes sick—it would be the most
horrible tragedy!!! *Ramsch* was dull. N. D. was dozing. Sasha was
melancholy. I left at nine-thirty. Theater. Boring and loathsome
German filth. In a café. Punch did not help—I am awfully upset
just the same and *something* worries me more and more in my left
side. A week from today I hope to be on the eve of departure.

18 August Today, the ray of freedom beamed on me, for I will
not be here *any longer* in a week. There is egoism, of course,
in this; but I really suffer terribly and mornings it seems to me
that I am quite sick and will not last. At N. D.'s there was a consultation today. I ran off, being afraid of excitement and a repetition
of Sunday's horrors. Returning, found N. D. and Sasha in silence
in the reception room; near by, the doctors were deliberating. I ran
off again upstairs, foreseeing something evil. Actually, Meier had
the heart to tell N. D. that he is very bad off. His despair. Luckily
Schuster said that he does not share Meier's opinion. That calmed
N. D. for the whole day. But God, how terribly bad he is! Return-

ing from dinner and a walk (eyeing of Russians in the Elisenbrunnen) I found N. D. in the *Schwitzbett*. How pitiful he was! At Sasha's, who is ill and depressed. After the steaming (unsuccessful) N. D. experienced an awful weakness. His dinner. Appetite. He drank half a bottle of champagne and became drunk. All this is terribly painful. The dentist and his delicate treatment of the dying man. My supper. *Ramsch* a complete failure (after a short visit by Schuster), as N. D. was dozing all the time. Sasha is upset to the last degree. N. D. stubbornly wanted to play, although he actually did not have strength enough to hold the cards. I went off disturbed, but the *ray* continued to gleam. Eyeing of Russians (a thin Polish type of gentleman, a handsome, slim one with beautiful hands and a blond one, sweetly good-looking, uncertain whether he was their comrade or not). Landed in a concert on the Hartmannstrasse. Home.

19 August Sasha made me happy in the morning with the news that N. D. slept well and that he is better in general. However, in the course of the day the improvement was extremely relative. He was quiet and submissive. In such a condition, he especially arouses my pity. Wanted to cry at times. His only joy now is *food*, but even for that, the spark, i.e. the appetite, was lacking today. As a matter of fact, I wept a little, while working on the orchestration of the piece ('cello), when he tried to relish his food and could not. . . . In the morning after a walk waited for Schuster and had a talk with him; he has not lost hope. Sasha is better today. After dinner and a walk sat at N. D.'s and was writing. At seven o'clock, while I went to wash my hands, Stroganov appeared and stayed a whole hour. And Schuster came while he was there. I had supper upstairs in my place. Coming down, found Schuster. *Ramsch*. N. D. was not sleepy and was in a rather excited condition. At ten o'clock I went walking; was drinking afterward in the Viennese café. Lying in bed, I began to think about N. D., about his endless agony and suffering, and sobbed for a long time like a child. Somehow today he is especially pitiful.

20 August Rose with a little headache. The whole day went very badly. N. D. was weak and suffered from difficult breathing. It was settled that I would come as soon as possible after dinner and decide whether or not I would be at the *Schwitzbett*. Returning at three o'clock, I arranged with Sasha not to allow the steaming, but N. D. wanted it no matter what happened. Sasha's face today, particularly at that moment, was so terribly pale that I trembled at the thought that he would get sick. The *Schwitzbett* took place. I was there. There was no perspiration but Zimmermann and Hubert lied to him that there was. After that, N. D. had such a spell of coughing, and was gasping so, that I thought that he was dying. Frightened me. I ran for water. Later it was better. He dined without enjoyment. We waited for the doctor. He came at eight o'clock, then at ten, and afterward I went out with him and spoke about N. D.; after that, he wanted to go back once more with me and find out what the reaction of the antipyrine was. Thank God! N. D. was sleeping. Conversation with Sasha.

21 August An abominable day for N. D. although in the morning it was not bad. I received a letter, a scolding letter, from Mary, which angered me very much. At N. D.'s. A stroll. A consultation. Mlle. Tasbender warned Doctor Meier and this time he did not alarm N. D. My dinner. Returning, found Count Stroganov at N. D.'s. The chattering of the former about music and about Russian gloom, in particular. N. D. is very weak. There was practically no urine. He had no appetite. Now and then he was complaining and crying. Agonizing, horrible hours! Oh, never will I forget all that was suffered here. I had supper with Sasha and treated him, poor fellow, to oysters. A talk with the amiable Tasbender about Schuster, Dremel, etc. N. D. informed us that he had decided on the draining of water. We played a little *Ramsch*. Pick is very much out of favor. A walk.

22 August A hard day! In the morning "acupuncture" was decided upon (draining of the water). I was so excited that I wandered through Aachen like mad, had the idea of drinking four glasses of beer and had to pay dearly for it. When I came, the operation was over. N. D. felt, of course, greatly relieved, but is very weak. I was too late for the dinner at our place and dined at Klüppel's. Coming home, felt a pain, had diarrhea, and was nauseated. It became worse and worse and finally I began to get awfully sick. The doctor came twice. Sasha called many times, also kind Josephine. A disgusting condition. The swallowing of ice. Toward night it was better. I slept feverishly, but slept nevertheless.

Sunday, 23 August Woke practically well. Tea. Went downstairs. The doctor. Expectation of Zasyadko; his arrival. N. D.'s joy. Conversation. I went with Mitya [Zasyadko] to the table d'hôte, but I

myself ate almost nothing. A walk and coffee. Home. *Ramsch* with
N. D. Went to sleep. N. D. has no appetite and is sleepy. All day
today I seem to be in a nightmare. A towering egoism tortures me.
A single thought: to leave!!! No limit to impatience. Especially
when N. D. is coughing, I go through extraordinary suffering! The
doctor. I left for my place at nine-thirty. Zasyadko left with the
doctor. God! Is it possible the time will come when I shall no
longer suffer so! Poor N. D.! Poor Mitya! What is waiting for him!
For the water is already accumulating again. . . .

24 August In the morning N. D.'s disposition was more melancholy; he complained of nausea, which tormented him all night,
and attacked especially the *cooking* (the identical thing he recently praised). I continued to have diarrhea. The doctor came
when Zasyadko and I were there. N. D. cried at that time. At dinner
I ate almost nothing again. Took a short walk with Zasyadko. N. D.
waited impatiently for us. *Ramsch.* N. D. was cranky all the time,
as though he wanted to appear worse than he is. Stroganov. In
his presence, he suddenly became very lively. Stroganov about
music. N. D.'s dinner during which he ate two plates of soup, a
whole sole and two baked apples, and to the doctor he said that
he *ate nothing.* In general, he was exaggerated and cranky the
entire day for some unknown reason. The doctor. After he left,
Zasyadko and I caught him and we spoke about the possibility of
a trip to St. Petersburg. He answered evasively, but gave the impression that he himself would gladly go. *Ramsch.* There were no
tears. In a café with Mitya. I do not feel well.

TRIP FROM AACHEN TO MAIDANOVO

25 August Slept feverishly. Rose at six-thirty. Packed. Sasha.
Mitya. At N. D.'s. Farewell without any unusual crying. The doctor.
Mitya saw me off. I am sick and drunk. In the *coupé,* a Frenchman
and a Hollander. The latter left soon. I slept. A nonpaying passenger. The Frenchman's attempts to converse. I kept quiet and read.
Very long journey. Berlin. Hôtel St. Petersbourg. Supper without
appetite, although did not eat the whole day. Walked along Unter
den Linden. Read Gnedich's fascinating story. Wept. Slept feverishly.

26 August Rose early. Tea, newspapers. Roamed about the streets.
Diarrhea. At the railroad station. Friedrichstrasse. Tickets. Home.
Lunch in the new dining room. The proprietor, Herr Hendtlass,

took a seat next to me and as is customary with the Germans began to talk about politics. In Café Bauer. *Moskovskiye Vedomosti.* Home. Do not feel well. Slept. Drank tea. Squandered money, and searched. Look at myself in the mirror and am amazed at my gauntness and paleness. Preparation for the departure. The usual fuss and excitement of departure. Marvelous sleeping car. No sooner did I sit down in my compartment (solo), than I felt a severe diarrhea and had a bad feeling accompanied by nausea. A vile night.

27 August Toward morning it became better and I fell asleep wonderfully. Rose at ten o'clock and the conductor gave me some tea. Became better and better. At Königsberg, had several spoons of soup without any aversion. Verzhbolovo. Felt able to eat something and had no more nausea. Crowded in the train. Passengers are Englishmen among whom an old man is especially typical. Their stout neighbor, spitting on the floor, turned out to be Mr. Makalinsky. The other young Russian made it loudly known that he lives in Paris. They became acquainted with one another. Opposite me sat a modest, thin gentleman with a severe tubercular cough. He turned out to be unusually nice and gentle. In Kovno, Vilna, and in Dünaburg drank tea at night.

28 August Throughout the trip read *André Cornélis* by Bourget and wondered what Modya could have liked in this long drawn-out work. Late in arriving. Two long stops. During the second of these, took a walk and it's impossible to express what a sweet feeling I experienced from this Pskov-Great Russian nature, which I like even when it's poverty-stricken. In Siver, more passengers came in (an energetic grandfather, a German with a nurse and child, etc.). Finally we arrived at eight o'clock instead of six. Grand Hotel. Rather dirty, although my rooms are good. Tea. Changed clothes. On foot along the Nevsky. Nikolaiev railroad station. Telegram to Lena. Supper at Palkin's. Went home on foot. Slept well.

29 August Tea and newspapers. At St. Isaac's Cathedral. Services conducted by a bishop in the right chapel. Endless "blessings" especially at the beginning. Lunch downstairs in the hotel. *Drigo* and my horror. Fled from him; then returned. Trip to Peterhof.[24] An attractive lyceum student of the type of Vasily I. Danilov. At Mary's. Talks. Learned with surprise that Modest is here, i.e. in

---

[24] *Where he went to visit Kondratyev's wife.*

St. Petersburg. We took a ride. Glorious weather. Returning, packed, dined in my room, and arranged about the ticket and baggage; went on foot to see Modest. To my surprise, found him in. Nara was so surprised that I think she took me for a ghost. At the railroad station. Was angry at Modest for the way he keeps silent, concealing and avoiding something. It passed later. Traveled marvelously and slept well. How much I looked forward to this moment, and, now, as it comes nearer, I find in myself a certain indifference and mournful coldness. . . .

MAIDANOVO

30 August Klin. Alesha. Bad weather. But still it was awfully pleasant to see the ugly mug of my Alesha. Home. Everything seems today dim, small, and insufficiently lived in. . . . Appetite for the first time at tea. For, the whole week, I either ate nothing or with a certain distaste. Hardly had I managed to dress, take a walk, and write two or three letters, hardly had I begun to enter into my norm and get some enjoyment out of my home, when Simon, who still lives here, appeared. How I despised him as he sat talking. At last, dinner was served and he left; a minute longer, and I would have asked him to leave. Dinner. A walk. Letters. Tea. Unusual amount of tenderness toward Alesha. *Russkaya Starina.* Took a stroll in the fields. The weather is gray and autumnlike—quite pleasant. Home. Wrote the diary for many days. Walked. Played Schumann's *Genoveva.* Played again after supper. Wrote my will.[25]

31 August A gray day. Took a cold bath for the first time since 10 May. A walk. Reading, attempts at composing. After dinner a walk and a visit to Novichikha. Her chattering. Bibikova. With Novichikha in the park. At home, talk with Alesha during tea about various homesteads he has seen and reading of replies to my advertisement in the newspapers.[26] At Simon's. Did not find him in. A stroll with Egorka. In the distance, saw the Sobolevsky house; it gets on my nerves as I am tortured by jealousy. For that is my ideal.

---

[25] *In a letter to Mme. von Meck, he wrote that due to his ordeal at Aachen, he had aged very much, felt tired of life, and had a feeling that he would die soon. With such thoughts, he prepared a new will, which was revised again on September 30, 1891. The latter was his last will.*

[26] *At this time, Tchaikovsky was advertising for an estate—to ascertain what was available for purchase within his limited means.*

Worked a bit. *Genoveva.* During suppertime Simon appeared. Played me his concerto [27]—a pretty piece.

1 September A trip with Alesha to Khimki to inspect the country houses of Enaleyev and Shchelkov. Sobolevsky at the railroad station. Egor Egorovich's story about Mendelyeev. Simon with his little girl in the train. Conversation with them. Khimki. A beggar boy the guide. Enaleyev's country house. The proprietor with fingernails several inches long. Filth and mediocrity. Mr. Enaleyev's haughtiness. Fifteen hundred rubles!!! We went on to Khovrino. Lunch in the forest near an empty country house. Shchelkov's house. Filth and abomination. Oh beloved fatherland, how dirty you are!!! Tea at a stand at a flag station. On foot to Khimki. A long way. Mr. Dushen and his nonsense. Darkness. Home. Supper. Reading.

2 September Beautiful weather. A walk and at Novikova's. She advises me to buy woodland from her and build a house. I am enthusiastic, but conceal it. Bibikova. Home. Newspapers. After dinner with Alesha to Sobolevsky—where Novikova also arrived. We inspected the house. Gleb. Marvelous view. We went to the mill. The daughter of the miller's wife. Kolya conducted us toward the place where Novikova suggests building a house, but it was impossible to get there as we were walking along the embankment and, to the right, water interfered. And so along the embankment we reached home. Poor Novikova got awfully tired. Tea. Busied myself. At Simon's. He had news about Taneiev, Arensky (he is better) [28] and about Moscow in general. Home. *Genoveva.* Supper. Alesha admits that he loves the country even more than I.

3 September After tea went to look at those places among which the intended site for the house would have to be. Could not imagine where it would be. Returned shortly before dinner. Letter from Pavlovskaya. After dinner rode with Novikova and Alexei to look over *my* woodland and the site for the house. We inspected them. There are lovely places, and I like the site for a house. Have de-

---

[27] *Piano Concerto, Op. 19, by Anton J. Simon.*

[28] *Tchaikovsky had heard that Arensky was mentally ill. He was very shaken by the news, as he believed it to be a religious mania, which he thought incurable.*

cided to buy. (And money???) [29] Went home. After tea stopped in at Novichikha's and gossiped with her and Bibikova. Home. Alexei, as is his habit, rebels unreasonably against buying but at the same time is happy about it. Read after supper. Telegram from Modest about the surprising improvement in Kondratyev's condition.

4 September The weather is divine. Slept restlessly somehow and did not feel well in the morning. Took a walk toward Sobolevsky's forest but more to the right. On the way back, was so tired that I rested sitting on the road. A Madino boy; Alesha going for mushrooms. Home, read the newspapers in the garden. Letters. Alexei was late to dinner. I was angry, all the more, because he placed the blame on me. In general, I was irritable. News from Emma about Kondratyev. His incomprehensible telegram. He is much better as Modest telegraphed yesterday. After dinner walked along the river and the brook. Avoiding the boys and hiding among the reeds by the brook. At Novikova's. Talks about the Pestoviks and Dash. Tea. Worked. Strolled. Beautiful evening. Before supper, read the new *Russky Vestnik* and the section about Katkov. Simon came and stayed until supper. I pointed out to him the deficiencies in the orchestration of the concerto. Before going to sleep, thought much and long about Edward.[30] Wept much. Is it possible *he* is not here now at all??? Don't believe it.

5 September The weather is divine. After tea took a walk. Worked briefly at home. At twelve o'clock went to meet the guests. They arrived. Laroche (whom I invited) and S. I. Taneiev. After dinner Simon dropped in and we four went to Sobolevsky for the illumination but there was neither illumination nor Sobolevsky himself. His lovable boy and dog Shah, still more lovable, were there. We sat a while. Tea home. S. I. [Taneiev] then played all he had composed and that not being enough, read, in addition, his research

---

[29] *On this day, he wrote his brother Tolya, telling him of the opportunity to purchase about 150 acres of woodland from Novikova where a house could be built in a few months. He decided first to ask for the five thousand rubles, the initial expenditure, from Tolya's wealthy wife, before turning to others, offering to pay 10 per cent interest on the money and to discharge the whole debt within two to three years.*

[30] *Edward Zak. All efforts to identify this individual have proved fruitless.*

about Russian folklore style. Unexpectedly P. I. Jürgenson arrived. Supper. Taneiev departed earlier. Novikova. Conversation about buying. Whist. When Novikova left, we considered the matter and I saw with sorrow that P. I. is right in thinking that N. V. N. wants "to skin" me.[31] Was recalling and thinking about *Zak* again. How amazingly lifelike my memory of him is: the sound of his voice, his motions, but, in particular, the rarely beautiful expression of his face at times. I cannot realize that he is *not* here *at all* now. Death, i.e. *his* complete nonexistence is beyond my understanding. It seems to me that I never loved anyone so intensely. God! what they did not say to me *then;* and no matter how I console myself, my guilt is terrible regarding him! And in the meantime, I loved him, i.e. did not love, and also love him now and his memory is sacred to me!

6 *September* Tanya would have been twenty-six years old today! Took a grand walk with Laroche along the railroad tracks in the direction of St. Petersburg. We rested in the forest and returned through it. Dinner at Simon's. At his place were the Pabsts, Remezov, and Bartzal. Tea in my place. Everybody escorted me to the railroad station. Left on the mail train. Children in the compartment next to mine. Had supper in the train.

ST. PETERSBURG

7 *September* In the train near Maly Vishera, saw and conversed with A. A. Rimsky-Korsakov. Arrived at ten o'clock. Modya and Kolya. Talk about Kondratyev, etc. Lunched at home. Modya informed me that they want to dismiss him; I got very excited. Went walking. Returned and went with Modest to the Summer Garden, conversing about the same matter. At Pavlovskaya's. Kondratyev,[32] of course, was there. Remained there during their dinner. But I myself dined in a hurry at Pivato's in a private room. Rain. Dropped in at a third-rate tavern. Marinsky Theater. *The Enchantress.*[33] The incident with Maria Alex. Slavina. Everybody found, as indeed I

---

[31] *The practical Jürgenson, after inspecting the property at Tchaikovsky's request and discussing it with Novikova, found the price too high and discouraged its purchase.*

[32] *Not N. D. Kondratyev but G. P. Kondratyev, head producer of the Marinsky Theater at St. Petersburg.*

[33] *The first general vocal rehearsal of his opera.*

did myself, that the duet of the third act is too long. I was tired. Vsevolozhsky was present. We drank tea. Drove up to the Pavlovskys' after twelve and sat about an hour in their place. Returned home very late.

8 September Rose early. Went out at nine o'clock. Dropped in at Rahter's. Walked home after a drive. Brandukov. Bob and Mitya at lunch. Bob's amazing coolness. Dressed in a tail coat and went off to the Conservatory. A. Rubinstein, Gerke, etc. Korsakov and Liadov. At the *Te Deum*. The annual meeting. I, an honorary member. Fled. Home. Changed clothes. At V. V. Butakova's. At the Kondratyevs'. Mitya and Kolya there. Threesome dinner at home. At the railroad station. Bibikov. Brandukov. They saw me off. The Pavlovskys. In a Pullman. A neighbor, an actor type, was spitting terribly. Went to chat with Brandukov in his car. Bouillon in Luban. Slept somehow, with difficulty. It is cold.

MAIDANOVO

9 September Woke before Tver. Tea. Klin. Rain. Home. Took a walk. Dinner. A short walk and still in the rain. At Novikova's. At Bibikova's. A futile attempt to reconcile them. The story of Alexei's courtship. Home. Tea. The unsuccessful second theme of "Hamlet." [34] Mikhail arrived. Supper. Reading. Awful weather. Slept with difficulty.

10 September Rain all day and a powerful thunderstorm in the evening. Was busy all morning until dinner with the changes in the duet in the third act. Went after dinner to Sobolevsky's forest. After tea fussed with changing the end of the duet in the second act. Thunderstorm. After supper, no sooner was I in my study than Mikhail I. appeared (who has been getting on my nerves all day for some reason) and pressed me for money. Played Schumann's *Das Paradies und die Peri*. What a divine work!!! Was struggling with sleep.

11 September A rainy day. Throughout the morning worked over the changes. Mikhail Sofronov finally departed. He tired me but, then, essentially he is very obliging when one recalls all that has happened. After dinner, the bell rang. It turned out to be Andrey A. Sokolov,[35] sent by P. I. J. in regard to buying. Clever chap. With

---

[34] *Overture Fantasy, Op. 67, for orchestra.*

[35] *A real estate expert.*

him at Novichikha's. Then and there he knocked off forty rubles
on about every three acres. A walk. Rain. A young man from whom
I lit a cigarette in the field. Handsome and deformed. Tea. I am in
a bad mood and am not myself, God knows why. Worked. The
feeling in my left side which I have considered, for a long time,
the beginning of a fatal disease. Supper almost with aversion. Do
not feel well. Played the fourth act. It's long all the same. Solitaire.
Gymnastics.

MOSCOW

12 September Slept restlessly with a pain in the back of my head.
Rose at seven-thirty. With Alesha to the railroad station. Delay.
The woman newspaper seller; coffee. Traveled in a compartment.
The good Huberts met me. At the Hotel Moscow. Lunch in a
private room with candelabras in the daytime. The Huberts and
Laroche. With Laroche to Jürgenson. A complete alteration in his
place and found only Anna Vasilyevna, by herself. Conservatory.
Taneiev and Karlusha in the director's office. At Anna Leontevna's.
Karlusha junior is undertaking to make the plans for the house. At
my place. Tea. Drowsiness. At the Uspensky Cathedral. At the
Jürgensons'. P. I.'s new office. Inspection of the changed quarters
of the lithography department. Zverev, Kashkin, the Huberts. Whist.
I was lucky. Supper. Drinks in the Hotel Moscow. At my place.
Regretful of the supper. Heavy feeling.

Sunday, 13 September The weather is beautiful. In the Kremlin.
Ostrovsky, the student. Uspensky Cathedral. Saw the choristers,
but there was no singing in the Cathedral. Grand Duke Vladimir
Alexandrovich. In Jürgenson's store and before that at Pechkovskaya's. Home. A. A. Sokolov. Laroche, Kashkin and Brandukov
lunched at my place. At Taneiev's with Laroche. Shestoperov, and
Koreshchenko. At Safonov's. K. J. Davidov. Chopin's sonata, Beethoven's sonata and works by Davidov.[36]

---

[36] *The famous 'cellist and at one time director of the St. Petersburg
Conservatory played these works. The musical example is the theme from
Davidov's Nocturne, Op. 41, No. 3, for 'cello and piano. Its daring har-
monies amazed musicians at the time.*

Hubert. Dinner at the Hermitage. I paid. Whist. Laroche and Kash-kin in the tavern at my place.

MAIDANOVO

14 September At nine o'clock at the railroad station. Laroche. In the car with us a woman passenger in a hood. A courteous colonel of the sappers. Klin. Vasily. Alesha. Home. Dinner. A walk to *my* site. We were late. Tea. Letters. Supper. Read Renan. Early to bed. Nightmares.

15 September Took a walk with Manya in the garden after tea. It is cold and damp. Worked painstakingly on the orchestration of the changes. Dinner. Afterward with Laroche to Klin. At Skokov's. In Praslovo was very happy to see Egorka. At home, feeding the dogs. Soon after tea, we got down to the dictation of the article.[37] It was good, but I did not feel well: *that place* pained severely. After supper we read Gogol and Renan. We played Mozart's concerto. I wrote the diary for three days.

16 September Slept again with great difficulty. What does it mean? Drank tea alone. Laroche slept until dinnertime. I worked until I was tired. After dinner (I was angry at Manya on account of a political discussion) strolled by myself. Met Egorka and *tutti quanti* near the Klin grove. Tea. I had already finished tea when Laroche got up. Became tired from the strain of searching for a way of making cuts. Took a walk with Laroche in the garden. Dictation. It went slowly. My eyes are tired, nervous, and painful. Supper. Reading of *The Nose*.[38] Killed time and slept until twelve o'clock.

17 September Took a little walk with Manya and went to the *Te Deum* in the school. Twenty-six children. A boy with scrofula and his mother, an intelligent woman. Worked on the condensations. Dinner. Walked alone. Was in the forest near Sobolevsky. After tea, we walked about the garden. The article until supper-time. Manya dictated better today. Supper. We walked to the park in the moonlight. Playing of Mussorgsky and Mozart four hands!!!!

---

[37] *Laroche had come to Maidanovo, where Tchaikovsky was helping him write an obituary article on Borodin.*

[38] *A story by Gogol. Shostakovich wrote his first opera (Op. 15) on this satire.*

Wrote Tolya in regard to the loan. The matter about buying worries me. Serious negotiations are going on—and I have no money at all.

18 September Beautiful weather. Laroche slept all morning. I was busy with pasting up and adjusting the changes in the fourth act. After dinner walked by myself and was wavering whether or not to go to the railroad station where poor Magnitzkaya seemed to miss me; she unexpectedly burst in on me today during dinnertime, creating a whole riot. However, did not go. The dictation was very unsuccessful—little of it and not good. Telegram from Jürgenson about the purchase of the property. To this event, we drank champagne. After supper Gogol's *The Carriage*. Sad news concerning N. D. Kondratyev.

19 September God! What excitement! Telegrams without end! Now from Makhina, now from Jürgenson, now a letter from Sobolevsky with an invitation for the illumination, now a letter from Pavlovskaya which disquieted me! Now guests! All morning *pasting up* the changes. With Laroche to meet the guests. Only Brandukov and Kashkin arrived. Dinner. At Sobolevsky's. Rain. Priests and so on. Returned with Brandukov. About his concert. Telegram from Jürgenson that eight thousand in cash is demanded. Upset. Headache. Walked up and down in the gallery. Karlusha junior. The plan. Not enough. Sobolevsky. Whist. Supper. Kashkin drunk. Ridiculous negotiations of Laroche with Sobolevsky. I am tired.

Sunday, 20 September Rising, drank tea with Kashkin, Karlusha, and Brandukov. The latter departed. Went with the first two to *my* woodland. We decided where the house should stand and made a tour of my parcel of land. Dinner. Another walk all together. Tea. Kashkin gets drunk and becomes, as usual, a terrible chatterbox; simply drove us to exhaustion. And yet what a good and smart person! Laroche went off to sleep. Pulled through with difficulty until their departure. Kashkin departed absolutely drunk. Laroche dictated excellently today (about Borodin). Supper. Letter from J. [Jürgenson]. My eyes are opened now. To buy is insanity. Won't buy. With Manya, Brahms' symphony. Recollections about the Conservatory.

21 September Bad weather. Slept poorly. While walking in the morning met Novikova. To congratulations on the purchase answered that, because of Golikova's refusal to transfer the debt, I have not decided as yet. She began to chatter, obviously to defend herself. Wrote N. F. Was nervous and in a bad mood. After dinner went walking with Laroche, not far. At Novikova's. Their familiarity. Tea. I walked up and down in the gallery while Manya was sleeping. Writing the article. It went very well. Expectation of Novikova. Supper. Threesome whist game. Poor Novikova lost all her money. Sat around with Laroche, we chatted, and we played *durachki*. And what is happening in Aachen? It's frightening even to think of it.

MOSCOW

22 September Trip to Moscow. With Laroche and Alesha in the second class. Drank too much. At P. I.'s. Makhina and her eternal harping on the idea that she is a great artist. Hardly had P. I. and I begun to talk things over than Fitzenhagen came to bully us. *News about the death of N. D. Kondratyev* which occurred yesterday. Home (Myasnitzkaya Street). Kolya von Meck. Walked. At the Bolshoi Theater. *Robert*.[39] I sat in the orchestra with Laroche. In a gloomy state of mind. Supper with Laroche in the Hermitage. Karlusha.

23 September Lunch in the Tartar restaurant. Conservatory. The Huberts. He is ill. Tea. At the Synod choristers. Dobrovolsky and Orlov. At Katerina Vasilyevna's. Dinner in the Hermitage with Kolya von Meck and Dima. Professors' meeting. The question about Fitzenhagen. At Patrikeyev's with Taneiev. Zverev there with the whole family. We were in a private room with the Huberts.

24 September Visits by: Polya, Arends, Makhina. Arends with the *overture*(!!!). Lunch at Laroche's. At the meeting. Met Vanka, the coachman. Glad. At the railroad station. Laroche. A talkative passenger. Crowded. Polish women. Supper. Decided not to buy the la. . . .[40]

MAIDANOVO

25 September Met Novikova and informed her that I'm not buying. Wrote letters. After dinner went, in the rain, to the railroad station to send off telegrams. Tea. Dictation. Soso. Novikova. Sup-

---

[39] *Meyerbeer's opera*, Robert le Diable.

[40] *It appears that Tchaikovsky, his dreams shattered by his final decision not to buy, did not have the courage to complete the word "land"* (zemlya) *but wrote* zem. . . .

per. Card game. Lay down to sleep very late. The matter with Khludov is not settled.[41]

26 September All morning worked over the first two acts of *The Enchantress,* i.e. preparing for conducting. At dinner, an argument with Laroche about Burenin. Went walking alone. Egorka solo. We both looked for mushrooms. In the morning, received a telegram about renting Krivyakino. Replied that I wished to very much. To remain here is impossible. The Volkovs are going to settle here. Dima arrived. Worked a little with Laroche! Whist.

> Oh, my God! Why all this?
> Am quitting!!!!
> Why, I'm forty-seven!!!
> Enough!

---

[41] *Another piece of property (named Krivyakino) belonging to a certain Khludov was offered for sale and Jürgenson was negotiating for its purchase by Tchaikovsky. In the course of time, this project also fell through.*

Diary Seven

December, 1887 — March, 1888

After a lapse of about three months, this diary begins with the record of Tchaikovsky's concert tour of Germany as a conductor. He appeared in Berlin, Leipzig, and Hamburg, giving many concerts and meeting the leading musical personalities of the time. After his appearances in the German cities, he went by invitation to Prague and thence to Paris and London. Tired by the tour, he returned to Russia.

15 December, 1887 Departed [from St. Petersburg]. Was seen off by Modya, Kolya [Konradi], the Napravniks, Pogozhev (*Te Deum* at the railroad station). Lunch. The imperial train and the tsar, whom I saw scurrying past us. Large compartment—a favor by the conductor. Passengers: an officer horse guardsman, an old Frenchman, a German diplomat count, etc. Drank much and read.

16 December Eydtkuhnen. Dinner in Königsberg. Drunkenness and reading continued. Homesick.

BERLIN

17 December Hôtel St. Petersbourg. A room downstairs. Read with horror in the *Fremdenblatt* about the *Frühstück* arranged by Friedrich.[1] A walk. At the museum. Dinner at the table d'hôte. T. Hendtlass sat opposite me and entered into a conversation. An old count and economic problems. A walk through the city. Very cold weather. Read at home.

18 December Expectation of Friedrich. While expecting him, was homesick and excited. He turned out to be not especially repulsive

---

[1] *Tchaikovsky's concert agent at Berlin.*

on first impression. Dropping him, went to the Passage to read the newspapers. Strolled. Dinner at the table d'hôte. Hendtlass again tortured me with conversation. Friedrich. Concert. Requiem by Berlioz. Scharwenka. Misunderstanding with Schneider. Acquaintance with Scharwenka and Wolff. Old Frenkel. Friedrich and his young lady escorted me and even stepped in with me. Homesickness and drunkenness.

19 December With Friedrich, who is more and more repulsive to me, to Bock. Bock is very nice and courteous. At Davidov's (K. J.). Awfully glad to see him. Grünfeld, Frenkel, Meyer-Helmund, etc. Lunch in my place with Friedrich. He saw me off. Alone in the compartment. Drunkenness. Excited. Leipzig. Brodsky, Siloti, Krause, Friedheim.[2] At the hotel. At Brodsky's. His charming wife and *belle-sœur*. Christmas tree. Supper. Home. Slept well.

LEIPZIG

20 December Homesick. A walk through unfamiliar localities and incredible suffering. With Sasha (Sil[oti]) to Brodsky. Meeting with Brahms, Grieg, Fritzsch, etc. Suffered greatly. Grieg and his wife awfully charming. Brahms' trio. My interference in the performance. Napped at home. With Brodsky and Sasha at the Gewandhaus.[3] Director's box. Meeting with lots of people. My sufferings became simply unbearable when Consul Limburger announced that the rehearsal is tomorrow. After the concert, had supper with Sasha and Brodsky. Slept abominably.

21 December Rehearsal. Suffered, of course, unbearably, especially at the beginning. The musicians very amiable. Reinecke introduced me to the orchestra; I made a little speech(!!!!).[4] Reinecke and Brahms were listening. After the rehearsal a visit to Reinecke and at Friedrich's with Sasha—dined at Sasha's. Friedheim. Vera [Siloti] with the child. Noticed that Sasha is very cold to her. After dinner, we sat awhile in her room and then went to Krause. From

---

[2] *The three pianists and Brodsky, a distinguished violinist, met the composer at the train.*

[3] *The principal concert hall in Leipzig.*

[4] *Tchaikovsky's speech in German was as follows: "Gentlemen, I cannot speak German, but I am proud, that I with such a . . . such a . . . that is . . . I am proud . . . I cannot . . ."*

there, we drove to the city. Brodsky's quartet concert in the evening. Brahms' trio. Supper with Sasha.

22 December All morning was busy with the revision of the new parts (the extra parts). Dinner at Sasha's. Vera. Friedheim. At Krause's. Came home by horsecar. New acquaintances. (The affair with the gloves and the inspector when we were riding there.) Home. Friedrich's visit and the argument about the Dresden concert. Friedrich is disgusting. At the opera with Sasha Siloti. Change of performance. Evening at the Brodskys'. Sweet and kind women. I met Brodsky himself on the way back from Siloti and he was at my place. Retired early.

23 December Terribly excited in the morning, although expected to be completely calm in the evening. Dress rehearsal with public. Sasha called for me. Brodsky. *A great success.* Russian students. Immediate invitations from them, Reinecke and Limburger. With Brodsky and Sasha to Auerbach's *Keller*. Dinner at Brodsky's. Shopping on the way. It was very enjoyable at their place. Kind people. Went home on foot passing through the main streets. Home. Sasha. At the opera. Wagner's *Das Rheingold.* Supper with Sasha. Friedheim, taking two hundred marks, promised to come but did not.

24 December After rising and reading the newspapers, went walking. At Grieg's (who left an enthusiastic note for me yesterday). Lovely, cultivated people, well acquainted with our literature. Home. Lunch in my room. Drunkenness. Slept. Am calm. Siloti. Excitement. Concert. Conducted well. A success *à la* Gewandhaus. Acquaintance with Haliř and others. Evening reception at Reinecke's. Gouvy. Supper. Reinecke's stories about Schumann. On the whole, not especially boring. Russian evening reception. The mother and the sisters of Goldstein with their fiancés. The wife and the *belle-sœur* of Brodsky. Home. Slept with difficulty.

25 December With Sasha Siloti at the old Gewandhaus. *Tschaikowsky-Feier.*[5] The Griegs. Zimmermann. Laurel wreath. Haliř,

---

[5] *The Liszt-Verein honored Tchaikovsky by arranging a program devoted entirely to his works. These were the Trio performed by Siloti, Haliř, and Schroeder; First String Quartet performed by the Petri Quartet and a barcarolle and fantasy on themes from Eugene Onegin arranged for piano, performed by Siloti. The composer sat on a platform with Grieg and his wife as neighbors. There was much enthusiasm and the society presented him with a laurel wreath.*

Schroeder, the Petri Quartet, etc. Dissipation. Siloti. Halǐř played my concerto. He is a genius. At Vera's, upstairs. In a party at the Krystallpalast. Box. Musical clowns. Supper. Champagne. Went home. Slept restlessly.

26 December [*Berlin*] Packed. A messenger from the Gewandhaus brought the music. Sasha Siloti. At the photographer's. We had a picture taken. At Mme. Klamrot's. Dinner reception at the Brodskys'. The news of the success of Brodsky in Berlin.[6] At dinner, Grieg and his wife, and two Norwegians. One of them is a composer. We played his quintet after dinner. Barbarous progressions in fifths. Home. Was almost late. Besides Sasha Siloti, who doesn't leave me, Krause came to the railroad station. Departed. Alone in the compartment. As usual, drunkenness. In Berlin, Brodsky met me. Supper with him at Dressel's. Russian vodka and appetizers.

27 December, 1887 Morning at home. At Brodsky's in the Askanischer Hof. A telephone. *Philharmonie.* Meeting with Schneider, Köhler, Wolff's wife, Ochs, etc. Discussions about the program in the bureau. At Wolff's. Talks about Siloti and Friedrich. Wolff is full of kindness. Dinner with Brodsky at Dressel's. In the Passage. Rain. The newspapers about Brodsky. Concert *with refreshments* at the Philharmonic. I am in a box with Brodsky, Wolff, his wife and another lady, Schneider, the concertmaster, the first soloist, etc. Went home. Read without having supper but went to sleep late on account of foolishness: what to do about the parts of *Francesca* [*da Rimini*]? Whether to give to Schneider, etc.?? But slept—not badly.

28 December, 1887 In the morning, after reading the newspapers, went to Bock. As always, very nice and courteous. Home. Expected Brodsky to lunch. His letter declining. At Brodsky's. He escorted me home. The story about *Die Walküre.* A *tail coat* was requested!!! Letters. Solo dinner at Dressel's. Home. Departure. Brodsky arrived before the signal. Compartment in the first class. Slept *beautifully* sitting up.

HAMBURG

29 December, 1887 At six o'clock in Hamburg. Tea with Brodsky. Napped. At the rehearsal. Von Bülow on the street; very surprised and kind, but . . . somehow I am uncomfortable with him. Mme.

---

[6] *In performing Tchaikovsky's Violin Concerto, after it had been pronounced unplayable.*

von Bülow. Lunch with Brodsky in a *Rathskeller*. Together to the *Halle*. I was at Rahter's. His wife and son. At von Bernuth's. Did not find him in. Home. Table d'hôte. In a café. Home. With Brodsky to the concert. Box. Overture by Méhul. Raff (Brodsky). Mendelssohn. Saint-Saëns. Eroica Symphony. Von Bülow conducted more with his left hand, but superbly. Farewell with Brodsky. In Mme. von Bülow's box. Dissipation in a café. Home. Intemperance.

LÜBECK

30 December, 1887 Rose late. A fog. Departed at ten o'clock. Parlor car first class. Two of us; later I am alone. Lübeck.[7] Stadt Hamburg. Oh it's terrible—to forget the black suitcase!!! Poor room. Afterward transferred to a good one. Table d'hôte. Strolling. Home. It is heated. The *suitcase* is returned!!! Letters. Baths. Home. Supper. Writing of this diary for many days. I am glad that I am here alone, but a little feeling of homesickness is coming on.

31 December, 1887 Crammed the Variations,[8] wrote letters. At twelve o'clock went out for a stroll. The weather is divine. At the table d'hôte was obstinately silent again, watching the actors and actresses. A walk. Dropped in at a beer hall in an ancient building, with frescoes on the walls and ship models. Wrote, crammed, and read Muravlin's novel with pleasure. Performance at the Stadttheater. Barnay played in *Othello*. In places, I was enraptured by his unsurpassed acting, but what a tragic work!!! And what a villain is Iago, especially played so abominably as yesterday. Supper at home. Reading. Cramming. *New Year's* greeting!!!!

1 January, 1888 Rose at nine o'clock. Crammed the Variations; letters. A walk beyond the city. The weather is wonderful. At dinner, it was very interesting to watch the actors. Strolled. Read and wrote letters at home. At the theater. *L'Africaine*. A colossal but not a bad Selika. A ludicrous little tenor with his snout poked forward, comically amusing basses and chorus. A tiny orchestra and a *Kapellmeister* lanky as a pole. During the intermission after the second act, a great unpleasantness was awaiting me: I was recognized. The composer Ogarev(!!!), *Musikdirektor* Stiehl, the conductor, von Fielitz. They dragged me to the buffet: no longer did

---

[7] *He sought seclusion in Lübeck for several days in order to find some freedom and rest.*

[8] *Theme and Variations from the Third Suite, Op. 55, for orchestra.*

I hear the opera. Deep despair and antipathy toward Ogarev. Stiehl was being very ingratiating with him, but when he was escorting me back he spoke of the *Herr Staatsrat* unflatteringly. With difficulty got rid of that repulsive Stiehl, lying that I was ill, was leaving, etc. Told the clerk not to receive anyone. Out of misery, overdrank and felt bad.

2 January Rose at nine, a telegram from Pogozhev with congratulations (I still did not know what it was about). Read, busied myself a bit; at eleven o'clock stole out like a thief for a stroll and took a beautiful walk beyond the city. On returning, found a telegram from Vsevolozhsky. *The tsar gave me a pension.*[9] Of course, I am deeply happy and glad, but I am—what shall I say, too grateful, i.e. I am somehow conscience stricken, as though it were undeserved. . . . Dined at my place. With great difficulty wrote letters to the tsar, the secretary of state, Vsevolozhsky, and Pogozhev. Went for a walk and bought some *Branntwein*. The weather is freezing, beautiful. Returning, had supper, read a great deal and, as a result, my head was heavy (of course, there was extreme drunkenness).

3 January God! How much time still remains until May! Is it possible I will endure it all? I felt unwell in the morning. It is cold out of doors; took the same walk as yesterday to that place where I watched a squirrel for a long time and looked for it today, but did not find it. After dinner (in the room) walked long up and down in the room, then dozed. And afterward such a *homesickness* and *boredom* set in that it was utterly unbearable. Is it possible I will endure four more months??? Read de Maupassant (*Pierre et Jean*). At seven o'clock went walking. Dropped in at a café where, as with us, an orchestrion was playing. My God! How I love our dear, precious Russia! Now it's ten o'clock; again there will be reading, again drunkenness. . . . Oh God! . . .

4 January Did not feel well. A walk. Dinner at my place. Franz is very obliging and kind. Packed. Departed on the six o'clock train. Avoided Leipzig acquaintances. With me in the first class is an old man. I fell asleep and did not notice how the trip went by. Streit's Hotel [Hamburg]. Went to the *Keller* and was so drunk there that I do not remember how or what. Slept with difficulty.

---

[9] *Through the efforts of Vsevolozhsky, Tsar Alexander III bestowed upon Tchaikovsky an annual pension of three thousand rubles for life.*

5 January The excitement kept getting crescendo all the time. Cognac. Expected Rahter. *Conventgarten.* Rehearsal in the small hall. Soon the uneasiness passed. The musicians sympathetic. A success. Bernuth. Rahter escorted me home. Lunch downstairs in the *Keller.* At Mme. von Bülow's. Home. Napped. Not well. In a carriage with Rahter. Dinner with his family. Nice people. An old lady of eighty-six years. Together to the concert. Mme. Joachim.[10] Went to the Kunstlerium to see Schroeder and Petri. Became acquainted with Mme. Joachim. Home.

6 January Rehearsal at nine. In the Piano Concerto disorders. Lunched with Sapelnikov. Home. Laube and Bernuth at my place. Dined alone in the restaurant at my place. With Sapelnikov at the Ludwigsgarten. We listened to Laube's orchestra; he came over during the intermission. In addition, we went to a snapshot photographer's and a *café chantant.*

7 January First rehearsal. After it, weary, went to have lunch and a walk. At two o'clock, the dress rehearsal. Excitement. It went well. Celebration dinner at Rahter's. Endless drunkenness and speeches. Cannot remember all who were present. Most interesting of all Gurlitt. From there with Bernuth, Doctor Riemann, etc. we went also to the *Bierhalle.* Went home at three o'clock.

8 January Burmester with his attractive son and daughter. At Bechstein's. Willy [Burmester] played my concerto very nicely. Lunch in the *Keller.* Sapelnikov, poor soul, came for money. A kind, nice boy! I walked. Slept. Concert.[11] I conducted well. A large reception and supper at Bernuth's. I made a speech in German. From there to the Wiener Café. We dissipated until three o'clock.

9 January An awfully hard day. Visit of old Ave-Lallemant. At eleven o'clock at the Ludwigsgarten. *Romeo and Juliet. Capriccio Italien, Tristan and Isolde.* A luncheon in my honor downstairs.

---

[10] *Wife of the famous violinist, Joseph Joachim.*

[11] *The program consisted of Tchaikovsky's Serenade for String Orchestra; the First Piano Concerto (with Sapelnikov as soloist) and the Theme and Variations from the Third Suite. The first of these three works was best received. In general, however, the Hamburg critics were not friendly; to his friend Napravnik, Tchaikovsky wrote that one critic stated that one of the variations represented a session of the Holy Synod, while another a dynamite explosion!*

Tchaikovsky and his wife in 1877

At the photographer's. At von Bülow's. For some reason, went away from him chagrined. Home. Hardly had I taken a nap, when it was necessary to go to Bechstein with the composer, Jenner. He played me his trio and songs. Home. Tired to distraction. Downstairs in the *Keller*. Sittard's article. Am very happy. Went home. Rahter. At the *Tonkünstler-Verein*. A session. Sapelnikov played beautifully. *Frau* Nathan sang nicely. Terrible redoubled dissipation at two taverns. I drank so much that I do not remember anything.

Sunday, 10 January Rising, I felt very gloomy, indeed; even the weather was gloomy, rainy. My head was heavy and at the same time empty from drunkenness. Went out at twelve-thirty and, expecting Sapelnikov, walked along the Alster. By horsecar with him to see Rahter. Dinner at Rahter's. Extraordinarily charming are his wife, children, and the old lady Lapré. Rahter's brother and his son. Dinner, borsch. Speech by Rahter's brother. After dinner visit to Ave-Lallemant. The old man touched me by his invitation *nach Deutschland zu übersiedeln.*[12] His wife, with a little belly. *Die Enkelin.* We returned and, taking Sapelnikov, we went out with Rahter. We found a *Droschke* and rode off. I packed in my place. Letter to Sittard. Visit of the violinist, Marwege, was very touching to me. A still more unexpected visit of Sittard (I bluffed him—did not go to the theater) and Ambrust. Departure. At the railroad station. Sapelnikov and his relative (a nihilist). I gave him fifty marks. Three in the compartment. I dozed all night, sitting up.

EN ROUTE TO LEIPZIG

11 January Berlin at 6 A.M. Room downstairs. That Sapelnikov is lovable. I am down in the dumps. Napped. With Sapelnikov at the *Philharmonie*. Rehearsal. We are upstairs. Symphony by Strauss. His lack of talent.[13] Appointment with von Bülow, Wolff, Schneider,

---

[12] *A director of the Philharmonic Society in Hamburg who was particularly friendly to Tchaikovsky, although he did not like the composer's compositions that he had heard. Tchaikovsky dedicated his Fifth Symphony to him. Ave-Lallemant invited Tchaikovsky to settle in Germany where the Russian composer's faults would be corrected under the influence of German culture. He felt Tchaikovsky was a product of a backward country and all Tchaikovsky's rebuttals to the contrary had no effect.*

[13] *The Symphony in F Minor, Op. 12, made a very poor impression on Tchaikovsky. When he heard it he thought it the trashiest of works but*

etc. Acquaintance with Ehrlich and Strauss. The program of my concert. They exclude *Francesca*. With Sapelnikov to Dressel's. Nervousness. A walk. In the Passage. *Novoye Vremya*. I am at Wolff's, coffee, Mme. Wolff, her sister. I am unnaturally lively. About Strauss. Home. On the telephone with Wolff. Invitation from Nicodé to Dresden. Home. Packing. A walk with Sapelnikov. Wax figures. Home. Supper. Departure. Drank until Magdeburg. An abominable room.

12 January, 1888 It turned out that my room was not only obnoxious but very dark as well. Rage. Candles. Strolling. Beautiful city. Beyond the fortress. Home. A new, beautiful room. Letter to Friedrich, who again telegraphed me in Berlin yesterday. Dinner at the table d'hôte. Boredom. Strolling. At home, letters without end. Performance at the Stadttheater. *Tannhäuser*. A boring opera. Shocking singers, both men and women, but the production was good. Supper at the railroad station near by. The waiter was a lover of the French language. Went home on foot.

13 January Spent all morning at home with letters. Went out for a walk; gazed at the Elbe and crossed several bridges. Went to dine in the *Keller;* unusually vile food, sickening to recall. Roamed through the beautiful Magdeburg streets; was in a café. Home. Read *Mensonges* by Bourget. Departure. On the way, it was hot. Leipzig. Newspapers. An obliging porter with overpolite manners. Letters. A letter from Colonne,[14] trailing me for a long time. Was drinking shamefully. Went to bed very late.

LEIPZIG

14 January Rose awfully late. Letters. Went out at twelve-thirty. Dined alone at Keil's. Went on foot to see *Siloti* but got off the path. A frightful diarrhea. To a café. By *Droschke* to Siloti. He is sick. Stayed at their place; we drank tea. Was glad to see them. At the Brodskys'. Found the ladies, he wasn't there—he was at my place. Conversation. Lovely women. On foot. Supper in a new res-

---

the following day, calming down, he began to think that perhaps he did not understand it or grasp its meaning.

[14] Colonne invited Tchaikovsky to conduct at two of his concerts, a very pleasant surprise. Tchaikovsky accepted the invitation, receiving no payment for his appearances, because Colonne assumed all financial responsibilities in connection with the concerts.

taurant, which turned out to be Keil's again. Went home. Home-sickness agitated me. Want to abstain from drunkenness. Slept excellently, thanks to that circumstance.

15 January Home. Remained until ten-thirty. At Forberg's. Walked with the agent to see Brodsky. Sat a while in their place. Dinner at Sasha Siloti's. Vera with us. Arthur [Friedheim] (I gave him money again). Afterward dropped in at Krause's and met him at his door. I went home on foot alone. Performance. *Don Juan.* Supper at Bormann's with Petri, his wife, Busoni (composer of a quartet), Konetzky, etc. Busoni is very charming. We all went home together. Sapelnikov. Meeting. Telegram from Siloti. Nervousness, drunkenness, a bad dream.

16 January At Sapelnikov's. Busoni. With him to the Gewandhaus. Rehearsal of the quartet. Very talented. At Limburger's—did not find him in. At Reinecke's—found him in. With Sapelnikov to Brodsky's. Dinner. Debate about Brahms. With Sapelnikov to Siloti. He is better. Krause. His duel with Friedheim. Went home on foot. Got off my path. Today, snow and a storm as in Russia. Glad that I can remain half an hour at home. Futile efforts to sleep. Quartet evening. Busoni. His success. Sonata by Brahms. Quartet by Haydn. Evening reception at Petri's. Magnitzkaya. The conductor, Mahler. Busoni's suite. Escorted Magnitzkaya. Perplexed. Home, after that to Sapelnikov.

Sunday, 17 January Rising, read the newspapers. Went in for Sapelnikov and together we started out to Brodsky. It is absolutely winter. We came too early; however, the Norwegians were already there. I took a walk again. The Griegs. Grieg's sonata. Sapelnikov played. Dinner. Sapelnikov again. Sinding's quintet. Grieg's quartet. With Sapelnikov to the theater. *Die drei Pintos* by Weber.[15] During the intermission, Petri dragged me onto the stage. In the box of the directress. The request about *Die Meistersinger.*[16] Busoni. Mme. Petri. We left during the third act. I escorted Sapelnikov to the Panorama restaurant. A walk. Supper at Keil's. Opposite me two

---

[15] *Unfinished opera by Weber which was completed by Mahler. Tchaikovsky liked the music but the subject seemed stupid to him.*

[16] *Tchaikovsky requested that a performance of Wagner's opera be given and on January 29 this was done under the direction of Nikisch whose conducting greatly impressed Tchaikovsky. His comment on the opera was "very interesting."*

gentlemen with a lady—just like Testov's after the theater. Went home. It is freezing. Sapelnikov at coffee. Talks. Many have found today that he is highly gifted and I myself am of the same opinion.

Monday, 18 January Went to arrange about the coin promised to Mme. Petri.[17] At Blüthner's regarding Sapelnikov. Went home for him and on foot to Siloti's. Dinner. Magnitzkaya. Krause. A walk. In a rustic café, an eggnog with liquor. Home. At the theater. Four *Lustspiele.* Supper with Sapelnikov (Mr. Jarno).

19 January Letters. I am at Siloti's. With him after dinner (Krause) to the woman singer, *blank,* to Blüthner (old man) and home. Sasha's solicitations about the *singer.* At the theater. *Doctor Wespe.*[18] Sontag. Threesome for supper at Keil's.

20 January With Sapelnikov for a hat. At Brodsky's. Dinner. The Griegs. His two sonatas. Miss Smyth. Conservatory concert. Brodsky the conductor. Supper with his wife, *belle-sœur* (lovely women) and Sapelnikov. Home. Packing.

21 January Did not go to *die öffentliche Probe.* Strolled. I gave a dinner reception at Keil's. Brodsky, Grieg, Siloti, Krause, Fritzsch, two conductors, Sapelnikov, etc. Departure. Chatted with Vasya.[19] What a sweet personality! Arrival at Berlin. Home. Friedrich's card. Supper. Home. In addition, Grieg's rude card. What a consolation Vasya is to me!

BERLIN

22 January Excitement. Friedrich did not come. Rehearsal. Went off well. Tired. The musicians were very friendly. Lunch with Vasya. A walk in the Tiergarten. Home. Homesickness. Dinner at Wolff's. A lot of people. Vasya played, Lauwers sang, an actress recited, Vasya played again. The hosts very warm. Left at twelve o'clock with Vasya.

---

[17] *Mme. Petri was a collector of autographs on coins. From the many celebrated people who visited her home, she would request a coin and an autograph. Then she would take both to her jeweller and have one side of the coin polished and the autograph engraved on it. She strung these autographed coins on a silver chain.*

[18] *Comedy by Julius Roderick Benedix.*

[19] *Vasya Sapelnikov accompanied the composer to Berlin. This gifted pianist was twenty years old at the time.*

Saturday, 23 January Reading of newspapers and tea in the salon at my place. Friedrich. I shouted at him. At Wolff's. Frau Schilder and Fernow. Conversation over the telephone with Brodsky in Leipzig. Meeting with Sauer. Lunch at Hiller's. A walk. Home. Homesickness. Vasya sick. Dinner at Bock's. Artôt.[20] Taubert. Radecke. Bloch. Sauret with his wife.

24 January Rather pleasant day. Finished with Friedrich.[21] With Vasya to the aquarium. Lunched at Dressel's. I rode to the Blochs' to free myself from the dinner. Before that, visited the consul's niece. Magnitzkaya. Tea. Home. Dined alone at Hiller's. Home in the evening.

25 January Dress rehearsal of von Bülow's concert. On the way from there came across Sasha Siloti who had just arrived. Dinner at the Fernows'. Grigorovich. Charming Mme. Fernow and the spinster who once painted a picture for me. Grigorovich is very handsome. Concert in the evening. Huge success of Stanford's symphony. Supper at Bloch's. Schultzen von Asten and her sister.

26 January Rehearsal. Von Bülow appeared and was warm. Siloti's recital. Lunch with Sasha Siloti and Vasya. A walk through the streets and to the entrance of the railroad station to see—with delight—where you leave for Russia. Home. The Griegs arrived. With them at Artôt's evening reception. Singing. It was enjoyable. Festive supper.

27 January With the Griegs and Vasya to my last rehearsal. We all lunched together afterward at Dressel's. The Brodskys also with us. The lady from Dresden and poor Vasya. A walk. Slept a little in the excitement. Concert. Success. Supper tendered me at Dressel's. With Vasya in Café Bauer. I am in seventh heaven.

28 January A pail of cold water (*au figuré*). Lunch at Baroness Senfft von Pilsach's. The woman composer, Becker. Dinner at

---

[20] *Desirée Artôt, French soprano with whom Tchaikovsky had been in love twenty years before and now met again for the first time. Writing to his brother Modest, he said that he was inexpressibly glad to see her; that they became friends immediately without mentioning a word of the past, and that she was just as enchanting as twenty years ago.*

[21] *Tchaikovsky put an end to his relations with Friedrich; it cost him 500 marks (about $120).*

Kudryavtzev's. We addressed one another familiarly! Seeing off my sweet Vasya.

29 January Woke late. Packing. Lunch in the room. Left on the two-thirty train. At the railroad station Magnitzkaya, the consul's niece, a Berlin priest. Two gentlemen with me. Napped. Coffee in Bitterfeld. Leipzig. Sasha. Home. *Die Meistersinger.* Friedheim. A. L. Brodskaya. Weariness. Supper at Keil's. Brodsky and I addressed one another familiarly.

30 January The *serenade* which awakened me. A whole hour at an open window. Dinner at the Brodskys'. The Griegs. Miss Smyth. Home. Evening at Siloti's.

31 January Departed with Sasha. Welcome by a delegation and a crowd in Kralupy. Welcome at the railroad station.[22] Speeches at the hotel. Performance at the opera. Urbánek, Strakatý, etc., etc. During the intermission, Rieger, Dvořák, Rieger's daughter, etc. During the following intermission, on the stage. Supper reception in the hotel after the performance. Weariness.

1 February After lunch Patera arrived for us. The Father from here. A delegation from the Kytice. Visit to the castle and the cathedral on the hill. Tired. Home. Valečka. Supper reception at his place. (His wife in a rose dress and everyone laughs.) A ball at the Kytice.[23]

2 February At ten-thirty, Patera. Visit to the ancient temple. In the Russian church. Singing. Dinner at Dvořák's. His wife is a simple, charming woman and an excellent hostess. Went home at three o'clock. Went for a walk to the hill on the other side of the river. Home. Napped a little. We were waiting for them to call for us. Patera (kind Adolf Osipovich) and Doctor Buchal arrived. At the Umělecká Beseda.[24] Thank God it went off without speeches. Smetana's quartet, Kovařovic's quartet and Dvořák's quintet were played. The latter is very nice to me and I like his quintet. A great many introductions (an old *general* with scars on his face, an old

---

[22] *Tchaikovsky was greeted at Kralupy, a small station just before the main one in Prague, in order to avoid great crowds.*

[23] *A society that gave a ball in Tchaikovsky's honor.*

[24] *The Arts Club that had honored him with a musical evening.*

musician resembling Berlioz, Peshkau from Moscow, etc.). I became awfully tired from talking. My portrait was being displayed, surrounded by laurel wreaths.

3 February Rose early. Sleep little, for the most part. Newspaper articles about us. The French-Czech and amiable Patera drove up for me. Rehearsal. Dvořák and many others were present there. It did not go badly. At the director's in the theater. Discussions about the concert at the theater. Lunch together at home. Sasha not quite well. Expected Patera. With him to Doctor Strakatý and to the Bertramka.²⁵ Mr. Popelka and his wife. *Mozart's* room. The garden. Tired. Home. Poor Sasha was fussing with the parts of the concerto. The French-Czech and Patera. Theater. *The Bartered Bride.* During the second and third acts sat with the intendant. During the intermissions, introductions. Conversation with Rieger's daughter. After the theater went home. Had supper solo. Sasha went to sleep.

4 February Went to bed late, but rose, for all that, at eight o'clock. Am getting old; when I look in the mirror I am horrified. Rehearsal. Again, the same French-Czech drove up for me. It was all right. Many interested people. Dvořák was present and was awfully friendly. Home. Lunch with Sasha (who played excellently today). The suite. Kind Patera at three o'clock. At the Town Hall. At the watchmaker's. The old university. At the Town Hall again. Kind Doctor ? . Inspection. Very interesting. The Diet hall, where all rose and greeted me. The archives. The clock. The *apostles.* The mechanism. Bought a *small organ* from the watchmaker. Home. Slept. Began to compose the speech. Patera. At the Russian Circle. Mme. Cervinková-Riegerová, Mme. Tomson, etc. Dvořák and his wife. There was singing. *The Bear as Matchmaker* ²⁶ in Russian by Czechs. Rode home, where P. I. Jürgenson was waiting. Was awfully glad to see him. Supper downstairs. Drunkenness. Received a telegram today from London. Agreed on 10 March.²⁷

5 February Awakened by P. I. Jürgenson. Drank tea with him and Sasha. Dvořák. Patera. With P. I. and Patera to the museum.

---

²⁵ *A villa near Prague in which Mozart lived as a guest of Dušek, and where he completed* Don Giovanni.

²⁶ *Comedy by Krylov.*

²⁷ *To conduct in London.*

It is very cold, but interesting. Dinner at the Father's. Vodka, hearty eating. The Father (Nikolai Petrovich Apraksin) talked to me about his quarrel with Sasha, my sister. On the Hradčany. The view. Home. *Haliř arrived.* Slept. Was hurrying with the speech. Patera, and little by little a lot of people. The Hlahol Society. The serenade on the street. I was very embarrassed. They sang. My two speeches. Supper reception downstairs in a large company. Chvála, Doctor Strakatý, Slavkovský and a lot of others were present. Was studying the [Violin] Concerto at my place for tomorrow.

6 February, 1888 Rose in a terrible frame of mind. Jürgenson, Sasha, Haliř. Then Dvořák, Hantich.[28] With both of them to the photographer's. Pictures were taken. Home. Patera. Urbánek. Sasha was practicing. To the Slovakian students. A celebration welcome, touching me deeply. The student's speech. My speech. The library. Send-off and cheering. At the *Rudolfinum.* Dress rehearsal. Bother with the Violin Concerto. Tired. Dinner home. We four (Sasha, Haliř, Jürgenson and I) and two doctors ?? . Went off to sleep, but did not sleep. Instead, went walking. Bought a clock. In a café. Newspapers. Home. In Jürgenson's room. All our people there. Patera. Translation of my speech and a lesson in the Czech language. At the Civic Club. Ovation. The chief conductor, Nováček. The Kytara Quartet. Mme. Cervinková-Riegerová. Endless ovations. Went home with Urbánek. My people in the restaurant. J. [Jürgenson] was a bit tipsy. And I too. How will it be tomorrow?

7 February Patera. At our church. Jürgenson with me. Went in, before Mass, to the watch expert. After Mass (where there was a big crowd) went home on foot. The collector of Slovakian songs (he is very charming) lunched at our place. Lunching with me were Haliř, P. I. [Jürgenson] and he. Learning my speech in Czech in my room. Concert. The usual excitement.[29] Slept at home. The

---

[28] *Hantich was the French-Czech mentioned previously. While the composer wrote Dvořák's name in his diary for this day, he failed to note that Dvořák presented him with the orchestra score of his Second Symphony inscribed in memory of his visit to Prague.*

[29] *It was an all-Tchaikovsky program consisting of his Romeo and Juliet; the First Piano Concerto with Siloti as soloist; the Elegy from the Third Suite; the Violin Concerto with Haliř playing the solo part and the 1812 Overture.*

banquet. Beside me, Jürgenson and Mayor Solc. Speeches. My speech. Went home at eleven o'clock. Slept. On the whole, I believe this is one of the most noteworthy days of my life. I have become very fond of these good Czechs. And, indeed, with reason!!! God! How much enthusiasm there was and of course all that is not for me, but for dear Russia.

8 February Halíř departed yesterday. In the morning, we three gathered; no longer four now. Rehearsal of the theater concert on Sophien Insel.[30] No rhythm. Lunch home. All three in a bad mood. They left; I waited for kind Patera. With him to Mme. Cervinková-Riegerová. Charming woman. We three to the museum of a private collector. Durdík. The Women's Club. M. Fedor. Apraksin. Went home on foot (after escorting Mme. Cervinková-Riegerová). In a café. Home. Weariness. Jürgenson and Sasha. Stayed during their dinner. Dvořák. Patera. In the *Bierhalle,* which Dvořák's friends visit. Old Kolář. Other amiable fellow countrymen. The Czechs are very likable. Went home with P. I. Supper. Sáller. Drunkenness.

9 February Rehearsal at the theater. The Serenade was still unsuccessful—they rushed it. We three together (i.e. P. I. J., Siloti, I) lunched at home. Awaited Dvořák. To the Conservatory with him and Bendl. Bennewitz. Excellent performance of Grieg's suite and Dvořák's symphony. Went home. Concert at the Divadlo.[31] Huge success. In a box. *Swan Lake. A moment of absolute happiness.* But only a moment. Supper. Speeches. I, Strakatý, Šubert, etc., etc.

10 February. Saw Sasha and P. I. off, with sorrow. Slept. Letters. Dvořák came and interfered a good deal. I am very irritated. Lunch. A walk. In Café Slave. Pišna and a balletmaster. At Urbánek's. František [Urbánek]. At Valečka's. Visited with him and his showy, pleasing wife. Home. Patera. With him to his place. His young wife and son, Volodya. Tea. Home. All possible visits and mad commotion. Durdík and a student beggar. The Father. Autographing of photos (good and charming N. P. Apraksin was helping). Pišna, Dvořák, Urbánek, etc., etc. Departure. The send-off. Bouquets. I

---

[30] *A charming island in the Vltava River on which there is, among other attractions, a concert hall.*

[31] *Theater in Prague where the following all-Tchaikovsky program was given: Serenade for String Orchestra; Theme and Variations from the Third Suite; piano solos by Siloti and the 1812 Overture. As a finale, the second act of his* Swan Lake *was performed.*

was very sad. Doctor Buchal said a beautiful thing: *"Die schönen Tage von Aranjuez sind vorbei!!"* [32] Departed. Sleep. Transferred twice at night. Slept splendidly even though sitting up. Glad to have solitude.

11 February Coffee in Nuremberg. Lunch in Bietigheim. Transfer. But, in general, the traveling was very good, and I was alone all the time. Read a delightful article by Rachinsky, as well as one by Strakhov on Darwinism. Dinner in Strasbourg. Avricourt. Inspection. Transfer. French railway car in which I was not alone. Spent the night rather badly. Cold.

PARIS

12 February Paris. Dark and very cold. Belard, despite the early hour, met me. Rooms on the mezzanine. Tea. Newspapers. Settled myself. Went out at nine o'clock. Meeting with Mme. Belard. At Brandukov's. He was telling me about his troubles. Freezing weather. Absinth. At Mackar's. Condemine. Mme. Mackar. Lunch at Colonne's. Mme. Colonne was alone. She was extremely pleasant. Colonne came at twelve forty-five. He rehearsed the serenade. He was awfully nice and pleasant. After lunch, discussions about the program. Left with Mackar for his place. Home. Visit of Benardaky. Was busy with the orchestration of the song. [33] Brandukov. Lemoine. At the Belards' Dinner at the Dîner de Paris. In a café. Freezing weather. At Belard's. With him and Brandukov in the Café Américain. Home.

---

[32] *Either the doctor or Tchaikovsky misquoted Schiller's lines from* Don Carlos:

> "Die schönen Tage in Aranjuez
> Sind nun zu Ende."

Although frightfully tired Tchaikovsky enjoyed his visit immensely. In a letter to Mme. von Meck he stated that the Czechs received him not as the representative of Russian music only but of Russia itself. He never suspected, he wrote further, to what a degree the Czechs were attached to Russia. But Tchaikovsky was to be very disappointed. For the newspapers in Russia wrote nothing of his Prague triumphs and the Russian people remained in darkness regarding the fervent tribute paid them by the Czechs.

[33] *"Always Thine," Op. 47, No. 6, which was to be sung at the concert on February 16.*

13 February Went walking; it was freezing, and drank absinth. Dropped in at Mackar's. (Taffanel.) Home. With Brandukov to Benardaky. The young lady, Olga Pavlovna.[34] The songs with her. Benardaky, his wife, lunch. In the Café de Londres, absinth. Visits to Marmontel, to Diémer. Did not find them in. At Mackar's. The *littérateur*, Delines. At Marsick's. Played through the concerto with him. Home. Dined with Brandukov at the Dîner de Paris. At La Trompette.[35] Lemoine and his wife. Quartet, sonata, singing (a bass from the opera and Boulanger), the pianist, Chansarel, etc. In the Café de la Paix. Home. Retired fairly early. Very tired.

Sunday, 14 February Visit of the *rédacteur* of *Le Gaulois*. Lunched alone in the Taverne de Londres. At Mackar's. With him to the Châtelet. Concert. In Mme. Colonne's box. Eroica, Grieg's concerto, *Les Troyens* by Berlioz, etc. In Colonne's box. He is awfully affectionate. Commotion. Lemoine. With Anatoly Brandukov and Mackar at the Café de la Régence. Brandukov with a proposal about a concert. I am angry. With him to dine at Mackar's. Lovely Mme. Mackar. She played. Went home.

15 February Rehearsal at Benardaky's. Colonne rehearsed and then I conducted. Singing. Olga, Benardaky herself, Lassalle, Taffanel, etc. Lunch. I at Mme. Conneau's. She sang. At Diémer's. His wife. Fantasy.[36] Absinth. Home. Grippenberg and Pryanishnikov. Discussion about the Société Franco-Russe and about Danilchenko's concert. With him and Brandukov dinner at the Sylvain restaurant. Tramped about alone and was very happy that I had freed myself from the dinner and the opera at Benardaky's.

16 February Received no one in the morning except Danilchenko who called before his departure. Cold weather. At Mackar's. Various ladies and gentlemen. Lunch at the Maire restaurant solo. At the Belle Jardinière. Purchase. At Mackar's. Rehearsed with Brandukov. Home. Could not sleep. Went out. The incident at the *coiffeur's*, my rage. Terrible drunkenness in various places. Begin-

---

[34] *Olga Pavlovna Leibrock, opera singer and sister of Mme. Benardaky, who was to sing some of Tchaikovsky's songs at the same concert.*

[35] *A musical society organized by Lemoine. There Tchaikovsky's First String Quartet, Op. 11 and Piano Sonata, Op. 37, among some of his other works were played.*

[36] *The Concert Fantasy, Op. 56, which Diémer was to perform at the concert on February 21.*

ning of the fire at the Grand Hôtel. A purchase while drunk. Home. At ten o'clock with Brandukov to Benardaky. Memorable evening reception.[37] I was half drunk. Made mistakes while accompanying Lassalle. However, everything all right. Weariness. Supper. The de Reszke brothers are nice people. Rode off with Colonne at four-thirty.

17 February Slept little. Visits of: Fauré, Grippenberg, Bogoliubov, Chashnikov, M. Joly, etc. Lunch at the Sylvain restaurant. In a very bad mood. At Esipova's. At the ambassador's. His talk with me concerning his successes in public life. Esipova's concert. A gentleman with compliments, a noisy lady. Delsart, Rémy, Paderewski, etc. Home. Slept. In a bad mood. Dinner at Colonne's. De Greeg and two representatives of Pleyel. Mme. Colonne's niece. With Colonne about conducting. His advice.

18 February Very hard day. Excitement (however, not very much before the rehearsal). Mackar drove up. Rehearsal. Introduction. Speech. Went excellently. With Colonne and his wife to them. Lunch. *Ma petite amie Alice.* Friendship. Conversation about religion and about future life. From them to the confectionery shop (some candy for Alice and dropped in at home). Condemine. With him to Mme. Langé. With Mackar to Magnard, the director of *Le Figaro.* He proposes to arrange an evening reception. He is very obliging. Réty-Darcours. At his place. At the *chamber music* matinée at Taffanel's. Gounod. Acquaintance with him. He is very nice. Bach's Flute Concerto. Rémy again. Absinth. Home. Pryanishnikov. Dinner at Princess Urusova's. She is a sister of Meshcherskaya (Tolya's). Her curious, rather strange, unmarried daughters. Dinner with pancakes in the upper rooms of the Sturdza palace. Boredom. Mme. Benardaky. She sang. Her accompanist is the secretary of the Madrid Embassy and a pessimist in politics. With Brandukov to a café. Grog.

19 February Thank God! A good day! Received no one until 11 A.M. Simone. Joly (from San Remo). He drove me to distraction with his chattering. Gave him forty francs. Lunch with Brandukov

---

[37] *The program consisted of compositions by Tchaikovsky for orchestra, voice, 'cello, flute, and piano. Benardaky was a very wealthy Russian who lived with his singer wife in Paris. He led the honors to Tchaikovsky, engaged Colonne's orchestra, invited the outstanding musicians of Paris to perform at his soirée and had all the social élite (more than three hundred persons attended) present.*

at the Sylvain restaurant. At Mackar's. A seamstress, who was in Russia. Mme. Mackar's shyness. Girs, Kotzebue, Viardot. The latter received me. At Mme. Colonne's. He and his advice. Singing with Mme. Colonne. Her tea reception. With the Colonnes to Mackar. Letters. Absinth. Modest's strange telegram. At the Belards'. Bogoliubov and Roman. I dine solo at Pierre's. Attractive omnibus. Tramping. At Mackar's. At the Variétés. Décoré.[38] It seemed very boring. Could not endure it after the second act; left. Grog in the Café de la Paix.

20 February Was expecting Mackar. Rehearsal at the Châtelet. Large audience. Went well. Lunch with pancakes at Ben'ardaky's. Weariness. Rehearsal at Colonne's of his evening concert reception. My quartet; monstrous parts. Wolff; the singer, Lauwers, etc. Home. Danilchenko. Dined threesome at the Sylvain restaurant. At Mackar's. Paderewski's concert. Magnificent pianist. I was in Blondel's box with Esipova. Lamoureux and Colonne. At Blondel's. His lovely ladies, punch. With Brandukov to the Café de la Paix. On the way, bought the novel *Le Froc,* in which, I learned from *Le Gaulois,* there is something about me.[39] Golitzin and a blond lyceum student, a friend of Sasha Zhedrinsky.

Sunday, 21 February A memorable day. After a good sleep, went for a walk at ten o'clock. Drank absinth and lunched near the Palais-Royal (alone). Home. Danilchenko. At two o'clock, started out with Brandukov to the Châtelet. Hot in our artist's room. My appearance. Brilliant welcome. The Serenade—a success, particularly the Waltz. The Fantasy (Diémer) less, etc. But, on the whole, very good. Complimentary visits in the room. Dinner with Brandukov and Danilchenko at the Sylvain restaurant. Home. Evening reception at Colonne's. Endless music. I accompanied. A lot of guests. With Tolya (Brandukov) and Le Borne at the Café de la Paix. Retired at two o'clock.

22 February Very burdensome day. Newspapers. *Le Gaulois* offended me unexpectedly; however, not much.[40] At Colonne's.

---

[38] *Comedy by Meilhac.*

[39] *Tchaikovsky's success had risen to such a height that Emile Goudeau wrote a novel in which Tchaikovsky's song "None but the Lonely Heart" was given great importance.*

[40] *The reception in the Paris newspapers was not favorable. Some critics found that he did not come up to the other Russian composers, while others thought his music too German.*

Francesca four hands with Diémer. Widor's luncheon at the Café Foyot. Taffanel, Philipp, etc. Home. At Leroux's from *Le Temps.* Again at Colonne's. Giraudet. At Mackar's. Home. Dinner reception at our ambassador's. All sorts of honors. Esipova, Yev. Nik., Korf, Kotzebue and his wife. Fredericks with his wife, etc. Café de la Paix. At Brandukov's. Went to bed at two o'clock.

23 February Home. Le Borne, Liebrecht from Moscow and his friend like Bonaparte. Solo lunch at Durand's restaurant. A walk. At Colonne's (after the first rehearsal of *Francesca*). Alice. At Mackar's. At Gounod's (did not find him in). At Mme. Adam's. At Mme. Bogomoletz's (found her in, it was her "at home"). At Massenet's. At Mme. Langé's. *Le Temps.* The article (of Leroux). Home. Letters and telegrams. Dinner at Benardaky's. Evening reception at the Russian Club. Playing, singing, stuffiness, boredom, a lot of people.

24 February Am writing much later. What happened on this day, don't remember clearly. Believe I lunched alone at the Durand restaurant. Dinner and evening reception at Diémer's. A lot of people and unusually hot. Benjamin Godard.

25 February Rehearsal. Colonne got on my nerves with his rapping. Lunch at the Café Riche. Visits. Dinner with Brandukov and Kharlamov at the Sylvain restaurant. This day was *Mi-Carême.* Masks and excitement on the streets. Declined the invitation to the evening reception at Kotzebue's. Strolled through the streets. In a *café chantant* on the Boulevard Sébastopol.

26 February Kaiser Wilhelm died.[41] At Mackar's. Solo lunch at Café Riche. At Benardaky's. Mackar. At Lassalle's, etc. Dinner and evening reception at Viardot's. Her *beaux-fils.* Singing. Viardot's beautiful song.

27 February Dress rehearsal. *Francesca* unsuccessful. Walked home. Lunch (pancakes) at Benardaky's. Esipova, Taffanel, etc. Home. Slept. Dinner and evening reception at Bogomoletz's. A terrible, maddening tiredness.

Sunday, 28 February At Magnitzkaya's. Lunch in a cheap restaurant. In the Passage Jouffroy. Home. Concert. Grand welcome. Big

---

[41] *Kaiser Wilhelm I died on March 9, 1888, New Style Calendar.*

success.[42] Dinner with Brandukov and Danilchenko at the Maire restaurant. Home. Evening reception at Colonne's. Paladilhe. Thomé, Joncières. Tiredness and boredom. Guiraud (he is very nice). With Brandukov in a café. Home.

29 February From bad to worse. Visits. I gave a luncheon reception at the Maire restaurant: Fauré, Le Borne, Philipp, Widor, Esipova, Benardaky, etc. Together on the boulevard. Diémer's concert. I was tired and slept. Retired early.

1 March All sorts of visits. M. Payen Souchon with a Turkish pianist. Krotkov, Simmonet, etc. They (especially Krotkov) exasperated me so that I simply lost my head. Went off to have lunch, forgetting about Condemine. Flew to them. The blood rushed to my head. Walked to Mackar. Slept at home and did not go to Esipova's concert. With Brandukov and Danilchenko dinner at the Sylvain restaurant. Home. With Benardaky to the *Vicomtesse de Trédern*. Musical evening. Luxurious interior on the Place Vendôme. Boredom. Marquises, duchesses, countesses, etc. Grog. Russian aunts [43] are repulsive.

2 March In the morning fled in a state of frightful homesickness and despair. The weather is awful. Drank something. Lunch with pancakes at Benardaky's: I, Brandukov, Shelkin, Korf. The *genius* of Maria Pavlovna in sending me away to be by myself awhile, in solitude. Went home with Brandukov. Home. The good Maria tired me. Dinner with Danilchenko and Brandukov at the Lucas restaurant. Populus. Evening reception at *Le Figaro*. Very interesting. Judic and Granier together.[44] Drunkenness with Brandukov. At the Sylvain restaurant. One girl from . . . he liked. I went home.

---

[42] *This concert had a very interesting program of Tchaikovsky's works: Theme and Variations from the Third Suite; the Violin Concerto with Marsick as soloist; the songs, "A Tear Quivers" and "Don Juan's Serenade" sung by Giraudet; Francesca da Rimini; Nocturne for 'cello with Brandukov as the 'cellist; "Song Without Words," Humoresque and the Polonaise from* Eugene Onegin *for piano played by Diémer, and the Elegy and Waltz from the Serenade for String Orchestra. Francesca da Rimini was the only number that had a comparatively small success.*

[43] *In Russian, "aunt" is also used in a reproachful tone toward women.*

[44] *The Paris newspaper,* Le Figaro, *gave a semiprivate affair in honor of Tchaikovsky. Besides many of Tchaikovsky's works, some songs by Massenet, the third act of Tolstoy's* The Power of Darkness *and a duet from the operetta* La fille de Mme. Angot *by Lecocq were performed.*

3 March In the morning, a meeting with Krotkov and my nerves horribly upset. He is stupid and impudent. With Brandukov to Widor at St.-Sulpice. The Mass. He is an excellent organist. Mme. Trélat his mistress. Lunch at the Foyot restaurant. Mme. Trélat sang. I was in a bad mood. At Colonne's in order to talk over about Krotkov. Mme. Colonne. He himself and the Grünfelds. Went home. Talk with Krotkov. More peaceful. At Belard's. Letter to Guiraud. Drunkenness. Went home. At Kotzebue's. Charming Mme. Kotzebue, Esipova, Antokolsky (incredibly repugnant and stupid). With Esipova to the Salle Erard. Sauntering. At the Palais-Royal. *La Boule.*[45] Second rate and not entertaining. Drunkenness at various stops. Went home. Zorin's card about Grippenberg.

4 March Received various people. Beggars, Zorin (explanation about the concert), Le Borne, etc. Lunch at Colonne's with Brandukov. Benjamin Godard. At Mackar's. Home. Solo dinner at an Italian restaurant. Rue Montmartre. A demonstration. Boulanger. Home. Evening reception at La Trompette. Boredom. Accompanied *Diémer.*[46] Offended. Went away. At the Café de la Paix. Benardaky, Tolya, and the marquis.

5 March Packing. At Brandukov's. At Krotkov's (absolutely insane, but his wife is pretty). At Mackar's. His sweetness. Lunch with Brandukov at the Café Riche. Candy for Alice. At Colonne's. Bade good-by. At Mackar's. Confession that I will not return. At Diémer's in the Salle Erard. *Audition.* His pupils and he played about forty of my pieces. Was touched, but became tired. At *Paul Collin's,* the poet. Home. Dinner at Benardaky's. Portraits. Together at Caran d'Ache's.[47] *Ombres françaises.* The cream of society. Maria Pavlovna and Alice. We rode off to see Marchesi. Supper in a café. Home.

---

[45] *Farce by Meilhac and Halévy.*

[46] *La Trompette honored Tchaikovsky with a concert and many works other than his were performed among them being Brahms' Sextet for Strings, Op. 18. Tchaikovsky played his Concert Fantasy four hands with Diémer.*

[47] *Caran d'Ache, E. Poiré's pseudonym. In January, 1871, Tchaikovsky began attending a gymnasium in Moscow owned by J. Poiré. He became acquainted with the latter's family and now, meeting Caran d'Ache, who was a famous caricaturist, he recognized him as the son of J. Poiré, whom he had known as a boy seventeen years ago.*

6 March Vile weather, snow. Wrote a letter to *Le Figaro*. At Brandukov's; at Krotkov's. At Reutlinger's; pictures taken with Tolya. *Macaroni* at an Italian restaurant. I am at *Auclair's* in Bicêtre. Am depressed and homesick. Home. At the Belards'. A loan. At my place Mackar with his wife, Blondel, Krotkov, Pryanishnikov. Dinner at the Café Riche with Brandukov. A walk. At the Vaudeville Theater. *Les surprises du divorce*.[48] Café de la Paix and supper. Home.

LONDON

7 March Departure for London. Krotkov. At the Belards'. Brandukov saw me off. Mackar. Silent passengers (thank God!). Lunched in the dining car. Amiens. Before Calais, we were standing a long time on account of the snow (the weather was awful). Finally, Calais. The ship. The tossing awful. Everyone vomited; I was all right. Slept a little. Boys with pans for vomiting; one was very kind. Dover. Alone in the compartment, later people sat down next to me. London. Cab. Hotel. Supper downstairs. It was very pleasant; chatted gladly with the servants. A coal-burning fireplace. Futile search for the toilet. I will probably travel via Berlin. Am still thinking how, where, why.

8 March Rising, read the *Daily Telegraph* and wrote letters. Lunched at the hotel. Strolling. A French Jew pestered me, but I got rid of him in the Strand. Walked. Rode in a *cab* to Berger. Found him in. Went home. Repaired [the orchestra] parts of the Suite and the Serenade. A smoking stove. Dined at the table d'hôte alone. Alhambra. Bessone.[49] Boredom. Went home. Worked a little over the parts. Slept well.

9 March Arose. Was very little excited over the rehearsal. Berger. With him to St. James's Hall. Rehearsal. They read excellently at sight. The acoustics worse than at the Châtelet, something was lacking. Lunched alone in a restaurant. Walked long. Home. Smoke from the stove. Drowsiness. Slept and then sat downcast, conscious of inability to do anything, even to write letters. Dinner at Berger's. His wife, *belle-sœur* and a Jewish lady. Homesickness. Ondříček.

---

[48] *Comedy by Alexandre Bisson and Antony Mars.*

[49] *At the Alhambra Theater he saw Georges Jacobi's* The Enchantment Ballet *with the* danseuse *Bessone.*

Not especially attractive. His wife. We left at eleven o'clock. I went to the Café Empire. Various goings on. Boredom.

10 March Slept restlessly; my tooth pained very much. Felt terrible in the morning. Conquered myself and went to the rehearsal. Ondříček. There was a small audience. My work went well. Lunched at my hotel with the Ondříček couple and a Jewish journalist, posing as a Czech. Strolled about the city and was drinking. Returning, received Ondříček's visit with difficulty, slept afterward. Dressed and went to the concert. A woman singer. Upstairs. Conducted well. The Serenade a big success; the Suite less.[50] Supper at home with the Ondříčeks and the Jew. Mme. Dieudonné and her sister. The latter sat with us and chatted. Janson, the correspondent of *Le Figaro* and his wife. Slept with difficulty, restlessly.

11 March Feel ill. Wrote letters. Went out at twelve o'clock. At the banker's received twenty-five pounds. A mistake (five instead of twenty-five). Lunched at a restaurant in the Strand. Gatti's. Ate unwisely and felt sick. Decided not to travel today. Home. Fever. Visit of Ondříček. Slept in bed, after which became better. Wrote Mme. Benardaky. Solo dinner downstairs. At the theater. *Tartuffe.* Coquelin. A marvelous troupe. On foot. Grog. Pestering. . . . Read at home *Le Figaro* and *Le Gaulois.*

EN ROUTE TO VIENNA

12 March In the morning, Ondříček visited and invited me to the Crystal Palace. Hesitating. Wrote letters. Lunched with the Ondříčeks at my place downstairs and escorted them to the railroad station. From there went home on foot through unfamiliar streets. The weather cleared up. Bought various things. Home. Packing and weariness. Solo dinner at six o'clock downstairs. The Ondříčeks dropped in. Bade good-by to them, to the sister of the proprietress, to the staff and then started out for the railroad station. Commotion and my fears. All the way to Dover it was rather crowded. On board ship, it was still more crowded. The crossing excellent. Made two acquaintances: 1) with an English aristocrat from Nice and 2) with a Russian cattle merchant, very talkative, who managed to tell me all the details about himself. Calais. We three rode together;

---

[50] *The program contained only two of Tchaikovsky's works, the Serenade for String Orchestra and the Theme and Variations from the Third Suite. The London press received him very well.*

I was magnanimous and, as a result, slept sitting up. Unattractive passengers. Washed myself and changed clothes in the toilet.

13 March While passing by Aachen, thought of *Nik. Dm.* [Kondratyev]. Cologne. Lunch. Got in a compartment with another silent gentleman. Along the Rhine. Recalled the summer trip. Ate twice, frequent drinking of coffee and beer, in order to kill time and homesickness, which was killing me all the more because the book I got was the despicable *La terre* by Zola. I absolutely hate this beast, in spite of all his talent. Slept very little and from Mainz on was alone all the time. Woke before Passau at 4 A.M.

VIENNA

14 March Passau. Customs inspection and transfer of trains. Alone until Vienna. Slept much. Dull. Vienna at eleven o'clock. Hôtel Ungarische Krone. Changed clothes and went walking and to exchange the money; for some reason all the money exchanges were closed. What eternal boredom Vienna causes me. Dined at my hotel. *Zadonskaya;* she did not recognize me. Strolling. Exchanged the money; bought a coat and some other clothes. Home. Read Zola and the newspapers. Performance at the theater *An der Wien. The Mikado;* could barely endure two-thirds of an act. Walked out. Had supper on the Opern-Ring. Returned home bored.

15 March All morning wrote letters. Went out at twelve o'clock in the new coat. Beautiful day. Got a haircut in the neighborhood. Dinner at my hotel. A trip on foot to the Prater. Had pictures taken at a cheap photographer's; went in to a show booth, etc. Trash. Home. Letters. Tea. Went out at seven o'clock; wanted to go to the baths, but was late. Dropped in at a café on the way back. Russian newspaper. Disgust aroused by it??? . . . Why is that? What's in it that seemed to me sickeningly vile? Don't know. Had supper near the opera. Cheap and good. Went home. Packing. Am faced with a long journey to Russia. Write for the future? Hardly worth while. Probably with this I am finishing the diary forever. Old age is knocking, perhaps even death is not far away. Is it worth while?

Diary Eight

Journal: 1886, 1887, 1888

The nature of the entries in the present diary is entirely different, as will be seen, from those in the preceding diaries. Tchaikovsky kept this diary apart from yet at the same time with the others, making entries at irregular periods. It is interesting that he also wrote in the preceding diaries on the same dates as in the present one, with the exception of the last two.

22 February, 1886 What an infinitely deep abyss between the Old and the New Testament! Am reading the Psalms of David and do not understand why, first, they are placed so high artistically and, second, in what way they could have anything in common with the Gospel. David is entirely *worldly*. The whole human race he divides into two unequal parts: in one, the *godless* (here belongs the vast majority), in the other, the *godly* and at their head he places himself. Upon the godless, he invokes in each psalm divine punishment, upon the godly, reward; but both punishment and reward are earthly. The sinners will be annihilated; the godly will reap the benefits of all the blessings of earthly life. How unlike Christ who prayed for his enemies and to his fellow man promised *not earthly blessings* but the *Kingdom of Heaven*. What eternal poetry and, touching to tears, what feeling of love and pity toward mankind in the words: "Come unto me all ye that labor and are heavy laden." All the Psalms of David are nothing in comparison with these simple words.

29 June, 1886 When one reads the autobiographies of our great people or recollections about them, one constantly encounters feelings, impressions, and artistic sensitivity frequently experienced by oneself and fully understandable. But there is *one man* who is

not understood; unattainable, he is alone in his inscrutable greatness. That is *L. N. Tolstoy*. Not infrequently (especially after drinking) I am inwardly angry at him, almost despise him. Why, I think
to myself, has this man, knowing, as no one else does or ever did
before him, how to attune our souls to the highest and most wonderfully harmonious pitch; a writer on whom was freely bestowed
from above the power, never before bestowed on anyone, to make
us of meager intellect comprehend the most impenetrable recesses
of our secret moral being—why has this man become addicted to
teaching, to a *mania for preaching and for the enlightenment* of
our obscured or limited minds? Formerly, from his description of
the most simple and everyday scene, an unforgettable impression
was created. Between the lines one read a kind of highest love
toward mankind, a highest *pity* toward its helplessness, limitations,
and insignificance. One would weep, not knowing why. . . . Because for a moment, through his intermediary, one came in con-
tact with a world ideal in its absolute goodness and humanity. . . .
Now he annotates his texts; claims the exclusive monopoly of understanding questions of faith and ethics (or whatsoever); but from
all his present writings there blows a cold wind; one senses a *fear*
and feels vaguely that he, too, is *human* . . . that is, one who is
involved in questions about our destiny, about the meaning of life,
about God and religion; as irrationally presumptuous and, at the
same time, as insignificant as some ephemeral insect that arrives
at noon on a warm July day and, at evening, ends its existence.

The former Tolstoy was a demigod—the present one, a *priest*.
But priests are essentially *teachers, by a role they have taken upon
themselves, and by virtue of a vocation*. And yet, I am not resolved
to pass judgment upon his new activities. Who knows? Perhaps it
should be so, and I am simply not capable of understanding and
evaluating appropriately the greatest of all artistic geniuses, who
has changed from the calling of a novelist to that of a preacher.

1 July, 1886 When I became acquainted with *L. N. Tolstoy*, I was
seized with fear and a feeling of embarrassment before him. I
imagined that this great explorer of hearts, with one glance, would
penetrate into all the secrets of my soul. Before him, I imagined,
one could not successfully conceal all the rot existing in the depths
of the soul and display only the pleasant side. If he is good I
thought (and such he *must be* and is, of course), then he would
delicately and gently, like a doctor examining a wound and know-

ing all the painful places, avoid hurting and irritating them; but in the same way, would also make me feel that nothing is hidden from him; that if he is not particularly merciful, he will poke his finger directly in the center of the pain. I was awfully afraid of one and of the other. But neither one nor the other happened. The profound explorer of hearts in his works—turned out, in his relations with people, to be a simple, pure, sincere character, disclosing extremely little of that *omniscience* I had feared. He did not *avoid hurting* but also did not *cause* intentional pain. It was obvious that he did not see in me an object for his researches—but simply wanted to chat a little about music, in which, at that time, he was interested. Incidentally, he liked to *disavow* Beethoven and frankly expressed doubts about his genius. This trait is not at all characteristic of great people; to reduce to one's own *incomprehension* a genius acknowledged by all is a characteristic of *limited people.*

Perhaps never in my life, however, was I so gratified and my creative ambition so touched as when L. N. Tolstoy, sitting beside me and listening to the andante of my First String Quartet, burst into tears.[1]

11 July, 1886 It is said that to abuse oneself with alcoholic drink is harmful. I readily agree with that. But nevertheless, I, i.e. a sick person, full of *neuroses,* absolutely cannot do without the alcoholic *poison,* against which *Mr. Miklukho-Maklai* protests. A person with such a strange name is extremely happy that he does not know the delights of vodka and other alcoholic drinks. But how unjust it is to judge others by yourself and to prohibit to others that which you yourself do not like. Now I, for example, am drunk every night, and cannot do without it. What should I do then, in order to get into the Maklai colony; should I seek that??? . . . And is he right? In the first stage of drunkenness I feel complete happiness and *understand,* in such a condition, infinitely more than I do when I am without the Miklukho-Maklai poison!!!! Also, I have not noticed that my health suffers particularly from it. But then: *Quod licet Jovi non licet bovi.* As yet, God knows who is more right: I or

---

[1] *Tchaikovsky first became personally acquainted with Tolstoy toward the end of 1876. The composer was then thirty-six; the novelist was forty-eight. Very soon after their acquaintance, N. G. Rubinstein arranged, at Tchaikovsky's request, a musical evening especially for Tolstoy at the Moscow Conservatory. It was on that occasion that Tolstoy heard the famous* Andante *cantabile.*

Maklai. It's still not such an incomparable calamity—not to be accepted by his colony!!! . . .

12 July Read *The Death of Ivan Ilyich.* More than ever I am convinced that the greatest of all artist-writers, whenever or wherever existing—is *L. N. Tolstoy.* He alone is sufficient so that a Russian does not bow his head in shame when he hears enumerated all the great contributions that *Europe* has given mankind. And in this, my conviction of the eternally great, almost divine, significance of Tolstoy, *patriotism* does not play any part at all.

20 September L. Tolstoy never speaks about a single prophet of truth (with the exception of Christ) with love or enthusiasm or with contempt or hatred. We do not know his attitude toward Socrates, Shakespeare, Pushkin, Gogol. We do not know whether he likes Michelangelo or Raphael, Turgenev or Dickens, George Sand or Flaubert. Perhaps his intimates know his likes and dislikes (in the realm of philosophy and art), but, in print, this genius did not slip in a single word which might illuminate his relationship toward the great who are comparable to him or near him in significance. To me, for example, he said that *Beethoven is without talent* (in contrast to Mozart)—but neither in the field of music nor in any other field has he given his opinion in print. I think that fundamentally this man is capable of bowing only before *God* or before the *folk*, before the *masses* of the people. There is no *person* before whom he would bow. Siutaev, fundamentally, in *Tolstoy's* eyes was not an individual, but the *folk* itself and the incarnation of one aspect of folk wisdom. But it would be interesting to know what this giant likes and does not like in literature.

20 September Probably after my death it will not be uninteresting to know what were my musical predilections and prejudices, especially since I seldom gave opinions in verbal conversation.

Shall start gradually and shall speak to the point, touching upon musicians living at the same time with me and about their personalities.

Shall start with Beethoven, whom it is usual to praise unconditionally and whom it is commanded to worship as though he were a god. And so what is Beethoven to me?

I bow before the greatness of some of his works—but I do not *love* Beethoven. My attitude toward him reminds me of what I experienced in childhood toward the God Jehovah. I had toward

Him (and even now my feelings have not changed) a feeling of wonder but at the same time also of fear. He created Heaven and earth, He too created me—and still even though I bow before Him, there is no *love*. Christ, on the contrary, inspires truly and exclusively the feeling of *love*. Though He was *God*, He was at the same time man. He suffered like us. We *pity* Him, we love in Him His ideal *human* side. And if Beethoven occupies a place in my heart analogous to the God Jehovah, then Mozart I love as the musical Christ. Incidentally, he lived almost as long as Christ. I think that there is nothing sacrilegious in this comparison. Mozart was a being so angelic, so childlike, so pure; his music is so full of unapproachable, divine beauty, that if anyone could be named with Christ, then it is he.

Speaking of Beethoven, I come to Mozart. According to my deep conviction, Mozart is the highest, the culminating point that *beauty* has attained in the sphere of music. No one has made me weep, has made me tremble with rapture, from the consciousness of my nearness to *that something* which we call the *ideal*, as he has done.

Beethoven has also made me tremble. But rather from something like fear and the pangs of suffering.

I cannot *discourse* on music and shall not go into details. However, I shall mention two details: 1) In Beethoven I love the middle period, at times the first, but I fundamentally *detest* the last, especially the last quartets. Here there are *glimmers*—and nothing more. The rest is *chaos*, over which, surrounded by an impenetrable fog, hovers the spirit of this musical Jehovah. 2) In Mozart I love *everything*, for we love *everything* in a person, whom we love truly. Above all *Don Juan*, for thanks to it I learned what *music* is. Until that time (until my seventeenth year) I did not know any music except Italian, semimusic,[2] however charming. Of course, loving everything in Mozart, I shall not start asserting that every insignificant work of his is a *chef-d'œuvre*. Yes! I know that none of his sonatas, for example, is a great work, and *still* I *love* every one of his sonatas because it is *his*, because this musical Christ imprinted it with his serene touch.

Concerning the forerunners of both, can say that I play *Bach*

---

[2] *Long before Tchaikovsky was seventeen, he had already heard parts of Mozart's* Don Giovanni *as well as Glinka's* A Life for the Tsar *and other operas by non-Italian composers. The works of Bellini, Rossini, and Donizetti were semimusic to him.*

gladly, for to play a good fugue is entertaining, but I do not recognize in him (as some do) a great genius. Handel has for me an entirely fourth-rate significance and he is not even entertaining. Gluck, despite the relative poverty of his creation, is attractive to me. I *like* certain things of Haydn. But all these four Muses are amalgamated in Mozart. He who knows Mozart, also knows what is good in these four, because being the greatest and most potent of all musical creators, he was not averse, even, to taking them under his wing and saving them from oblivion. They are rays lost in the sun of Mozart.

21 September, 1887   How short life is! How many things I would like to do, to think over, to express! One postpones, imagining that there is still so much time ahead, while death is already beginning to lie in ambush around the corner. It is exactly one year since I have touched this diary and how many things have changed! How strange it was for me to read, that 365 days ago I was still afraid to acknowledge that, despite all the fervor of sympathetic feelings awakened by Christ, I dared to doubt His Divinity. Since then, my religion has become infinitely more clear; I thought much about God, about life and death during all that time, and especially in Aachen the vital questions: why? how? wherefore? occupied and hung over me disturbingly. I would like sometime to expound in detail my *religion* if only for the sake of explaining my beliefs to myself, once and for all, and the borderline where, after speculation, they begin. But life with its excitement rushes on, and I do not know whether I will succeed in expressing that *Creed* which recently has developed in me. It has developed very clearly, but still I have not adopted it as yet in my prayers. I still pray as before, as they taught me to pray. But then, God hardly needs to know how and why one prays. God does not need prayer. But *we need* it.

27 June, 1888   It seems to me that letters are never entirely sincere. I judge, at least, by myself. Regardless to whom or why I write, I always worry about what impression the letter will produce not only on the correspondent but even on some casual reader. Therefore, I am posing. Sometimes, I *try* to make the tone of the letter simple and sincere, i.e. make it *seem* so. But, except for letters written in a moment of emotion, I am never myself in a letter. On the other hand, the latter kind of letters are always a source of regret and sorrow, at times even very tormenting. When I read the letters of famous people, published after their deaths, a vague feeling of falseness and mendacity always disturbs me.

27 June Am continuing the account, commenced earlier, of my musical likes and dislikes. What feelings are awakened in me by Russian composers?

Glinka An unparalleled, amazing phenomenon in the realm of art. A dilettante, who played now on the violin, now on the piano; who composed absolutely colorless quadrilles and fantasies on stylish Italian themes; who tried his hand both at serious forms (quartet, sextet) and songs, but composed nothing except banalities in the taste of the '30's—who suddenly, in the thirty-fourth year of his life, produces an opera, which by its genius, breadth, originality, and faultless technique, stands on a level with the greatest and most profound in art! The astonishment becomes still greater when one recalls that the composer of that opera is at the same time the author of the *Memoirs,* written twenty years later. The author of the *Memoirs* produces the impression of a man who is kind and amiable, but empty, insignificant, and ordinary. I am sometimes disturbed simply to stupefaction by the question—how was it possible for such a colossal, artistic power to be combined with such a nonentity and by what means, after being long a colorless dilettante, Glinka, suddenly with one stroke, stood on a level (Yes! On a level!) with Mozart, with Beethoven, or with anybody one chooses? This may be said without any exaggeration about the man who composed the Gloria!? [3] But let this question be decided by people more able than I to delve into the mysteries of the creative spirit, which elects for its temple a vase so fragile and apparently incongruous. But I will say only that certainly no one appreciates and loves the music of Glinka more than I. I am not an absolute *Ruslanite* and am even inclined to prefer *A Life for the Tsar,* although the musical values in *Ruslan,* are perhaps actually greater. But the elemental power of the first opera makes itself felt more strongly, while the Gloria is something overwhelming, gigantic. And there was no model at all; antecedents do not exist in Mozart, in Gluck, or in any of the masters. Amazing! Wonderful! No less a manifestation of rare genius is the *Kamarinskaya. Merely in passing,* not in the least setting out to compose something surpassing on a simple theme, a playful trifle—this man (out of nothing) gives us a short

---

[3] *A chorus in* A Life for the Tsar.

work in which every bar is the product of great creative power. Almost fifty years have passed since then; many Russian symphonic works have been written; it is possible to state that there exists a pure Russian symphonic school. And what is the result? All of it is in the *Kamarinskaya,* in the same way as the whole oak is in the *acorn!* And long will Russian composers borrow from this rich source, for much time and much strength is needed in order to drain all of its richness.[4]

Yes! *Glinka* is a real creative genius!

23 July Dargomyzhsky? Yes! Of course that was a talent! But never has the dilettante *type* in music expressed itself so clearly. Glinka too was a dilettante, but his colossal genius serves to screen his dilettantism; indeed, if not for his fateful *Memoirs,* we would not even be aware of his dilettantism. Dargomyzhsky is another matter; with him the dilettantism is in the creations themselves and in his forms. To be average in talent and in addition to be technically unequipped and imagining oneself an innovator—that is real dilettantism. Dargomyzhsky wrote *The Stone Guest* [5] near the end of his life, fully believing that he was demolishing old foundations and was building on their ruins something new, colossal. A pitiable delusion! I saw him in this last period of his life and in view of his sufferings (he had heart disease) it was not, of course, the time for arguing. But if anything is more dislikable and *false* than this unsuccessful attempt to introduce *truth* in a branch of art where everything is based on *pseudo* and where *truth,* in the usual sense of the word, is not required at all—I do not know it. Mastery D. did not have at all (not even a tenth of that possessed by Glinka). But he had a certain piquantness and originality. He was especially successful in harmonic *curiosities.* But not in *curiosities* is the *essence* of artistic beauty, as many among us believe. Something ought to be said about the personality of D. (I saw him rather

---

[4] Kamarinskaya, *named for a Russian folk dance. A short fantasy for orchestra which Glinka wrote on two Russian themes. It was composed about forty years (and not almost fifty) before Tchaikovsky wrote the present entry.*

[5] *Dargomyzhsky's last opera which he left unfinished. It was completed by Rimsky-Korsakov and Cui and when produced was not a success. "I desire that the music express exactly what the words express" was what Dargomyzhsky wrote as the aim of his opera, in which he endeavored to achieve truth.*

often in Moscow during the time of his successes), but it is better not to recall that he was very harsh and unjust in his opinions (as, for example, when he abused the Rubinstein brothers), but was inclined to talk about himself in a praising tone. During the period of his fatal illness he became much more good-natured, even displayed considerable *warmth* to his younger colleagues. I will remember only that. Unexpectedly, he behaved sympathetically (about the opera, *The Voyevoda*[6]) to me. He probably did not believe the gossip that *I* was supposed to have *hissed* (!!!) at the first performance of his *Esmeralda*[7] in Moscow.

---

[6] *Tchaikovsky's first opera composed when he was twenty-eight.*

[7] *Dargomyzhsky's first opera which was unsuccessful.*

Diary Nine

January, 1889 — June, 1889

The present diary, for 1889, was written when Tchaikovsky was living in a house which he rented at Frolovskoye, a village near Klin he thought more picturesque and beautiful than Maidanovo. On April 24, 1888, he moved into his new home, completely satisfied with it. In January he started on his second European concert tour as a conductor giving concerts at Cologne, Frankfurt am Main, Dresden, Berlin, Geneva, and Hamburg. After appearances again in Paris and London, he returned to Frolovskoye by way of the Mediterranean and Tiflis. During this period he was occupied with the composition of the "Sleeping Beauty" ballet.

FROLOVSKOYE

1 January [1889]   Celebrated so that, in due time, I did not even remember. Worked all morning (entrance of Aurora)

Did not drink vodka during dinner. It's a good thing! . . . Worked after tea. *I am not satisfied with my domestic.* I think he is not very honest! (Nine hundred!!!)

2 January   The day went by, as always, when I am absorbed in work. Was writing the *grand adagio* in the second scene and it came hard!!! Even in the evening my head ached. Walked before supper in the courtyard. Was with Feklusha[2] at Gavrila Alex-

---

[1] *The musical example is from the* Sleeping Beauty, Act One, Scene One (*second scene in the ballet, the Prologue being the first*).

[2] *The wife of Alexei Sofronov, Tchaikovsky's valet and house manager.*

eyevich's. The moon!!! Today Petya arrived unexpectedly, the surgeon's assistant whom I have not seen in thirteen years. Talk about the devil—yesterday I spoke about him with Alesha. The weather continues beautiful.

3 January The work went soso. But then I did not strain myself too much and for that reason my head did not hurt. Before supper, received the news about the death of D. V. Razumovsky.

In the morning I read Jahn and looked over those works about which he speaks. Thanks to Jürgenson for the present.[3] A letter from Wolff,[4] an invitation to Berlin.

4 January How beautiful the days continue! Not very frosty, bright, and, starting about three or four o'clock, the moon! Was angry in the morning at Alexei because of the fireplace. Worked, as always now, beyond my strength. It seems to me I am played out!!! Letters from: Jürgenson, Wolff, Nadezhda Filaretovna, etc. After dinner walked long and was down below by the river. Wonderful! Worked after tea—but very differently. It's not the same! . . . After supper walked about the courtyard and the garden. The view at the back toward Klin and the house in the distance is stunning. Strange, something is wrong with my bowels.

5 January Still the same amazing, beautiful, bright, winter weather. Worked well today on the whole. Finished the second scene. Played it through (lasts half an hour). Letter from Shpazhinskaya and that's all. It is painful to receive her letters. Felt especially well during the day as I did not drink any vodka. Waited in vain for the appearance of the moon at four o'clock. It deigned to be late!!! Declared my decision of going to Moscow tomorrow.

6 January Two *priests* officiated at my place and both had lunch. There were also Gavrila Alexeyevich and his wife and Alexei and Feklusha. Walked. Departed at seven o'clock for Moscow. Hotel Moscow. Supper.

---

[3] *Jürgenson gave Tchaikovsky, as a Christmas gift, a collection of all Mozart's orchestra scores and other works in the Breitkopf & Härtel edition. A small Christmas tree was included with this gift.*

[4] *Hermann Wolff, the Berlin concert manager.*

MOSCOW

7 January Moscow. At Jürgenson's. Meeting with Klimenko after a seventeen-year separation. The session. Dinner at Jürgenson's with Klimenko. Gay. *Eralash* [5] (!!!) Supper. Home.

8 January Moscow. Either a headache or the effects of drunkenness. At the Uspensky Cathedral. A stroll. Home. Dobrovolsky and Orlov. Luncheon (mine) at Lopashov's restaurant with Jürgenson, Klimenko, Kashkin, Laroche, Katerina Ivanovna, and Sasha Siloti. Went home at seven-thirty. Dinner. Departed. Vasily to Klin. Snowstorm. Knocking at the door. Quarrel with Alexei.

FROLOVSKOYE

9 January Frolovskoye. Wrote letters all day—seventeen in all. Decided in the evening to ask Vsevolozhsky about the payment.[6] A certain horrible feeling.

10 January The work went well; wrote the entire *entr'acte* to the Sleep Scene, and I think it's all right. Took a pleasant walk after dinner. It was not cold. My domestic is very cold with me. In the evening played the Overture to *The Voyevoda* (located at the request of Jürgenson) and examined the orchestra scores of the ballets given to me once upon a time by Gerber.

11 January The work went especially well today, as of old. Did many things. Finished the second scene of the second act. The experiment with Booby (rode with Alesha to the paved highway, leaving her on the chain, while Feklusha released her five minutes after we left). Read Dostoyevsky (*The Twin*). Chocolate. Eavesdropping.

12 January Jürgenson and Klimenko arrived. I expected a lot of guests, but no one else came. Dinner, discussions, playing, walk, again playing. About Tolstoy. Slept poorly.

13 January Rose very early, i.e. managed to drink tea with those departing. Started Tolstoy's *What I Believe*. Walking, met the children coming from school. A telegram came from Vsevolozhsky about the three thousand as well as a telegram from Panchulidzeva.

---

[5] *A card game similar to whist.*

[6] *Of the annual pension of three thousand rubles which Tsar Alexander III granted Tchaikovsky for life.*

14 January Worked, still just as painstakingly. Hope arises of finishing the first four scenes before my departure.

15 January Siloti, Taneiev (before the others—played Mozart with him) and Klimenko arrived. Debate about Tolstoy. The Fifth Symphony [7] four hands.

16 January The snow has piled up considerably. Both yesterday and today it was hard to walk. The school children in the forest. Worked until I was tired out. A passion for chocolate.

17 January Worked beyond my strength—how very tired I am. Kept sinking into the snow during the walk. Read *What I Believe* in the mornings and am astonished by its combination of wisdom and childish *naïveté*. A letter from Panchulidzeva. Comical solution to my expectations.

18 January It seems to me that never has there been such a divine, beautiful winter day. The beauty was truly stunning. Finished the work, i.e. the first four scenes. Letter from P. I. with an accounting which plunged me in a quandary. Upset. After supper *une querelle avec der Diener. He is not delicate.*

19 January Preparations for the departure. Left in the evening for St. Petersburg. It was sad to leave. On cold terms with Alexei.

ST. PETERSBURG

20 January St. Petersburg. Arrival. Tzet. Vasya. Lunch at home with him. At Buettner's. To the directorate. Visited the sick Pogozhev at his apartment. Dinner at Angèle's and Guitry's. *Eugene Onegin* with Figner and Medeya.[8] Sat in the orchestra.

21 January Rehearsal of the ballet at the Bolshoi Theater. Sat all the time with O. E. Napravnik. Dinner at our place (Bob, Anya, Tzet, Vasya). At the Mikhailovsky Theater (*Marion Delorme;* [9] in a box with Anya and Modya) and at the Society of the Nobles. Russian concert. Glazunov's *Stenka Razin.* Tea at home.

---

[7] *By Tchaikovsky which Taneiev arranged for piano four hands.*

[8] *He witnessed a performance of his opera at the Marinsky Theater with Figner and Medeya May, his wife, in the leading roles.*

[9] *Play by Victor Hugo.*

Tchaikovsky at the age of forty-eight

22 *January* At Panteleimon's. At V. V. Butakova's. To the directorate at Vsevolozhsky's. Discussions with him and Petipa about the ballet. Dinner at Figner's. At Palkin's restaurant with Vasya.

23 *January* At Napravnik's at eleven o'clock. I gave a luncheon at Palkin's for Korsakov, Glazunov, etc. Various visits. At five o'clock at the director of theaters; played the second act of the ballet. Dinner at Kondratyev's. Tea at *Bob's* (a hundred times divine).

24 *January* Departure for abroad. Lunch at the railroad station with Anya, O. E. Napravnik and Volodya, Tzet, Modya. Alone in a (large) compartment. Spaniards for neighbors. The usual boredom and drunkenness. Chocolate.

BERLIN

25 *January* We crossed the border. In a sleeping car compartment. Read Daudet's *L'Immortel*.

26 *January* Arrival at Berlin. At Wolff's. Solo lunch at Dressel's. At Klindworth's, at Bock's, at Bloch's. Home. Did not feel well (my tooth ached due to the cold). Dinner in a new restaurant. Roamed about. Home.

27 *January* At Wolff's. At Artôt's. Lunch at Dressel's. Am ill. Home. Jedliczka. Wolff. With him at the *Singakademie*. Bach. Supper at Wolff's brother's. Conversation about Russian literature with the old man.

28 *January* After being at Wolff's, remained at home and repaired the parts of the Suite.[10] Did not feel well. However, lunch and dinner at Dressel's.

29 *January* Departure from Friedrichstrasse. A rather big crowd. A disagreeable German opposite me (his wife saw him off). Reading. Dinner in Hannover. Arrival at ten-thirty at Cologne. Hotel du Nord. Charming room. Supper. An attractive personality.

COLOGNE

30 *January* Uncertainty about the place and time of the rehearsal. Homesickness and dejection. Too early to the Gürzenich. The

---

[10] *Third Suite, Op. 55, for orchestra.*

honest agent with red eyes. Finally the rehearsal. Wüllner.[11] Excellent orchestra. Table d'hôte (there are but three of us). In the evening again a rehearsal. A supper for me by the Musicians' Society. The joy of meeting Haliř.

31 January Rehearsal. It went off excellently. Dinner at Wüllner's. Homesickness. Haliř is upset. Home. Drunkenness. Slept. The concert.[12] Queer artists' room. Haliř. The singer Meyer. Went off very well and it was a big success. Supper reception at Neitzel's (Baron, the director of the theater). Neitzel's pretty wife.

FRANKFURT AM MAIN

1 February Departure from Cologne. Packed. Lunched at eleven o'clock. Haliř and Neitzel came. In the train. Alone at first; then an attractive youth and alone again. Frankfurt am Main. Hotel Schwan. Dinner. Mischievous boys. A walk. At Doctor Sieger's. Home.

2 February Was not unusually excited. Director Müller and Doctor Sieger. Museum.[13] Rehearsal. Cossmann. The coolness of the musicians; the orchestra not as good as Cologne's. The Suite. 1812 Overture. Evidently an unfavorable impression. Discussions. Decided not to play it.[14] Dinner at Cossmann's. He has aged awfully. Pleasing wife and daughters. At Müller's. Wife thin as a reed. Coffee. Boredom and homesickness. Home. Unpleasant realization of failure. At Cossmann's. Supper. Their warmth and kindness.

3 February Rehearsal. The audience. The musicians attentive. Knorr (married to a Russian), Gustav Erlanger. Home. Solo lunch. The composer Urspruch. A stroll. Home. Drunkenness. Sleep. The concert. Huge success. The Cossmanns in the artists' room. Sat with two young ladies in the hall. Supper reception at Doctor Sieger's.

---

[11] *Franz Wüllner, leader of the Gürzenich concerts in Cologne.*

[12] *At this concert, held in the Gürzenich Hall, Tchaikovsky conducted his Third Suite which was enthusiastically received by the orchestra, public, and critics.*

[13] *Museum Society concerts in Frankfurt am Main.*

[14] *The Third Suite and the 1812 Overture were rehearsed but the bombastic Finale of the latter frightened the managers who timidly suggested that another work be chosen. Since no other was on hand, only the Suite was performed.*

Attractive furnishings. Mme. Kwast—daughter of Hiller. Went home at one o'clock.

4 February Packing. Visits (Stasny, Lamond, Vede and the nephew of André, the Cossmanns). The debt paid by Gustav Erlanger (*stukolka* [15] once upon a time, about twenty years ago). With Mme. Cossmann to the railroad station. Lunch. Knorr, he and his wife, and old Cossmann. Compartment. Dissipated throughout the trip. Transfer in Leipzig. A talkative German. A pretended but later a real sleep. Dresden at night.

DRESDEN

5 February Rose at eight. Repairing (superficially the parts of the [Fourth] Symphony). Visits of Messrs. Pražek and Sauer. Dinner at the table d'hôte. A neighbor recognized and talked to me a little. A walk through the city. Home. Repairing. At the theater *Die Königin von Saba.* [16] I disliked the music very much. Poor singers, especially the tenor. Falseness and conventionality. Home. *Kalter Aufschnitt* and tea. Lay down to sleep early.

6 February A sad day. Rehearsal. The orchestra turned out to be third rate. The symphony went off abominably. The impoliteness of Mr. Ries. The singing of the young ladies and the tenor from Prague. Home. At Sauer's. He and his wife (pretty) are a pair of cooing doves. They are very sweet. Fine dinner. Home. (Sauer escorted me.) Homesickness. Roamed about after sleeping. Did not know how to kill time. Home. Supper. Brilliant illumination.

7 February Second rehearsal. Fussed to exhaustion. The absence of the management. Dinner alone at the table d'hôte. A stroll. Slept at home. Evening reception at Sauer's. Müller. Went home with him. Punch.

8 February Third rehearsal. The careful work of the musicians; the treat to beer. Continued absence of the management. Ploetner appeared only toward the end. I was preparing uselessly for *Ah, perfido.* [17] Dinner at a restaurant. Slept. The concert. [18] Was terribly

---

[15] *A Russian card game.*

[16] *By Carl Goldmark.*

[17] *Beethoven's aria for soprano and orchestra. Tchaikovsky did not conduct it at the Dresden concert.*

[18] *The program consisted of the Fourth Symphony and the First Piano*

afraid and felt bad especially in the beginning. Much less success than at Cologne and Frankfurt am Main. However, a fanfare. Supper reception at Sauer's with guests and speeches.

BERLIN

9 February Berlin. Packed. The Dobrov girl with fans. Visits to Grützmacher and Schuch. Dinner at Sauer's with the old lady and Müller. At Scholz's. Autographs. His works. Strange wife. All three of us together to the hotel and to the café. Beer. Newspapers. Hartmann's article. At the railroad station. Beer. Departed. At eleven-thirty at the hotel. Supper in the room.

10 February At Wolff's. He is out. Letters. At Mme. Klindworth's. Lunch at Dressel's. Winter weather. At Schneider's—found him out. At Bock's in the store. Home. Transferred to the first room. Dinner reception at the Blochs'. Kumanin. The Bocks. With Bock to the Opernhaus. Ninth Symphony. Home. Supper. Telegram to Bernuth.

11 February Doubts concerning Schneider. Bock at my place. Awful weather. I at Schneider's. Changes. I am satisfied. At Dressel's. Visits to Kumanin and Kudryavtzev. Evening reception at Artôt's.[19] Kumanin toward the end of the supper; he came directly from a dinner at which the kaiser was present. An American woman singer. The Bernstams. Went home with Kumanin.

12 February When I went out, I found that there was no announcement of the concert. Furious. At Wolff's. Certain things were cleared up. Payment of the two hundred marks received from Wüllner. Dinner reception at Klindworth's. The Jedliczkas. Beer. Went home. Evening reception at Kudryavtzev's. Card playing. Late supper. Svyatlovskaya. Escorted her.

13 February First rehearsal. Uncertainty as to the soloists. Serenade. The orchestra is stunning. Lunch at Rummel's. His little dog. The concert. Home. The dream about father. The dinner reception

---

Concerto with Emil Sauer as soloist. The audience liked the First Movement of the symphony little, the Andante more, the Scherzo still more and after the Finale it was a real success.

[19] *During his stay at Berlin, Tchaikovsky met Désirée Artôt de Padilla at all the receptions to which he was invited. She was his only comfort (the tour was tiring him).*

at the Bocks' is excellent. Artôt. Her problem concerning the child.[20]
Little Hofmann. Went home with Kumanin.

14 February At eleven o'clock dress rehearsal. Matilda Ivanovna
and the Kudryavtzev girls. Lunch downstairs at my place. Hendtlass. Cossmann did not come. A stroll. Drunkenness at home. The
concert.[21] Not so good. The hall was filled. Left with Cossmann.
Supper at Kudryavtzev's. The native woman fish dealer. Café Bauer.
Telegram from Ducastel.

15 February Agonizing homesickness. Lunch at the ambassador's.
He is very charming. The parrot. The secretaries. Passage. A stroll.
Home. Maddening homesickness and weeping. Dinner at Dressel's,
solo. Home. Evening reception at Klindworth's. Very pleasant and
touching. Supper at the Bellevue with Artôt, the Bocks, Jedliczka,
etc. Homesickness.

16 February Packed. Jedliczka. Wolff (money from Wüllner and
the offer to play *Eugene Onegin* next season). News about the
death of K. J. Davidov. With Jedliczka to the Kudryavtzevs'. Pancakes. Count Muravyev. At Klindworth's. Home. Paid my bill.
Dinner at Dressel's (the Bocks, Artôt, Bohlmann, Wieniawski).
Seeing me off were Bock, Jedliczka, Baroness Senfft von Pilsach.
Alone in the car. Eleven-thirty at Leipzig. I was received like an
old friend.

LEIPZIG

17 February Leipzig. Albert, Max [von Erdmannsdörfer], and
Emma. In the same room (No. 43). All this is pleasant to me.
Letters. Kogel smelled me out and came. His proposal to enter into
business negotiations with Doctor Abraham (Peters). Dinner with
both of them downstairs at the table d'hôte. A stroll. Home. Cold
weather. At the theater. *Der Barbier von Bagdad* and *Puppenfee.*[22]
Supper. Home. Letter from Bernuth. Decided to go to Hamburg
after Geneva.

---

[20] *She had a daughter, slightly over three years, Lola Artôt de Padilla,
later a well-known soprano.*

[21] *Tchaikovsky conducted his Serenade for String Orchestra and Francesca da Rimini.*

[22] *Comic opera by Peter Cornelius and ballet by Josef Bayer.*

18 February Scheffer (Vertreter Rahter's) came. The publisher Payne. Walked to the Brodskys'. Everything as before except Olga Lvovna is not here. Lovely people. Dinner. Nováček and Sinding. A stroll. At seven o'clock again to them. My Third Quartet phenomenally performed. Supper. Klengel (his wife just gave birth). Went home at 1 A.M. My homesickness has calmed down a little.

19 February Packed. Brodsky at ten-thirty. Walked to the railroad station. Cold weather. Alone in the compartment. Lunch in the train and drunkenness. It was very melancholy. More than an hour in Frankfurt am Main. Had supper. Girls and women one of whom (resembling a nurse) was sick. Sleeping car. Alone. It is cold and sad.

20 February Basel. Hustle-bustle. Seven o'clock in the train. The girl with her companion (from the Frankfurt am Main passengers); an old man who came over to smoke. Lunch in Berne. Read Count Tolstoy's [23] *Prince Serebryany.* Lausanne. Traffic and commotion. Excitement. Geneva. Gr. Hôt. de la Paix unattractive. Had dinner alone. A stroll. Liqueur at a café. To the Russian church—closed. Went home. Visit from Hugo Senger.[24] Alone in my room with the lamp burning. Enjoyable evening.

GENEVA

21 February Passed the whole morning in expectation of Senger. Read and wrote letters. Went downstairs at twelve. In the reading room. Began to walk along the quay. The weather is marvelous. Senger. To the rehearsal. M. Ducastel. Cui's portrait. Rehearsal in some kind of attic. A small and bad orchestra. The musicians are very amiable and enthusiastic. With Senger in music stores. Home. Dinner alone without enjoyment. A walk. Home. Senger. At the Russian church. At the theater. *Rigoletto. The sacristan.* At the director's. Made the acquaintance of the men singers and the woman singer. Went home with Senger. Supper in my room.

22 February After tea read the newspapers and wrote letters. The visits of Mr. Bonade, the sacristan (Spassô) and one more guest. The 1812 Overture for military band. A stroll. Wonderful weather.

---

[23] *Not the great novelist and philosopher, but Alexei K. Tolstoy, the poet.*

[24] *Conductor in Geneva.*

Preconsecration Mass at the Russian church. Rehearsal. Went home with Senger, Bonade, and the sacristan. Solo lunch. The peculiar, stupid, but good-natured sacristan with effeminate manners. My photo of 1875. A stroll. Visited the owner of my photo (a friend of Rabus). Home. Rehearsal again. The serenade. (Three viola players—good for nothing.) Went home with Senger. Supper, fireplace; a pleasant short hour.

23 February The weather is amazing again. After tea and reading a walk beyond the city on the Savoy side. Lunch in a café. Absinth. Rehearsal. Music from Mackar. "Mozartiana." After the rehearsal, in the director's office. The program. Beer. To the Plainpalais Square. Had a picture taken at the *photographie instantanée*. Went home. About six o'clock Bonade and Senger came for me. Dinner in a restaurant. It was very enjoyable. We stayed until eleven o'clock. Bonade and his friend escorted me home. Gossip about Geneva affairs.

24 February Made cuts in the Finale of the [Fifth] Symphony. Lunched at eleven o'clock. The weather is marvelous. Was late for church. Rehearsal. At Spassô's, the sacristan. Home. Dinner in a tavern, given in my honor by Consul Barton. English people and Bonade. At the *Cercle nautique*. My overture. Very good. At a café. Prokesch, the pestering Czech. Good Spassô but somewhat . . . peculiar. Became acquainted with a charming priest.

25 February At Prokesch's. Rehearsal. At the Café du Nord restaurant alone. Drunkenness. At the steamship agency. The concert.[25] Huge success. Golden laurel wreath. Fee. Champagne. With Senger and N. N.[26] at a café.

26 February A lot of visitors in the morning; one cannot remember them all. Departure. Seeing me off were Rey, Senger, and the old consul. Was angry at the passengers (old men) as far as Lausanne and at the new ones (a red-headed man and a thin man) from Neuchâtel on. Homesick. In Basel an hour and a half. Read in the train. Traveled alone.

27 February Two whole hours in Frankfurt am Main. Traveled alone in a compartment. Read Belot and finished *Prince Serebryany*.

---

[25] *The all-Tchaikovsky program contained the Serenade for Strings, Don Juan's Serenade sung by Dauphine and the First Suite for orchestra.*

[26] *Tchaikovsky used the initials N. N. as one of his pseudonyms.*

Slept much and *drank* much. Arrived in Hamburg at 10 P.M. A small room. Brahms as neighbor. Repairing the parts of the symphony.

28 February First rehearsal. Affectionate reception by the musicians. Brahms at the rehearsal. The Burmesters. Laube at my place. Lunch with Brahms [27] and Bernuth at the Pfordte restaurant. At Mme. Rahter's. Home. Dinner. Alone in the evening. A strange thing! Strive for solitude, and when it comes, I suffer. Read *Les Petites Cardinal.* [28]

1 March Second rehearsal. It went off excellently. With Laube and Sittard in the Wintergarten. Abominable weather. Home. Slept. Dinner at the Rahters'. (Mme. Krantz, etc.) Benefit concert for Laube. An ovation for me. Rode back with Sittard and Bernuth.

2 March At ten o'clock to the rehearsal. The musicians like the symphony more and more. Burmester played. Lunch at the Pfordte restaurant solo. Public dress rehearsal at two o'clock. Big success. Burmester is becoming more and more repulsive to me. Dined downstairs at home, very well. Sittard. With him at a café. Homesickness. With him also at the Society of Musicians. German humor. However, nice people. In a café.

3 March Visit by Sapelnikov's cousin. He smelled of vodka. Asked for money. My stinginess. Awfully cold in the room. The Burmester girl. At Blüthner's. Solo lunch at Pfordte's restaurant and a stroll. Home. *Terrible* drunkenness, to such an extent that, the next day, I did not remember what had happened. At five o'clock the *lady* appeared with the shirts and I quarreled with her. I think Burmester came and I annihilated him, because of yesterday, but do

---

[27] *Tchaikovsky was surprised to learn that he had Brahms as his neighbor at the same hotel. But he was flattered when he later found out that Brahms stayed a day longer in Hamburg solely for the purpose of hearing the first rehearsal of his Fifth Symphony. Brahms expressed frankly and simply his opinion of the Fifth Symphony—he liked all the movements except the Finale. Tchaikovsky thought that the orchestra musicians had the same opinion, but what was more important, Tchaikovsky himself felt that the Finale was "awfully repulsive."*

[28] *By Halévy.*

not remember for certain. The concert. Success. At a beer hall with Bernuth and *tutti quanti*. At the Café Continental.

4 March I let it appear that I departed in the morning. Wrote letters, recollected, was terrified, homesick, perplexed—in a word, a horrible state. Lunch at Pfordte's restaurant. Packed. Departed. Somewhere on the way bought *Butterbrote* and was carousing in the train. Hannover. Unattractive hotel. Slept sweetly and well, despite the unbearable coughing neighbors.

HANNOVER

5 March Woke in a good mood. Wrote letters. Strolled about the city. Pretty but commonplace; however, there are some medieval houses. Dinner at the table d'hôte; I sit by myself and am very satisfied. A walk to the Schloss Herrenhausen. A remarkable hot-house with gigantic palms. *Bierbrauerei.* Home. Letters and reading. Supper at an elegant restaurant. Home. Read the lovable Mérimée (Colomba, etc.). Was carousing. Slept badly.

6 March In the morning paid for yesterday's excesses. Reading. Attempt at composing the ballet [*Sleeping Beauty*]. Wrote something but unwillingly and poorly. The weather is terrible, bleak, and misty. In my soul is gloom. Took a little walk. Dinner at the table d'hôte. Slept. Tea. At the theater. *Martha!!!* Supper at that same elegant restaurant and probably there I caught cold. . . .

7 March . . . for I woke in the morning with a dull pain in my tooth and an indefinite feeling of indisposition. Packed and prepared for the trip. No appetite at all at dinner and it was painful to chew. Departure. Almost for the first time in my life did not sit by the window. Passengers: A young man from Russia but not a Russian (a Jacobin type); a good-natured German and an Englishman, very repulsive. The pain and indisposition worse and worse. Arrangements in Cologne about a berth in the sleeping [car]. Got an upper. Suffered incredibly. Terrible night!

PARIS

8 March Early in the morning customs inspection in Jumont. Shortly after that felt better. Dozed all the time and had feverish dreams. Paris. Aversion and boredom. The friendly Belards (she herself left yesterday for the country). Brandukov. Slept in my room. Dressed with difficulty. Had lunch with disgust and the tooth

pained very much. Exchanged the money. Home. Sleep. Branduk-
kov. He went to dine and to the concert. Maria came and conversed
long. I napped and read. Toward the end of the evening felt much
better. Brandukov after the concert (of Diémer). Fires in the fire-
places.

9 March Spent a fair night, but still am not entirely well. Despite
the swelling, went out. Lunched with Brandukov at the Sylvain.
Strolled along the Palais-Royal and St.-Honoré. At home, reading
and writing. Dined with Brandukov at the Sylvain. At the Variétés.
Les jocrisses de l'amour.[29] Fairly amusing. (Dupuis, Baron, Raimond, etc.) At the Café de la Paix.

10 March Was at Mackar's. M. Noël. A boy clerk. Mme. Mackar.
Money from the Society of Composers. Lunched alone at the Café
Riche. Strolled. Got tickets at the *location* for the evening performance at the Opéra-Comique. Home. At Brandukov's for the rehearsal of Chaminade's trio. I do not care for it. We dined again at
the Sylvain. Opéra-Comique. *Le Roi d'Ys.*[30] I liked it very much.
At a café. The nostalgia and the aversion *to a foreign country* have
passed.

11 March Overslept. Rehearsal of the Concerts Châtelet. I am in
Mme. Colonne's box. Lefebvre's works. Very nice. *Parsifal.* Lunch
with Anatoly Brandukov at an Italian restaurant. Wonderful
weather. On foot to Benardaky. She is ill. Was in bed. I did not
feel well. At the Café Meyerbeer. *Novoye Vremya.* Home. Slept.
Dreamed that I was a *dancer.* Dinner with Brandukov at the Sylvain. All evening we loafed. I feel better.

12 March Lunched at the Riche with Brandukov. Concerts
Châtelet (*Parsifal,* Lefebvre, etc.). I was in Mme. Colonne's box.
With Mackar in a café on the quay. Dinner with Brandukov in the
rue Royale. Also at a café in the open. Widor. Evening reception
at Colonne's. Stifling. My songs. Acquaintance with Massenet.

13 March Still do not feel well and am rather dull (it may be
due to the quinine which I finally took). Lunched at the Lucas
restaurant with Brandukov. At Benardaky's. She is better. Still in
bed. At Diémer's. Did not find him in. Slept at home. Glazunov's

---

[29] *Comedy by Barrière and Thiboust.*
[30] *Opera by Lalo.*

letter. (He is ? *Wagnerite!!*) Dinner at the Dîner de Paris. Musée Grévin. Roaming. Retired early.

14 March Lunched at the Maire restaurant (after the baths). Made visits to Lalo and Mme. Bogomoletz, but did not find them in. Ordered some clothes and underwear. Dinner with Brandukov at the Dîner de Paris. *Gymnase. Belle-Maman.*[31] Soso. At a café.

15 March Went in for Mackar (after getting rid of Mr. Ogonchikov and his concert) and we started for lunch to Lefebvre's. It was enjoyable. He played *Eloa*. Strolled. Dined with Brandukov at the Sylvain. *Grand opéra.* We were in a box. *Roméo et Juliette.* Charming Eames.[32] At a café.

16 March Mi-Carême. At the rehearsal of the Concerts Châtelet. *Holmès* and her [*Une vision de*] *Ste.-Thérèse.* The musicians received me cordially. Lunch at Mackar's. At Blondel's. Did not find him in. Could hardly elbow my way home through the crowds. Dinner with Tolya Brandukov at the Dîner de Paris. We roamed about. Went home early.

17 March Until twelve o'clock, stayed at home and made corrections.[33] Coquard. Lunched in a luxurious café on the Avenue de l'Opéra. Was captivated by the beauty of a certain lady. Visits to the tailor (a fitting). To Viardot (did not find her in) and to Benardaky (also out). On foot to the Trocadéro. Searched for Pascal, whose traces are no longer visible. At the Trocadéro looked at the *Tour Eiffel* and went up in the *ascenseur* with some little *commissionnaire*. Home. Dinner with Brandukov at the Dîner de Paris. *Audition.* Duvernoy, Massenet, Delibes. At a café.

18 March Vasya Sapelnikov arrived. I was at the rehearsal before an audience. They reacted very indifferently to my work. I was a little hurt. Home. Modest's *terrible* letter about the *storm* that nearly killed him. Lunch with Brandukov and Sapelnikov at the Café de Paris. At Colonne's. Found him with Holmès at lunch. At Blondel's with Vasya. Lemoine. At the Café de la Paix. I was at

---

[31] *Comedy by Sardou and Deslandes.*

[32] *Emma Eames, the famous soprano, was making her appearance in Gounod's opera.*

[33] *In the Theme and Variations from the Third Suite for orchestra for the concert on the nineteenth.*

Benardaky's. A marquise. Home. Dinner at Diémer's with Branduikov. Rather boring and very long, but the people are nice. The pupils of Diémer. Stojowski, the Pole, and a Peruvian.[34] Mme. Damcke. Went home.

19 March Woke in a very bad mood. At M. Coquard's. His opera. Home. Lunch with Brandukov and Sapelnikov at the Lucas. At the Concerts Châtelet. With Brandukov in Mme. Colonne's box. My composition.[35] Success. Back stage. Diémer. Colonne. Massenet's enthusiasm. Strolled. Drunkenness at two places. Home. Paderewski. Lemoine. Paderewski played his concerto. Nice person. Dinner with Sapelnikov at the Dîner de Paris. At a café. Along the boulevard. Magic lantern. Escorted him home. Café again. At the Belards'. Bade good-by to Jean-Marie. Sapelnikov played me the Overture to *Tannhäuser*. Learned of the death of V. P. Taneieva and wept.

20 March Lunched with Brandukov and Vasya at the Italian restaurant. Escorted Vasya to the Salle Erard. Strolled. To the Salle Erard again. The incident with Mme. Montigny-Rémaury regarding her rehearsal. Upstairs. Diémer and the Marquise de St. Paul. *Caniche.* Vasya played. Home. Dinner at Mme. Benardaky's. We carried her downstairs. After dinner playing and singing. At a café.

21 March Mr. Ogonchikov and the singers. With Brandukov to the Café de Paris. We lunched. I roamed about and drank slightly. Home. Threesome dinner at the Lucas. Went home. Tail coat. At Diémer's concert. I was in Mme. Diémer's box. Widor, Delsart, etc. Evening reception at M. Fuchs'. Mme. Lalo, my duet, Fauré, a lot of guests. At the Café de la Paix. Vasya and Brandukov played chess.

22 March I lunched alone at the Café de Paris. Fish pie. Ordered the dinner. Roamed about and drank heavily. (Before lunch a visit to Detroyat; he is in bed.) Home. Slept. The weather is awful. My dinner at the Café de Paris. The Mackars, Noël, Brandukov, Vasya, Fauré. I was not gay. At a café with . . . and at the Café de la Paix. Chess. I napped. Went home alone. A Negro. He came in to me.

---

[34] *The pianist, Victor Henri Staub, born at Lima, Peru.*

[35] *Theme and Variations from the Third Suite which Colonne conducted.*

23 March Am writing now in London after almost a week and it is very hard to remember. I think Sanya appeared at my place for the first time in the morning. Solo lunch at the Italian restaurant. Dinner with Vasya and Brandukov at the Lucas. I attended a *choral* concert. Vile. At a café. Vasya and Brandukov played chess.

24 March I think I was with Brandukov at the Café de Paris. They pay no attention. At the rehearsal of *Jeune France*.[36] D'Indy. At Detroyat's. Galée.[37] Home. Dinner at Colonne's. Vasya created a furor. At a café. (Conversation about religion with Mme. Choudens.)

25 March Got rid of Paul Dultis. Ogonchikov exhausted me. At Sanya's at the Hôtel de Paris. Shilg. Lunch with them and Brandukov. Do not recall what happened. Home. Threesome dinner at the Café de Paris. At the *Jeune France* concert. Trash. D'Indy, etc. . . . Fauré—fascinating! The three of us together at the Café de la Paix.

26 March With Vasya to Lemoine. Paderewski *"Je ne me laisse pas pincer."* Lunch at Lemoine's. *Frogs' legs.* Pierné, d'Indy. Concerts Châtelet. *Damnation [de Faust].* Was avoiding Grieg. At Colonne's. (Reyer.) Home. Dinner at M. P. Benardaky's. Lassalle —Hérisson (!!!) Russian singers. Playing. Late at a café with . . . The three of us together at the Sylvain.

27 March They gathered one after another (not counting the horrible Ogonchikov), Fauré, Diémer, Pierné, Taffanel, Le Borne, etc. (In the morning Sanya came over.) Lunch at the Café de la Paix. Various visits. Mackar is intrusive. At Erard's. Vasya played the [First Piano] Concerto with me (Diémer). Home. Dinner at the Café de Paris. Performance at Viardot's.[38] Tiredness. At the Café de la Paix. To sleep.

28 March Rose at seven o'clock. Packing. Bills, Farewells, etc. Mackar saw me off. Sanya von Vizin appeared. How lovely she is.

---

[36] *A rehearsal of works by young French composers; Tchaikovsky thought they were all strong Wagnerites.*

[37] *To his nephew Bob, Tchaikovsky wrote that he would compose a French opera to be called* La Courtisane *to a libretto written by Detroyat and Galée. The opera was never composed.*

[38] *A performance of Viardot-Garcia's opera,* Le dernier sorcier, *composed twenty years previously to a libretto by Turgenev.*

In a separate *coupé de luxe*. Lunch in Amiens. All the while playful and fantastic talk with Vasya. Boulogne. The sea. Vasya was nauseated. The marvelous steamship "Folkestone." Separate cabin. London. Hôtel Dieudonné. Pleasant reception. Dinner. Playful talk. Rain. Strolling. At Berger's. *"Grieg ist unartig."* Home. Drunkenness in private.

LONDON

29 March Rehearsal. *Extraordinary fog,* like night. I lunched alone. Strolled during darkness and rain. Home. Dinner with Vasya. We strolled along the Strand. Nana. Home in my room. Retired early.

30 March Second rehearsal. [Reginald De] Koven took up too much time. I was furious. The musicians, as yesterday, very cold. Lunch with Vasya at a restaurant. Home. Letters. Drunkenness. The *concert*.[39] Vasya had a huge success. A lot of people came to the artist's room. Supper at home with an old Jewish acquaintance.

TRIP FROM LONDON TO TIFLIS

31 March Kissed sleeping Vasya and departed. Clever and pleasant porter. Compartment to Dover. Lunch on the steamship. Alone in the compartment all the way to Paris. Transfer to a *train de luxe*. Kolya Korsakov[40] and Bazilevsky. Dinner in the dining car with Bazilevsky. Slept well. Marseilles.

1 April Marseilles. Marvelous weather. Waiting for the baggage. Anxiety. Did everything that was necessary. The incident with the gold pince-nez. [S.S.] "Cambodge." Passengers not very interesting. The charming youth Sklifasovsky[41] and a student. Tossing of the ship. Dinner. Tossing of the ship. Fear. Bad night.

2 April Eight o'clock. The tossing is terrible. I am terrified! It subsided toward twelve when we were crossing the Strait of Bonifacio.

---

[39] *The program had the First Suite and the First Piano Concerto on it with Tchaikovsky conducting and Sapelnikov as soloist.*

[40] *On the train, Tchaikovsky met N. A. Rimsky-Korsakov, who was related to the composer of the same name and was the husband of his niece, Vera L. Davidova.*

[41] *The fourteen-year-old son of a famous Moscow surgeon who was traveling with a Moscow University student named Hermanovich. Tchaikovsky became very fond of the boy.*

In the evening it became stronger again. The weather was clear. Sklifasovsky and his student friend were sick all the time; only for a short while during the day did they feel better. During dinner, when the pitching started, all, one after the other, began to leave. I am invincible so far. But I am melancholy and there is still too long a wait before the end.

3 April Slept restlessly, as the creaking and crackling irritates me. The weather, since morning, is dreary, gray; it is beginning to rain; the tossing is quite bearable. Sklifasovsky and the student strolled on deck. Pretty boring. The weather cleared up little by little and became excellent. Fishing. The Lipari Islands. The volcano and eruption. The Strait of Messina. Storm (it was frightful). After we passed the strait, the storm was over but it was still very rough. Mockery at an old Greek.

4 April Slept well with an open porthole. Performed all the ablutions from evening on. Tea. Sklifasovsky. The student. Both well. Wind. Composed the Polonaise.[42] At lunch was shy as always; somehow especially so today. Talks with the captain. Read *Capitaine Fracasse* [43] upstairs. It is becoming interesting. Writing the Polonaise. Napped. Before dinner listened to the Greek's story of a fire at sea. Dinner. Expectation of the lighthouse. Sailing is still a very good thing, most of the time.

5 April In the morning it was quite calm. Finished the Polonaise. Syra.[44] Went ashore with Volodya [Sklifasovsky] and Hermanovich. A square in antique style; palm trees. At a café. Through the city. Hot weather. Some purchases. Sailed at four o'clock. Noisy loading of vegetables. During dinnertime, the tossing started; it was very severe. Later it broke out into a real storm. Fear gripped me. Drank a good deal. Began to calm down after midnight. Went to sleep when all was quiet.

6 April, Smyrna Woke with a headache. With Volodya and Hermanovich to the city. A Greek guide speaking Russian. Two churches, in the first of which a metropolitan was conducting the services very unimpressively. Through the city and at a caravansary. Purchase of fezzes. Lunch in a restaurant on the seashore.

---

[42] *From the third act of* Sleeping Beauty.

[43] *Novel by Gautier.*

[44] *A Greek island.*

Along the quay in a horsecar. Aboard ship. A lot of new passengers (Cook). Half of my cabin is taken away from me. My despair. Was quite upset by that. The weather is wonderful. A babbling old man with refined manners. After dinner on the upper deck. Beautiful weather. I slept downstairs in the salon.

7 *April* A cold wind and the sky is covered with clouds. In the cabin almost all day, until we arrived. Poor appetite. The courteous priest, who occupied the second berth in my cabin. Finished *Capitaine Fracasse*. Both bad and excellent at the same time. Constantinople. With Hermanovich and Volodya to the city. The kind *Greeks in panamas* obliged us during the transfer. To the agency. Closed. Dinner in a restaurant above a pastry shop. We strolled. We took a ride in a boat. Twice through a tunnel. At the Café Luxembourg. Aboard ship. Volodya's chattering in the middle of the silence of the night.

8 *April* It is very cold. Woke with a headache and was in a bad mood all day. Transfer of Volodya's and Hermanovich's baggage to the "Tsarevitch." A guide. In the city. At the barber's. Lunch. In a carriage to the St. Sophia. Cook's tours. Savage singing—some fanatic crying out. Trip by carriage through some wonderful places. The underground colonnade. Aboard the Russian ship. My young friends are permitted to remain overnight. Café Luxembourg. On foot through Pera. Dinner. Aboard the "Tsarevitch." Champagne. Farewell to the two lovely friends.[45]

9 *April* Rose with a headache, probably due to the fact that after returning to the ship yesterday and hearing the talk of *company* in the *cabin,* I hid on the upper deck and wept there for a long time. (*Some bread for the dogs and a boy who got their leftovers*); that resulted in drunkenness. Woke at six o'clock. Springing out on deck, I was delighted by the sight of the Bosporus. At lunch there appeared only one other passenger besides myself; all the others were the personnel. I am well yet somehow sad. Sorry not to hear any more of Volodya's chattering, his jolly laughter and the high-pitched voice of Hermanovich. Read Sainte-Beuve. At dinner con-

---

[45] *Tchaikovsky was moved to tears at parting with Volodya. Did he perhaps have a premonition that he would never see him again? The youth died only ten months later. Three years after his death, Tchaikovsky dedicated the piano piece,* Chant élégiaque, Op. 72, No. 14, *to the memory of his young friend.*

versation about literature. The doctor's bezique. A new passenger (a young man in a fez) pestered me all day.

10 April The farther I travel, the more burdensome becomes the journey. Slept vilely at night. The ship tossed a little. All morning the passenger in the fez pestered me. He is thoroughly antipathetic to me; especially his manner of pronouncing the French language. After lunch (I took a lively part in the conversation) I was anticipating Samsun. The passenger followed me like a shadow. Samsun. We stopped briefly; there was no loading. Sailed at two-thirty. There was no tossing at all. The last dinner on board ship. Kerasund at 11 P.M. I am on deck. Tumult. Went to sleep late. Good François.

11 April Early morning Trebizond. Sailed between nine and ten o'clock. A French actor. The last lunch; packing; distribution of tips; waiting. Batum. They did not let us off the ship for quite a long time. Hôtel Impérial. Everything is filthy and the dinner bad. At a café on the shore opposite the ships. Strolling. Tea and early to sleep.

TIFLIS

12 April Departure. An obliging porter. In the compartment, at times alone, at others with a French newspaper publisher and a governess. Slept. The Rion valley. After the descent slept almost through to Tiflis. Was met by my people. Rain. Supper at home and conversation. Attractive Arsenty.

13 April Bykov at our place. At the Ivanovs'. Their adopted child —delightful. Lunch at home. (Vyrubov.) Lovely Alice.[46] Strolled a little. Tea in the children's room. Dinner. Whist with Vyrubov and the baron.

14 April Walked in the Mushteid. Felt a little ill. Read the newspapers. Am under the effect of a very unpleasant letter from Modest. Lunch at home. Slept at home. Wrote letters. Dinner at home (without Kolya[47] who later appeared with Karnovich, both drunk). I went with Kokodes to the Circle (my people were at the operetta). Whist with Vasily Vasilyevich and M. M. Ivanov. My people. Mme. Karnovich. Supper.

---

[46] *The governess of the children of Tchaikovsky's brother, Anatoly (Tolya).*

[47] *Kolya (Nikolai) Peresleni whose nickname was Kokodes.*

15 April At eleven-thirty, after a short stroll, to the Ivanovs'. They gave me lunch. Mikhail Mikhailovich's *Azra*.[48] A stroll. Home. Dinner at the Bykovs'. Drunkenness. Vishnevsky. Evening at the Ivanovs'. I play whist with them and their two hangers-on.

16 April Liturgy at the Zion Cathedral. The High Priest conducted the services. Lunch at home. At the annual session of the girls' high school. Volodya Argutinsky. Visit to his parents with Tolya. Home. Tea on the balcony. Vyrubov and the baron. Game of badminton. In the Mushteid. Dinner at home. Whist at two tables. Panya's fun during whist. A poor supper and I was angry (however, not on account of myself).

17 April A walk uphill in the direction of Kodshor. An attack of panicky fright. Lunch at home. With her [Panya?], Tata, and Alice to the handicraft exhibition at the Sheremetev castle. Mirsky, etc. Home. Slept. With Tolya on the balcony. Dinner at home with Gakel. At the amateur performance of the Artists' Circle. *The Genius Custodian. Les Charbonniers. Monologue de M. Lassale*.[49] I went home with Panya and Tolya. Kokodes with . . . at Count Steinbach's at the Vaz.

18 April Went for a wonderful walk to the hills in the direction of Kodshor. Fright while ascending the footpath. Return on the paved highway. Worked after lunch (ballet) [*Sleeping Beauty*]. Bad weather. With Kokodes for some hors d'œuvres. At Mme. Loth's. Threesome dinner. Tata is ill. Saradzhev's concert. Lack of audience. Cancellation. At the theater with V. M. Zarudnaya, etc. Also empty. *Lili*.[50] Supper at the Artists' Circle. Stepan. Lody.

19 April I feel somehow out of sorts since morning. A walk along the wall. (Gray weather.) Went home. Lunch. Slept. Visits with Panya. At Sheremetev's, he was out, and at the Andronikovs'. Her sister. Prince Baryatinsky. To the Chelokaevs', but I went home. Worked. Tata is ill. Dinner. Whist. Later Svyatopolk-Mirsky. Caucasian calendar. Supper. Svyatopolk is a handsome and interesting old man. Panya. I was carousing.

---

[48] *Opera by M. M. Ippolitov-Ivanov.*

[49] *The author of the comedy,* The Genius Custodian, *is anonymous;* Les Charbonniers *is an operetta by Costé; Lassale recited a poem by Coppée.*

[50] *Operetta by Hervé.*

20 April Since morning I have felt a kind of heaviness, uneasiness, almost feverish. Probably the gray, bad weather. After rising and drinking tea (Kokodes rising early of course in order to get what he needs) went walking and read the newspapers in the Alexandrov Garden. Home. M. M. Ippolitov-Ivanov. Unwillingly, played four hands. Vyrubov. Napped a little after his departure, and worked afterward. A stroll in the rain with Kokodes. We dropped in at a side show. Girls (an electrical one and another kind). Dinner at home. Gakel, Vyrubov, and the baron. Tata is still ill. Whist at two tables. Ivanov felt insulted by Kokodes. *Passe.* Mezentzev unexpectedly.

21 April Went to buy newspapers in the morning and read them in the Alexandrov Garden. Went for a walk to the left on an unfamiliar street, near the Kura, got to an old cemetery and could hardly get out to the Golovinsky Prospect. Lunch at home. Remained at home doing nothing. Took a short walk with Kokodes and to Baron Maidl's for dinner. Dinner. Panya created an awful scene on account of Kokodes. Whist. Home.

22 April A stroll. After lunch with Panya and Vyrubov to the *silkworm breeding house* in the Mushteid. The courteous director. Thunderstorm. Home. Idleness. After dinner I went with Tolya to Teryan's concert. From there to the theater. Faust parodied.[51] Boredom. Threesome tea at home. Rain.

23 April Mass at St. George's from ten to one. Hot weather. Procession with the cross. Home. Early dinner. On the balcony. Bykov (with whom I drank to our addressing one another intimately the other day at the baron's). Slept. The magnetism of Panya's eyes. Unsatisfied desire for solitude. At the parade. Panya selling. Boredom. Misha Bykov and Volodya Argutinsky. Saradzhev's concert at the school of music. I was with Kokodes. Supper party at the Hotel London. Mezentzev was the life of the party.

24 April In a bad mood since morning. A stroll and read the newspapers. Home. Official visit by the head of the Artists' Society. With Panya to the sick Korganov. At the Goncharovs'. A crowd. Colonel Vestman and discussion about music. Fled home on foot. Got a haircut. The wait for my people. Conversation with Alice. At seven-fifteen sat down to dine alone. Vyrubov. At Varvara Mikhailovna's.

---

[51] Le Petit Faust *by Hervé, an operetta.*

Home. My people still not here. Will go to bed now (ten-thirty o'clock).

25 April Forty-nine years. Congratulations. A telegram from Vasya. A stroll. Lunch. Kolya Peresleni visiting and shopping with me. In the Mushteid. Lordkipanidze. Home. Whist on the balcony. Volodya Argutinsky. Autographs. Guests. At seven o'clock my big dinner. It was gay. Opochinin introduced the pianists. Literary discussions. Early to sleep.

26 April Am in a very bad mood as a result of some trivial matters. Walked to the Mushteid. Newspapers. Home. Had to wait for the lunch. At Goncharov's in his chambers. Home. Vyrubov. Tea. Letters with terrible difficulty. With Panya on the balcony. Toward dinner, Tolya and Mezentzev returned from the hunt. The baron. Quartet evening concert. (Haydn, Grieg, Volga.) [52] Home. Whist. Tolya was angry at Panya because of her *egoism*.

27 April After tea a walk (newspapers in the Alexandrov Garden) on the other side past the Metekh Castle. Tired. Nausea. Tolya is at the hunt. After dinner I went with Kokodes to the Mushteid. Met Tolya in the Dedubian Temple. He was returning from the hunt. Home. Whist and supper at Khalatov's. The drunken Gakel.

28 April The usual walk. Lunching at our place was Goncharov. Tolya dined at Prince Dundukov's. In the evening, guests at our place. Whist. Supper at home.

29 April A walk. Newspapers. Home. With Panya, visits to the Shatilovs' and the Izvolskys'. I went home. Dinner at the Goncharovs'. On their watch tower. Bykov is a *philosopher*. Went home late.

30 April Waiting for Volodya Argutinsky. At the Armenian church. In the Alexandrov Garden. At Ippolitov-Ivanov's; V. M.[53] sang my songs. Home. Coffee. Celebration at the Artists' Society.[54] Opochinin's speech, etc. Dinner at the Artachal restaurant. Very

---

[52] *Besides Haydn's and Grieg's string quartets, he heard The Volga, a string quartet by Afanasiev.*

[53] *Varvara Mikhailovna Zarudnaya, wife of Ippolitov-Ivanov.*

[54] *As part of the send-off to Tchaikovsky, the society organized a concert devoted exclusively to the composer's works.*

gay. Speeches. Drunkenness. Opochinin's poems. Whist. Speeches again. Supper at the Hotel London. I drank a great deal.

1 May Tolya's birthday. Went walking, became hungry, and lunched alone at the Hotel London. Home. Discussion about an evening party between myself, Tolya, Panya, and Vyrubov. Dinner at Prince Dundukov-Korsakov's. Kavelin. Singing. At our place, whist on the balcony and supper. Packing. The Cossack's singing.

TRIP FROM TIFLIS TO MOSCOW

2 May Departure from Tiflis. Secular clergy. The send-off. Photograph. Prince Andreyev. Departed. Longing, on the way. In Mlety at eight-thirty. Was permitted to pass the night in the imperial rooms. Slept with feverish dreams.

3 May Departure from Mlety at six o'clock. A *lady* in my postchaise between Kobi and Gudaur. At three o'clock in Vladikavkaz. A large room, formerly Sorokoumovsky's. A walk. Dinner. Safonov.[55] Could not escape him. Drunkenness in his room. Delightful old man.

4 May Departure from Vladikavkaz. In a compartment. All the time an Englishman kept forcing himself upon me. All day ate and slept. Read a little. It was very boring.

5 May Rostov. Lunch. A compartment in the train. In Novocherkassk meeting with Tartar Misha (1876, Bellevue). Hid from a boring officer, Ippolit's friend.[56]

6 May At Voronezh a marvelous Pullman car. A little girl with her mother and governess; the French language. Mud. Eating. Kozlov. An hour's waiting.

MOSCOW

7 May Arrival at Moscow. Conservatory performance at 1 P.M. at the Maly Theater. *Waffenschmied.*[57] Dinner at Zverev's. Evening at Safonov's. Batasha.

---

[55] *General Safonov, father of V. I. Safonov, conductor and director of the Moscow Conservatory.*

[56] *Younger brother of Tchaikovsky.*

[57] *Opera by Lortzing.*

8 May Lunch at Jürgenson's. Dinner at the Maslovs'. Stayed a long time.

9 May Performance at the Maly Theater. Repetition of *Waffenschmied*. Dinner for the students at the Conservatory. At Batasha's with Taneiev.

10 May Remember poorly (am writing on the fifteenth). In the evening dropped in for Batasha and we went to the Maslovs' to play whist. Taneiev at the bank. During the day Taneiev and I consulted with Jürgenson about the Albrecht incident.[58] I dined at home.

11 May First meeting of the directors with Rukavishnikov at Jürgenson's. Lunch at the Bazaar. Second meeting at Rukavishnikov's. I explain to Albrecht. A painful situation. Third meeting at the Conservatory. Supper at my hotel. Taneiev's and Siloti's tears.

12 May I was at Karlusha's [Albrecht's]. Explained what happened. Lunch at the hotel. Do not recall what else. Dined at home. (I think I slept before dinner as I was carousing the day before.) A performance at the Maly Theater. *The Guiltless Guilty* [59] and vaudeville. I was alone in the box. At Brius'.

13 May The meeting. Ham and vodka in the director's office. Examinations in counterpoint and free composition. The Koniuses. Dinner at my place. 110 rubles in silver. Kashkin. Departure. Batasha saw me off.

ST. PETERSBURG

14 May St. Petersburg. The new apartment of Modya and Kolya [Konradi]. Lunch. Slept. Tea. With Modya. His story. . . . Thunderstorm. At Butakova's. At Laroche's. Dinner at the Contant

---

[58] *When Taneiev resigned as the director of the Moscow Conservatory, the directorship was offered to Safonov, who accepted on condition that Albrecht, supervisor at the Conservatory, be released. Tchaikovsky, acting as intermediary, threatened to resign as a director if Albrecht were released without a pension after many years of service. The affair was finally adjusted to the satisfaction of all. Taneiev remained as instructor in counterpoint; Safonov succeeded him as director and Albrecht resigned, receiving a very large pension.*

[59] *Play by Ostrovsky.*

restaurant. Volodya Shilovsky.[60] Scandal. With Modya and Laroche to the Arcadia. Konstantinov made us laugh.

15 May At Osip I. Jürgenson's. At the notary's. At Rahter's. Kündinger. His stories about lessons in Gatchina. Lunch at our place. Zasyadko, Laroche, Vasilyev. At Vsevolozhsky's. He was designing the costumes.[61] Petipa, etc. At Kondratyev's. The baths. Dinner at our place. At the Aquarium Concerts with Annette and Vera Vasilyevna. Engel, Franke, etc.

16 May Lunch at Konstantinov's. I, Laroche, Modest. It was very gay and entertaining. On foot to the Conservatory. Could not see Rubinstein. Home. Dinner at the Kondratyevs'. Meeting of the Rubinstein Committee[62] at the Mikhailovsky Palace. We stayed until eleven-thirty o'clock.

17 May Had lunch early at Kiub's restaurant. At the Conservatory. Anton Rubinstein. Very friendly. Examinations in violin playing. At Gerke's. He was out. Tea at home. Unexpected meeting with Vasya Sapelnikov. With him at Korsakov's (he was out) and at Glazunov's. Dinner at our place. Malya with her family, Laroche with Katerina Ivanovna, Konstantinov, Anna Merkling. We sat on the wonderful balcony. At eleven o'clock made an effort and went to Palkin's restaurant. Rimsky-Korsakov, Glazunov, Liadov, Lavrov, Yevgeny Albrecht and Verzhbilovich. We had to leave at two o'clock.

18 May A headache and nausea. Could hardly get up. In the Summer Garden and on the pier. Home. Lunching at our place were Rahter, Tzet, Vasya. Felt better. Slept. At brother Kolya's. Dinner at Donon's restaurant: Modya, Vasya, Tzet. (Makovsky, Bogomoletz, *tutti quanti*.) Departure. Seeing me off were brother

---

[60] *Vladimir (Volodya) Shilovsky was a friend and pupil of Tchaikovsky when the latter was a young man. There is reason to believe that a homosexual relationship existed between them at that time. About ten years prior to the present entry, Tchaikovsky had a disagreement with his wealthy friend over financial matters. Three years later there was a reconciliation but it was in name only. It is likely that there was another disagreement when the two met at this time.*

[61] *For the forthcoming production of the* Sleeping Beauty.

[62] *Formed to celebrate the fiftieth anniversary of Anton Rubinstein as a pianist.*

Kolya with his family, Anna, Liadov, Verzhbilovich. Slept excellently even though not immediately.

FROLOVSKOYE

19 May Arrival at Frolovskoye. Beautiful day. After the dinner on the balcony (a new woman cook) and a walk, wrote letters. Lukyan, the nurse's brother, arrived. I began to reprimand him. He started to cry. I was awfully touched. In the evening Legoshin arrived from Moscow.

20 May Commenced to work in the morning. Walked a little after dinner. Slept. (All this time I sleep vilely at night on account of the heat and something else.) Work. Every now and then something like melancholia and discontent. Strange!

21 May Lukyan departed furnished with a letter to V. D. Konshin and money. Toward dinner S. I. Taneiev appeared. After that I strolled alone, while he slept. Mozart. He departed between six and seven o'clock. I worked a little! Played after supper. The weather is beautiful, but the mosquitoes and the heat spoil it.

22 May It has become somewhat colder. Wrote letters all morning. Oh! These letters! After dinner went to the *felled* forest. Fury and hatred toward those guilty of such meanness! After tea worked excellently. Took a walk. Read after supper. (Klera's [63] screams.) Slept better last night than the previous nights.

23 May Somehow felt well, probably because it has turned cold. Worked strenuously and successfully (*Pas de deux*). After tea conversed a long time with my people in Feklusha's room. What a delight Klera is. Worked until seven o'clock and again with unusual success. At supper chatted with Pasha (Alexei was in the city). Read.

24 May It has grown very cold. Felt perfect in the morning. Worked successfully. A telegram from Safonov about Batasha's position as supervisor.[64] A walk through the forest that is being felled. Picked several lilies of the valley. Pashenka served tea (Alesha is not here and Feklusha was doing the laundry). Work. After supper read the orchestra score of *Giselle* too zealously, also books,

---

[63] *Legoshin's three-year-old daughter.*

[64] *Batasha was the widow of Tchaikovsky's good friend, N. A. Hubert. She was a pianist and was appointed supervisor to succeed Albrecht.*

later; and because of that my head was heavy. Yes, also ate too much.

25 May It is as cold as autumn. Out of sorts. My head ached a little. But worked just the same. Writing the last number of the ballet: the Mazurka. Did not sleep well at night.

26 May Finished the *composing* of the ballet, in spite of the headache and bad frame of mind. Decide to go down to Moscow.

MOSCOW

27 May Took the express to Moscow. Lunch at the railroad station. At Jürgenson's. Found his office workers at lunch. The orchestra score of *Swan Lake*.[65] Boris and Sasha Osipovich. Nina Valentinovna and her typing. Conservatory. In a bad mood. Tretyakov. The meeting. Dinner at Zverev's. With Batasha at the Church of the Assumption on Mogiltza Street. At the Maslovs' all evening. Fyodor Ivanovich's stories about certain mysterious happenings.

28 May Felt bad from drunkenness. Beautiful day. Not long at the Friday church. Lunch at V. D. Konshin's. (Before that I was at Karlusha's. His insinuations and, on the whole, I see Karlusha in a new light). After the lunch at V. D. Konshin's, was at Batasha's and, with her and Taneiev, at Safonov's. Evening at the Maslovs'. Home. Dined at Testov's restaurant alone.

FROLOVSKOYE

29 May Left on the morning train. At home for dinner. Letters. During the evening walk two drunken muzhiks (overseers) pestered me. Alexei returned drunk from the city. He had what was almost a brawl with one of the overseers who forced himself upon me about money for drinking. Overheard that the peasants were rebelling against Alexei.

30 May Worked diligently all day, namely, orchestrating the March. The walk wonderful; the weather cool.

31 May Bob's arrival. Worked just the same. After dinner a walk with Bob through the forests. Felling of trees. Worked. A walk before supper. Fishing.

1 June With Bob all day. We talked a lot. His musical feeling is a surprise to me. We strolled after dinner along the brook, and

---

[65] *Tchaikovsky's earlier ballet.*

in the evening downhill through the open country. The superintendent arrived. The banishment of poor Gavrila. I am aroused.

2 June Bob left on the express. I stood with a white flag while the train passed. Worked all day very well. After dinner went past Davidkovo to the left. Klera charmed me. Wonderful child. A thunderstorm was beginning, but happily it passed over.

3 June Worked very well. After dinner took a marvelous walk. After my tea was at Alexei's. Feklusha is ill. Klerochka is enchanting. Before supper walked marvelously. *In general, am experiencing wonderful days.* After supper conversed with Feklusha and Pashenka for about two hours. The latter related many interesting things.

4 June In the morning parted with poor Gavrila Alexeyevich and Alexandra Dmitriyevna. Sorry for them. Worked. Had a drop too much at dinner. A stroll after the rain. From Davidkovo uphill and home via the forest. Heat and flies. Evdokim with the papers from the Conservatory. After tea worked diligently. A walk. After supper a long conversation again with Pasha, Feklusha and Klera. What a delight this child is! Beautiful evening. Mozart's [cantata] *Davidde Penitente.*

5 June Glorious day. Rose with a feeling of heaviness in my head. Worked well. (The end of the *Pas de six*.) After dinner walked through the remains of the forest. A guest at Alexei's (a former postman). Tzivinsky was telling Alesha about Gavrila's dishonesty. Klera before supper and during supper. Her charming questions: "And what is that?" "And what is that you have?" etc. Such a beautiful child! Feklusha is still ill.

6 June Slept well. The day beautiful and just warm enough to be moderate. A strange letter in the morning from Novikova. Wrote several letters until time for the morning walk. Worked desperately. Newspapers and letters. One from Tolya, irritating me: asks a favor from Grand Duke Konstantin Konstantinovich. A stroll after dinner to the remains of the forest. Flies. Tea. Worked desperately; finished just before supper. Klera with me while I washed and at the beginning of the supper. Her bewitching questions. After supper (overdrank a bit) walked.

7 June Good sleep. Worked with a mad diligence. Both our women (Feklusha and Pashenka) sick. Klera is alone and was singularly bewitching. After dinner a short walk. Sat in the forest. Wrote letters until teatime (to the grand duke about Tolya). Worked intensely. Feklusha has broken down completely. Am afraid that she has a serious illness.

8 June Alesha, despite her weakness, drove Feklusha to the doctor in Klin. But surprisingly she felt better after her return. I worked all day like a madman.

9 June Worked, worked, and worked. Nothing unusual. A walk with adventures. Fell into slime while crossing the stream. Strolled along the Sestra. Washed my trousers. Made friends with a peasant with a gun from the felled forest. He is very likable. Worked.

10 June Nothing unusual. Since morning have felt very tired. Worked with less strain. Alesha went to the city. I became acquainted with the new clerk. The weather was rainy, although it rained only a little. (Lately I have been tempted by an intense fondness for chicory.)

11 June Felt more sprightly than for days past. After dinner and a short stroll was writing the autobiography(!!!) [66] for Neitzel. Feklusha's mother arrived. In the evening just before supper, the young Chernyaev appeared unexpectedly. Very untimely. Played several of Mozart's symphonies.

12 June It is cold and grayish weather. So much the better for me. In the morning wrote letters to Siloti and Ippolitov-Ivanov. After a stroll worked more calmly than on the preceding days. After dinner was perturbed because I did not receive the newspapers. (News about the concert in Paris.) [67] Went to meet the *clerk* who had to return. Met him. All is well. Home. As usual, after my tea, at Alexei's. Feklusha's mother. Klera was sleeping. Work. Peaceful. Mozart (*Idomeneo* and *Don Juan*). How good! Rain.

13 June The day of mother's death thirty-five years ago. Slept little (as all this time and woke frequently). It is cold and rainy. The little girl finished weeding the flowers and after her departure the gardener appeared with a boy with fresh flowers. Worked diligently

---

[66] *The manuscript of his autobiography was lost.*

[67] *The first of a series of Russian concerts taking place in Paris under the direction of Rimsky-Korsakov. The first program contained the First Movement of Tchaikovsky's First Piano Concerto.*

as usual but with less strain. After dinner walked on the paved highway despite the rain. In the evening orchestrated the Valse with enjoyment. I was marvelously fed today. The radishes we have are amazing. Contrived to write some letters. Complaint against the woman cook and a quarrel.

14 June It is cold, although less so than yesterday, and rainy. After tea wrote letters. The work went well. Unpleasant feeling as I recalled yesterday's scene with the woman cook. After dinner (unusually fine dinner, must be the result of the quarrel) went walking. Egorka Tabach. Both glad and not glad. Escorted him up to the paved highway. Sat in the forest. Went home along the stream. After tea, work again. Gavrila Alexeyevich arrived from Podsolnechnaya. Work. Supper. Stroll in the garden. Flowers. Zelenski's opera.[68] Tiredness.

15 June The cold weather continues. As a result of a letter from Siloti, who is gladly taking upon himself the [piano] arrangement of the ballet, was busy all evening indicating the markings in the first act. Feared for the flowers. Chocolate and drinking to excess. After dinner strolled up and down on the balcony.

16 June Incredible cold and dampness. All morning was indicating the markings in the Prologue. How difficult that is for me! After dinner got my feet wet on a walk. Newspapers. Modest informs me that he is coming one of these days. In the evening became very exhausted from work. Think Feklusha's mother will stay. Klera was angelic today.

17 June Woke ill; think it the result of gluttony. Lounging now on the divan, now in my room. All day it rained and it was very cold. Forced myself to make the markings in the first act.

18 June Modest's arrival. The weather somewhat better. After dinner (I wrote ten letters before that) we went walking together. In the evening went on with the second act.

19 June Begin to work now somewhat more calmly. After dinner strolled alone. Beautiful evening. Fishing.

20 June A good day. Worked well and calmly. The evening marvelous. Went strolling in the open country until suppertime. Read

---

[68] Konrad Wallenrod, *an opera dedicated by its composer to Tchaikovsky.*

newspapers and played *Das Paradies und die Peri.* Read Filaret's correspondence. Poor Feklusha is still ill.

21 June Work, Klera, two meals—all as usual. In the evening newspapers and letters were received and as always they excited me. Played, with Modya, Rubinstein's Fifth Symphony four hands. Read the new *Russky Arkhiv*. Rejoicing in the coolness of the night; went to bed very late and as a result of that:

22 June —my head ached. Even after an hour and a half's work lay down for a nap in the dressing room and slept through until dinner. After dinner strolled at first unwillingly but afterward enjoyed the forest very much, contemplating a threatening cloud moving over Demyanovo and Klin. Worked. Telegram from Safonov. Am going to Moscow tomorrow. Remarkable night.

Diary Ten

January, 1890 — May, 1890

This diary begins with an entry made in St. Petersburg. Tchaikovsky had moved from his Frolovskoye home to a Moscow apartment for the winter where he had been living since October 1, 1889. In December, 1889, he attended a meeting of the directorate of the Imperial Theaters and undertook to compose an opera to "The Queen of Spades" by Pushkin, with a libretto by the composer's brother Modest. Tchaikovsky decided to compose the opera away from Russia where he felt he would have more peace and selected Florence, Italy, as the place. The greater part of this diary, then, was written in Florence and concerns his work on "The Queen of Spades."

ST. PETERSBURG

1 January, 1890 Monday. The New Year. Celebrated the New Year at Leiner's restaurant with Modest, Guitry, and Angèle.

2 January Tuesday. Rehearsal of the ballet [*Sleeping Beauty*] with the tsar present. "Very nice" [1] !!!!! His Majesty treated me very haughtily. God bless him.

3 January Wednesday. First performance of the ballet.

4 January Thursday. Departure for Moscow with Tolya and Panya.

MOSCOW

5 January Friday. Moscow. Straight to the rehearsal. At home, the dying Feklusha. All sorts of complications and dissatisfaction with Moscow.

---

[1] *The tsar's comment regarding the ballet. Neither he, his court which accompanied him nor the audience of the first performance were impressed by the music.*

6 January Saturday. The concert. I conducted for Rubinstein. A string broke. Supper.

7 January Sunday. Lunch at the Konshins'. Rubinstein's recital. Dinner. Safonov's tactlessness.

8 January Monday. Dinner at the Konshins'.

9 January Tuesday. At the Konshins'. Went home with Tolya and Volodya Konshin. Visit and explanation by Safonov. Dinner at the Konshins'. Bade good-by to Tolya and Panya. Tatusya. Will not go "for anything" to Petya, etc.

10 January Wednesday. With Alesha to Podsolnechnaya. Spasskoye and Milovidovo.

ST. PETERSBURG

11 January Thursday. St. Petersburg. At Vsevolozhsky's. Friendliness. At the Mikhailovsky Theater; to dinner at the Kondratyevs'. ·

12 January Friday. In the evening at *Eugene Onegin.* In a box with G. P. Kondratyev. Glazunov. (Lunching at my place were Siloti and Sapelnikov.)

13 January Saturday. In the evening at the Mikhailovsky Theater. *La Boule.*[2] Supper with Pogozhev and Co. as well as Guitry and Angèle.

14 January Sunday. Departure from St. Petersburg. Homesickness in the train.

15 January Monday. Eydtkuhnen. Sleeping car. Homesickness. Sleepiness.

16 January Tuesday. Berlin. Hôtel de Rome. With Nazar [3] through the city. Lunched together. Strolled alone. Dined together. Departure at nine o'clock. In the sleeping car; very comfortable (but they fleeced me).

17 January Wednesday. Munich. We were alone in a coach car. At Kufstein, inspection of small baggage. Lunch. Mountainous road. Homesickness!!! At nine-thirty the border (Ala). We traveled all night by ourselves. Slept badly.

---

[2] *Farce by Meilhac and Halévy.*

[3] *Nazar Litrov, Modest's valet, who accompanied Tchaikovsky. Alexei, Tchaikovsky's valet, remained with his dying wife, Feklusha, in Moscow.*

FLORENCE

18 January Thursday. Arrival in Florence. The weather damp but warm. Bad room. Inspected an apartment in the hotel, rented it and agreed on the terms. With Nazar to the San Miniato church. Lunch at the Gilli e Letta café. Home. We were arranging our things. First dinner. Separate table. Good. Orzhevskaya.

19 January Friday. Started work and not bad. (Stole the beginning from Napravnik.) [4] The day passed first rate. After lunch roamed about. A cold wind was blowing, but we have the sun in our place. After dinner went to the *Celebrissimi Circus*. Mariani. The fat man. Cigars.

20 January Saturday. Worked well. Less homesickness. Everything as it should be. In the evening at the Pagliano Theater. Stout Singer (Amneris). A scoundrel conductor. Despicable choruses. In general everything is provincial. Left after the second act.

21 January Sunday. Worked in the morning well, but after lunch badly. Strolled, went to the Cascine Park—to the very end. Dined *badly* as a result of tiredness and exertion in work. Roamed in and out of cafés. A letter at home. The fireplace. Conversation with Nazar.

22 January Monday. Still cold but clear weather. Rising, read the newspapers, drank tea with honey as usual. Worked well. During lunch, conversation with Luigi about the king, the pope, etc. A walk through the city; shopping. From my window watched people riding by with Nazar. Worked well. Got rather emotional. Dined excellently (Orzhevskaya has guests and a chattering little girl). With Nazar to the Arena. My Mariani. Everything as before. Walked there and back. Beautiful, but cold, moonlight night.

23 January Tuesday. During lunchtime, Orzhevskaya was sitting with a Russian lady, who later came over to me. It turned out to be Platonova. I behaved very coldly to her. In the evening wrote letters. The work went along all right. Telegram to Sapelnikov concerning Modest's letter about his refusal to go to Paris and a reply. Angry at Nazar twice.

---

[4] *Napravnik did not know from which of his works the beginning of* The Queen of Spades *could have been stolen.*

Tchaikovsky's home in Klin, subsequently the Tchaikovsky Museum

24 January Wednesday. Worked with intensity. After dinner was at the Alfieri Theater. *Il giro del mondo* with *Stenterello;* impossibly stupid and clownish.

25 January Thursday. Worked with intensity (the ensemble). The weather is warm. Via Lungo del Mugnone. Telegram from Modest; proposes to come here.[5]

26 January Friday. Worked not badly. Letters from Riemann, Nata, and Shpazhinskaya. After lunch walked on the road to Fiesole. Purchase of a pipe and tobacco for Nazar. Worked well. After dinner in a café (Via Cerretani) as usual and at the Niccolini Theater. They were giving *Messalina*.[6] Hardly sat through an act. Bad and ridiculous.

27 January Saturday. The work was going a little hard (the finale of the first scene). After lunch, at the request of Nazar, went to look for the Russian church—had a hard time finding it. After dinner was at the Pagliano Theater; the first two acts of *Aïda* again. (The ludicrously stout Singer with a voice like a huckster's.) This time the orchestration of *Aïda* seemed vilely coarse to me in places. As ever, was delighted with the beginning of the scene between Aïda and Amneris.

28 January Sunday. Celebration for the unveiling of the monument to Manin. In the morning received letters from Laroche and Jürgenson. During lunch saw the Venetian guests, who were also lunching. Went to the Cascine. But there was no unveiling. On returning, watched the crowds going by with Nazar from the window. Work. Dinner. Sitting in various cafés. A talk with Nazar on returning home. Read [the score of] Grétry's *Richard Cœur de Lion*. In the depths of my soul there is a frightful boredom and a feeling of desolation.

29 January Monday. In the morning started the second scene. After lunch walked on the other side of the river to the left. A *dog* set upon me. At our hotel there is still a commotion and people are gathering because of the Venetian guests. Letters from Alesha, Emma, Modya. Worked well. Dinner. Drunkenness at a café. A

---

[5] *Tchaikovsky told his brother that he could not invite him to Florence as his guest. He was very short of money and in fact had requested financial support, in the form of a loan, from the Musicians' Aid Fund.*

[6] *Opera by Pallavicini.*

fiera and a lottery in which I had luck. Home. Sent Nazar to the *fiera*. Read the old orchestra scores taken from the directorate.[7]

30 January Tuesday. The letter of P. I. J. with the news about A. I.[8] upset me terribly. Like a madman all day. Slept badly. Did no work.

31 January Wednesday. The work went better; in the evening before dinner real inspiration came to me. As always, roamed about and caroused. Dropped in at the *fiera*. Distributed all the prizes.

1 February Thursday. Was working well. After lunch (today it is warmer) walked on the Viale dei Colli. Tea. A carnival. Crowds, masks, traffic. Worked unsuccessfully. During dinner was excited, as Mme. Orzhevskaya was expected with the guests. Was roaming about. Nazar dissipated today. Read the satires of Juvenal. What an awful translation by Fet.

2 February Friday. Worked well today even though it was an exertion. Many people appeared in the dining room. The Palens dine at a separate table now near me. Went walking today in the Cascine Park. After dinner, café; another café and the *fiera*. Was lucky; won something good at once. Nazar has been dissipating all day today with the new acquaintance.

3 February Saturday. *Je crois que Nazar qui est un excellent garçon est très curieux et qu'il s'amuse à déchiffrer ce que son maître provisoir écrit sur ces feuilles. Dorénavant j'écrirai en français. Ça n'a pas très bien marché (le travail). Mais il est vrai que c'est difficile (fin de la scène dernière du deuxième tableau). Après déjeuner grande promenade vers les montagnes. A cinq heures je voulais aller au bain; c'était fermé. Après dîner café (pince-nez). Vêpres à la chapelle russe. Différent cafés et assommoir. La fiera.*

---

[7] *Of the Imperial Theaters. Besides Grétry's orchestra score, he also took with him those of operas by Salieri and probably by Astaritta.*

[8] *P. I. Jürgenson, who had been empowered by Tchaikovsky to act in matters pertaining to his wife Antonina Ivanovna Miliukova, wrote that she was appealing to various well-known persons for material aid, despite the fact that she was receiving a fixed allowance from the composer. Tchaikovsky was completely unnerved by this news and wrote her a long letter, which was never sent and is the only one of his letters to his wife that has been preserved.*

Mandoline et charmant accompagnement. Lecture à la maison des partitions de Salieri et Grétry.[9]

4 February Sunday. Shrovetide. What a climax to Shrovetide. I finished the second scene. Am not particularly satisfied. After lunch a stroll on the Viale dei Colli. Drank tea alone. Played through the second scene. A carnival. Masks. Went out at five-thirty. Crowds on the Via Tornabuoni. Dinner at the Capitani restaurant. Poor, yet pretentious. Pagliano Theater. Stayed almost to the end. Singer and *Aïda* (Boronat) are vile. Decadence of singing. Poor *maestro.* Apropos: received a letter from kind Drigo.[10]

5 February Monday. Nazar came limping in to me. It was a serious leg injury. Worry. Hardly worked at all. Waiting for the doctor. The doctor. Thank God! There is no fracture. Strolled after lunch. Today the weather is unusually beautiful—it was impossible not to be enraptured. In the Cascine Park, but in the shade where there are few people. Two little dogs chained together. Visited Nazar. Worked. It comes hard (scene of the death from fright). After dinner just what I had feared happened: Palen came over and conversed with me. Walked without carousing. Home. Read Kostomarov's *Mazepa.*

6 February Tuesday. Mardi gras. The weather is most splendid; quite summery. Nazar still the same—unable to walk. Worked with great intensity and exertion. After lunch experienced considerable enjoyment in the Cascine Park. Found a violet. Procession of the masks, *chars* with flour [*sic*] throwers, etc. I worked as always. On the way to dine, had to go over to the Palens' and converse. After dinner walked as usual. Wrote letters and was at Nazar's. Now

---

[9] *"I think that Nazar, who is an excellent fellow, is very curious and that he amuses himself with deciphering what his temporary master writes in these pages. In the future, I will write in French. It (the work) did not go very well. But, it is true that it's difficult (the end of the finale of the second scene). After lunch a long walk to the hills. At five o'clock I wanted to go to the baths; they were closed. At a café (pince-nez) after dinner. Vespers at the Russian chapel. Various cafés and a tavern. La fiera. A mandolin with a charming accompaniment. Reading at home of scores by Salieri and Grétry."*

[10] *Riccardo Drigo, who conducted the* première *of the* Sleeping Beauty *and was the composer of the ballet* Les Millions d'Harlequin.

(11:30 P.M.) someone has been ringing the bell frantically for half an hour. What can that mean???

7 February Wednesday. The weather is divine. Nazar is little better. The doctor. During both meals talks with the Palens. Very nervous from work and at lunch became angry because we were not served for a long time. Probably for that reason had a severe pain near the heart while strolling, which I felt yesterday, too, in a slight degree. Curiously, I am experiencing both mad inspiration and difficulties. Letter from Alesha about the renting of Frolovskoye and the theft.

8 February Thursday. The weather is not as good. Nazar feels better. The Palens. After lunch bought a lot of books. Worked well. After dinner drank a little. Read *Le Termite* [11] a long time; a lampoon on naturalists.

9 February Friday. Shrovetide. Am writing one week later; remember poorly. After dinner was at the Palens' and passed an hour at their place. Amiable, lovely people but still I am glad that they are leaving.

10 February Saturday. Shrovetide. The Palens left. Nazar is just as before. Do not recall whether it was this day or the day before that I was unusually nervous.

11 February Sunday. Shrovetide. Finished the fourth scene and started the *Intermède*. At first it came hard; then it went well. In the evening caroused *terribly*. Got in again at the *repelling Aïda* and where only didn't I roam.

12 February Monday. Beginning of Lent. Continued the *Intermède*. At times it seemed to me that I was living in the eighteenth century and that after Mozart there was nothing.[12] Nazar is *worse*. The rubdowns and massages have commenced.

13 February Tuesday. The weather has become worse; rain. Received magazines and have started to read them gradually in the evenings. The rain did not hinder me from taking a walk along the Viale dei Colli. *Flowers*.

---

[11] *By Rosny* aîné.

[12] *The action of the opera takes place in the eighteenth century and Tchaikovsky composed the* Intermède *in the style of that period.*

14 February Wednesday. There was no rain, but the weather is bad just the same. Cascine Park. Right to the end. The pain in the side, which I suffered last week, has almost completely disappeared.

15 February Thursday. Wrote well. The aria of the Prince. Strolled on the Viale dei Colli. After dinner, at church. Evening prayers. At home with Nazar heard a boy singer. Americans are expected at our place. The doctor every day. Nazar still must not walk.

16 February Friday. The cold today is awful. It even tried to snow. Received a lot of letters, everything piecemeal. That irritated me. Because of it, the work did not go so well. Wrote some answers. Before dinner, the work lagged terribly. Dined with aversion. After dinner, despite the infernal cold, went walking; drank coffee as usual in my near-by café. Afterward at the Alhambra Theater. Vaudeville singers. Boredom. Nazar is at Olga's.

17 February Saturday. The cold was surprising and unbearable, particularly in view of spring being near. Wrote with great effort. In the evening at the Niccolini Theater. *I Puritani;* [13] the singing not bad, but the orchestra and production awful. Returned at twelve o'clock. In the morning wrote a long letter to Moscow about resigning from the directorate. [14]

18 February Sunday. Continuation of the vile cold. Worked with effort. Strolled on the Viale dei Colli, but in the opposite direction. Holiday trial of the steam tramway. Work. After dinner still the same long drawn-out, boring routine. Never has Florence seemed so foul to me, during this stay, as today. In the morning Safonov's insolent (as I regard it) letter.

19 February Monday. Finished the third scene and played it through. Read in the evening. Retired early. Worrying because there is no news from Sapelnikov.

20 February Tuesday. Received [libretto of] the fifth scene and immediately began to work. It went extremely slowly. But then it's hard. After lunch walked in the direction of Tramvia del Chianti.

---

[13] *Opera by Bellini.*

[14] *Of the Moscow branch of the Russian Musical Society. He was resigning because Safonov, the director of the Moscow Conservatory, had refused to accept his choice of Brandukov as professor of 'cello at the Conservatory.*

Terribly cold and windy. In the evening, near the Hotel New York, listening to the boy singer. He rode off wrapped in a coachman's sack. Poor thing, how cold he is! Wrote Modya about my changes.[15]

21 February Wednesday. In the morning letters from Alesha and Bob. Alesha writes that Feklusha now "begs God that He quickly take her." Poor, poor, suffering woman!!! Started to write the beginning of the fifth scene; did the end mentally yesterday but actually this morning. After lunch got on the road to Certosa again but today it was warmer. Before dinner worked well. At the end of dinner the proprietor was telling about the young man who fleeced him yesterday (I thought that he was an impostor). Strolled. The little singer was not around. Sweets. Nazar and I were eating them.

22 February Thursday. Distributed money according to custom. Finished the fifth scene. Somehow am not entirely satisfied with it—cannot reconcile myself to certain places, yet feel unable to make changes. Strolled on the Viale dei Colli. The weather today is excellent. Exchanged money. Tea. Worked. (Both during the stroll and after I did not feel very well.) Dinner without appetite. Orzhevskaya made me angry. A walk. The boy singer. I found him singing under my window. Conversation. Reading of Gogol's letters to Danilevsky. How little charming our great people are, except for Pushkin.

23 February Friday. Grand weather. Suffering all morning until lunch composing the *words* to Lisa's arioso. Decidedly, I am no poet. Strolled in the Cascine Park; enjoyed the walk very much today. Wrote the arioso. Letters from Siloti and Klimenko. After dinner (how tired I am of the cooking here!) the usual walk. Singers, but Nazar's and my favorite did not come. Read Renan.

24 February Saturday. Received the news of Feklusha's death from Alesha. Wept. A sad morning, generally. Am worried about Sapelnikov. However, worked. The weather is warm, gray; it rained intermittently. A beautiful walk in the Cascine Park. In the evening, one act of *I Puritani*. Really, this Bellini is delightful in spite of all the ugliness.

25 February Sunday. Finished the sixth scene, and yet did not finish it. Letter from Modest and Laroche. Sapelnikov had a *succès*

---

[15] *He made a number of changes in Modest's libretto and also wrote some of his own words for the Prince's aria.*

énorme in Paris. Rain. Walked to the hills. *Torre del Gallo*. Work. Dinner at the Doney restaurant. Bad and dull. Letter to Modya.

26 February   Monday. Finished the sixth scene; after the walk, started the Overture. In the evening, listened to Ferdinando [16] a long time.

.... *richiè*   .... *richiè*   .... *v'ascondere* ....

New sweets. A joking letter to Emma.

27 February   Tuesday. Mr. Khitrovo turned up (a foppish, but not very good-looking young man with St. Petersburg slang) and completely upset me. Received the seventh scene. Modest is a clever fellow.

28 February   Wednesday. The work went well. Unexpectedly eight hundred francs; from whom, I don't know. Buffalo Bill [17] at lunch. Strolled on the other side of the suspension bridge to the right. After tea the work went excellently. The dinner tiresome. The usual café and walk. Ferdinando sang Pimpinella [18] for the first time. Sat a long time at the open window, wondering where to go from here; [19] was very nervous thinking about the last scene of the opera, etc.

1 March   Thursday. Did not sleep well. Had a terrible nightmare at the beginning of the night (rustling of paper and motion in my room). Worked assiduously. The weather beautiful. After lunch to the Cascine Park in the heat (for the first time perspired as in the summer). Nobody was there, as today was the first performance of Buffalo Bill; Nazar even picked a hole there. Enjoyment of solitude

---

[16] *A boy street singer who captivated the composer. Efforts to identify the musical example have proved futile.*

[17] *William F. Cody was making a European tour with his Wild West Show.*

[18] *When Tchaikovsky was in Florence in 1878, he heard another boy sing an Italian folksong. He was so impressed with it that he noted down the words and the melody and made a Russian translation of the text, under his pseudonymous initials of N. N. He embodied this melody in his Op. 38, No. 6, entitled Pimpinella.*

[19] *Tchaikovsky wished to start work on the piano and vocal score of the opera in some other Italian city, perhaps Rome or Naples.*

(???) at tea. Worked zealously. After dinner a walk. Ferdinando did not sing. Read the *Russky Arkhiv.*

2 March   Friday. Do not sleep well, probably due to tiredness from work. The king's birthday and lots of soldiers with vile music. Worked. After lunch went to the Viale dei Colli from the lower side. At the Piazzale a great crowd was watching Buffalo Bill. Finished the seventh scene today (the aria still remains). Wept terribly when Hermann breathes his last. The result of weariness, but perhaps too because it is really good. After dinner the usual roaming about. Saw the mandolin player and his attractive companion probably for the last time. A rejection from the Pension Française in Rome.

3 March   Saturday. Slept excellently, thanks to the fact that I did not carouse and went to sleep early. Woke at six o'clock. Rose early, long before Nazar came. Until dinner, fussed with the *Brindisi.*[20] After dinner went to the Poggio Imperiale, then up the hill, came out at the Torre del Gallo and descended to the Piazzale; watched Buffalo Bill. After tea finished the Introduction [Overture]. Before dinner *finished everything.* After dinner bought music paper; roamed about a little. At home wrote Modest and Jürgenson business letters. I thank God that He has given me strength to complete the opera. It was as hot as summer. Rain.

4 March   Sunday. Started the piano and vocal score. The weather is gray. Very tired from work. Walked along the Mugnone.

5 March   Monday. Worked diligently. Less tired. A rejection from the Hotel Royal at Rome. Hesitation. A stroll in a pouring rain . . . [three lines crossed out.] I do not even expect. Decide to remain in Florence. Nazar is in favor of it.

6 March   Tuesday. The work went well. Infernal weather. Strolled nevertheless. In the evening saw Ferdinando, but on account of the bad weather did not ask him to sing. Read. Was distressed about sixty francs I thought were lost; but it seems I imagined it. Wrote Annette and Kolya.

7 March   Wednesday. The weather is horrible. The Arno is turbulent. After lunch strolled farther than I should and did not feel well.

---

[20] *This was the composer's name for the last scene which took place in a gambling house amidst singing and drinking.*

However, was in the Cascine Park. The work did not go so well.
Church in the evening. Went home with Nazar. Read the *Vestnik
Evropy*.

8 March   Thursday. Sick.

9 March   Friday. Sick.

10 March   Saturday. Sick.

11 March   Sunday. Sick!

12 March   Monday. Sick!

13 March   Tuesday. Sick!

14 March   Wednesday. Sick! Disgusting to recall this time. Only
today toward evening, I think, I am better, thank God! [21]

15 March   Thursday. Worse, much worse!

25 May   Friday. Filatovo, Baranovsky station on the Ryazan-
Kazan line.

[Tchaikovsky brought to Florence several orchestra scores of
operas including Astaritta's *Rinaldo d'Aste* about which he made
the following remarks, at the end of the present diary.]

In *Rinaldo d'Aste* two themes in the Overture are not bad. In the
first number the accompaniment is unpianistic at the beginning and
later at the end of the fifth. (The accent is poor on "not press,"
better to extract the repetition and change the rhythm slightly in
the parts.) It ought to be here:

Oh, do not press them!

The song is nice and the mood rendered faithfully.
   The second number is very nice in its craftsmanship and warmth
(a successful suspension).

---

[21] *He described his illness to Modest on this day, saying that it was a
combination of fever, pressure on the stomach, sleepiness, weakness, lack
of appetite, etc. He attributed all this to his horrible aversion to making
the arrangement (for piano and voice of the opera) although the composing of the opera itself was a pleasure to him.*

Such fifths as in the fourth number, for example, in the second bar on the second page or in the next to the last one on the same page, as evidently was the *intention,* I admit.

In the fourth number, the dismal mood is sustained very well; in places the harmony is as though it were a little strained, as, for example, in the *più animato.* For instance, the beginning of the third bar: for piano it is all right as the B and the D do not sound, but it would have been otherwise for the orchestra.

In the fifth number there is a beautiful harmonic progression at the beginning.

Diary Eleven

April, 1891 – May, 1891

*In 1891, Tchaikovsky was invited by Walter Damrosch to
come to New York to conduct at the opening festival concerts of Music Hall, the original name for Carnegie Hall.
He was also engaged to conduct in Philadelphia and Baltimore. The present diary is entirely devoted to a record of
his American trip. Tchaikovsky wrote in a letter to his
nephew Bob that he was not writing letters in detail since
everything would be recorded in his diary and Bob could
read it there. The diary is much more complete and narra-
tive in style than any other and describes vividly his
American experience. It should be noted that the dates in
this diary have been given according to the New Style
calendar in order to synchronize them with American
records of these events. The diary ends with Tchaikovsky's
sailing for Europe—and with it ends the writing of his
diaries altogether, for on returning to Europe he discontinued the practice. His own life ended not long after his
return. He died on October 25 (November 6), 1893.*

NEW YORK

26 April, 1891 When finally the endless procedure of *landing* was
over and I descended from the steamer, Messrs. Reno, Hyde, Mayer
(Knabe's representative), the daughter of Reno and some young
man came up to me. They quickly helped me to fulfill all the
formalities of the customs, seated me in the carriage alongside the
pretty Miss Alice and drove me to the Hotel Normandie. On the
way, I carried on an unbelievably amiable and an incredibly animated conversation (as though I were pleased with all that was
happening) with my companions. But in my soul there was despair
and a desire to flee from them to the world's end. However, to tell
the truth, all these dear people gave me a most cordial reception.

At the hotel, an extremely comfortable apartment (with toilet and bath) was awaiting me in which, after the departure of the welcomers, I made myself at home. First of all, I wept rather long.[1] Then took a bath, changed, and went downstairs to the restaurant. The French waiter entrusted with serving me was very gentle (which cheered me immensely) but he seemed silly. I dined without any enjoyment at all. Went out on the street (it's the main one: Broadway) and wandered quite a long way on it. As it was Sunday, the street was not especially lively. I was surprised by the number of Negro faces. Returning home, took to whimpering again several times. Slept excellently.

27 April Drank tea downstairs. Wrote two letters in my room upstairs and began to await visitors. Mayer came first. The sincere friendliness of this nice German surprises and touches me. Being the representative of a piano factory, he does not have the slightest interest in paying attention to a musician who is not a pianist. Following him, came a reporter with whom I was able to converse only because Mayer was present. Certain of his questions were very curious. Then Reno and another very fine and courteous gentleman appeared. Reno informed me that I was expected at the rehearsal. Getting rid of the reporter, we (Reno, Mayer, and I) went on foot to Music Hall.[2] The building is magnificent. At the rehearsal they were finishing the finale of Beethoven's Fifth Symphony. Damrosch (conducting without a frock coat)[3] seemed very charming to me. At the finish of the symphony, I started to go to Damrosch but had to stop immediately to respond to the loud greeting of the orchestra. Damrosch delivered a little speech; another ovation. I succeeded in rehearsing only the first and third movements of the [Third] Suite. The orchestra is splendid. After the rehearsal I went with Mayer to have lunch and after lunch he took me along Broadway, helped me buy a hat, presented me with one hundred cigarettes, showed me the extremely interesting bar of the Hoffman House, decorated with rare paintings, statues, and tapestries, and

---

[1] *Tchaikovsky's arrival in New York was sad. Shortly before leaving for America, he had read quite accidentally in a Russian newspaper in Paris that his sister, Alexandra (Sasha) Davidova, had died.*

[2] *The name of Carnegie Hall came into general use in 1894.*

[3] *In Russia it was customary always to wear a coat while conducting, even at rehearsal.*

finally brought me home. Unbelievably tired, I lay down to sleep. Waking, began to dress in expectation of Reno, who appeared presently. Tried to persuade him to release me from going to Philadelphia and Baltimore. He seems to have no objection to granting my request. Went to his home with him on the *Hochbahn*. His wife and daughters are very sweet and obliging. He also took me to Damrosch. Damrosch married the daughter of a very wealthy and influential [4] man a year ago. We three dined together; both host and hostess are very charming. With Damrosch to see Mr. Hyde and Mr. Carnegie. The latter, affluent, possessing thirty million dollars, and resembling Ostrovsky, is an elderly man whom I liked very much, mainly because he adores Moscow, which he visited two years ago. No less than Moscow, he loves Scottish songs, and Damrosch played a considerable number of them for him on an excellent Steinway. His wife is young and extremely sweet. After these two visits I was also at the Athletic Club with Hyde and Damrosch and at another, a dignified club resembling our English Club. The Athletic Club surprised me; especially the swimming pool, where members were bathing, and the upper gallery where in winter they skate. At the dignified club we had some refreshing drinks. Finally at eleven o'clock they drove me home. Is it necessary to say that I was completely exhausted?

28 April Slept very well. Reinhard, the representative of Mayer from Knabe, visited me solely for the purpose of finding out whether or not I needed anything! Amazing people, these Americans! Compared with Paris, where, at every approach, in every stranger's kindness one feels an attempt at exploitation, the frankness, sincerity, and generosity of this city, its hospitality without hidden motives and its eagerness to oblige and win approval are simply astonishing and, at the same time, touching. This, and indeed American customs, American manners, and habits generally are very attractive to me—but I enjoy all this like a person, sitting at a table set with marvels of gastronomy, devoid of appetite. Only the prospect of returning to Russia can awaken an appetite within me.

At eleven o'clock went sauntering! Had lunch in some rather elegant restaurant. Was home at 1 P.M. and napped. Reinhard (a very attractive young man) came for me so that we could go together to see Mayer. We dropped in at the magnificent Hoffman

---

[4] *James G. Blaine, secretary of state in 1891.*

House bar. Knabe's store. Mayer took me to a photographer. Having risen to some floor, the ninth or the tenth, we were received by a little old man in a red cap who turned out to be the proprietor of the photograph studio. A more eccentric person I believe I have never seen. This parody on Napoleon III (resembling the original very much but in the sense of a caricature) at first turned me around in search of the good side of my face. After that he developed for a long time the theory of the "good side" and made experiments with this art also on Mayer. Next I was photographed in various poses; during the intermissions between *posing* the old man amused me with some almost clownish tricks. In spite of all these peculiarities, he is unusually likable and genial, once again in the American way.[5] From there, went to the park with Mayer in a carriage. The park is young but grand. A great number of elegant carriages and ladies. We called for Mayer's wife and daughter and continued the ride along the high shore of the Hudson. It was becoming cold; conversation with the kind German-American ladies was tiring me. . . . At last we drove up to the famous Delmonico restaurant. Here Mayer treated me to a lavish dinner. He and his ladies escorted me to the hotel. Having changed into a tail coat, I was expecting Mister Hyde. With him, his wife, Damrosch, the Reno couple, and young Tom, we sat through an extraordinarily boring concert at a large opera theater. They performed *The Captivity*, an oratorio, by the American composer, Max Vogrich, with an orchestra and chorus of five hundred singers.[6] More banal and poor music I have never yet heard. The boredom was terrible. Wanted to go home, but the good Hyde couple dragged me and young Thomas to Delmonico's for supper. We ate oysters, a sauce of small turtles(!!!), and cheese. Champagne and some kind of peppermint drink with ice supported my sinking spirits. They drove me home at twelve o'clock. A telegram from Botkin, inviting me to Washington.

29 *April*   Slept restlessly. After tea wrote letters. Took a walk on Fifth Avenue. What mansions it has! Had lunch at home alone. At Mayer's. The kindness and attention of this nice person simply amaze me and I, by *Parisian* habit, still try to imagine: what does

---

[5] *Napoleon Sarony. This photograph is reproduced facing page 321. (Brown Bros.)*

[6] *This concert took place at the Metropolitan Opera House. Vogrich was Austrian and not American.*

he need of me? But indeed, nothing! He sent Reinhard in the morning to find out whether or not I needed anything and it was necessary to turn to him for help, for without him I would not have
known what to do about the telegram to Washington. Was at home
at three o'clock in expectation of Mr. *William de Sachs*,[7] a very
kind and cultivated gentleman, a lover of music and a writer on it.
While he was here, there also appeared my French friends from
the steamer, May, Buso and some friend of theirs. I was very much
pleased and went to drink some *absinth* with them. Returning, slept.
At seven o'clock Hyde and his wife drove up for me. What a pity
that I have not the words and color to describe these two charac-
ters who are so affectionate and kind to me. Especially interesting
is the language in which we converse: it consists of a most curious
mixture of English, French, and German. Each word that Hyde
pronounces in talking to me is the result of an enormous mental
effort during which sometimes, literally, a whole minute passes until
finally there is uttered from out of the vague muttering some inconceivable word—from which one of the three languages it would
be impossible to say. And all the time, Hyde's expression is so
earnest and so good-natured! They drove me to the Renos', who
were giving a big dinner for me. The ladies were dressed in evening gowns. The table was almost covered with flowers. Beside each
lady's service lay a bouquet, while for the men there were little
bunches of lilies of the valley, which each inserted into his buttonhole after being seated. Near the service of each lady stood my
portrait in a graceful frame. The dinner started at seven-thirty
o'clock and finished exactly at eleven. I write this without the least
exaggeration; such is the custom here. To recount all the courses
is impossible. In the middle of the dinner, an ice was served in
some kind of small boxes to which were attached small slates, with
pencils and sponges, on which excerpts from my works were finely
written in pencil. Then I had to write my autograph on these slates.
The conversation was very lively. I sat between Mme. Reno and
Mme. Damrosch, the latter a very charming and graceful woman.
Opposite me was seated little, elderly Carnegie, the adorer of Moscow and the possessor of forty million dollars.[8] Amazing, his resemblance to Ostrovsky. All the time he talked about how our singing

---

[7] *Better and correctly known as Willy von Sachs.*

[8] *According to Tchaikovsky, Carnegie had accumulated an additional
ten million dollars in two days, for on the fifteenth he had thirty million!*

chorus must be brought to New York. At eleven o'clock, tortured
by the need of smoking and nauseated by the endless eating, I decided to ask Mme. Reno's permission to rise. Half an hour after that,
all dispersed.

30 April It is becoming very difficult to write—do not find the
time. I lunched with my French friends at their place, the Hotel
Martin. A rendezvous with von Sachs near the post office. We
walked on the Brooklyn Bridge. From there we set out for Schirmer's, the owner of the biggest music store in America; however,
the store and particularly the engraving plant yield to Jürgenson
in many respects. Schirmer asked for some compositions for his
firm. At home, in my room received the woman journalist, Ivy Ross
who had come to ask me to write a piece for her newspaper,[9] and
the pianiste [10] Wilson, who tired me pretty much. After her departure I sat on the divan as though I were made of stone for about an
hour and a half, indulging in the delights of peace and solitude.
Did not dine. By eight-thirty, I was at Music Hall for the chorus
rehearsal. The chorus greeted me with an ovation. They sang very
well. On leaving there I met, near the exit, the affable architect
who designed the hall; he introduced to me a nice, rather corpulent
man, his chief assistant, whose talent and business ability he could
not praise enough.[11] This person turned out to be a full-blooded
Russian, who had become an American citizen. The architect informed me that he is an anarchist and socialist.[12] I chatted a little
with this fellow countryman in Russian, and promised to call on
him. An interesting acquaintance. Here also saw the amiable Reno
family. Gave the remainder of the evening over to a light supper
and stroll. Read and reread the letters received. Wept, as usual.

1 May Rose late. Sat down to compose an article for Miss Ivy.
Reno appeared with the news that he has arranged a cabin for me

---

[9] *The* New York Morning Journal. *Tchaikovsky wrote an article for her
newspaper titled "Wagner and His Music" which appeared in the issue
of May 3, 1891. Miss Ross was the original Cholly Knickerbocker for this
was her pseudonym when writing about society later on for the* New
York Journal.

[10] *Better known as Helen Hopekirk (Mrs. William Wilson).*

[11] *The architect of Carnegie Hall was William Burnet Tuthill. His first
assistant was Waldemar R. Stark.*

[12] *It must be borne in mind that these terms were loosely applied in
Russia to any, even mildly, liberal person.*

on the "Fürst Bismarck," sailing the twenty-first [May]. God! How far away still!!! Stopped by for the good Mayer, with whom I had lunch at a first-class Italian restaurant. Started downtown on the elevated. Only then did I see what a rushing crowd there is on Broadway at certain hours. Up to now this street, judged from the part in the neighborhood of the hotel, seemed only slightly animated. But this is an insignificant section of a street about five miles long.[13] The buildings downtown are ridiculously colossal; at any rate, I refuse to understand how anyone can live on the thirteenth floor. Mayer and I ascended to the roof of one of these buildings; the view from there is glorious—but I felt dizzy looking down on the Broadway pavement. Then Mayer obtained permission for me to see the government subtreasury and its vaults in which are kept hundreds of millions in gold, silver, and new bank bills and paper currency. Important officials, exceptionally courteous, guided us through these vaults, opening massive doors with secret locks and with equally secret turnings of some sort of metal knobs. Bags of gold, looking like bags of flour in granaries, repose in handsome tidy drawers, illuminated by electricity. They permitted me to hold for some time a package of new bills valued at ten million dollars. At last I understood why gold and silver are not in circulation; only now was this oddity explained to me. It turns out that Americans prefer the soiled, disagreeable bank bills to metal, finding them more convenient and practical. On the other hand, these bank bills, thanks to the huge quantity of precious metals kept in the subtreasury, are valued at *more* than gold and silver, and not as with us. From the subtreasury we started out for good Mr. Hyde's place of business. He is a director of some other banking institution and he too guided me through the vaults, showing the mountains of valuable bank bills kept at their place. We visited the Stock Exchange, which seemed to me somewhat quieter than the one in Paris. Hyde treated us to a lemonade at a neighborhood café. Finally we set out for home on the elevated again.

All the time I was on this interesting tour, I felt a certain peculiar, probably senile, disquieting tiredness. Having got home, I still had to finish writing the article (on Wagner) for Miss Ivy. And at five o'clock I was already rushing to Mr. William von Sachs'. He lives in a gigantic building in which only single men may rent rooms. Women are admitted only as guests in this strange American mon-

---

[13] *Broadway is actually fourteen and one half miles long.*

astery. Both the building itself and Sachs' apartment are very elegant and tasteful. At his place I found a small company which gradually became larger as a good many of us gathered. It was a *five o'clock tea*. The pianiste Wilson played (she was at my place yesterday)—a great worshiper of Russian music, who, by the way, performed Borodin's delightful serenade. Having evaded invitations, I spent the evening alone and, God, how pleasant it was! Dined at the Hoffman House restaurant, as usual without any enjoyment. While walking farther up along Broadway, came across a meeting of socialists in red caps. Here were, as I learned the following day from the newspapers, five thousand people with banners and huge lanterns and something like the following inscriptions on them: "Comrades! We are slaves in free America! We do not want to work more than eight hours!" [14] Nevertheless, the whole demonstration seemed to me like some buffoonery; indeed, I believe people here look at it that way also, judging by the fact that few appeared interested and folks moved about just as on any other day. Went to sleep physically tired, but somewhat refreshed spiritually.

2 May At ten-fifteen was at Music Hall for the rehearsal. It was already going on in the large hall amidst the noise of workers, the knocking of hammers, and the excitement of the managers. The orchestra is spread across the entire width of the huge stage, the result of which is that the tone is bad, not even. These things reacted badly on my nerves and several times I felt a rage coming on and a desire to drop everything indignantly and run away. Carelessly played through the Suite and the March, while the Piano Concerto, as a result of disorder in the music and the tiredness of the musicians, was dropped in the middle of the First Movement.[15] Returned home terribly tired, took a bath, changed and went off to Mayer. Lunched with him in the Italian restaurant again. Slept at home. The pianiste *von der Ohe* [16] came at five o'clock and

---

[14] *This was the traditional May Day holiday. Tchaikovsky must have made his entry after May 1, since he states that he read about the meeting the following day in the newspapers.*

[15] *Carnegie Hall was not yet completed but despite that, Tchaikovsky tried to rehearse his Third Suite, his* Marche Solennelle *(composed for the coronation of Tsar Alexander III) and the orchestral part of his First Piano Concerto.*

[16] *Correctly Adele Aus der Ohe.*

played me the Piano Concerto so unsuccessfully rehearsed this morning. Wrote Napravnik (an answer to his kind letter). Dined downstairs with aversion. Strolled along Broadway. Went to bed early. Thank God, sleep does not desert me!

3 May A cablegram from Jürgenson: "Christ is Risen."[17] It is raining outside. Letters from Modya and Jürgenson. "Yes, only he who knew"[18] what it means to be far away from one's own knows the value of letters. Never yet have I experienced anything like this. Mr. Narrainov visited me with his wife. He is a tall, bearded, half-gray man, very carelessly dressed, complaining about his spinal disease, speaking Russian well though not without an accent; cursing the *Jews* (although he looks very Jewish himself); she—an ugly Englishwoman (*sic*, not an American!), speaking no language other than English. She brought a pile of newspapers, and pointed out her articles in them. Why these people came to me—I do not know. He asked whether I had composed a fantasy on the "Red Sarafan." At my negative answer, he exhibited surprise and added: "Strange! Thalberg composed one and you didn't! As a Russian you must do one. I will send you Thalberg's fantasy and please do one like his!"[19] I could hardly get rid of these strange visitors. At twelve o'clock von Sachs dropped in for me. This fine, short man, who speaks French excellently, knows music perfectly, and is very affectionate to me, is almost the only person in New York whose company is not burdensome, is even pleasant. We went on foot across the park. This park, where Mayer, who is not an old man, remembers the cows grazing, is now one of the finest parks in the world, though the trees are still comparatively young. At this time of the year, when the trees are covered with fresh leaves, and the lawns excellently cared for, it has a special charm. At twelve-thirty, we ascended in the elevator to the fourth floor of a colossal building to the apartment of Mr. Schirmer. Schirmer is the Jürgenson of this country, i.e. the proprietor of the best store and a first-class publisher. He is sixty-three years old, but looks no more than fifty. He

---

[17] *The Easter greeting in Russia.*

[18] *The opening words of Tchaikovsky's famous song best known under the title of "None but the Lonely Heart," which he composed at the age of twenty-nine. He was inspired by Goethe's poem as was Beethoven.*

[19] *The "Red Sarafan" (Russian national women's dress) is a popular Russian folksong which a number of composers have used in their works.*

has been in America since he was twelve,[20] and although very Americanized, has still retained many German customs and has remained, in general, a German at heart. He is very wealthy and lives in considerable luxury. With him live his charming daughter Mrs. White and her children, and his son with his wife. His wife and two younger daughters are now living in Weimar for the second year, where he had also sent the older children to study, as he was afraid that they would cease being Germans. At dinner, besides myself and von Sachs, were the famous conductor, Seidl (a Wagnerite) and his wife; the pianiste, Adele Aus der Ohe, who will play my Concerto at the festival, with her sister and the Schirmer family. Preceding the dinner some kind of mixture of *whiskey, bitters* and *lemon* was served—extraordinarily delicious. The dinner was hearty and very tasty. On Sundays, Schirmer always dines at 1 P.M. and likes to pour an extra glass then. The conversation at first burdened me, but the whole Schirmer family and especially Mrs. White is so nice, simple, and cordial that I felt easier at the end of the dinner. Conductor Seidl informed me that my *The Maid of Orleans* will be given next season.[21] At four o'clock I had to be at the rehearsal. They drove me to Music Hall in Schirmer's carriage, accompanied by von Sachs. Music Hall was illuminated and put in order today for the first time. While *Sulamith,* an oratorio by Damrosch's father was going on, I sat in Carnegie's box. Then Schütz's boring cantata, The Seven Words of Our Savior was sung. My turn came. My choral numbers[22] went off very well. Rather reluctantly I rode with von Sachs to Schirmer again, as he had exacted a promise from me to return. There I found a large company invited for the purpose of seeing me. Schirmer led us to the *roof* of the house in which he lives. The immense nine-story building has a roof so constructed that it offers a fascinating and spacious walk with views commanding all four sides. The sun was setting at that hour and it is impossible to describe all the glory of the majestic spectacle. On descending, we found only an intimate circle left, in which, quite unexpectedly, I felt very comfortable. A. Aus der Ohe played several pieces extremely well and,

---

[20] *The founder of G. Schirmer, Inc. was not quite sixty-two and came to the United States when he was slightly over eleven.*

[21] *Tchaikovsky's opera* The Maid of Orleans *was not performed.*

[22] *Two* a capella *choral works by Tchaikovsky, "Our Father" and an arrangement of "Legend," Op. 54, No. 5, were rehearsed.*

with me, my Concerto. Toward nine o'clock we sat down to supper. At ten-thirty we, i.e. I, von Sachs, and Aus der Ohe and her sister, were presented with gorgeous roses, taken down in the elevator, seated in Schirmer's carriage once more and conveyed to our homes. One must give credit to American hospitality; only in our own country would one encounter anything like it.

4 May Received letters from Kolya Konradi, Annette, Sapelnikov, and Konius. Drank tea in my room. Visit by Mr. Romeike, the proprietor of a newspaper clipping bureau. Probably, he too is one of our anarchists, like the two mysterious Russians who talked to me yesterday at the rehearsal. Wrote letters and the diary. Having dropped in for Mayer, rode downtown with him on the elevated. We went in for Hyde who took us to the Down Town Club for lunch. After taking us up unbelievably high in the elevator, he showed us first the quarters of five lawyers and a law library attached to his Trust Company.[23] The Down Town Club is nothing other than a most superb restaurant, in which, however, none but members of the club are admitted. All are business people for whom it is far to get home, and for that reason they have their *lunch* there. After a splendid lunch, I went on foot along Broadway, alas, with Mayer. This kind German cannot at all understand that his sacrifices for my sake are superfluous and even painful to me. What a pleasure it would have been to walk alone! But Mayer is ready to neglect his many duties in order not to leave me alone. And so, despite my suggestion to ride home and attend to business, he dragged along with me for an hour and a half on foot! There is a walk that gives an idea of the length of Broadway! We were walking an hour and a half, and had barely walked a third of this street!!! After refreshing ourselves in the men's lounge, we started out for Chickering Hall to the recital of the famous English singer, Santley. The famous singer turned out to be an elderly man who sang arias and songs in English in very strict time and very colorlessly, with a British pronunciation and with British stiffness and restraint. Was greeted by various critics, among them Finck, who wrote me enthusiastically about Hamlet[24] last winter. Not

---

[23] *Hyde was the vice president of the Central Trust Company.*

[24] *Henry T. Finck, music critic of the* New York Evening Post *had written the composer regarding his fantasy overture Hamlet, which was performed by the New York Philharmonic Orchestra on February 14, 1891.*

waiting for the end of the recital, started for home where work was
waiting for me with A. Aus der Ohe and my Piano Concerto. She
appeared with her sister and I pointed out to her various nuances,
details and refinements in which her powerful, crisp, and brilliant
playing was lacking, judging by yesterday's rather coarse performance. Reno informed me of the interesting details concerning the
American career of Aus der Ohe. She arrived here four years ago
without a penny, but armed with an invitation to play Liszt's Concerto (she was his pupil) with the Symphony Society. Her playing
was liked; invitations poured from everywhere; huge success followed her all over; in the course of four years she roamed about from
city to city through all America and now she possesses a fortune
of *one half million marks!!* [25] That's what America is! After her departure, I barely had time to change to a tail coat and start out
to Reno's for dinner. I walked and found the house without difficulty. On this occasion we dined in a family circle. Only Damrosch
came after dinner. I played four hands with sweet Alice. The evening went by rather pleasantly. Reno escorted me to the tramway.
It has suddenly become very cold.

5 May Max the waiter, who serves me tea in the mornings, spent
his entire childhood in Nizhnii-Novgorod and attended school there.
Since the age of fourteen he has lived now in Germany, now in
New York. He is thirty-two years old now and has forgotten the
Russian language to such an extent that he expresses himself with
great difficulty, but knows most of the everyday words. It makes
me feel very pleasant to talk a little Russian with him. At eleven
o'clock the pianist Rummel appeared (an old Berlin acquaintance)
still with the same pestering to conduct at his concert on the seventeenth, regarding which he has already visited me once before. A
journalist came, who was very obliging and warm. He asked
whether my wife likes living in New York. That question has
already been asked of me frequently. It turns out that on the day
following my arrival, it was stated in several newspapers that I had
arrived with a young and pretty wife. That happened because two
reporters saw me entering the carriage with Alice Reno at the
steamship pier. Lunched downstairs in the hotel. Strolled on

---

[25] *About $120,000. This was an enormous sum to Tchaikovsky who
received $2500 for conducting four times at Carnegie Hall. He refused
a subsequent invitation calling for twenty concerts in America for a fee
of $4000.*

Broadway. Dropped in at a Viennese café recommended to me, but had the ill luck to encounter Seidl, the conductor, and was obliged to converse with him—and I was in no mood for conversation. I was excited on account of my imminent first appearance at the evening concert, before an audience of five thousand. On returning home, had the extreme displeasure of receiving M. Buso (one of the French friends from the steamer), who forced himself upon me. He stayed endlessly long, affecting a sad expression as though expecting that I would ask why he was upset. When I finally put that question to him, Buso said that he had been robbed of all his money yesterday in Central Park and that he came to ask me for two hundred francs. And a rich father? And the billions of *corks* that are manufactured and distributed all over the world? All these extravagant stories of his then are rot? I informed him that I do not have any money now, but could probably give it to him at the end of the week. All this is very suspicious and I am beginning to wonder whether he didn't steal my wallet on the ship. Will have to consult Reno. At seven-thirty Reno's brother-in-law came for me. In an overcrowded trolley car we reached Music Hall. Illuminated and filled with an audience, it has an unusually effective and grandiose appearance. I sat in a box with the Reno family. It started with Reno delivering a speech (on account of which the poor man was terribly excited yesterday). After him the national hymn was sung. After that a pastor made a long and, they say, unusually boring speech in honor of the founders of the hall and of Carnegie in particular. Following that, the Leonore Overture was performed very well. Intermission. Went downstairs. Excitement. My turn. Was welcomed very loudly. The March went off excellently. A big success. Listened to the remaining part of the concert in Hyde's box. Berlioz's *Te Deum* is somewhat boring; only toward the end did I find great enjoyment in it.[26] The Renos carried me away with them. An impromptu supper. Slept like a dead man.

---

[26] *The program of the inaugural concert on the evening of May 5 was "Old Hundred" sung by the Oratorio Society; an oration (the dedication of the Hall) by the Right Reverend Henry C. Potter; national hymn "America" also sung by the Oratorio Society; Leonore Overture No. 3 by Beethoven conducted by Walter Damrosch;* Marche Solennelle *by Tchaikovsky, conducted by the composer; the* Te Deum *by Berlioz for tenor solo (sung by Italo Campanini), triple chorus and orchestra. The Hall was filled to capacity and the concert was attended by celebrities in the social, artistic and financial world.*

6 May "*Tschaikowsky* is a tall, gray, well-built, interesting man, *well on to sixty* (?!!) He seems a trifle embarrassed, and responds to the applause by a succession of brusque and jerky bows. But as soon as he grasps the baton his self-confidence returns." That is what I read today in the *Herald*.[27] It angers me that they write not only about the music but also about my personality. Cannot bear it when my embarrassment is noticed and surprise shown at my "brusque and jerky bows."

Started out on foot at ten-thirty to the rehearsal. Found the entrance to the hall only through the aid of an employee. The rehearsal went off very well. At the end of the Suite [28] the musicians were shouting something like *Hoch!* Completely drenched with perspiration, had to converse with Mme. Reno, her oldest daughter, and with two other ladies. In Reno's office. A steamship ticket; instructions regarding the trip to Philadelphia and Boston [Baltimore?]. Having changed, hurried to Mayer, where Rummel was waiting for me a whole hour and a half, in order to play through my Second Concerto. However, we did not play it, and instead of that I exercised my eloquence, i.e. I showed that there is no reason at all for me to accept his proposal to conduct in some concert on the seventeenth *free*. Lunched with Mayer in the Italian restaurant. Slept at home. About seven o'clock, the good P. S. Botkin appeared unexpectedly from Washington. He came purposely for the concert. At seven-thirty Hyde and his wife drove up for me. The second concert. Mendelssohn's oratorio *Elijah* was being given. An excellent work but somewhat long and drawn-out. During the intermission was dragged to the boxes of the various bigwigs here. Carnegie (charming millionaire; founder of Music Hall) invited me to dinner at his home *Sunday,* but I could not accept, as I must go to Mr. Holls' for the whole day out of town. Went home on foot, after having gotten rid of everyone. Had supper in the restaurant downstairs. Letters from Modya and Kolya, my brother. A big fire somewhere.

---

[27] *From the* New York Herald *of May 6, which reported the concert in detail. He neglected to quote the following regarding his conducting:* "There is no sign of nervousness about him as he taps for silence. He conducts with the authoritative strength of a master and the band obeys his lead as one man."

[28] *Third Suite rehearsed for the concert to take place on May 7.*

7 May Am fifty-one years old. Awfully excited in the morning. At two o'clock the concert is to take place, with the Suite. An amazing thing is this odd fright. How many times have I already conducted this same Suite! It goes excellently; why be afraid? But still I suffer unbearably!

My sufferings continued *crescendo*. Never, it seems, have I been so afraid. Is it not because they scrutinize my outward appearance here and therefore my shyness will be noticeable? Be that as it may, after experiencing several painful hours, especially the last, when I was obliged to carry on a conversation with Frau Mielke, etc. while waiting to appear, I finally went out, was again splendidly greeted, and created, as is said in today's newspapers, a sensation.[29] After the Suite was in Reno's office, giving an audience to reporters (Oh, these reporters!), among them the very famous Jackson. Went into Mme. Reno's box; she sent me a lot of flowers this morning, with exact foreknowledge that today is my birthday. Felt the necessity of being alone and so, forcing myself past the crowd of ladies surrounding me in the corridor in whose wide eyes I could not fail to read enthusiastic and pleasing interest, and declining an invitation from the Reno family, I ran home. There, wrote a note to Botkin that I could not dine with him in accordance with my promise; then, relieved and happy, as far as I can be, went out to saunter, dine, drop in at a café, in a word, give myself over to the enjoyment of silence and solitude. Retired very early.

8 May Am beginning to have difficulties finding time for letters and this diary. Visitors besiege me: reporters, composers, librettists, one of whom, an elderly man who brought me an opera *Vlast*, touched me very much with the story of the death of his only son; but the main thing is whole piles of letters from all parts of America with requests for *autographs* to which I reply very conscientiously. Was at the rehearsal of the Piano Concerto. Was angry at Damrosch, who, taking up all the best time, leaves me the remainder of the rehearsal. However, the rehearsal went off all right.

---

[29] *This afternoon concert, on May 7, had on its program the Overture and the Grand Finale, Act II, from Mozart's* Figaro, *conducted by Walter Damrosch; Third Suite, Op. 55, by Tchaikovsky, conducted by him; aria from Massenet's* L'Esclarmonde, *sung by Mlle. De Vere; aria from Massenet's* Le Roi de Lahore, *sung by Theodor Reichmann and the Prelude and Finale from Wagner's* Tristan and Isolde, *conducted by Walter Damrosch.*

Having changed at home, lunched alone about three o'clock. Was
at Knabe's. He was with Mayer at Martelli's restaurant (where I
found them in company drinking champagne); thanked them both
for the excellent gift presented yesterday (a Statue of Liberty).
Only how are they going to allow this piece into Russia? Hastened
home. Visitors without end, among them two Russian ladies. The
first of these: Mrs. MacGahan, the widow of the famous correspondent during the war of 1877, and herself the correspondent of
the *Russkiye Vedomosti* and *Severny Vestnik*. Since it was the first
time that I had had occasion to indulge in a heart to heart talk with
a Russian woman, a shameful thing happened. Suddenly tears came,
my voice trembled, and I could not keep from sobbing. Ran into
the other room and did not come out for a long time. Burn with
shame to recall this unexpected incident. The other lady, Mrs.
Neftel, was talking about her husband, Doctor Neftel, as though
everyone must know who he is. But I don't know. There was also
Mr. Weiner, the president of a chamber music society (which in-
cludes [besides strings] the flute), with whom I corresponded from
Tiflis. Slept a little before the concert. The choral numbers went
off well, but were I less abashed and excited, they would have gone
better. Sat in the boxes of Reno and Hyde during the performance
of the splendid oratorio *Sulamith*, by *Damrosch's father*.[30] Went on
foot with Reno and Carnegie to the supper at Damrosch's. This little
multi-millionaire is awfully gracious to me and talks all the time
about an engagement for next year. At Damrosch's, a very original
supper: only the men went to the table while the poor ladies remained near by. The supper was hearty, but the cuisine is American, i.e. unusually repugnant. Much champagne was drunk. I sat
next to the host and to the concertmaster, Dannreuther. While
talking with him about his brother I must have seemed, for two
whole hours, either crazy or a hopeless liar. He opened his mouth
in amazement and was mystified. It turned out that my memory
confused Dannreuther, the pianist, with Hartvigson, the pianist.
My absent-mindedness is becoming unbearable and I imagine bears

---

[30] *The program of this concert on the evening of May 8 contained the
cantata, The Seven Words of Our Savior by Schütz, conducted by
Walter Damrosch; two a cappella choruses, "Our Father" and an
arrangement of "Legend," Op. 54, No. 5, by Tchaikovsky, conducted by
him and the oratorio* Sulamith *by Leopold Damrosch, conducted by
Walter Damrosch.*

witness to my old age. Incidentally, all those at the supper were surprised when I said that I was fifty-one years old yesterday. Carnegie was particularly surprised; they all thought (except those knowing my life) that I was much older. Have I aged during recent years? Extremely possible. I feel that something within me is crushed. They drove me home in Carnegie's carriage. Influenced by the conversation about my aged appearance, I had horrible dreams all night. [Ten lines crossed out here.] Along a gigantic, rocky descent, I was tumbling down irresistibly into the sea and was clinging to a small projection of rock. I believe all that was the aftermath of the evening's conversation about my old age.

Mr. Romeike sends me daily piles of newspaper clippings about myself. All of them without exception are laudatory in the highest degree. The Third Suite is praised to the sky, but hardly more than my conducting. Is it possible that I really conduct so well? Or do the Americans exaggerate?!!!

9 *May* The weather has become tropical. Max, the nice German from Nizhnii-Novgorod, has now arranged my apartment so that it has turned out to be ideally comfortable. There is no doubt that nowhere in Europe may one have so much absolute comfort and peace in a hotel. He has added two tables, vases for lots of flowers sent up, and has placed the furniture in another way. Unfortunately, it is just before the beginning of my tour. In general, I observe a curious difference in the behavior toward me of all the employees in the hotel at the beginning of my stay and now. At first, they treated me with that coolness and rather offensive indifference that bordered on enmity. Now they all smile, are all ready to go to the four corners of the earth at my first word, and even the young people serving on the *elevator* begin to talk about the weather every time I go up or down. But I am far from the thought that all this is the result of *tips* which I hand out rather liberally. Besides, indeed, all servants are very grateful when one acts in a friendly way to them.

I was visited by Messrs. Howson and Smith, representatives of the Composers' Club, which is preparing to give an evening concert devoted to my works. Lovely Mrs. White sent me such a great quantity of beautiful flowers that, due to lack of vases and room, I had to give them to Max, who was completely enraptured as his wife adores them. I was also visited by the violinist Rietzel, who came for my portrait and related how the orchestra players had got

to like me. That touched me very much. Having changed, went to
Mayer with that other large portrait. From there to Schirmer, while
from there hastily to Music Hall where my last appearance before
the public was due. These visits before the concert prove how little
I was *excited* this time. Why? I absolutely do not know. In the
artists' room, became acquainted with the *woman singer* who sang
my song, "Both Painful and Sweet," yesterday.[31] A marvelous singer
and a sweet woman. My Concerto went magnificently in the excellent performance of Adele Aus der Ohe. The enthusiasm was such
as I never succeeded in arousing even in Russia. They called me
out endlessly, shouted "Upwards," [*sic*] waved handkerchiefs—in a
word, it was evident that I had really pleased the Americans. But
especially dear to me was the enthusiasm of the orchestra. Owing
to the heat and to the profuse perspiring caused by waving the
baton, I was not able to remain at the concert and, unfortunately,
did not hear the scenes from *Parsifal*.[32] At home took a bath and
changed. Lunched (or dined) at five o'clock downstairs at my
place. Sat in turn in the boxes of Carnegie, Hyde, Holls and Reno
at the final evening concert of the festival. Handel's oratorio, *Israel
in Egypt* was performed in its entirety and the performance was
distinguished. During the middle of the concert an ovation for the
architect of the edifice. After the concert went with Damrosch to
the supper given by von Sachs. This luxurious supper was held at
the Manhattan Club. The building is grandiose and splendid. We
were in a private room. Although the cuisine of this club is renowned, nevertheless, it still seemed repugnant to me. On an exquisite vignette *menu* there was written, for each guest, an excerpt
from some composition of mine. The guests, besides Damrosch and

---

[31] *The singer was the contralto, Mrs. Carl Alves, who also rehearsed
on April 26 (May 8) Tchaikovsky's song, "Both Painful and Sweet," Op.
6, No. 3, in preparation for her appearance on May 9 on the same program with Tchaikovsky. On the program the song was listed as "So
Schmerzlich."*

[32] *This was Tchaikovsky's final appearance at Carnegie Hall. The concert was held the afternoon of May 9 and performed were Beethoven's
Fifth Symphony, conducted by Walter Damrosch; two songs, "To Sleep"
by Walter Damrosch and "So Schmerzlich" by Tchaikovsky sung by Mrs.
Carl Alves, orchestra conducted by Walter Damrosch; First Piano Concerto, Op. 23, by Tchaikovsky, Adele Aus der Ohe, soloist with the composer conducting, and the Prelude and Flower Maiden Scene, Act II,
from Wagner's Parsifal, conducted by Walter Damrosch.*

myself, were the pianist, Van der Stucken, the Hungarian, Korbay;
Rudolph Schirmer, von Sachs' brother and finally the very famous,
extremely revered and loved Schurz. Schurz, the friend of Kos-
suth, Hertzen and Mazzini, fled Germany in '48. Little by little
he made a great reputation for himself and became a senator. A
man truly very wise, cultured, and interesting. He sat next to me
and talked much about Tolstoy, Turgenev, and Dostoyevsky. The
supper went off very gaily, on the whole, and there was no lack of
evidence of interest in me. We dispersed at two o'clock. The Hungarian, Korbay, escorted me to the hotel.

10 May This was a very hard and burdensome day. In the morning I was besieged by visitors. Who didn't come! The courteous,
interesting Mr. Korbay, and the young, very handsome composer,
Klein, and von Sachs, and the pianiste, Friend, with gold teeth, and
Mr. Sutro with his beautiful wife, a doctor of laws and I do not
recall who else. Was driven simply to insensibility. At one o'clock
went out to visit the nihilist, Stark-Stoleshnikov,[33] but he lives so
far away and the heat was so awful, that I had to postpone it.
Dropped in at the Hoffman House and there met Mr. Parris, the
steamer companion, the one who provided me with cigarettes. He
detests America and thinks only about leaving. From there hastened
to lunch at Doctor Neftel's. Barely managed to arrive in time.
Doctor Neftel is a Russian or at least was educated in Russia. His
wife, as I finally learned, is a Georgian princess, a cousin of Egor
Ivanovich. They have lived in America since 1860. Travel often to
Europe, but have not been in Russia since that time. Why they
avoid it, it was awkward to find out. Both are fervid patriots; love
Russia with a genuine love. The husband is more to my liking than
the wife. Something soft, kind, fine and sincere is felt in each
Russian word, uttered not without effort, and in every sluggish
motion of the tired and rather sad old man. He spoke about Russia
all the time with the idea that despotism and bureaucratic administration prevent it from becoming the leader of mankind. He repeated that idea with different variations a countless number of
times. His wife is a type of energetic, Moscow mistress. Wishes to
appear clever and independent but, in reality, I think she is neither
clever nor independent. Both love music very much and are well
acquainted with it. Neftel, at one time and in some way, was famous
in the field of medicine and he is very much esteemed in New

---

[33] *Doubtless Waldemar R. Stark.*

York. I believe that he is a freethinker who at one time incurred the wrath of the government and escaped from Russia in time; but, to all appearances, his present liberalism is very far from nihilism and anarchism. Both repeated several times that they do not associate with the nihilists here. After lunching at their place (about three o'clock!!!), ran (as it's necessary to run about here constantly due to the lack of hackneys) to V. N. MacGahan. If it may be said that the Neftels live luxuriously, then the furnishings of this correspondent of Russian newspapers and magazines is quite student-like. She lives in a boardinghouse, i.e. in a neat, furnished house where downstairs all have a common reception room and a common dining room, while the living quarters are on the upper floors. At her place I found a very strange Russian young man, Griboyedov, who spoke broken Russian, but perfect French and English. He has the appearance of a contemporary *dandy* and is a little affected. Later, the famous sculptor, Kamensky, appeared; do not know why he has lived twenty years now in America. He is an elderly man, with a deep scar on his forehead; ailing and rather pitiful looking. Placed me in a quandary by asking me to relate *all* that I know concerning present-day Russia. I was on the point of losing my self-composure entirely before the magnitude of that task, but, fortunately, Varvara Nikolaievna [MacGahan] began to talk about my musical affairs, and then I looked at my watch and saw that it was time to run home and change for the dinner at Carnegie's. On account of its being Sunday, all the cafés were closed. Inasmuch as they are the only places where 1) one may buy cigarettes, and 2) satisfy Nature's little need, and I being in extreme in want of the one and the other, one can then imagine how great were my sufferings until I at last reached home. These remnants of English Puritanism, shown by such absurd trifles as, for example, the impossibility of obtaining a drink of *whiskey* or a glass of *beer* on Sundays except by deceit, make me very indignant. It is said that the legislators who made this law in New York state, are themselves awful drunkards. Barely managed to change and reach Carnegie in a carriage (which I had to send for and paid very high). This multi-millionaire lives, in the main, no more luxuriously than others. Dining were Mr. and Mrs. Reno, Mr. and Mrs. Damrosch, the architect of Music Hall and his wife, an unknown gentleman and a stout lady friend of Mme. Damrosch. I again sat next to this very aristocratic and refined looking lady. Carnegie—that amazing character, who has developed in the course of years from a telegraph messenger into one of the leading American men of wealth, but who has remained simple, modest and not in the least turning up his nose at people—inspires within me unusual affection, probably because he is filled with interest in me too. Throughout the whole evening, he displayed his regard for me in an unusual manner. He grasped my hands, declaring that I am the uncrowned but true king of music; embraced me (without kissing—here men never kiss), expressed my greatness by standing on tiptoe and raising his hands up high, and finally threw the entire company into raptures by showing how I conduct. He did it so seriously, so well, so similarly, that I myself was delighted. His wife, an extremely simple and pretty young lady, also displayed her interest in me in every way. All of that was pleasant but, at the same time, somehow embarrassing to me. I was very glad to start for home at eleven o'clock. Reno escorted me home on foot. Packed for the coming trip tomorrow.

TRIP FROM NEW YORK TO NIAGARA

11 May Mayer called for me at eight-fifteen. Well, what would I have done without Mayer? How would I have gotten for myself just the kind of ticket I need? How would I get to the railroad station? How would I find out at what time, where, how, and what I had to do? I got into the drawing room car. It is like our Pullman car only the easy chairs are placed closer to one another and with backs to the windows, but in such a way that it is possible to turn in all directions. The windows are large and the view on both sides is completely unobstructed. Next to this car was the dining car, while several cars away was the smoking car with a buffet. The connection from car to car is quite easy, much more convenient than with us, since the passage-ways are covered. The employees, i.e. the conductors, the waiters in the dining car and in the buffet in the smoking car, are Negroes who are very obliging and polite. At twelve o'clock I lunched (the price of the lunch is one dollar) from a menu giving one any choice of food from among all of the dishes indicated. Dined at six, and again in exactly the same way, that is, from a score or two dishes I could select whatever and as much as I desired, and again for one dollar. The cars are much more luxurious than ours, despite the absence of *classes*. The luxuries are entirely superfluous even, as, for example, the frescoes, the crystal ornamentations, etc. There are numerous dressing rooms,

i.e. compartments, in which are the washstands with hot and cold
water, towels (regarding towels, there is an amazing supply here,
in general), cakes of soap, brushes, etc. You can roam about the
train and wash as much as you like. There is a bath and a barber
shop. All this is convenient and comfortable—but, for all that, our
cars nevertheless are more attractive to me for some reason. But
probably that is a reflection of my longing for home, which oppressed and gnawed at me madly again all day yesterday. We
arrived in Buffalo at eight-thirty o'clock. Here two gentlemen were
waiting for me whom Mayer asked to show me from one train to
the other, as it is rather difficult to orientate oneself in the labyrinths of this junction of various lines. One of them is a Polish
pianist. The meeting with these gentlemen lasted but ten minutes.
Fifty minutes after leaving Buffalo, I was in Niagara Falls. Stopped
at the Hotel Kaltenbach where accommodations were already prepared for me, again thanks to Mayer. The hotel is unassuming,
something like the small Switzerland kind, but very neat and, most
important to me, convenient, as everyone speaks German. Drank
tea, unfortunately, with some gentleman who annoyed me with his
talking. Felt unusually tired, I think because it was awfully stuffy
in the train, for Americans and especially American women are
afraid of drafts, as a result of which the windows are closed all
the time and there is no passage for the outside air. And then one
has to sit longer than with us. There are almost no stops at all. It
was all the more tiresome, since only the first hours of the trip,
along the Hudson River, were interesting to the eye; all the rest
of the time the territory is flat and not very attractive. Retired
early. The roar of the waterfalls in the silence of the night is very
impressive.

NIAGARA

12 May, Niagara Rose about eight o'clock. Breakfast at eight. Became acquainted with the proprietor, Mr. Kaltenbach. A somewhat
reserved, but extremely courteous and distinguished German. A
landau was already waiting. There are no guides here—and that is
grand! The driver goes wherever it is necessary and, partly by
words, partly by gestures, shows those who do not know English
what to do. At first we started out for Goat Island, crossing an old
bridge. There, turning to the right, we stopped, and the driver invited me to descend to the level of the American Fall. Will not

Tchaikovsky at the age of fifty-one, from the photograph taken by
Sarony in New York City

describe the beauty of the Falls, as such things are difficult to express in words. The beauty and majesty of the sight are truly breath-taking. After walking about and viewing this part of the Falls, which is divided, in general, into several separate waterfalls of which two are colossal (especially the second), we set out along the edge of the island to the Three Sisters Islands. This whole excursion is enchanting, particularly at this time of the year. The verdure is quite fresh and in the grass the *dandelions*, my darlings, are showing off. Wished terribly to pick several of these yellow beauties with the fragrance of freshness and spring, but at every step there sticks out a board with a reminder that even *wild flowers* cannot be picked. Then I gazed at the main waterfall, the Horseshoe Fall. A grandiose picture. From there, after returning to the mainland, we went across a marvelous, daring, and beautiful bridge to the Canadian side. This bridge was constructed, or better, thrown across the Niagara but two years ago. One feels dizzy when looking below. On the Canadian side I had to consent, so as not to be tortured by the thought that I was cowardly, to a very ugly change of clothing; to descend in an elevator below the Falls; to walk through a tunnel and finally to stand right below the Falls—all of which is very interesting, but a little frightening. Above, there was the pestering to buy photographs and all other kinds of nonsense. The pressure and impudence of those leeches would have been incomprehensible had I not observed from the facial features of both sexes tormenting me with offers of service that they are Jews. Besides, *Canada* is no longer America. From here we rode down the river to a view of the rapids. The Niagara, a river wider than the Volga and dividing into branches, falls from enormous cliffs and then suddenly contracts to the size of the Seine; and soon afterward, as though having restored its energies, it rushes against the rapids and enters into battle with them. Next, I descended with a boy guide by a cable railway and walked rather long on the shore, level with the roaring river. The sight reminded me of the Imatra on a big scale. After that I walked for a while, got into my landau again near the bridge, and arrived home shortly before dinner. At the table d'hôte, I sat at a distance from the others; the dinner was European, very delicious. After dinner, I walked to the waterfalls and about the small city in general. During this walk, however, as also in the morning, I could not manage to conquer a certain unusual tiredness, probably nervous, which hindered me from enjoying the walk and the beauty of the surroundings as I should

have. It was just as though something was shattered within me
and the machine wasn't operating quite easily. At six-fifteen, I left
in a Pullman in a separate compartment. The Negro porter is not
especially obliging and is unintelligent. On account of him I could
not get any food and went to sleep hungry. There are all possible
comforts: washstand, soap, towel, and a splendid bed. But I slept
badly.

NEW YORK

13 May At five o'clock awoke, tired and with tormenting thoughts
about the dreadful coming week. Arrived at my place at eight
o'clock. Took a bath, was glad to see good Max but was sad on
reading in the newspaper the news about the attempt on the life
of the tsarevitch. It is also saddening that there are no letters from
home—and I was expecting very many of them. Visitors: Reinhard,
Howson, Smith, Huss, etc. In view of the distances between the
various places in New York in which I had to be today, I hired
a private carriage. First of all I drove to bid good-by to Damrosch,
who is leaving for Europe. He asked me to take him as a pupil. I
refused, of course, but unintentionally showed my horror too much
at the thought of Damrosch coming to me in the village for the
purpose of studying!!! From there I hastened to Reno's for lunch.
The coachman was completely drunk and positively refused to
understand where he had to drive me. It is a good thing that I can
now orient myself in New York. The Reno family displayed much
hospitality, as usual. From there to Mayer's, where I was to meet
Mr. Keidel, Knabe's partner. This took place. After that, Mayer and
I hurried, still with the same drunken coachman, to the huge steam
ferry that transports horses and carriages and people across the
East River, and from there to his *summer home* by train. I felt so
tired, irritated, and unhappy that I could hardly keep from crying.
Mayer's summer home and the neighboring summer homes remind
me very much of the summer homes near Moscow in style. The
only difference is that near Moscow there are groves, grass, and
flowers; here there is nothing except sand. Nothing can be more
desolate than these *summer homes* and it would be impossible to
imagine, were it not for the *ocean*, which compels forgetfulness,
all that in our view goes to make up the attractions of summer or
country life. Soon after our arrival we sat down to dine. The
younger son of Mayer, that thorough German, a boy of fourteen

years, has already become so Americanized that he speaks German like this: *"Du haben kalt in Russland."* The family is pleasant and kind, but their intellectual level is very low, as a result of which I was unusually and intensely bored and listless. In the afternoon we strolled in the sand right by the sea, which was a little rough. The air here is fresh and clean and this walk afforded me pleasure and relief. Passed the night at their place, and slept badly.

14 May Rose about six o'clock. Went to the ocean and was enthralled. After *breakfast* we left for the city. I longed to be alone even for a little while—but it was difficult. Miss Ivy Ross appeared. My letter about Wagner sent her, and published, created a sensation and Mr. Anton Seidl, the famous conductor and Wagnerite, answered it rather lengthily in a very courteous tone.[34] She came to request that I reply to Seidl's letter. I was about to write the reply, but Mr. Ditman appeared and stayed unusually long, relating very uninteresting local musical gossip heard already a hundred times. Then there was the correspondent of a Philadelphia newspaper, an especially sincere admirer of mine, I think. I had to speak English: I made progress; said certain things exceptionally well. Wrote letters. Lunched downstairs in the hotel alone. Walked through Central Park. In accordance with my promise, dropped in at Mayer's in order to write the testimonial for the Knabe pianos. So there is finally the answer to Mayer's attentions!!! All those presents, all the spending of Knabe's money for my sake, all that incomprehensible attentiveness—is merely payment for future advertisement!!! I proposed to Mayer that he compose the requested testimonial himself; he sat for a long time but for some reason could not think of anything and asked to postpone the matter until the next meeting. After that, visited Mr. Tretbar, the representative of Steinway, who, notified in advance by Jürgenson, had been waiting for me all this time with a letter from Peter Ivanovich— not wanting to come to me first. I purposely postponed the visit to this punctilious German until a time when there would no longer be occasion to become better acquainted. Was packing at home.

---

[34] *Tchaikovsky wrote his article about Wagner in the form of a letter. One week after his article appeared, Seidl replied to him in an article entitled "A Defense of Wagner" also in the New York Morning Journal. The substance of Tchaikovsky's article was that he considered Wagner's music essentially symphonic. Seidl, a fervent Wagnerite, answered that the Russian composer had failed to understand the "music of the future."*

Soon Reinhard appeared with a letter from Mayer in which the latter asked me to sign the testimonial for the Knabe pianos. In the draft of this testimonial it was stated that *I* find Knabe's pianos indisputably the best in America. Inasmuch as I really not only do not find it so, but recognize the Steinway as undoubtedly superior (despite the comparative unfriendliness of its representative, Tretbar, toward me), I, therefore, rejected this wording of my *testimonial-advertisement.* I entrusted Reinhard to tell Mayer that in spite of all my gratitude, I do not want to lie. The reporter from the *Herald* came; a very charming person. At last Thomas Junior appeared with whom we started out in Hyde's carriage to his place. I am sorry that I am absolutely incapable of describing all the fascination, charm, and originality of this couple. Hyde greeted me with the words: *"Kak uashe zdaroiue, sidite pozhaliust."* [35] At the same time, he himself was laughing like a lunatic, his wife was laughing, and Thomas and I were laughing. It came out that he had bought a Russian self-tutor and memorized several phrases in order to surprise me. Mme. Hyde bade me instantly to smoke a cigarette in *her* drawing-room—the height of hospitality for an American lady. After the cigarette, we went to dine. The table was lavishly adorned with flowers; each of us had a little bunch of flowers for his buttonhole. With this, Hyde became quite unexpectedly solemn and lowering his eyes read the Lord's Prayer. I did as the others, i.e. also lowered my eyes. Then began an endlessly long dinner having enormous pretensions (for example, an ice was served to everyone in the form of a really huge, lifelike rose, in the middle of which was the ice). In the midst of the dinner Mme. Hyde invited me to take a smoke. All this lasted very very long, so that I was tired to complete inertia, especially because it was necessary to speak English all the time or listen to the unsuccessful attempts of both hosts to say something in French. At ten o'clock I left with Thomas. Reinhard was already waiting for me at home. We drank some beer downstairs and started downtown on the elevated with my valises; there we crossed the Hudson on a steam ferry and finally reached the railroad station. Here Reinhard (without whose help I would have been lost) settled me in a comfortable compartment; a courteous Negro made up the bed for me—I threw myself on it with my clothes on, not having the strength to undress and immediately

---

[35] *Broken Russian, meaning "How do you feel? Sit down, please."*

fell asleep like one dead. Slept soundly but for only a little time. The Negro awoke me one hour before the train's arrival in Baltimore.

15 May Was received at the hotel with indifference and neglect, as usual. Finding myself alone in my room, I felt unusually pitiable and unhappy, chiefly because no one speaks anything but English here. Slept a little. Went to eat breakfast in the restaurant and was very irritated by the Negro waiter who did not want to understand at all that I simply wish tea with bread and butter. I had to go to the office, where also no one understood anything. Finally some gentleman understanding German saved the situation. Hardly did I sit down, when stout Knabe came, and soon after I saw Adele Aus der Ohe with her sister and was awfully cheered by them; at least musically we have something in common. Went together with them to the rehearsal in a carriage. The final glory took place on the stage of the Lyceum Theater. The orchestra turned out to be small (there were four first violins in all!!!) but not bad. There was not even a thought of the Third Suite. We decided to play in its stead the Serenade for Strings, which the musicians did not know at all, while Mr. Herbert [36] (the conductor) did not even think of playing it through beforehand, as Reno had promised me. The Concerto with Aus der Ohe went well at once, but it was necessary to fuss considerably with the Serenade. The musicians were impatient, and the young concertmaster [37] was not even particularly courteous, for he displayed too vehemently that it was time to finish. True, this unfortunate touring orchestra is very tired from traveling about. After the rehearsal went home with Aus der Ohe again. We changed in a half hour and drove at once to the concert. As is customary at concerts during the day, I conducted in a frock coat. Everything went perfectly well, but I did not notice any unusual enthusiasm in the audience, at least, in comparison with New York. After the concert we drove home to change, and not even a half hour passed when Knabe, colossal in figure and colossal in hospitality, drove up for us. This beardless giant had arranged a banquet in my honor at his home. I found a large company there. Mlle. von Fernow, a

---

[36] *The orchestra was the touring Boston Festival Orchestra of forty men, conducted by Victor Herbert.*

[37] *Emil Mollenhauer.*

former friend of Kotek, who turned up as a music teacher in Baltimore; the composer and the director of the Conservatory, Hamerik; the extremely old pianist, Courlaender; Burmeister, the composer; Fincke, professor of singing, very witty and an eloquent after-dinner speaker; Knabe's two sons; his two nephews; the music critic of the *Sun* (the newspaper here) and several others whose names I do not recall, one of whom had been in St. Petersburg. The latter entertained us with tricks after dinner. The dinner was endless, awfully delicious, and generous in both food and wine, which Knabe kept pouring zealously throughout the course of the dinner. By the second half of the dinner I felt an unusual tiredness and an unimaginable hatred of everyone, particularly of my two neighbors: Mlle. von Fernow and the sister of Aus der Ohe. After dinner conversed a little with everyone, most of all with the venerable old Courlaender; watched the tricks of the gentleman mentioned above; listened to the piano concerto of the young pianist, Burmeister; smoked and drank without end. At eleven-thirty Knabe drove me and the Aus der Ohe sisters home. I dropped on the bed like a log and fell asleep at once like one dead.

16 May Awakening early and breakfasting downstairs, wrote the diary and awaited, not without horror, Knabe, with whom I was to see the city and the sights. Mr. Sutro came, the brother of the one who is married to a beauty, a doctor of laws. Knabe appeared and together with the Aus der Ohe sisters we started out to run around Baltimore in his carriage. The weather is bad, rainy. Baltimore is a very pretty, neat city. The houses are not large, all red brick with white marble steps at the entrance. First of all we drove to the Knabe factory and inspected its huge piano plant in every detail. In the main, it is very interesting and certain machines especially I liked extremely; indeed, the sight of so many workers with serious, intelligent faces, so clean and carefully dressed despite the manual labor, leaves a fine impression. But I felt that peculiar American morning fatigue, which has troubled me here ever since the day of my arrival. Even spoke and understood with difficulty what others were saying. The glass of beer offered by Knabe after the inspection heartened me exceedingly. From there we went to the central square with its beautiful view of the *harbor* and the city. From there to the Peabody Institute. This is an enormous, handsome building built with the money of the wealthy Peabody. It contains: an enormous library, open to all; a painting and sculpture gallery (extraordinarily poor and pitiful, which does not prevent the Baltimoreans from being proud of it) and a *conservatory*. The latter, from the outside, is splendid. Besides marvelously arranged classrooms it has two concert halls, its own music library, many instruments, etc. Its director, Hamerik, greeted and escorted me around very warmly. The professors—all my boon companions of yesterday. Young Burmeister was consumed with a desire to play me his symphonic poem [38] and I had to agree to stay and listen to it despite my imminent departure at three o'clock. This composition is proof of the composer's adherence to the *Liszt* group of young musicians, but I cannot say that it delighted me. Burmeister asked that I make it known in Russia. Immediately after that we drove off for home to pack and prepare for the departure, but on the way Knabe took us to look at some sights. The good giant helped me to pack, treated Aus der Ohe and me to lunch and champagne, and seated me in the carriage to leave for the railroad station. They left for Philadelphia, and I, five minutes after them, for Washington. Rode only three-quarters of an hour. Was met by Botkin. After kissing one another, had the misfortune of losing my loose front tooth and heard, horrified, the sibilants from my lips, with an entirely new and special hissing sound. It's very unpleasant. Botkin conveyed me to the Hotel Arlington where he had reserved for me most splendid, indescribably comfortable accommodations, furnished with taste and refined simplicity. Declining a trip to the races, I asked Botkin to call for me before the dinner and on his departure took a bath and changed to a tail coat. The dinner was given for me in the Metropolitan Club, where Botkin and his colleagues are members. We four dined together: he, I, Greger, the counselor of the Embassy, and Hansen, the first secretary. Greger is a sportsman and only today he won the first prize at the races. Hansen is a musician. Both are very nice, engaging. In manners, Hansen reminds me a little of Mr. Nikitenko and St. Petersburg men of that type in general. They are young people, but Hansen is already bald. The dinner was very gay, and I was enjoying the happiness of speaking nothing but Russian, though this happiness was dampened by the sad fact that my *ch*, *sh*, *shch* hiss and whistle like an old man's. During the dinner came the information, first by telegram and then by telephone, about the return of Ambassador de Struve, especially for me, from a business trip

---

[38] *The Chase After Happiness, Op. 2.*

to New York. At about ten o'clock, we started for the Embassy, where Botkin had arranged a musical evening in the reception hall. Invited were about one hundred people. The ambassador appeared. He turned out to be a very hospitable, elderly man, simple in behavior and exceedingly charming generally. The company, gathered at the Embassy, was exclusively *diplomatic*. All were ambassadors with their wives and daughters and personalities from the higher administration. Almost all the ladies spoke French, as a result of which it was not particularly bad for me. I conversed especially long with the very clever and elegant Miss Williams. The program consisted of my trio and Brahms' quartet.[39] The piano part was performed by Secretary Hansen who turned out to be an exceedingly good pianist. He played my trio extremely well. The violinist was rather poor. I became acquainted with everybody. After the music a superb cold supper was served. When most of the guests dispersed, we, ten in number (besides Russians, there were the Belgian ambassador, and the secretaries of the Swedish and Austrian embassies), sat long at a big, round table, sipping most excellent wine. De Struve evidently likes to drink an extra glass of wine very much. He creates the impression of a man, shattered and sad, who seeks oblivion for his sorrows in wine. I came home about three o'clock escorted by Botkin and Hansen. Slept well.

WASHINGTON

17 May Woke with a pleasant impression of yesterday. It was unusually comforting for me to be among Russians and have a chance to do without foreign languages. After drinking tea downstairs, strolled a bit through the city which is very nice. All of it abounds in luxuriant, spring verdure. Returning home (the American morning fatigue makes itself felt, all the same) indulged in a semisleep in an extraordinarily comfortable easy chair. At about twelve o'clock Botkin came for me and we went to the luncheon of Ambassador de Struve. As he is a widower and does not maintain a household, the luncheon took place again in the same Metropolitan Club, where all these people spend the greater part of their lives. After the luncheon I went with Botkin and Hansen in a landau to see Washington. We visited the famous obelisk (the tallest struc-

---

[39] *The program of this musicale consisted of Tchaikovsky's Trio, Op. 50, for violin, violoncello and piano and the First Quartet, Op. 25, for piano and strings by Brahms.*

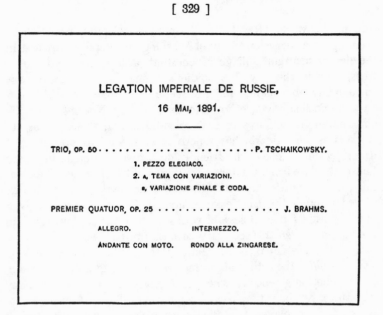

LEGATION IMPERIALE DE RUSSIE,

16 MAI, 1891.

———

TRIO, OP. 50 · P. TSCHAIKOWSKY.

1. PEZZO ELEGIACO.

2. A, TEMA CON VARIAZIONI.

B, VARIAZIONE FINALE E CODA.

PREMIER QUATUOR, OP. 25 · · · · · · · · · · · · · · · · J. BRAHMS.

ALLEGRO.   INTERMEZZO.

ANDANTE CON MOTO.   RONDO ALLA ZINGARESE.

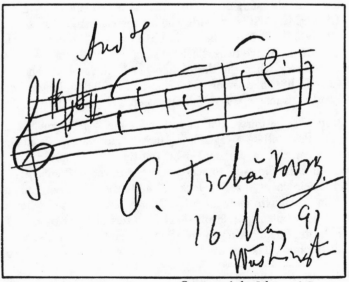

Courtesy of the Library of Congress.

Front and back of the program card for the musicale at the Russian Legation with a quotation from the first two bars of the second movement of the Trio.

ture in the world after Eiffel Tower); the Capitol, from where
there opens a marvelous view of Washington, literally drowned in
the dense, luxuriant foliage of chestnut, acacia, oak, and maple
trees; outside the city, the Soldier's Home (a magnificent park
surrounding the shelter for war veterans); some of the better
streets; and finally we returned to the Embassy. Not only does the
ambassador himself live in that splendid building but all his co-
workers as well. Botkin has superb accommodations upstairs. We
drank tea in his place; the friendly de Struve also came in to see
him and related many interesting things out of his past. Incidentally, he is very friendly with Mitrofan Tchaikovsky, with whom he
served through the Khivinsky campaign. Greger also came over.
With Hansen I played several works on two pianos downstairs in
the hall, and then this secretary-virtuoso played several solo pieces
excellently. We dined in the Metropolitan Club. Read in the *New
York Herald* [40] the article about me, of course with a picture again,
by the charming reporter who was at my place on the day of my
departure. At about nine o'clock we went to the local music school
where Hansen played two Beethoven concertos with the student
orchestra. In the audience were all Hansen's friends, among them
my friend, Miss Williams, with whom poor Hansen, it turns out, is
hopelessly in love. From there we drove to the Club once more, in
a very curious, native two-wheeled *fiacre*, which lets the passengers
out at the rear when the destination has been reached. There we
conversed a little and, escorted by Hansen and Botkin, I came home.
Had bad nightmares before falling asleep.

18 May At ten-thirty, Botkin called for me. I paid my bill and
left. Besides Botkin, Greger and Hansen saw me off. Rode in a
Pullman car. Sat in the smoker all the time, being afraid of conversation with the lady to whom Greger introduced me. Arrived
in Philadelphia at three o'clock. Visited Aus der Ohe. Lunched
downstairs. An extremely intrusive Odessa Jew came and wheedled
some money out of me. Strolled. The concert at eight o'clock. The
huge theater filled. [41] After the concert, at a club, in accordance with
an old promise. The return to New York was very dull and com-

[40] *John P. Jackson's article was entitled "Tschaikowsky on Music in
America." The article, in the form of an interview, was very laudatory
of American customs, etc. in general, and, in particular, of American
audiences and musicians.*

[41] *The concert was held at the Academy of Music on May 18. The
orchestra was the same as the one at the Baltimore concert (Victor*

plicated. In the sleeping car it was stifling and crowded. Woke with a headache. Rode home with Aus der Ohe, an endlessly long way. It is becoming impossible to write in detail.

NEW YORK

19 May Slept until nine o'clock and my head felt better. Visits by Reinhard and Holls. Became torpid from tiredness and excitement; understood nothing and sustained my energy only with the thought of my coming departure tomorrow. Letters with requests for autographs overwhelmed me. At twelve-thirty, started out to see Mayer. Wrote the notorious *letter-advertisement* with the omission of the phrase about *pre-eminence.* Lunched with him and Reinhard in the Italian restaurant. Expected the composer, Bruno Klein, at home. He appeared and played me several of his things, which were very nice. At four o'clock Mr. Holls came for me. With him and the Aus der Ohe sisters we went to Central station, joined Mr. and Mrs. Reno there and set out along the Hudson. After half an hour we were out of the train and settling into a gig. We started out for *Holls' summer home* along a wonderful, picturesque road. This summer home-villa, of exceptionally fine construction, stands on the high shore of the Hudson and the view unfolding from the balcony, the arbor, and especially from the roof of the house is incomparable. At six o'clock we sat down to dinner. The conversation was lively and it was not distressing to me, for what can I not endure now, in view of my departure so soon!!! Aus der Ohe played after dinner. At ten-thirty we got into the gig again and returned home by train. Reno talked about my engagement for next year. Went in to see the Aus der Ohe sisters and bade good-by to them. Was packing.

20 May The elderly librettist. I was very sorry to tell him of my reluctance to write an opera to his text. He was visibly grieved. No sooner did he leave when Dannreuther called for me in order to take me to the rehearsal of the quartet and trio,[42] which are to be performed this evening at the gala concert of the Composers' Club. Had to ride rather far. The quartet was played insignificantly and the trio quite poorly even, for the pianist (Mr. Huss, bashful and timid), is altogether inferior; he cannot even count. Did

Herbert, conductor) and Tchaikovsky conducted the same works as at Baltimore. The concert was received very well by the Philadelphia press.

[42] *Third String Quartet in E-Flat minor, Op. 30, and the Trio, Op. 50, for violin, violoncello and piano, both by Tchaikovsky.*

not succeed in doing anything at home in the way of preparations
for the departure. Went to Reno for lunch in a carriage. More
than ever they, i.e. Mme. Reno and the three daughters, were full
of enthusiastic cordiality toward me. The oldest (Anna, who is
married) presented me with a splendid cigar case. Mme. Reno
with lots of eau de Cologne; Alice and her sister with cookies for
the journey. After them, hurried to Hyde's. Mme. Hyde was expecting me. Here too there was much sincere enthusiasm, expressed
with her characteristic humor. Finally I could busy myself with
packing at home—hateful work. Besides my back pained severely.
Tired, I went to Mayer. I treated him and Reinhard to a fine dinner
at Martelli's. At eight o'clock hastened home to change. At eight-
thirty, Howson came for me. The Composers' Club is not a club
of *composers,* as I thought at first, but a special musical society,
the purpose of which is to arrange hearings, from time to time, of
works by *one* composer. Yesterday [43] the concert was devoted to
me and it took place in the splendid hall of the Metropolitan Opera
House. I sat in the first row. The E-Flat minor quartet and the
trio were played, some songs were sung, certain of which were
performed excellently (Mrs. Alves), etc.[44] The program was too
long. In the middle of the concert, Mr. Smith read a speech addressed to me; I responded briefly in French; an ovation, obviously.
One lady threw a gorgeous bouquet of roses straight into my face.
Was introduced to a lot of people, among them to our consul-
general. After it was over, I had to converse with about a hundred
people, and write about a hundred autographs. Finally, tired out
to exhaustion and suffering extremely from the pain in my back,
went home. Inasmuch as the steamer sails at 5 A.M., it must be
boarded during the night. Packed hurriedly, changed; Reno, Mayer,
and Reinhard were present during this. Downstairs we drank two
bottles of champagne, after which, bidding farewell to the personnel of the hotel, we rode to the steamer. We rode a very long
way. The steamer turned out to be just as magnificent as the

---

[43] *Tchaikovsky must have made the entry for this day on May 21 for
the concert took place on May 20.*

[44] *The quartet was performed by the Beethoven String Quartet whose
members were Gustav Dannreuther, Ernst Thiele, Otto K. Schill and
Adolf Hartdegen while the trio was played by Dannreuther, Hartdegen
and Henry Holden Huss. Mrs. Carl Alves sang some of Tchaikovsky's
songs. Mrs. Gerrit Smith, Purdon Robinson, Ferdinand Dulcken and
Frank Taft also appeared.*

"Bretagne." My cabin is an *officer's* one, i.e. officers on these steamers have the right to sell their accommodations, but also fleece outrageously. I paid three hundred dollars (1500 frs.) for my cabin!!! But then it's really good and spacious. Bade farewell to my dear American friends and went to sleep soon after that. Slept poorly and heard the steamer sail at five o'clock. Came out of my cabin as we were going past the Statue of Liberty.

TRIP FROM NEW YORK TO GERMANY

21 May Despite the desperate pain in the back, dressed unwillingly, drank tea downstairs, and walked a little through the steamer so as to become acquainted with the location of its sections. There are many passengers, but they are of a different character from those who were aboard the "Bretagne." The most striking difference is that there are no immigrants. At eight o'clock they called us for breakfast. My place had been indicated earlier. Have as a neighbor a middle-aged gentleman who immediately began a conversation. Slept all morning. Am indifferent to the sight of the ocean. Think about the coming journey without terror and with homesickness: would like it to be over sooner! The steamer flies with unusual speed: it is the new, luxurious "Fürst Bismarck" making its first return voyage. It arrived last week in New York from Hamburg, after a passage of only six days and fourteen hours. God grant that we too cross the vast distance just as fast! It is not as quiet as the "Bretagne" while in motion. The weather so far is beautiful. At *lunch* became better acquainted with my vis-à-vis. He is a gentleman of indefinite nationality (possibly a Jew—and I, on purpose, told him the story of the intrusive Jew) who speaks all languages perfectly. He lives in Dresden and sells tobacco *en gros*. He has already succeeded in finding out who I am, or if he speaks the truth, he actually saw me conduct in New York; but, in any case, he launched into compliments and raptures about my fame and talents. Having become accustomed in New York to constant talking despite the desire to be quiet, I soon got used to his company, though it had burdened me in the morning. The singer, Antonia Mielke, whom I knew was sailing on this steamer and of whom I was rather afraid, fortunately does not sit at the same table with me, which, I believe, she was trying to arrange. I met her just before dinner. Wanted to read after lunch, but instead of that fell asleep and slept through three good hours. On the whole, I slept surprisingly much today, and in the evening, soon after dinner, I was so attacked by drowsiness again that I went to bed about

ten o'clock and slept until seven o'clock in the morning. Nothing unusual happened in the course of the day. Mr. Aronson and his young wife came up to me and became acquainted; he is the owner of the Casino Theater, a favorite of von Bülow, as is proved by an autograph album sent me the other day for my signature and some lines of music. The steward in my cabin, Schroeder, is a very kind young German; two other *gracious* Germans serve at table; this is *very important* to me. In general, I am satisfied with the steamer, the cabin, and the food. Since there are no immigrants, it is possible to walk on the lower deck, which is very enjoyable, for there I do not meet my traveling companions in the first class and can be silent.

22 May A day not distinguished by anything unusual. The weather was somewhat foggy, as always near the Banks of Newfoundland, but calm. I have already become accustomed to the steamer and the passengers, and my attitude has been set. I keep myself at a distance and, thanks to the wonderful cabin, where it's even possible to walk without difficulty, I feel much more free than on the "Bretagne." With my neighbor at table, I converse without tension. With the other neighbors, an American family, have a, so to say, bowing acquaintance. With Mielke, I converse once a day about the opera, singers, and St. Petersburg where she sang two years ago at the Livadia. Aronson and his wife I just greet. Of the remaining about three hundred passengers am not acquainted with any as yet. Go to the smoking room and watch them play cards. My neighbor at table plays *skat* there all day. Look in at the salon mornings, when no one is present. There stands a fine Steinway grand. There's a not bad music library with it. My works are there also. The order of the day is as follows: in the morning, after dressing, ring and Schroeder brings me a cup of tea. At eight o'clock, breakfast. Eat an omelet and drink tea with *Pfannkuchen*. The tea is good. Then take a walk on the lower deck, work, and read. At work, I am conceiving the sketches for a future symphony.[45] At twelve o'clock the tom-tom sounds: it is the call for lunch. Two hot and a lot of cold dishes are served. After that, walk again, read, and converse with Mielke. At six o'clock, dinner. It lasts until seven-thirty. Drink coffee in the *Rauchzimmer*, roam

---

[45] *This was probably the Symphony in E-Flat Major which he commenced to compose about one year following the present entry. The symphony was never finished but he used its sketches for the composition of his Third Piano Concerto also in E-Flat Major, Op. 75.*

about the steamer, especially on the lower deck, where only the third-class passengers are—not many. I go to sleep early. Twice a day the orchestra plays. It consists of *stewards* from the second class, of whom there are about sixteen, and they play quite well, though the selections are poor. They play first at two o'clock, second, during *dinnertime*. Am little pleased by the sea. It is magnificent, but I am too filled with yearning for home. My health is excellent. An appetite, the kind I haven't had for a long time. Three times a day I devour an enormous quantity of food. For some reason, I slept badly last night; was waking continually. I am now reading Tatishchev's book, *Alexandre et Napoléon*.

23 *May* I was told so often in New York that the sea is splendid at this time of year that I was convinced of it. Oh, what a disappointment! In the morning the weather turned bad; it rained, the wind began to blow, and in the evening a storm. A terrible night! Didn't sleep. Sat on the divan. Napped toward morning.

24 *May* A disgusting day! The weather is horrible. The sea is raging. Seasickness. Vomited. Ate one orange the whole day.

25 *May* Last night, completely exhausted from tiredness and sickness, I fell asleep dressed on my divan and slept through the whole night like that. The tossing is less today, but the weather is disgusting, just the same. My nerves are inexpressibly tense and irritated by the noise and crash, not stopping for one moment. Is it possible that I will decide on torture like this once more?

In the course of the day the tossing grew less and less, and little by little, the weather became very good. Repulsion to the company of passengers seized me; the very sight of them angers and terrifies me. Remain in my cabin almost without going out. However, at meals, besides the usual conversational tobacconist, I converse by now in English with the American party sitting at our table. They are extremely nice people, particularly the tall, plump lady. They are going to northern Norway to see the midnight sun. From there they intend to go to St. Petersburg.

26 *May* The night was magnificent, calm, moonlit. Having read enough in my cabin, I strolled long on deck. It was amazingly pleasant. All were asleep without exception and I was the only one of the three hundred passengers in the first class who went out to admire the night. The beauty was indescribable and words cannot express it. It is strange to recall now the terrible night on Sunday, when everything, even the trunk, was rolling from one corner of

my cabin to the other; when some kind of frightful jolts—causing a shuddering feeling that the steamer was making its final effort to battle the storm—filled my soul with tormenting terror; when, to complete the horror, the electric lamp and shade toppled over and crashed into bits . . . ! I promised myself that night never to travel again on the ocean. But my steward, Schroeder, says that every time the weather is bad, he promises himself to quit the steamship service and on each return to the harbor longs for the sea and is lonely without it. Perhaps that will also happen to me. The weather today has finally turned splendid. The passengers talk of a *concert* today in the salon and pester me to play. This is what spoils an ocean trip: it's the obligatory association in the company of the passengers.

27 May The weather has settled beautifully. Now and then a little rain fell. As we neared La Manche, the sea became more and more animated. Hundreds of small fishing vessels appeared in view of the steamer. About 2 P.M. the English coast became visible, in some places, rocky and picturesque, in other places, smooth and covered with fresh spring grass. Otherwise, nothing unusual happened, with the exception of the *ball* after dinner, at which I was present not more than five minutes. The circle of acquaintances has widened terribly. Fortunately, I can disappear into my splendid cabin for whole hours. At 2 A.M. we arrived in Southampton. Here part of the passengers, among them the Aronsons and the American family traveling to Norway, went off. I woke and went out to watch the departure of the small ship. Delighting in the superb sunrise.

28 May After Southampton and the Isle of Wight, I slept again and woke at seven o'clock with a slight cold. The weather continues to be splendid. Spent the greater part of the morning on deck in the company of the Tiedemann brothers, my new friends, admiring the English coast and the sight of lots of ships and sailboats scurrying about the channel. Folkestone and Dover appeared for a moment. The North Sea is very agitated. At night, Helgoland in the distance.

29 May Early in the morning, we came to Cuxhaven. At six o'clock, breakfast was served. At about eight, we transferred to a small ship and amid the notes of a march and shouts of "hurrah," we reached the customs. A very long inspection and waiting for the train. I sat in a coupé with Hülse, the Tiedemanns and Aramburo, the singer. At twelve we arrived in Hamburg. I stayed at the Hôtel St. Petersburg.

Additional Notes

Diary Three, page 23, 12 April, line 11, home:

Home was the expression used by the composer wherever he happened to stay: his own room; his hotel room; as guest with friends or relatives, etc.

Diary Six, page 185, 24 June, line 2, letters:

One was written to Jürgenson wherein Tchaikovsky declared how loathsome Moscow was becoming to him, "where Slavyansky's jubilee is celebrated; laurel wreathes are presented to Kashperov; Shostakovsky is taken seriously and the articles of Flerov are read." Tchaikovsky was obviously irked at these personages, now completely forgotten.

Diary Six, page 189, 9 July, line 1, July:

On one of the blank pages the composer entered the following remark in the upper right hand corner: "How old will I be if I reach this page? Kerch 9 July, 1887."

Diary Six, page 214, 17 September, line 7, four exclamation marks:

Tchaikovsky adored Mozart but had very little regard for Mussorgsky; playing together these composers, who had nothing in common except that their names started with M, called forth the four exclamation marks.

Register of Personalities

As a rule, persons mentioned only once and adequately identified in footnotes do not appear in the Register. First names, initials, and nicknames are listed separately only in cases where the person's identity is not clear from the context.

Abaza, Julia Fyodorovna (Stube) (?-1915), German-Russian singer and music patroness.

Abraham, Dr. Max (1831-1900). From 1880, sole owner of C. F. Peters, music publishers in Leipzig.

Adam, Juliette Lamber (1836-1936), French historical writer.

Adlerberg, Count Alexander Vladimir (1818-1888), secretary of the imperial court.

Albrecht, Anna Leontevna, wife of Konstantin (Karl) Karlovich Albrecht.

Albrecht, Evgeny Karlovich (1842-1894), Russian violinist, brother of Konstantin (Karl) Karlovich Albrecht.

Albrecht, Konstantin Karlovich, architect son of Konstantin (Karl) Karlovich Albrecht. He planned a house for Tchaikovsky.

Albrecht, Konstantin (Karl) (Karlusha) Karlovich (1836-1893), German-Russian violoncellist and professor at the Moscow Conservatory. Tchaikovsky dedicated two works to him.

Alesha, Alexei, see Sofronov, Alexei Ivanovich

Alexeyev, Konstantin Sergeyevich (1863-1938), Russian actor-director known by the pseudonym of Stanislavsky, one of the founders of the Moscow Art Theater.

Alexeyev, Nikolai Alexandrovich (1848-1893), merchant and a director of the Russian Musical Society.

Alice, niece of Edouard Colonne. Tchaikovsky mentions her in Diary Four.

Alikhanov, Konstantin Mikhailovich, associate chairman, Tiflis Russian Musical Society.

Altani, Ippolit Karlovich (1846-1919), Russian conductor with whom Tchaikovsky took some lessons in conducting. He introduced several of Tchaikovsky's works.

Amalya, see Litke, Countess Amalya Vasilyevna (Shobert)

Ambrust, Karl F. (1849-1896), German organist and music critic.

Angèle, French actress, wife of Lucien Guitry.

Anna, see Meck, von

Annette, Anya, see Merkling, Anna Petrovna

Antokolsky, Mark Matveyevich (1842-1902), Russian sculptor.

Antonina Ivanovna (Miliukova), *see* Tchaikovskaya, Antonina.

Apukhtin, Alexei (Lelya) Nikolaievich (1844-1893), Russian poet, whose poems inspired many of Tchaikovsky's songs.

Arends, Andrey Fyodorovich (1855-1926?), Russian composer and conductor.

Arensky, Anton Stepanovich (1861-1905), prolific Russian composer, best known for his piano works. Also the author of a well-known exercise book on harmony.

Argutinsky, Volodya, son of N. V. Argutinsky, mayor of Tiflis.

Arisha, Tchaikovsky's chambermaid.

Artôt, Désirée, *see* Padilla, Désirée Artôt de

Auber, Daniel François Esprit (1782-1871), prolific French composer of operas.

Auclair, M. and Mme., French family with whom little Georges was left. See note 41, Diary Four.

Aus der Ohe, Adele (1864-1937), German pianist, pupil of Liszt, resident in New York. Soloist on the occasion of Tchaikovsky's appearances in New York.

Ave-Lallemant, Theodor (1805-1890), German writer on music and director of the Hamburg Philharmonic Society. Tchaikovsky dedicated his Fifth Symphony, Op. 64, to him.

Balakirev, Mily Alexeyevich (1837-1910), Russian composer, one of the "Mighty Five" of the nationalist school of Russian music. Tchaikovsky dedicated three orchestral works to him.

Barbi, Alice (1862-?), Italian mezzo-soprano.

Baron, Louis Bouchenez (1838-1920), popular French actor.

Barrias, Louis Ernest (1841-1905), French sculptor.

Bartzal, Anton Ivanovich (1847-1927), operatic tenor.

Batasha, *see* Hubert, Alexandra Ivanovna (Batalina)

Bazilevskaya, Sasha (Alexandra Vadimovna), a distant relative of Tchaikovsky.

Bechstein, Friedrich Wilhelm Karl (1826-1900), German piano manufacturer.

Belard, M. and Mme., proprietors of Hotel Richepanse in Paris where Tchaikovsky stayed.

Belokha, Anna Porfirevna, Russian operatic contralto.

Benardaky, Maria Pavlovna (Maria Pavlovna Leibrock) (?-1913), opera singer and wife of N. Benardaky, music patron.

Bendl, Karel (1838-1897), Czech composer.

Bennewitz, Anton (1833-1926), Czech violinist and teacher.

Benoît, Camille (1851-1923), French composer and curator at the Louvre Museum from 1895.

Berger, Francesco (1834-1933), English pianist and composer, secretary of the Philharmonic Society of London.

Bernard, Jean Emile Auguste (1843-1902), French composer.

Bernuth, Julius von (1830-1902), German conductor and teacher.

Bertenson, Lev Bernardovich (1850-1929), Tchaikovsky's physician.

Bessel, Ivan Vasilyevich, brother of Vasily V. Bessel and co-owner of the Bessel music publishing firm in St. Petersburg.

Bessel, Vasily Vasilyevich (1843-1907), Russian music publisher, who wrote reminiscences of Tchaikovsky and was the composer's first publisher.

Bezekirsky, Vasily Vasilyevich (1835-1921?), Russian violinist and composer.

Bichurina, A. A., Russian opera singer.

Blaramberg, Pavel Ivanovich (1841-1907), prolific Russian composer.

Bloch, Georg (1847-1910), German composer and teacher.

Blondel, Albert (1854-1935), successor and director of Erard, Paris firm of piano makers.

Blüthner, Julius Ferdinand (1824-1910), well-known German piano manufacturer.

Blumenfeld, Felix Mikhailovich (1863-1931), Russian composer, pianist, teacher, and conductor.

Blumenfeld, Sigismund Mikhailovich (1852-?), Russian composer, brother of Felix.

Bob, Bobushka, Bobyk, see Davidov, Vladimir L.

Bock, Hugo (1848-?), owner of the music publishing firm of Bote and Bock in Berlin.

Bogdanov, Russian ballet master.

Bogoliubov, A. P., Russian painter.

Bogomoletz, Mme., a wealthy Russian music patroness resident in Paris.

Bohlmann, Georg Karl (1838-1920), Danish composer and organist.

Bonade, professor of clarinet and *solfège* at the Geneva Conservatory.

Boris, see Jürgenson, Boris Petrovich

Borisov, P. B., operatic baritone.

Bormann, Emil von (1864-?), Russian teacher and music critic, attached to German newspapers and journals.

Borodin, Alexander Porfirevich (1834-1887), Russian composer, one of the "Mighty Five." Best known for his opera *Prince Igor*.

Boronat, O., operatic soprano.

Botkin, Peter Sergeyevich, son of Dr. Sergey P. Botkin, attached to the Russian Embassy at Washington in 1891.

Botkin, Sergey Petrovich (1832-1889), famous Russian physician.

Bourgault-Ducoudray, Louis Albert (1840-1910), French composer and professor of music history at the Paris Conservatoire.

Brahms, Johannes (1833-1897). Tchaikovsky records his meeting with Brahms December 20, 1887, in Diary Seven.

Brandukov (Branduchek), Anatoly (Tolya) Andreyevich (1858-1930), Russian violoncellist and protégé of Tchaikovsky.

Brandus, Louis, French music publisher.

Briullov, Vladimir Alexandrovich (1846-1918), step-father of Nikolai H. Konradi.

Brodsky, Adolf (1851-1929), distinguished Russian violinist who first performed Tchaikovsky's Violin Concerto, dedicated to him.

Bülow, Hans von (1830-1894), distinguished German pianist and conductor, Liszt's son-in-law. He gave the first performance of Tchaikovsky's First Piano Concerto which was dedicated to him.

Buettner, A., music publisher at St. Petersburg.

Burenin, Victor Petrovich (1841-1926), Russian poet and critic.

Burmeister, Richard (1860-1933), German composer and pianist.

Burmester, Willy (1869-1933), German violinist, member of a famous family of musicians.

Busoni, Ferruccio (1866-1924), Italian composer and pianist, Tchaikovsky's friend. A profound thinker in music.

Butakova (Butichikha) Vera Vasilyevna (Davidova) (1840-1920), sister of Tchaikovsky's brother-in-law, Lev V. Davidov. Tchaikovsky dedicated two works to her.

Bykov, Fyodor Alexandrovich, prosecutor for the Tiflis Circuit Court.

Carnegie, Andrew (1837-1919), American steel magnate. The composer describes their meeting in Diary Eleven.

Catoire, Georgy Lvovich (1861-1926), Russian composer, aided and influenced by Tchaikovsky.

Cervinková-Riegerová, Marie (1854-1895), librettist and translator, daughter of F. L. Rieger.

Cesi, Beniamino (1845-1907), Italian pianist and teacher.

Chaminade, Cécile Louise Stéphanie (1857-1944), French composer and pianist best known for her songs and piano works in salon style.

Chansarel, René, French pianist and composer.

Chaumont, Marie Céline (1848-1926), French actress.

Choudens, Mme., wife of the Paris music publisher.

Chvála, Emanuel (1851-1924), Czech composer and critic.

Collin, Paul Adrien François (1843-?), French poet. His poetry inspired many of Tchaikovsky's songs.

Colonne, Edouard (1838-1910), eminent French conductor, leader of the Concerts du Châtelet.

Condemine, Henri, French pianist.

Conus, *see* Konius

Coquard, Arthur (1846-1910), French composer and music critic, originally a lawyer.

Coquelin, Benoît Constant (1841-1909), French actor.

Cornély, Jean J. (1845-1907), French journalist.

Cossmann, Bernhard (1822-1910), famous German violoncellist and teacher at the Moscow Conservatory for a time.

Courlaender, B., teacher at the Conservatory of the Peabody Institute, Baltimore.

Cui, Tzezar Antonovich (1835-1920), prolific Russian composer, critic, one of the "Mighty Five."

d'Albert, Eugène Francis Charles (1864-1932), one of the greatest pianists of his time and a successful, if ephemeral, composer. Born in Scotland. Husband of Teresa Carreño.

Damrosch, Leopold (1832-1885), German-American conductor and composer, father of Walter Damrosch. He conducted the first New York performance of Tchaikovsky's First Piano Concerto with the Symphony Society.

Damrosch, Walter (1862-   ), American conductor and composer, on whose invitation Tchaikovsky came to United States in 1891. See Diary Eleven.

Danilchenko, Peter Antonovich (1857-190?), violoncellist.

Dannreuther, Gustav (1853-1923), violinist and concertmaster of the Boston and New York symphony orchestras.

Dargomyzhsky, Alexander Sergeyevich (1813-1869), Russian composer. Tchaikovsky writes of him in Diary Eight.

Davidov, Dmitri (Mitya) Lvovich (1870-1930), Tchaikovsky's nephew, son of Lev V. Davidov and Tchaikovsky's sister Sasha.

Davidov, Karl Julyevich (1838-1889), violoncellist and composer, director of the St. Petersburg Conservatory. Tchaikovsky dedicated an orchestral work to him.

Davidov, Lev (Levushka) Vasilyevich (1837-1896), husband of Tchaikovsky's sister, Alexandra (Sasha).

Davidov, Nikolai (Koko) Vasilyevich (?-1917), brother of Tchaikovsky's sister's husband.

Davidov, Ury (Uka) Lvovich (1874-   ), Tchaikovsky's nephew, son of Lev V. Davidov and the composer's sister Sasha.

Davidov, Vladimir Alexandrovich (1816-1886), cousin of Lev V. Davidov, Tchaikovsky's brother-in-law.

Davidov, Vladimir (Bob, Bobyk) Lvovich (1871-1906), Tchaikovsky's favorite nephew, son of Lev V. Davidov and Tchaikovsky's sister Sasha. Tchaikovsky dedicated a set of piano pieces and the Sixth (*Pathétique*) Symphony, Op. 74, to him. See note 7, Diary Three.

Davidova, Alexandra Arkadyevna (1849-1902), wife of K. J. Davidov, publisher.

Davidova, Alexandra (Sasha) Ilyinishna (Tchaikovskaya) (1842-1891), Tchaikovsky's sister and wife of Lev V. Davidov.

Davidova, Alexandra Ivanovna, Alexandra Vasilyevna, Lizaveta Vasilyevna, Tchaikovsky's distant relatives.

Davidova, Natalya (Tasya) Lvovna (1868-?), Tchaikovsky's niece, daughter of Lev V. Davidov and Tchaikovsky's sister Sasha.

Davidova, Tatyana (Tanya) Lvovna (1862-1886), Tchaikovsky's niece, daughter of Lev V. Davidov and Sasha Davidova. See note 41, Diary Four. Tchaikovsky dedicated six vocal duets to her.

Davidova, Varya Nikolaievna, daughter of Nikolai Vasilyevich Davidov.

Davidova, Vera Lvovna (1863-1889), Tchaikovsky's niece and first wife of Nikolai Alexandrovitch Rimsky-Korsakov. Tchaikovsky dedicated a piano piece to her.

De Koven, Reginald (1859-1920), American composer, particularly of light operatic music.

Delibes, Clément Philibert Léo (1836-1891), prolific French composer of operas and ballets. Perhaps best known for his ballet *Coppélia* and opera *Lakmé*.

Delines, Michel (pseud. of Mikhail Osipovich Ashkinazi), Russian-French journalist and translator.

Delsart, Jules (1844-1900), French violoncellist.

Derichenko, Roman Efimovich, the doctor at Kamenka.

Diémer, Louis (1843-1919), French pianist and composer, who helped spread Tchaikovsky's music in Paris. The composer dedicated a piano work to him.

Dima, *see* Peresleni, Vadim Vadimovich

D'Indy, Vincent (1851-1931), as a composer the French counterpart of Brahms.

Dobrovolsky, N. F., director of the Synod school in Moscow.

Donskoy, L. D., Russian operatic tenor.

Drigo, Riccardo (1846-1930), Italian composer and conductor, who conducted the première of Tchaikovsky's *Sleeping Beauty*.

Ducoudray, Bourgault, Louis Albert, *see* Bourgault-Ducoudray

Dütsch, Georgy Ottonovich (1857-1891), Russian conductor.

Dupont, Auguste (1827-1890), Belgian pianist and composer.

Dupuis, José (1831-1900), French actor.

Durdík, Alois (1839-1916), Czech lawyer and translator.

Duvernoy, Victor Alphonse (1842-1907), French composer, pianist, critic, and professor at the Paris Conservatoire.

Egorka, Egorushka, a little boy living in Praslovo.

Ehrlich, Alfred Heinrich (1822-1899), Austrian pianist, composer, and writer.

Elizaveta Mavrikyevna, Grand Duchess (1865-1927), wife of Grand Duke Konstantin Konstantinovich.

Emanuel, N. B., Russian conductor.

Emma, see Genton, Emma

Epstein, Edward Osipovich (1827-1889), German-Russian pianist and teacher.

Erdmannsdörfer, Max von (1848-1905), German composer and, for a time, conductor of the Imperial Musical Society at Moscow. Professor at the Moscow Conservatory. Tchaikovsky dedicated his Third Suite, Op. 55, to him.

Erdmannsdörfer, Polina (Fichtner Oprawill) von (1847-1916), pianist and wife of Max von Erdmannsdörfer.

Erlanger, Gustav (1842-1908), German composer and music writer.

Esipova, Annette (1851-1914), Russian pianist and teacher. Pupil and wife of Theodor Leschetizky.

Ezer, K. F., violoncellist and professor at the Moscow Conservatory.

Fauré, Gabriel Urbain (1845-1924), celebrated French composer and organist, teacher of Ravel, Enesco, Schmitt, and many others.

Fernow, Sophie von, Russian pianist, who lived and taught in Berlin and Baltimore.

Fet, Afanasy Afanasyevich (1820-1892), Russian poet. Many of his poems inspired Tchaikovsky's songs.

Fielitz, Alexander von (1860-1930), German-Polish conductor, composer, and teacher who lived for a time in Chicago.

Figner, Nikolai Nikolaievich (1856-1918), Russian operatic tenor, who created the part of Hermann in Tchaikovsky's opera *The Queen of Spades*. The composer dedicated six songs to him.

Fincke, Fritz (1846-?), German violinist and composer. He also taught singing at the Conservatory of the Peabody Institute, Baltimore.

Fitingov-Shel, Boris Alexandrovich (1829-1901), Russian composer.

Fitzenhagen, Wilhelm Theodore (1848-1890), German violoncellist, professor at the Moscow Conservatory. Tchaikovsky dedicated his Variations on a Rococo Theme, Op. 33, to him.

Flegont, teacher of the children of Alexandra Davidova, sister of Tchaikovsky.

Flerov, Sergey Vasilyevich (1841-1901), Russian music and dramatic critic.

Forberg, Otto, Leipzig music publisher.

František, see Urbánek, František

Friedheim, Arthur (1869-1932), distinguished Russian-German pianist and teacher. Pupil, friend, and secretary of Liszt.

Friedrich, Dmitri, Tchaikovsky's Berlin concert agent.

Fritzsch, Ernest Wilhelm (1840-1902), forward-looking German music publisher, an able musician in his own right.

Frolov, V. K., Russian music critic.

Frolovsky, Alexander Filaretovich, brother of Nadezhda F. von Meck.

Fyodotova, Glikeriya Nikolaievna (1846-1925), opera singer.

Gakel, Mikhail Pavlovich, chairman, Caucasian censorship committee.

Galvani, professor of singing at the Moscow Conservatory.

Garcia, see Viardot-Garcia, Pauline

Gartung, Yakov (Yasha) Fyodorovich, Russian merchant.

Genichka, see Korganov, Gennady Osipovich

Genton, Emma, governess for the N. D. Kondratyev family. Tchaikovsky dedicated his Valse sentimentale, Op. 51, No. 6, for piano to her.

Georges, see Tchaikovsky, Georges-Leon

Gerber, July Gustavovich (1831-1883), supervisor of music in the Bolshoi Theater.

Gerke, August Antonovich, professor of piano at the St. Petersburg Conservatory. Tchaikovsky dedicated a piano piece to him.

Giraudet, Alfred Auguste (1845-?), eminent French operatic bass and teacher.

Girs, Alexander Alexandrovich (1850-?), Russian diplomat.

Glazunov, Alexander Konstantinovich (1865-1936), prolific Russian composer, teacher and conductor. Cambridge and Oxford universities honored him with the degree of doctor of music.

Glinka, Mikhail Ivanovich (1804-1857), Russian composer. Tchaikovsky discusses his art in Diary Eight.

Godard, Benjamin Louis Paul (1849-1895), French composer of rather light chamber music and operas.

Golitzin, Prince Alexei V., Tchaikovsky's friend.

Goncharov, Sergey Sergeyevich, chairman of the Tiflis Justice Department.

Gouvy, Louis Theodore (1819-1898), German-French composer and pianist.

Greger, Alexander, attached to the Russian Embassy at Washington in 1891.

Grétry, André Ernest Modeste (1742-1813), Belgian composer, chiefly of operas.

Grieg, Edvard (1843-1907). Tchaikovsky refers to his meeting with Grieg in Diary Seven. He dedicated his Overture Fantasy Hamlet, Op. 67, to the Norwegian composer.

Grigi, children's teacher at Kamenka.

Grigorovich, Charles (1867-1926), Russian violinist.

Grisha, see Jürgenson, Grigory Petrovich

Grünfeld, Alfred (1852-1924), Bohemian pianist and composer.

Grünfeld, Heinrich (1855-1931), Bohemian violoncellist.

Grützmacher, Friedrich Wilhelm (1832-1903), renowned German violoncellist and composer.

Guiraud, Ernest (1837-1892), New Orleans born French composer and teacher of much influence.

Guitry, Lucien, French actor. He gave the first performance of Shakespeare's *Hamlet* with incidental music by Tchaikovsky.

Gurlitt, Cornelius (1820-1901), German operatic composer and music director.

Haliř, Karl (1859-1909), excellent Bohemian violinist and leader of a distinguished quartet.

Hamerik, Asger (1843-1923), Danish composer and director of the Conservatory of the Peabody Institute, Baltimore.

Hansen, T., attached to the Russian Embassy at Washington in 1891.

Hanslick, Eduard (1825-1904), Austrian music critic, who supported Brahms and was anti-Wagner.

Hartmann, Ludwig (1836-1910), German music critic and pianist.

Hartvigson, Frits (1841-1919), Danish pianist, pupil of von Bülow.

Hendtlass, T., Berlin hotel proprietor.

Hilf, Arno (1858-1909), German violinist and teacher.

Hofmann, Josef (1876-   ). Tchaikovsky refers to Hofmann in Diary Nine, 13 February, 1889.

Holls, George Frederick William (1857-1903), American lawyer, author and music patron.

Holmès, Augusta Mary Anne (1847-1903), Irish-French popular composer of songs and piano pieces.

Howson, Frank A. (1841-1926), American composer and conductor.

Hubert, Alexandra Ivanovna (Batalina) (Batasha) (1850-1937), wife of N. A. Hubert and professor at the Moscow Conservatory, later appointed supervisor there. She arranged many of Tchaikovsky's works for piano.

Hubert, Nikolai (Tonichka) Albertovich (1840-1888), Russian professor of music theory at the Moscow Conservatory and later director there. Tchaikovsky dedicated a song to him.

Huss, Henry Holden (1862-   ), American pianist, composer, and teacher. A descendant of the Bohemian patriot John Huss.

Hyde, Edwin Francis (1842-1933), in 1891, vice president of the Central Trust Company, New York, and president of the New York Philharmonic Society.

Ilinsky, Alexander Alexandrovich (1859-1919), Russian composer and teacher.

Ippolitov-Ivanov, Mikhail Mikhailovich (1859-1935), Russian composer, at the time of Tchaikovsky's visit to Tiflis director of the Tiflis Conservatory of Music. He changed his name (Ivanov) so as not to be confused with the contemporary music critic, Ivanov. Best known for his Caucasian Sketches, Op. 10, for orchestra.

Iretzkaya, N. A., singer and professor at the St. Petersburg Conservatory.

Ivan, see Vanya

Ivanov, chorus master of the Moscow Choral Society.

Ivanov, Mikhail Mikhailovich (1849-1927), Russian composer and music critic, Tchaikovsky's pupil at the Moscow Conservatory.

Jarno, Georg (1868-1920), Hungarian composer and conductor.

Jedliczka, Ernst (1855-1904), Russian pianist and teacher, pupil of Tchaikovsky. He also taught in Berlin at the Klindworth-Scharwenka Conservatory.

Jenner, Gustav (1865-1920), German composer and conductor.

Joly, Charles, owner of a pension at San Remo where Tchaikovsky stayed in 1877-1878.

Joncières, Victorin de (1839-1903), French composer and critic, one of Wagner's earliest ardent apostles.

Judic, Anna (1850-1911), French actress.

Jürgenson, Alexandra (Sasha) Petrovna (1869-?), painter daughter of Peter I. Jürgenson. Tchaikovsky dedicated a piano piece to her.

Jürgenson, Boris Petrovich (1868-1935), Moscow music publisher and son of Peter I. Jürgenson. Successor to his father's business.

Jürgenson, Grigory (Grisha) Petrovich (1872-1936), Moscow music publisher and son of Peter I. Jürgenson. Successor to his father's business.

Jürgenson, Osip Ivanovich (1829-1910), St. Petersburg music dealer, brother of Peter I. Jürgenson.

Jürgenson, Peter Ivanovich (P., P. I., P. I. J.) (1836-1904), most important music publisher in Russia with a catalogue embracing over 20,000 numbers including noteworthy editions of the classics and works of the numerous Russian composers. Nearly all of Tchaikovsky's works were issued by him. Tchaikovsky dedicated a song to him.

Jürgenson, Sophia Ivanovna (S. I., S. I. J.) (1840-1911), wife of Peter I. Jürgenson. Tchaikovsky dedicated a piano piece to her.

Kamensky, Theodore (1836-1913), Russian-American sculptor.

Karlusha, see Albrecht, Konstantin (Karl) Karlovich

Karnovich, V. L., chairman of the Tiflis Circuit Court.

Kartzev, George Pavlovich (1861-1931), Tchaikovsky's cousin and husband of Alexandra V. Panaeva.

Kartzeva, Sasha (Alexandra V. Panaeva) (Tatusya, Tatyana) (1853-?), wife of George P. Kartzev. Amateur singer. Tchaikovsky dedicated seven songs to her.

Kashkin, Nikolai Dmitrievich (N. D. K.) (1839-1920), Russian music critic and teacher at the Moscow Conservatory. Tchaikovsky dedicated a song to him.

Kashperov, Vladimir Nikitich (1827-1894), Russian composer and professor of singing at the Moscow Conservatory.

Katerina Ivanovna, see Sinelnikova

Katerina Vasilyevna, see Peresleni

Katkov, Mikhail Nikiforovich (1818-1887), Russian publicist and literary editor.

Keidel, Charles, member of the Knabe Piano Company, New York.

Khomyakov, Alexei Stepanovich (1804-1860), Russian poet. Two of his poems were set to music by Tchaikovsky.

Kira, baby daughter of Nikolai and Anna von Meck.

Klamrot, Mme., wife of Karl A. Klamrot (1829-1912), concert-master of the Bolshoi Opera.

Kleeberg, Clotilde (1866-1909), gifted French pianist.

Klein, Bruno Oscar (1858-1911), German composer, organist, and pianist in New York most of his life.

Klengel, Julius (1859-1933), German violoncellist, the leading teacher of his instrument in central Europe.

Klimenko, Ivan Alexandrovich, Russian architect. Tchaikovsky dedicated a song to him.

Klimenko, Misha (Mikhail), an employee of Peter I. Jürgenson.

Klimentova, Maria Nikolaievna (1856-?), Russian operatic soprano. She created the part of Tatyana in *Eugene Onegin.*

Klindworth, Karl (1830-1916), renowned German pianist, teacher, and conductor (for a time at the Moscow Conservatory), is remembered as the arranger of excellent piano scores. He arranged Tchaikovsky's *Francesca da Rimini*. Tchaikovsky dedicated two piano works to him.

Knabe, Ernest (1837-1894), American piano manufacturer.

Knina, Leonid Fyodorovich, Russian pianist and composer.

Knorr, Ivan (1853-1916), German composer and writer, author of a Tchaikovsky biography.

Kochetov, Nikolai Razumnikovich (1864-?), Russian composer.

Köhler, Christian Louis Heinrich (1820-1886), German composer and teacher, principally known for his educational piano music.

Kogel, Gustav Friedrich (1849-1921), German conductor.

Koko, *see* Davidov, Nikolai Vasilyevich

Kokodes, *see* Peresleni, Nikolai Vadimovich

Kolář, Josef (1830-1911), Czech philologist and translator.

Kolya, *see* Konradi, Nikolai Hermanovich

Kolya, *see* Meck, Nikolai Karlovich von

Kolya, *see* Peresleni, Nikolai Vadimovich

Kolya, *see* Tchaikovsky, Nikolai I.

Kommisarzhevsky, Fyodor Petrovich (1838-1905), Russian tenor and professor at the Moscow Conservatory. Tchaikovsky dedicated a song to him. He created the part of Vakula in Tchaikovsky's opera *Vakula, the Smith.*

Kondratyev, Gennady Petrovich (1835-1905), head producer of the Marinsky Theater.

Kondratyev, Nikolai Dmitrievich (N. D., N. D. K.) (183?-1887), landowner friend of Peter I. Tchaikovsky. Tchaikovsky dedicated a piano piece to him.

Kondratyeva, N. D., mother of N. D. Kondratyev. Tchaikovsky dedicated a piano piece to her.

Konius (Conus), Georgy Edwardovich (1862-1933), Russian composer and theorist; pupil of S. I. Taneiev.

Konius (Conus), Jules Edwardovich (1869-?), Russian violinist and composer, best known for his Violin Concerto. Brother of Georgy E. Konius.

Konius (Conus), Lev Edwardovich (1871-1944), Russian pianist and composer. Brother of Georgy E. Konius.

Konradi, Nikolai (Kolya) Hermanovich (1868-1923), pupil of Modest I. Tchaikovsky.

Konshin, Nikolai Vladimirovich, son of Vladimir D. Konshin.

Konshin, Vladimir Dmitrievich (?-1915), Moscow merchant, father of Anatoly I. Tchaikovsky's wife.

Korbay, Francis Alexander (1846-1916), Hungarian tenor, composer, and pianist. Liszt was his godfather.

Koreshchenko, Arseny Nikolaievich (1870-1921), Russian composer and pianist, pupil of S. I. Taneiev.

Korganov, Gennady (Genichka) Osipovich (1858-1890), Armenian-Russian composer and pianist.

Korsakov, see Rimsky-Korsakov, Nikolai Andreyevich

Korsh, Fyodor Adamovich (1852-?), theater owner and dramatist.

Korsov, Bohomir Bohomirovich (1845-1920), Russian operatic baritone. Tchaikovsky dedicated two songs to him. He created the part of Mazepa in Tchaikovsky's opera *Mazepa*.

Kostomarov, N. I., Russian historian and publicist.

Kotek, Joseph Josephovich (1855-1885), Russian violinist and pupil of Tchaikovsky who dedicated a violin piece to him.

Kotzebue, counselor of the Russian Embassy in Paris.

Kovařovic, Karl (1862-1920), Czech composer and conductor.

Krause, Martin (1853-1918), German pianist and teacher.

Kross, Gustave G., Russian pianist. He gave the first performance of Tchaikovsky's First Piano Concerto, Op. 23, in Russia.

Krotkov, Nikolai Sergeyevich, composer and conductor.

Krutikova, Alexandra Pavlovna (1851-1919), operatic mezzo-soprano. She created the role of Olga in Tchaikovsky's opera *Eugene Onegin*. Tchaikovsky dedicated two songs to her.

Kündinger, Rudolf Vasilyevich (1832-1913), German-Russian composer and teacher. Taught Tchaikovsky as a boy.

Kwast, Antonie (Hiller), wife of James Kwast (1852-1927), Dutch pianist and composer, daughter of Ferdinand Hiller.

Ladukhin, Nikolai Mikhailovich (1860-?), Russian composer, pupil of S. I. Taneiev.

Lamond, Frederic (1868-?), Scottish pianist.

Lamoureux, Charles (1834-1899), distinguished French conductor of the Concerts Lamoureux.

Langer, Edward Leontevich (1835-1905), Russian professor at the Moscow Conservatory, pianist, organist, and composer. He arranged many of Tchaikovsky's works for piano.

Laroche, Herman (Manya) Augustovich (1845-1904), Russian music critic and composer. Intimate friend of Tchaikovsky, who dedicated three works to him.

Lassalle, Jean Louis (1847-1909), famous French operatic baritone.

Laube, Julius, German conductor, active in Hamburg and Pavlovsk.

Lavrov, N. S., pianist, professor at the St. Petersburg Conservatory.

Lavrovskaya, Elizaveta (Lizaveta) Andreyevna (1849-1919), operatic contralto. Tchaikovsky dedicated two works to her.

Le Borne, Fernand (1862-1929), Belgian composer and music critic.

Lefebvre, Charles Edouard (1843-1917), French composer, professor at the Paris Conservatoire.

Legoshin, Sasha, Nikolai D. Kondratyev's valet.

Lelya, see Apukhtin, Alexei

Lemoine, French musician and founder of the musical society La Trompette.

Lentovsky, Mikhail Valentinovich, Russian music promoter.

Lermontov, Mikhail Jurevich (1814-1841), prominent Russian poet whose poems inspired three of Tchaikovsky's works.

Leroux, Xavier Henri Napoléon (1863-1919), French composer and teacher.

Levenson, Anna Yakovlevna (1863-1930), Russian music teacher.

Levitzky, Sergey Lvovich (1819-1898), a photographer at St. Petersburg.

Levushka, see Davidov, Lev Vasilyevich

Liadov, Anatoly Konstantinovich (1855-1914), Russian composer and teacher at the St. Petersburg Conservatory. Pupil of Rimsky-Korsakov.

Liebling, Georg Lothar (1865-   ), American pianist and composer. Pupil of Liszt.

Litke, Count Nikolai (Niks) Fyodorovich (?-1887), Russian government official.

Litke, Countess Amalya Vasilyevna (Shobert) (?-1912), Tchaikovsky's cousin.

Litrov, Nazar, valet of Modest I. Tchaikovsky.

Litvinov, Alexander Alexandrovich (1861-1931), Russian violinist.

Liza, maid in the home of Nikolai I. Tchaikovsky.

Lody, Peter Andreyevich (1852-1920), operatic tenor.

Mackar, Félix, French music publisher, genuinely interested in Tchaikovsky's works. For a considerable sum, he acquired the right to publish Tchaikovsky's compositions from P. I. Jürgenson.

Magnard, Francis (1839-1894), French newspaper man, editor of Le Figaro.

Magnitzkaya, E. P., Russian pianist.

Maidl, Baron Artur, member of the Tiflis Court.

Maikov, A. A., director of the Moscow Theaters.

Makovsky, Vladimir Egorovich (1846-1929), Russian painter.

Malya, see Litke, Countess Amalya Vasilyevna (Shobert)

Mamontov, Nikolai Nikolaievich (1836-1890), Moscow merchant.

Mamontov, Savva Ivanovich, Russian industrialist and art connoisseur.

Manya, see Laroche, Herman Augustovich

Marchesi, Salvatore (1822-1908), Italian baritone and teacher, husband of Mathilde Graumann Marchesi.

Maréchal, Charles Henri (1842-1924), French composer.

Maria Pavlovna, see Benardaky

Marmontel, Antoine François (1816-1898), French piano professor at the Conservatoire, one of the most influential musicians of his time. Tchaikovsky dedicated a piano piece to him.

Marsick, Martin Pierre Joseph (1848-1924), Belgian violinist, composer, and professor at the Paris Conservatoire.

Mary (Maria Sergeyevna Kondratyeva) (1840-?), wife of Nikolai D. Kondratyev.

Maslov, Fyodor Ivanovich (1840-1915), jurist friend of Tchaikovsky.

Mayer, Ferdinand, representative of the Knabe Piano Company, New York.

Mayer, Wilhelm (pseudonym W. A. Rémy) (1831-1898), Bohemian pianist and teacher of many famous musicians, among them Busoni.

Meck, Anna Lvovna (Davidova) von (1864-?), Tchaikovsky's niece married to N. F. von Meck's son, Nikolai.

Meck, Nadezhda Filaretovna (Frolovskaya) von (1831-1894), Tchaikovsky's moral and financial benefactress, a widow with eleven children and nine years his senior. They never spoke to each other but saw one another on several occasions from a distance. Her desire was that they communicate only by letter, which was welcome to Tchaikovsky. Their correspondence lasted from 1876 to 1890, comprising 771 letters. Her financial support and letters were suddenly discontinued, leaving posterity to guess the motives. Tchaikovsky dedicated his Fourth Symphony, Op. 36, to her.

Meck, Nikolai Karlovich von (1863-1929), husband of Tchaikovsky's niece, Anna L. Davidova, son of Nadezhda F. von Meck.

Meck, Vladimir Karlovich von (1852-1892), son of Mme. von Meck.

Merkling, Anna (Annette) Petrovna, Tchaikovsky's cousin. The composer dedicated a piano piece to her.

Meshchersky, Prince Vladimir Petrovich (1839-1914), Russian journalist.

Meyer-Helmund, Erik (1861-1932), Russian-German composer and singer.

Mielke, Antonia (1852-1907), German soprano.

Mikhail, *see* Sofronov, Mikhail Ivanovich

Mikhail Ivanovich, *see* Sofronov

Mikhail Mikhailovich, *see* Ippolitov-Ivanov

Minsky, Nikolai Maximovich (1855-1937), Russian poet.

Mitya, *see* Davidov, Dmitri Lvovich

Molas, Lizaveta Mikhailovna, companion of Tatyana L. Davidova.

Montigny-Rémaury, Fanny Marcelline Caroline (1843-1913), French pianist.

Mozart, Wolfgang Amadeus (1756-1791). Tchaikovsky writes of him in Diary Eight.

Müller, Carl (1818-1894), German conductor and composer.

Muravlin, D. P., Russian writer.

Muromtzeva, *see* Klimentova, Maria Nikolaievna

Mussorgsky, Modest Petrovich (1839-1881), Russian composer, one of the "Mighty Five."

Napravnik, Edward Franzevich (1839-1916), Czech composer and conductor who introduced many of Tchaikovsky's works at St. Petersburg. Tchaikovsky dedicated his opera *The Maid of Orleans* to him.

Nata, *see* Plesskaya, Natalya A.

Nazar, *see* Litrov

Neftel, Dr. William Basil (1830-1906), Russian-American doctor of medicine.

Neitzel, Otto (1852-1920), German pianist, teacher, composer, and writer. He taught at the Moscow Conservatory and also visited the United States.

Nevedomskaya-Diunor, N. A., singer.

Nicodé, Jean Louis (1853-1919), German pianist and composer.

Nikolai, *see* Konshin, Nikolai Vladimirovich

Nikolai Ilyich, *see* Tchaikovsky, Nikolai I.

Niks, *see* Litke, Count Nikolai Fyodorovich

Noël, A., Paris music publisher, partner of Félix Mackar.

Nováček, Otakar (1866-1900), Czech violinist and conductor, pupil of Brodsky and second violinist in the latter's quartet.

Novikova (Novichikha), Nadezhda Vasilyevna, landowner at Maidanovo.

Ochs, Siegfried (1858-1929), German composer and conductor.

Olga, *see* Tchaikovskaya, Olga Sergeyevna

Olga Edwardovna, wife of Edward Franzevich Napravnik.

Olkhovskaya, Lidya Vladimirovna, Tchaikovsky's cousin.

Olya, see Tchaikovskaya, Olga Sergeyevna

Ondříček, František (1859-1922), eminent Czech violinist, composer, and teacher.

Opochinin, Peter Alexandrovich, Russian lawyer in Tiflis.

Orlov, Vasily Sergeyevich, Russian chorus master of the Moscow Synod.

Orlovsky, member of the Tiflis Justice Department.

Osipovna, Pelagea, music teacher at Kamenka.

Pabst, Pavel Augustovich (1834-1897), German pianist, composer, and professor at the Moscow Conservatory. Tchaikovsky dedicated a song to him.

Paderewski, Ignace Jan (1860-1941). Tchaikovsky met Paderewski in 1888, Diary Seven.

Padilla, Désirée Artôt de (1835-1907), gifted French operatic soprano. Tchaikovsky saw her in Rossini's opera *Otello* as Desdemona and was fascinated. He was then twenty-eight; she thirty-three. Mlle. Artôt was the first and the only woman that he loved and desired to marry. It appeared that the marriage would take place but about a year after they first became acquainted, she married the Spanish baritone Mariano Ramos y Padilla to Tchaikovsky's complete amazement. However, they remained friends to the end of their lives. He dedicated seven songs to her.

Padilla, Mariano Ramos y (1842-1906), Spanish operatic baritone, husband of Désirée Artôt.

Pakhulsky, Vladislav Albertovich, violinist and husband of Mme. von Meck's daughter, Julia. He was in the employ of Mme. von Meck as a musician, later assuming an important role in her household and possibly played a part in the estrangement between Tchaikovsky and Mme. von Meck.

Paladilhe, Emile (1844-1926), French operatic and song composer popular in the nineteenth century.

Palen, Count Konstantin Ivanovich, Russian minister of justice, an acquaintance of Tchaikovsky.

Panaeva, Alexandra Valeryanovna, see Kartzeva, Sasha

Panya, see Tchaikovskaya, Praskovya Vladimirovna (Konshina)

Papendieck-Eichenwald, Ida Ivanovna (1845-1918), harpist.

Patera, Adolf (1836-1912), Czech librarian and philologist.

Pavlovskaya, Emilia Karlovna (1857-1935), Russian operatic soprano. Tchaikovsky dedicated a song to her. She created the role of Maria in his opera *Mazepa*.

Payne, Albert (1842-1921), German music publisher, principally of miniature scores.

Pchelnikov, P. M., office director of the Moscow Imperial Theaters.

Peresleni, Katerina Vasilyevna, sister of Tchaikovsky's brother-in-law, Lev Vasilyevich Davidov and mother of Vadim (Dima) Vadimovich Peresleni.

Peresleni, Nikolai (Kolya, Kokodes) Vadimovich, son of Katerina Vasilyevna Peresleni. Distant relative of Tchaikovsky.

Peresleni, Vadim (Dima) Vadimovich, son of Katerina Vasilyevna Pereslini. Tchaikovsky's distant relative.

Peters, C. F., German music publishing firm in Leipzig.

Petersen, Pavel Leontevich (1831-1895), pianist and secretary of the Russian Musical Society.

Petipa, Marius Ivanovich (1822-1910), renowned ballet master of the Marinsky Theater.

Petri, Henri Wilhelm (1856-1914), Dutch violinist, teacher, composer. Pupil of Joachim. Leader of a famous string quartet.

Philipp, Isidor (1863-   ), eminent French pianist and teacher. Pupil of Saint-Saëns. Teacher of many outstanding pupils and the composer of numerous notable piano studies.

P. I., P. I. J., see Jürgenson, Peter Ivanovich

Pick, probably an attendant for N. D. Kondratyev.

Pierné, Henri Constant Gabriel (1863-1937), pupil and successor (as organist at Ste. Clothilde) of Franck. Although a prolific composer, he is better known as a conductor.

Pingaud, Léonce (1841-1923), French historian.

Pisemsky, Alexei Feofilaktovich (1820-1881), Russian writer.

Pišna, Johann (1826-1896), Czech pianist and composer.

Platonova, J. F., opera singer.

Plesskaya, Julia Ivanovna, wife of Vladimir A. Plessky.

Plesskaya, Natalya (Nata) Andreyevna, landowner neighbor of the Davidov family at Kamenka. Tchaikovsky dedicated a piano piece to her.

Plessky, Vladimir Andreyevich, neighbor landowner of the Davidov family at Kamenka.

Pleyel, famous French firm of piano makers.

Pobedonostzev, Konstantin Petrovich (1827-1906), Synod prosecutor at St. Petersburg.

Pogozhev, V. P., office director of the St. Petersburg Imperial Theaters.

Polina, see Erdmannsdörfer, Polina von

Popelka, Adolf, owner of the house in Bertramka near Prague where Mozart lived.

Popov, Ivan Petrovich, head of the Moscow Russian Choral Society.

Popova, Nastasya Vasilyevna, Tchaikovsky's cousin.

Prokesch, F., professor of piano at the Geneva Conservatory.

Prokunin, Vasily Pavlovich, compiler of Russian folk songs.

Pryanishnikov, Ippolit Petrovich (1847-1921), operatic baritone. He created the part of Lionel in *The Maid of Orleans*.

Pustarnakov, P. P., Russian violinist.

Rachinsky, S. A., Russian writer. Tchaikovsky dedicated his First String Quartet, Op. 11, to him.

Rachmaninoff, Sergei Vasilyevich (1873-1943), prolific Russian composer and pianist, who idolized Tchaikovsky.

Radecke, Albert Martin Robert (1830-1911), German composer and teacher.

Raff, Joseph Joachim (1822-1882), prolific German composer and teacher who went on a concert tour with Liszt.

Rahter, Daniel (1828-1891), Hamburg music publisher.

Raimond, Perrée (1850-1906), French actor.

Razumovsky, Dmitri Vasilyevich (1818-1889), professor of church music at the Moscow Conservatory.

Reinecke, Carl Heinrich Carsten (1824-1910), German pianist, composer, conductor, and writer, the influential and conservative leader of musical life in Leipzig for a quarter of a century.

Reinhard, William, representative of the Knabe Piano Company, New York.

Remezov, Sergey Mikhailovich, Russian professor at the Moscow Conservatory. Tchaikovsky dedicated a piano piece to him.

Rémy, W. A., *see* Mayer, Wilhelm

Reno, Morris, president of Music Hall (Carnegie Hall), New York.

Reszke, Edouard de (1855-1917), Polish operatic bass. Brother of Jean de Reszke and one of the most celebrated basses of all time.

Reszke, Jean de (1850-1925), Polish operatic tenor. Member of a famous family of singers. He was originally a baritone but at thirty-four made his first appearance as a tenor—with great success.

Réty-Darcours, Charles (pen name Charles Darcours) (1826-1895), French music critic.

Rey, Louis Théophile (1852-?), French violinist and teacher.

Reyer (right name Rey), Louis Etienne Ernest (1823-1909), French composer.

Rieger, František Ladislav (1818-1903), Czech statesman.

Riemann, Hugo (1849-1919), outstanding German musical theorist and writer.

Ries, Franz (1846-1932), German violinist and composer.

Rietzel, J., American violinist.

Rimsky-Korsakov, Alexei Alexandrovich (1860-1920), marshal of the nobility.

Rimsky-Korsakov, Nikolai Alexandrovich (1852-?), adjutant to Grand Duke Konstantin Nikolaievich.

Rimsky-Korsakov, Nikolai Andreyevich (1844-1908), famous Russian composer, one of the "Mighty Five." Tchaikovsky dedicated a song to him.

Rimskaya-Korsakova, Nadezhda Nikolaievna (1848-1919), pianist, wife of Nikolai Andreyevich Rimsky-Korsakov. Tchaikovsky dedicated a song to her.

Rimskaya-Korsakova, Natalya Lvovna (Davidova) (1868-?), Tchaikovsky's niece and second wife of Nikolai Alexandrovich Rimsky-Korsakov.

Rimskaya-Korsakova, Vera Lvovna (Davidova) (1863-1889), Tchaikovsky's niece and first wife of Nikolai Alexandrovich Rimsky-Korsakov. Tchaikovsky dedicated a piano piece to her.

Rogge, Vladimir Petrovich, director of the commander-in-chief's chancellery.

Romeike, Henry (1855-1903), Russian-American owner of a press-clipping firm, New York.

Rosny, J. H., pseudonym for Joseph H. H. B. Rosny (1856-1940) and Séraphin J. F. B. Rosny (1859-?), French novelists.

Ross, Ivy, New York newspaper woman.

Rubetz, Alexander Ivanovich, professor at the St. Petersburg Conservatory.

Rubinstein, Anton Grigoryevich (1829-1894), Russian pianist, composer, and teacher. Founder and director of the St. Petersburg Conservatory. His fame rests chiefly as one of the greatest pianists of all time. Tchaikovsky dedicated three works to him.

Rubinstein, Nikolai Grigoryevich (1835-1881), eminent Russian pianist and conductor, brother of the more famous Anton. Founder of the Moscow Conservatory of Music. He was of great help to Tchaikovsky in his early struggles. Tchaikovsky dedicated six works to him.

Rukavishnikov, Konstantin Vasilyevich, member of the directorate of the Moscow Russian Musical Society.

Rummel, Franz (1853-1901), English pianist.

Russell, Ella (1864-1935), American operatic soprano.

Ryabinin, G. I., amateur singer.

Sabaneiev, house manager on the Davidov estate at Kamenka.

Sachs, Willy von, American music critic.

Safonov, Vasily Ilyich (1852-1918), Russian conductor and director of the Moscow Conservatory. Also conductor of New York Philharmonic Orchestra. Tchaikovsky dedicated a piano piece to him.

Sangursky, Votya (1865-?), Tchaikovsky's protégé. Kamenka boy whose father (Vonifaty) worked in a sugar refinery. Tchaikovsky took much interest in his musical education but he became a drawing teacher.

Santley, Sir Charles (1834-1922), English baritone.

Sanya, *see* Vizin, Alexandra Petrovna von

Sapelnikov, Vasily Lvovich (1868-?), Russian pianist and protégé of Tchaikovsky. Tchaikovsky dedicated a piano piece to him.

Saradzhev, I. F., violoncellist and teacher.

Sarcey, Francisque (1828-1899), French novelist and critic.

Sasha, *see* Davidova, Alexandra I.

Sasha, *see* Jürgenson, Alexandra Petrovna

Sasha, *see* Legoshin, Sasha

Sasha, *see* Siloti, Alexander I.

Sauer, Emil (1862-1942), German pianist and composer; one of the best pianists of the Liszt-Rubinstein school of "grand" virtuosi.

Sauret, Emile (1852-1920), French violinist and composer.

Savanelli, Kharlampy Ivanovich, amateur singer friend of Tchaikovsky.

Scharwenka, Franz Xaver (1850-1924), German pianist, composer, and head of a well-known conservatory in Berlin which, in the nineties, had a branch in New York.

Schirmer, Gustav (1829-1893), one of the leading music publishers in the world. Founder of G. Schirmer, Inc., New York.

Schirmer, Rudolph E. (1859-1919), American music publisher and son of Gustav Schirmer.

Schneider, Otto, member of the directorate of the Berlin Philharmonic Orchestra.

Scholz, Bernhard (1835-1916), German composer and conductor.

Schroeder, Alwin (1855-?), German violoncellist.

Schuch, Ernst (1846-1914), German conductor for four decades the unquestioned ruler of opera in Dresden, a worthy successor to Weber and Wagner.

Schultzen von Asten, Anna (1848-1903), Austro-German soprano and teacher.

Schurz, Carl (1829-1906), German-American statesman.

Seidl, Anton (1850-1898), Hungarian conductor, Wagner's assistant in Bayreuth, next to Hermann Levi and Hans Richter the most authoritative interpreter of Wagnerian music. Conductor at the Metropolitan Opera House from 1885 to 1891 and again from 1895 to his death.

Senfft von Pilsach, Baroness, wife of Gottfried Arnold Senfft von Pilsach (1834-1889), German concert singer.

Senger, Hugo (1835-1892), German-Swiss conductor and teacher.

Senkrah, Arma (Anna) Loretta Hoffman (Harkness) (1864-1900), American violinist, who toured with Liszt.

Serov, Alexander Nikolaievich (1820-1871), Russian opera composer and critic who was strongly influenced by Wagner.

Shcherbachev, Nikolai Vladimirovich (1853-?), Russian pianist and composer.

Shchurovsky, Peter Andreyevich (1850-?), Russian conductor.

Sheremetev, Sergey Alexeyevich (1836-1896), commander of the Caucasus military district.

Shestakova, Liudmila Ivanovna (1816-1906), sister of Mikhail I. Glinka.

Shilovsky, Konstantin Stepanovich (1849-1893), dilettante poet and composer.

Shilovsky, Vladimir Stepanovich (Count Vasilyev Shilovsky), composer of popular valse, The Little Tiger, pupil and friend of Tchaikovsky. See footnote 60, Diary Nine. Tchaikovsky dedicated two piano pieces to him.

Shishkov, A. N., prosecutor for the Moscow Synod Bureau.

Shostakovsky, Peter Adamovich (1853-1916), pianist and conductor.

Shpazhinskaya, J. I., wife of Ippolit V. Shpazhinsky.

Shpazhinsky, Ippolit Vasilyevich (1844-1917), Russian dramatist, author of The Enchantress and librettist for Tchaikovsky's opera based on this play.

S. I., S. I. J., see Jürgenson, Sophia Ivanovna

S. I., S. I. T., see Taneiev, Sergey Ivanovich

Sieger, Dr. Friedrich, German music patron in Frankfurt am Main.

Silberberg, Cecile, Russian pianist.

Siloti, Alexander (Sasha) Ilyich (1863-), Russian pianist, composer, and conductor. Tchaikovsky's pupil and close friend.

Siloti, Vera Pavlovna (Tretyakova) (1867-1940), daughter of Pavel M. Tretyakov and wife of Alexander I. Siloti.

Simon, Anton Julyevich (1851-?), French-Russian composer and teacher.

Sinding, Christian (1856-?), famous Norwegian composer and teacher, principally known for his piano pieces.

Sinelnikova, Katerina Ivanovna, wife of Herman A. Laroche.

Singer, Teresina (1850-1928), operatic contralto.

Sitovsky, N. P., business manager of the Moscow Conservatory.

Sittard, Josef (1846-1903), German music critic.

Slavina, Maria Alexandrovna (1858-?), operatic mezzo-soprano.

She created the parts of the princess in *The Enchantress* and the countess in *The Queen of Spades*.

Slavkovský, Karěl (1846-1919), Czech pianist.

Slavyansky (Agrenev), D. A., Russian singer and choral conductor.

Smetana, Bedřich (1824-1884), celebrated Czech composer.

Smitten, N. P., member of the Tiflis Justice Department.

Smyth, Dame Ethel Mary (1858-1944), English composer, the first distinguished woman composer of modern times.

Sobolevsky, Vasily Mikhailovich (1846-1913), publicist, Tchaikovsky's neighbor at Maidanovo.

Sofronov, Alexei (Alesha) Ivanovich (1859-1925), Tchaikovsky's valet, Mikhail's brother.

Sofronov, Mikhail Ivanovich (1848-1932), first valet of Tchaikovsky, Alexei's brother.

Sofronova, Fekla (Feklusha) Grigoryevna (?-1889), wife of Alexei, Tchaikovsky's valet.

Sofronova, Pelagea Ivanovna, mother of Alexei I. Sofronov.

Šolc, Jindřich (1841-1916), Czech journalist and mayor of Prague.

Sollogub, Count Vladimir Alexandrovich (1814-1882), Russian novelist. Tchaikovsky wrote a song to his text.

Sontag, Karl (1828-1900), German actor.

Sonya, *see* Tchaikovskaya, Sophia Petrovna (Nikonova)

Sophia Ivanovna, *see* Jürgenson, Sophia Ivanovna

Stanford, Sir Charles Villiers (1852-1924), Irish composer and conductor, one of the leaders of the revival of music in Victorian England, was much esteemed by the Leipzig school.

Stark, Waldemar R., Russian-American architect, first assistant to William Burnet Tuthill, architect of Carnegie Hall.

Stasny, Karl Richard (1855-1920), German pianist and teacher.

Stasov, Dmitri Vasilyevich (1828-1918), Russian lawyer, brother of Vladimir V. Stasov.

Stasov, Vladimir Vasilyevich (1824-1906), famous Russian music critic and librarian. Tchaikovsky dedicated an orchestral work to him.

Stepan, valet of Anatoly I. Tchaikovsky.

Stiehl, Karl Johann Christian (1826-1911), German conductor and critic.

Stojowski, Sigismond (1870-), Polish-American pianist, composer, and teacher of many successful pianists.

Strakatý, Dr. Jan (1835-1891), Czech lawyer active in musical affairs.

Stroganov, Count Grigory Sergeyevich (1823-1910), large landowner.

Struve, Charles de, Russian ambassador at Washington in 1891.

Šubert, František Adolf (1849-1915), Czech playwright and theater director.

Sumbul, Leonid Nikolaievich (?-1900), member of the Duma.

Sutro, Otto (1833-1896), American music merchant prominent in the musical life of Baltimore.

Sutro, Theodore (1845-1927), American lawyer and brother of Otto Sutro.

Suvorin, Alexei Sergeyevich (1834-1911), Russian newspaper publisher.

Svyatlovskaya, Alexandra Vladimirovna, Russian operatic contralto.

Svyatopolk-Mirsky, Dmitri Ivanovich, member of the State Assembly.

Taffanel, Claude Paul (1844-1908), celebrated French flutist, teacher, and conductor.

Taneiev, Sergey Ivanovich (1856-1915), Russian composer, pianist, and professor at the Moscow Conservatory, later its director. Pupil of Tchaikovsky and arranged the latter's fourth and fifth symphonies for piano. Tchaikovsky dedicated an orchestral work to him. He introduced several of Tchaikovsky's works.

Taneiev, Vladimir Ivanovich (1840-1921), lawyer brother of Sergey I. Taneiev.

Taneieva, Varvara Pavlovna, mother of Sergey I. Taneiev.

Tanya, see Davidova, Tatayana Lvovna

Tarnovsky, Konstantin Augustovich (1826-1892), Russian dramatist.

Tasya, see Davidova, Natalya L.

Tatusya, Tatochka, see Kartzeva, Sasha

Tatusya, Taniusha, Tata, see Tchaikovskaya, Tatyana Anatolevna

Tatyana, see Davidova, Tatyana Lvovna

Tatyana, see Kartzeva, Sasha

Tatyana, see Tchaikovskaya, Tatyana Anatolevna

Taubert, Karl Gottfried Wilhelm (1811-1891), German pianist and composer.

Tchaikovskaya, Alexandra Andreyevna (Assier) (1813-1854), Tchaikovsky's mother.

Tchaikovskaya, Alexandra (Sasha), see Davidova, Alexandra I.

Tchaikovskaya, Antonina Ivanovna (Miliukova) (1849-1917), Tchaikovsky's wife. See note 65, Diary Four.

Tchaikovskaya, Olga (Olya) Sergeyevna, wife of Nikolai I. Tchaikovsky.

Tchaikovskaya, Praskovya (Panya) Vladimirovna (Konshina), wife of Anatoly I. Tchaikovsky, daughter of one of Moscow's leading merchants. Tchaikovsky dedicated an orchestral work to her.

Tchaikovskaya, Sophia (Sonya) Petrovna (Nikonova) (1843-1920), wife of Ippolit I. Tchaikovsky.

Tchaikovskaya, Tatyana (Tatusya, Taniusha, Tata) Anatolevna, Tchaikovsky's niece, daughter of Anatoly.

Tchaikovsky, Anatoly (Tolya) Ilyich (1850-1915), Tchaikovsky's brother, ten years younger than the composer, twin of Modest. He was an assistant prosecutor. Tchaikovsky dedicated six songs to him.

Tchaikovsky, Georges-Leon (1883-   ), adopted son of Nikolai I. Tchaikovsky. See note 41, Diary Four.

Tchaikovsky, Ilya Petrovich (1795-1880), mining engineer, Tchaikovsky's father.

Tchaikovsky, Ippolit Ilyich (1843-1927), Tchaikovsky's brother, three years younger than the composer. A naval officer, finally becoming an admiral.

Tchaikovsky, Modest (Modya) Ilyich (1850-1916), Tchaikovsky's brother, ten years younger than the composer, Anatoly's twin. The only brother artistically inclined—a critic, playwright, librettist, wrote the librettos for Tchaikovsky's operas *Pique Dame* and *Iolanta* as well as those of operas by Arensky, Rachmaninoff, and others. Wrote a biography of the composer. Was particularly close to Tchaikovsky. Also homosexual. Tchaikovsky dedicated twelve piano pieces to him.

Tchaikovsky, Nikolai (Kolya) Ilyich (1838-1911), Tchaikovsky's brother, mining engineer.

Tebenkov, Mikhail Mikhailovich, Russian newspaper editor in Tiflis.

Teryan-Korganova, E. O., opera singer.

Thalberg, Sigismond (1812-1871), Swiss pianist and composer, erstwhile rival of Liszt.

Thierry, Amédée Simon Dominique (1797-1873), French author.

Thomé, Francis Lucien Joseph (1850-1909), French composer, teacher and critic.

Timanova, Vera Viktorovna (1855-?), Russian pianist. Tchaikovsky dedicated a piano piece to her.

Tolstoy, Count Alexei Konstantinovich (1817-1875), Russian poet and dramatist, many of whose poems were set to music by Tchaikovsky.

Tolstoy, Lev Nikolaievich (1828-1910), great Russian novelist and philosopher. Tchaikovsky met Tolstoy in 1876 and describes his impressions in Diary Eight.

Tolya, *see* Tchaikovsky, Anatoly I.

Tolya (Tolichka), *see* Brandukov, Anatoly Andreyevich

Tonya, Tonichka, *see* Hubert, Nikolai Albertovich

Tretbar, Charles F., representative of the Steinway Pianos in 1891 in New York.

Tretyakov, Pavel Mikhailovich (1832-1908), merchant and founder of the Tretyakov Art Gallery.

Tretyakov, Sergey Mikhailovich (1834-1892), merchant and art collector, brother of Pavel M. Tretyakov.

Tretyakova, Vera Pavlovna (1867-1940), daughter of Pavel M. Tretyakov and wife of Alexander I. Siloti.

Trubetzkoy, Prince Vasily Andreyevich (1856-1920), Russian military officer.

Tzet, July, Tchaikovsky's Russian concert manager.

Uka, *see* Davidov, Ury Lvovich

Urbánek, František (1842-1919), Prague music publisher.

Urbánek, Velebín (1853-1892), Prague music publisher.

Urspruch, Anton (1850-1907), German pianist and teacher, a pupil of Liszt and Raff.

Usatov, Dmitri Andreyevich, Russian operatic tenor. Tchaikovsky dedicated a song to him.

Valečka, Eduard (1841-1905), Czech author and publisher.

Van der Stucken, Frank Valentin (1858-1929), American composer and conductor.

Vanya, Vaniusha, Vanka (Ivan), Tchaikovsky's coachman in Moscow.

Varvara Pavlovna, *see* Taneieva, Varvara Pavlovna

Vasily, manservant of Tchaikovsky.

Vasya, *see* Sapelnikov, Vasily Lvovich

Vera, *see* Rimskaya-Korsakova, Vera Lvovna (Davidova)

Vera, *see* Siloti, Vera Pavlovna (Tretyakova)

Vera Vasilyevna, *see* Butakova

Verinovsky, Ivan (Vanya) Alexandrovich, Russian artillery officer strongly attached to Tchaikovsky. He committed suicide in 1886.

Verzhbilovich, Alexander Valeryanovich (1849-1911), eminent Russian violoncellist.

Viardot-Garcia, Pauline (1821-1910), phenomenal French operatic mezzo-soprano and teacher, retired from the stage and lived in Paris.

Vinitzkaya-Budzianik, A. A., Russian authoress.

Vischer, Friedrich Theodor (1807-1887), German art critic and writer.

Vizin, Alexandra (Sanya) Petrovna von, Tchaikovsky's cousin.

Vladimir Alexandrovich, Grand Duke (1847-1909), son of Tsar Alexander II.

Vladimir Ivanovich, see Taneiev

Vogrich, Max (1852-1916), Austrian composer who lived for many years in the United States.

Vogt, Karl (1817-1895), German naturalist.

Vogüé, Eugène M. (1848-1910), French writer.

Vsevolozhsky, Ivan Alexandrovich (1835-1909), director of the Russian Imperial Theaters. Tchaikovsky dedicated his *Sleeping Beauty* ballet to him.

Weiner, Eugene, American flutist, president of the New York Philharmonic Club.

Widor, Charles Marie Jean (1845-1937), French organist and composer, the internationally accepted head of the modern school of organ playing.

Wolff, Bernhard (1835-1906), German pianist and composer.

Wolff, Hermann (1845-1902), Berlin concert manager.

Wurm, Wilhelm (1826-1904), German-Russian composer and cornetist.

Yakovlev, Sergey Pavlovich (1837-1906), a director of the Moscow Russian Musical Society.

Yasha, see Gartung, Yakov F.

Zarudnaya, Varvara Mikhailovna (1857-?), Russian operatic soprano, wife of Mikhail M. Ippolitov-Ivanov.

Zasyadko, Dmitri (Mitya), Nikolai D. Kondratyev's nephew.

Zelenski, Vladislaus (1837-1921), Polish composer.

Zhedrinsky, Vladimir Alexandrovich (1851-1891), associate prosecutor of the St. Petersburg Circuit Court.

Zverev, Nikolai Sergeyevich (1832-1893), pianist and professor at the Moscow Conservatory. Tchaikovsky dedicated a piano piece to him.

Index